"Greece, the captive, took her savage victor captive . . ." wrote the Roman poet Horace, and the assumption that Greece ultimately conquered Rome through its superior culture has tended to dictate past studies of Roman Greece. This book adopts a different approach, examining the impact of the Roman conquest from the point of view of the majority of Greek provincials. The author traces social and economic developments from approximately 200 BC to AD 200, drawing on a combination of archaeological and historical sources. Archaeological evidence, in particular the new data provided by archaeological surface survey, is especially emphasized. One result of this emphasis is the division of the work into four separate "landscapes" – rural, civic, provincial and sacred – each of which complements the others. This framework allows an exploration of conditions in the countryside, of the organization of the Early Roman city, of the provincial structure of Greece (the province of Achaia) as a whole, and of the repercussions of conquest upon Greek sacred geography. The book does not present a detailed political history, but attempts instead to question our usual preconceptions about the relationship of Greece and Rome by offering some insight into the many changes that accompanied Greece's passage into the Roman imperial sphere.

Both ancient historians and classical archaeologists will find this book of value to them.

D1353169

# GRAECIA CAPTA

# GRAECIA CAPTA

## THE LANDSCAPES OF ROMAN GREECE

Susan E. Alcock

*Assistant Professor in the Department of Classical Studies,*
*University of Michigan*

CAMBRIDGE
UNIVERSITY PRESS

Published by the Press Syndicate of the University of Cambridge
The Pitt Building, Trumpington Street, Cambridge CB2 IRP
40 West 20th Street, New York, NY 10011–4211, USA
10 Stamford Road, Oakleigh, Melbourne 3166, Australia

First published 1993
Reprinted 1994
First paperback edition 1996

Printed in Great Britain at the University Press, Cambridge

*A catalogue record of this book is available from the British Library*

*Library of Congress cataloguing in publication data*
Alcock, Susan E.
Graecia capta: the landscapes of Roman Greece / Susan E. Alcock.
p.    cm.
Includes bibliographical references and index.
ISBN 0 521 40109 7 (hardback)
1. Greece – History – 146 BC–AD 323   2. Greece – History – To 146
BC.   3. Greece – Antiquities.   4. Civilization, Greco-Roman.
I. Title
DF239.A65   1993
938′.09–dc20   92-19006   CIP

ISBN 0 521 40109 7 hardback
ISBN 0 521 56819 6 paperback

SE

For my parents

# Contents

# Illustrations

# List of illustrations

# Tables

# Preface

In an article published a decade ago, Stephen Dyson discussed current challenges to traditional approaches within the discipline of classical archaeology, in the course of which he remarked ironically that one sure path to academic obscurity would be to undertake "some social science oriented theme on the archaeology of third–fourth century AD Greece."[1] Until recently Dyson's choice would admittedly have been particularly apt, for the study of post-Classical Greece has long held the status of a clear also-ran in terms of popularity and prestige when compared with that of the Classical epoch, or indeed even of the preceding Archaic age. But times are changing: the Roman and Byzantine periods are increasingly finding favor, especially among younger scholars eager to explore new problems and fresh territory of their own. This book is an instance of the trend, which accounts for part of my interest in Late Hellenistic and Early Roman Greece.

However, as an American citizen resident in Britain, I also became intrigued by what – at least superficially – appeared a modern parallel to the ancient relationship of Greece and Rome. The meeting of an older, more sophisticated but weaker culture with a brash, yet powerful and younger nation seems actually to be something of an archetypal conflict. In the ancient case, scholarly attention for the most part has been firmly focused on the Hellenic cultural hegemony and the interaction of the Greek and Roman political and intellectual élite, whereas it was my curiosity about the possible effects of the Roman conquest in other spheres of economic and social life that inspired the specific direction of the present work. My own particular approach to Roman Greece differs from its predecessors in a number of significant respects, above all by the fact that it was only made possible by the introduction of an important new form of evidence which has very recently begun to become available for use in synthetic studies such as this. Archaeological surface survey, arguably the most important contemporary development in classical archaeology, provides a unique type of information about the past, allowing the material consequences of collective activity across the entire human landscape to be observed. Since it is diachronic in character, survey evidence is helping to expand the chronological horizons of classical archaeologists, as well as encouraging comparisons between periods hitherto treated in isolation. So recently available are these data that this study of early imperial Greece can claim to be among the first to bring various Greek survey results together upon a specific historical problem and in a comparative fashion. As I hope to demonstrate, this line of investigation is so promising that we can surely expect many further studies in the same vein to follow, gaining in quality as more and better survey results become available.

As is the case with any scholarly work that has been some time in the making, debts of gratitude are owing to institutions and scholars too numerous to thank by name, but some cannot pass without special recognition. A Churchill Studentship from Churchill College and a Junior Research Fellowship at Clare College supported much of my time at the University of Cambridge. Paul Cartledge, Antony Spawforth and Richard Saller read complete drafts of the finished text, while Frank Walbank, John Lloyd, Michael Jameson, Robin Osborne, Jack Davis, Stephen Hodkinson, Panayiotis Doukellis, David Gill, Barbara Levick, Tom Blagg and Paul Millett have at one time or another read (or heard) and commented on some aspect of this work: all have saved me from error and offered ideas in equal measure. Anthony Snodgrass and Peter Garnsey in particular deserve my special thanks for their unfailing support through the proverbial thick and thin.

The orginal line drawings for this book were prepared by Rosamond Otto; I must also thank John Cherry, Michael Fulford, Cynthia Kosso and Robin Osborne for help in acquiring further photographic material. All quotations from ancient authors are taken from Loeb Classical editions, unless otherwise cited, though I have taken the liberty of transliterating Greek names in such a way as to be consistent with my text as a whole. For Cambridge University Press Pauline Hire has proved a stalwart editor and I must especially thank Margaret Deith for her consistent efforts on behalf of consistency.

Directors of several survey projects in Greece have been extremely generous with their unpublished data and thoughts; without their aid this study would have proved impossible. I thank especially Curtis Runnels, Tjeerd van Andel and Michael Jameson (Argolid Exploration Project), William Cavanagh and Joost Crouwel (Lakonia Survey), John Lloyd, Eddie Owens and Jim Roy (Megalopolis Survey), Anthony Snodgrass and John Bintliff (Cambridge and Bradford Boeotia Expedition), Don Keller (Southern Euboea Survey), James Wright (Nemea

Valley Archaeological Project), John Cherry, Jack Davis and Eleni Mantzourani (Northern Keos Survey; Nemea Valley Archaeological Project).

Writing a book is only partly an academic enterprise, however, and I have been blessed with a notable support staff. My colleagues at the University of Reading, especially Professor Michael Fulford and Professor Andrew Wallace-Hadrill, have offered moral as well as academic support. Dr. J. G. Daley, Dr. H. E. Donais and Dr. W. G. Fisher came to the rescue at one particularly critical juncture. My husband, John Cherry, knows just how much I owe him without further elaboration here. Above all, my family (especially my mother) have been unwavering throughout in their confidence that the "paper" would turn out well and have provided every facility to ensure that it did.

# Abbreviations

| | |
|---|---|
| AA | *Archäologischer Anzeiger* |
| AAA | *Athens Annals of Archaeology* |
| AAAG | *Annals of the Association of American Geographers* |
| AAnt | *American Antiquity* |
| AD | *Archaiologikon Deltion* |
| AJA | *American Journal of Archaeology* |
| AJP | *American Journal of Philology* |
| AnnRevAnth | *Annual Review of Anthropology* |
| ANRW | *Aufstieg und Niedergang des Römischen Welt* |
| AR | *Archaeological Reports* |
| BCH | *Bulletin de correspondance hellénique* |
| BICS | *Bulletin of the Institute of Classical Studies, University of London* |
| BSA | *Annual of the British School at Athens* |
| CAH | *The Cambridge Ancient History* |
| CIL | *Corpus Inscriptionum Latinarum* |
| CJ | *Classical Journal* |
| CPhil | *Classical Philology* |
| CQ | *Classical Quarterly* |
| CR | *Classical Review* |
| CSSH | *Comparative Studies in Society and History* |
| EMC/CV | *Echos du monde classique/Classical Views* |
| GRBS | *Greek, Roman and Byzantine Studies* |
| HSCP | *Harvard Studies in Classical Philology* |
| IG | *Inscriptiones Graecae* |
| IGBulg | *Inscriptiones Graecae in Bulgaria repertae* |
| JFA | *Journal of Field Archaeology* |
| JHS | *Journal of Hellenic Studies* |
| JMA | *Journal of Mediterranean Archaeology* |
| JRA | *Journal of Roman Archaeology* |
| JRS | *Journal of Roman Studies* |
| OJA | *Oxford Journal of Archaeology* |

## List of abbreviations

| | |
|---|---|
| *PBSR* | *Papers of the British School at Rome* |
| *RA* | *Revue archéologique* |
| *SEG* | *Supplementum Epigraphicum Graecum* |
| *SIG³* | *Sylloge Inscriptionum Graecarum*, 3rd edition |
| *WA* | *World Archaeology* |
| *ZPE* | *Zeitschrift für Papyrologie und Epigraphik* |

# I

# The problem of Roman Greece

*Graecia capta ferum victorem cepit et artis intulit agresti Latio . . .*
[Greece, the captive, took her savage victor captive, and brought the
arts into rustic Latium . . .] (Horace, *Epistles* 2.1.156)

> Fair Greece! sad relic of departed worth!
> Immortal, though no more; though fallen great!
> (Lord Byron, "Childe Harold's Pilgrimage," II.lxxiii)

The history of Greece under foreign domination records the degradation and calamities of the nation which attained the highest degree of
civilisation in the ancient world. (Finlay [1857], ix)

Greece may be unique in the degree to which the country as a whole has
been forced to play the contrasted roles of *Ur-Europa* and humiliated
oriental vassal at one and the same time. (Herzfeld [1987], 19)

Captive Greece lies caught within a paradox: the sublimely gifted
Greeks, origin and inspiration of western culture, nonetheless fell to
other, and somehow lesser, civilizations. Rome was Greece's first
conqueror and the Greeks under Roman rule the first to be enmeshed.
The paradox has produced a curious ambivalence in the attitudes
brought to the study of Roman Greece. Put simply, the Greeks of the time
have been hailed as superior and impervious to Roman domination, yet
at the same time condemned for their weakness and decadent fall. This
ambivalence, as we shall see, is not solely a later construction, but is
rooted in contemporary sources, both Greek and Roman.
    Cultural superiority, of course, is what is being celebrated. Unlike the
barbarian west, the Greek east has generally been seen as advanced and
sophisticated, far beyond any need of Rome's civilizing power. A. H. M.
Jones began an article entitled "The Greeks under the Roman empire"
with the statement: "The most surprising feature of Roman rule in the

Greek East is that despite its long duration it had so little effect on the civilisation of the area." Not only did Greek culture preserve itself from Roman contamination; what is emphasized is the phenomenon of "reverse cultural imperialism" (or "reverse acculturation") with Greece (as Horace said) "bringing the arts to rustic Latium." This particular perspective on the (non-)effects of external conquest focuses largely on the response of the Greek political and intellectual élite. Individuals such as Plutarch of Chaironeia (fl. first century AD) or Herodes Atticus (fl. second century AD) loom large in discussions of the epoch, just as they dominate the extant contemporary sources. Compared with such figures, the fate of the majority of Greek provincials is either disregarded, or, as "Greeks," they are assumed somehow to possess the same protective cultural magic.[1] Moreover, from the perspective of the western Roman empire, the east (which did not "decline and fall") appears to remain the same; "in this view, the study of social change in the East is unnecessary because there *was* no substantial change."[2]

On the other side of the coin, however, is depicted a land in twilight, sunk in quiet obscurity. Its period of independent glory finished, Greece was now content to pass on the torch of leadership to a younger, more vigorous nation. This decline is implicitly considered a "natural" development, with weakness (even "senility") ineluctably following an epoch of strength. Essentially this reflects the nineteenth-century notion of civilizations, like organisms, possessing a natural life cycle, with appropriate organic metaphors (birth, maturity, decline) employed to describe its history. Such an evolutionary perspective invites an assumption that there is a "certain inevitability" about the development of any particular civilization.[3] In the Greek case, internal factors – moral decadence, internal disarray, spiritual inertia – are thought for the most part to have engineered this collapse, making the actual conquest somehow an inevitable occurrence, and one bearing only partial responsibility for Greece's parlous state of affairs. If anything, the Romans ("compelled," as one scholar put it, "by the masculine sense of order") did the forlorn Greeks a favor by sheltering them within their world dominion. From this perspective, Rome's main interest in the backwater was a desire to enjoy its cultural offerings, a predilection encouraged by the provincials themselves. In a slightly different context, Bowersock summed up this viewpoint well in his remark that "Old Greece" was "a country learning how to be a museum; cultivated Romans admired Greece romantically for what she had been."[4]

These twin verdicts, presented here in their starkest form, dominate the limited range of secondary works on the subject. Most striking of all, however, is how relatively little academic attention Roman Greece has received in the nineteenth and twentieth centuries. Some excellent historical analyses have, it is true, been produced, but nothing approaching the number and variety seen for other provinces, especially in the west. Numerous standard histories of the country take the loss of Greek independence, associated either with the battle of Chaironeia or the reign of Alexander, as their most natural stopping point. The disdain in which the subsequent centuries were held is generally clear; at this point the historian must, Grote argued, feel "that the life has departed from his subject, and with sadness and humiliation brings his narrative to a close."[5] Specifically *archaeological* exploration of Roman remains in Greece (or indeed of the post-Classical era as a whole) has lagged behind even more distressingly.[6] In general, the western empire, the territorial base for modern Europe, has been disproportionately emphasized at the expense of the east, the "oriental" domains of Byzantine and Ottoman civilization. For "captive Greece" in particular, a disinclination to stare at the unwelcome, to confront the paradox, has seemingly fettered free investigation.[7]

### ESCAPING THE PARADOX

This book offers an alternative look at Roman Greece (i.e. the province of Achaia) during the early imperial period (fig. 1). Several recent trends in anthropology, ancient history and archaeology have converged to prompt such a revisionist approach. Most fundamental, of course, is recognition of the hitherto dominant paradox for what it is: celebration of Greek achievement, coupled with shame at Greek failure, is a purely external, European construction of Hellenic history, written by outsiders in order to define their own modern and western identity. More generally, there is a greater sensitivity to the implications of imperial activity for subordinate societies, for, in the post-colonial world, accepting the conquest of one people by another as "natural" and "inevitable" is no longer so easy. Central to this development is a growing concern to recover the "people without history" (in Eric Wolf's phrase) – the silent majority of any pre-industrial population, which almost completely fails to figure in the predominantly élite-biased ancient sources. Such a concern may be especially necessary in the case of Greece: "Peasants and slaves did not speak or write, their condition denied them freedom of action. By good fortune, the Hellenes, although not always in possession of the liberty which they cherish even to excess, exhibit and avow a strong tendency to be active, visible and vocal."[8] Syme here characteristically strikes an extreme position, but he is not alone in his apparent disregard for those "Hellenes" who might also be "peasants

3

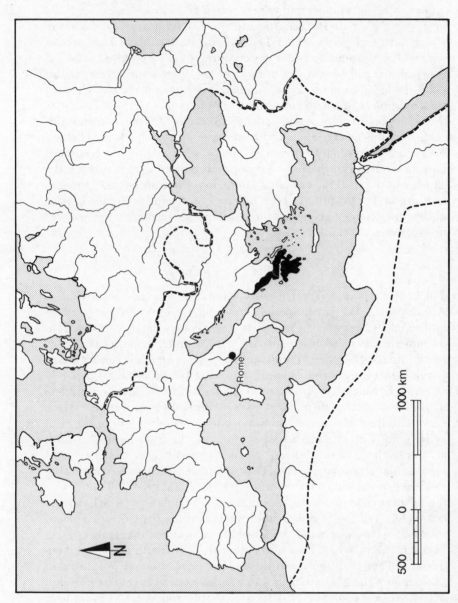

Rome

1000 km

500    0

N

1   The location of Achaia within the Roman empire of the second century AD

and slaves." Not all Greek provincials were "active, visible and vocal" in the documentary sources, and this is one reason why archaeological evidence plays such a vital role in this investigation.

Center–periphery relations (in the formulation of Immanuel Wallerstein, embracing an entire world system) have proven an influential concept in anthropological, sociological and archaeological circles in recent years, and it too has a bearing on this subject. Within this theoretical framework, the image of an isolated Greece, located within the empire but basically describing its own internal downward spiral, is open to severe criticism. Center– or core–periphery formulations stress the essential interrelationships existing between the individual parts of larger systems, of which an empire is only one particular example. No attempt is made here to apply a full-fledged model to the Roman empire – such attempts are problematic in the extreme – but the concept still possesses great heuristic value in prompting "the search for interconnectedness and structured interaction."[9] Large-scale, long-distance influences have the power to transform societies: even if Achaia is the specific subject for attention, its setting and role within the empire at large must continually be kept in mind. Such a theoretical perspective also helps to set aside distorting notions about the supposed "uniqueness" of Greece, allowing it to be viewed as just one peripheral unit, comparable to many others, both within the Roman empire itself and beyond. Comparisons with various imperial systems at other times and in other places can often be stimulating, and are brought into play from time to time throughout this book.

Archaeology, of course, has been fascinated by empire since the very beginning of the discipline's history, as research into the Assyrian, Aztec, Inca or Roman cases, among many others, serves to demonstrate. Yet for most of this history, it has been the élite, palace-based cultures, with their "Great Traditions," which have dominated archaeological attention: royal iconography, imperial architecture and prestige goods as specific objects of curiosity and connoisseurship. Today, instead of focusing upon the perquisites of the victor, archaeologists are engaging with the effects of imperialist expansion upon subject peoples, generating a new kind of "archaeology of imperialism." A battery of archaeological techniques is being turned upon issues such as shifting levels of exploitation, changes in economic and social behavior, acculturation, and resistance. Settlement studies, often made possible for the first time as a result of archaeological survey, have in many cases proved particularly crucial indicators of the life of a conquered population.[10]

Our ability to study imperial Greece in a similar fashion has only become possible with the recent proliferation of regionally based archaeological projects, arguably the most significant development to have had an impact on classical archaeology in recent years. Pedestrian surface survey is a remarkably successful technique in the Mediterranean basin; the amount and quality of work undertaken in Greece itself now ranks the country among the archaeologically best investigated parts of the world. Survey evidence necessitates a regional, rather than a specifically site-based, level of analysis, necessarily turning inquiry away from particular individuals or events and toward more general and long-run patterns of human activity; it has proved useful in particular on account of its unprecedented ability to shed light on rural settlement and land use conditions – major lacunae both in the documentary sources and in the more traditional excavation-oriented practices of classical archaeology. Such information does indeed allow some conclusions to be drawn about the life of a "people without history," and provides a diachronic record of human activity, encouraging the comparison between different periods. In this book, for example, the survey record of early imperial Greece (and thus, I argue, its patterns of settlement and social organization) is compared with that of the preceding Classical/Early Hellenistic and subsequent Late Roman epochs. Thus survey evidence, and the regional perspective it ensures, acts as the essential springboard for this study, which could not have been attempted even so recently as a decade ago.

### THE CONCEPT OF LANDSCAPE

The organizing theme for my analysis and discussion is the concept of landscape. The term "landscape" defies easy definition, and in various disciplines a range of meanings is currently in use. Often artistic representations are signified, with much interesting recent work conducted, for example, on the "iconography" of landscape, its use as a "cultural image, a pictorial way of representing, structuring or symbolising surroundings." The transition to capitalism, and changing European self-perceptions and self-representations, dominates this research.[11] Elsewhere, however, landscape can broadly denote the arrangement and interaction of peoples and places in space and time, and such is the meaning intended in the present context. Depending on the problems under examination, landscapes can vary in scale and in definition, while always stressing the spatial correlates of human behavior. Usages of the term are also bound together by an emphasis upon landscape as a *social* product, the consequence of a collective human transformation of the physical environment. Human activity, human involvement forms the key element: landscape is "never simply a natural space . . . always

6

artificial, always synthetic, always subject to sudden or unpredictable change."[12] Landscapes are inherently dynamic and historically sensitive, altering to accommodate change in the political and social order. At the same time, they serve as an active force in promoting and perpetuating cultural change, through their ability to structure and control human activity.

This focus upon spatial organization and reorganization reveals relationships of power and influence in a fashion quite different from any other form of evidence. For example, the restructuring of political authority or the redistribution of economic resources are perceptible in the ways in which settlement patterns or territorial boundaries come to be modified. Ecological and economic constraints play a part in shaping landscapes, but ideological and symbolic factors are equally active. Identifying just who or what forces initiate change becomes a central concern for any analysis of social change. The possible spatial correlates of domination offer an effective alternative approach to the consequences of imperial conquest and control.

The following five chapters attempt to define and explore several landscapes of a quite distinct character – although they are all in fact closely interrelated and interdependent. The chapters are arranged so that they "nest" together, moving very roughly in scale from the geographically localized to the more general. Chapter 2 begins with the rural landscape and the activity of people in the countryside. From survey data, inferences are made about the nature of landholding patterns, and how the division of land – the basic guarantor of economic and social position – was affected by the Roman conquest. The issue of demographic change, central in many previous interpretations of this period, is also raised. In one sense, this chapter provides a substratum for the remainder of the analysis, provoking arguments to be followed through in the remainder of the book. Chapter 3 ("The civic landscape") builds on this rural picture by including the urban centers. Together, they make possible an examination of entire civic units (the *poleis* of the early empire), the distribution of population within them, and the social and economic pressures dictating the residential preferences of Greek provincials. Effects stemming from the altered status of individual *poleis*, following their political incorporation, are sought in the relationship between town and country, as well as in attitudes to local frontiers and borders. "The provincial landscape" (chapter 4), taking as its scope the entire province of Achaia, continues to examine the implications of Greece's integration within a larger imperial system. We consider examples of external reallocations of population and resources, and the restructuring of territorial boundaries, before turning to the more

7

indirect consequences of Roman rule for the success or failure of various provincial cities. While these three chapters build directly one upon the other, chapter 5 ("The sacred landscape") adopts a slightly different vantage point. Its concerns include the location and significance of certain classes of sanctuaries, and the role played by cult in articulating various relationships within provincial society, such as between individuals and cities or between cities and the imperial power. Chapter 6 ("Greece within the empire") draws some general conclusions, while also expanding to an empire-wide perspective, briefly relating the particular development of Roman Greece to other provinces of the empire.

Though somewhat arbitrary, the treatment of the evidence in the context of these several "landscapes" brings with it, I would claim, certain definite advantages. The approach naturally embraces various kinds of archaeological evidence, in particular the results of surface survey. The past tyranny of the orthodox documentary sources is circumvented, while treating landscapes as equally valid "social documents" allows alternative histories to be constructed. Moreover, each of these landscapes carries within itself several layers of meaning; variant readings will generate other valid observations about the society and economy of Greece under the empire. Indeed, it should be emphasized at the outset that this is only one of several books that could be written about Roman Greece. Adopting landscapes as a controlling theme necessarily, but regrettably, excludes several worthwhile archaeological and historical subjects: the detailed study of individual cities or sanctuaries, trade and commerce patterns, or mortuary practices, for instance.[13] Nor is much time given to administrative and legal studies, or to political narrative (although a brief history of the province is provided below). What an exploration of different landscapes within this province can offer is a relatively comprehensive view of the nature of Greek society under Roman rule, in a way that eschews the "top down" perspective that has limited the value of many earlier studies. Not least, this permits us to observe the active involvement of Greek provincials in historical change, the collective response to imperial domination.

## A LITTLE HISTORY OF ROMAN GREECE

In the course of the book, I shall often use the term "early imperial" to indicate the period under study, very roughly the period from 200 BC to AD 200. The archaeological chronologies involved will be introduced in the next chapter. If one had to define this period in terms of specific historical events, the Second Macedonian War could stand as the starting point, Caracalla's declaration of universal citizenship in AD 212

8

(and in a way the "end" of the Roman empire) as the finish. Yet such milestones would be largely deceptive in a study such as this which, to use Braudelian terms, works rather at the level of *conjoncture* or the *longue durée* than at that of *événements*.[14] To some, this treatment may seem to glide too easily over important distinctions, for example in administration and taxation between the Republic and the Principate. For the exploration of human landscapes, however, a different and deeper – but equally valid – temporal frame is required. The remainder of this chapter provides a background sketch of the more important political and military developments in Greece from the first major "contact" period with Rome, into the first two centuries of the empire. By no means is this intended as a complete account, but rather as a guide to orient the reader and to provide some framework for the discussions that follow (fig. 2). A review of the principal ancient literary testimonia for Roman Greece, and a critical assessment of the evidence they provide, are likewise necessary preliminaries.[15]

It would be a grave mistake to accept the formal creation of the province of Achaia (generally agreed to have occurred in 27 BC) as the starting point for a history of Roman Greece: a Roman interest and presence in the region can be traced back at least to the beginning of the second century BC and the Second Macedonian War (200–197 BC). This conflict involved Greek states on both sides, and its conclusion saw Rome replacing Macedon as the principal influence in the Balkans. Following the war, at the Isthmian Games, T. Quinctius Flamininus declared the Greeks free and subject to no tribute. At the same time, however, Flamininus and other Roman officials became actively involved in the workings of numerous Greek cities, notably in respect of the reorganization of boundaries and the reconstitution of civic governments, usually in favor of the propertied classes. The early years of the second century continued to see substantial military activity in Greece, both with and without Roman involvement – for example, a war between Sparta and the Achaean League or that between Rome and the Aetolians, and the ally of Aetolia, Antiochus III. No Roman troops were left stationed in Greece after these clashes, but numerous embassies and letters reveal that intervention by Roman authorities in Greek affairs was not unusual. In the Third Macedonian War (172–168 BC), although the primary contest lay between Rome and Perseus of Macedon, perceived disloyalty to Rome by Greek cities was harshly punished, notably in Boeotia and Epirus, even to the extent of the physical destruction of certain communities. The settlement of 167 BC witnessed several territorial readjustments, with the resultant loss of land to hostile states, while those currently in Roman favor (such as Athens) were rewarded. Losers in all

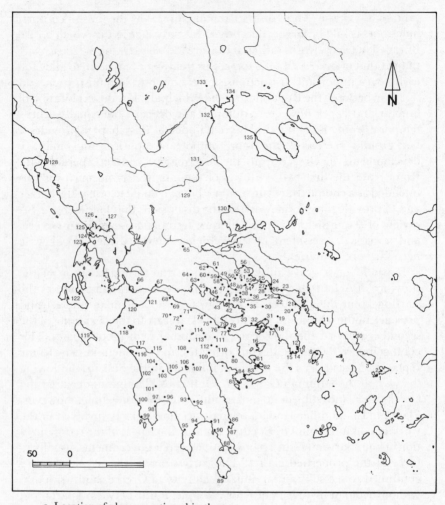

2 Location of places mentioned in the text

| | | |
|---|---|---|
| 1 Delos | 9 Melos | 17 Piraeus |
| 2 Mykonos | 10 Andros | 18 Athens |
| 3 Tenos | 11 Karystos | 19 Acharnai |
| 4 Gyaros | 12 Thorikos | 20 Marathon |
| 5 Karthaia | 13 Laurion | 21 Rhamnous |
| 6 Poiessa | 14 Sounion | 22 Oropos |
| 7 Ioulis | 15 Atene | 23 Eretria |
| 8 Koressos | 16 Aigina | 24 Chalkis |

| | | |
|---|---|---|
| 25 Anthedon | 62 Ledon | 99 Methone |
| 26 Aulis | 63 Delphi | 100 Pylos |
| 27 Harma | 64 Amphissa | 101 Messene |
| 28 Mykalessos | 65 Hypata | 102 Phigaleia |
| 29 Tanagra | 66 Kalydon | 103 Lykosoura |
| 30 Panakton | 67 Naupaktos | 104 Bassae |
| 31 Eleusis | 68 Aigion | 105 Megalopolis |
| 32 Megara | 69 Bura | 106 Pallanteion |
| 33 Pagai | 70 Kynaitha | 107 Tegea |
| 34 Salamis | 71 Aiga | 108 Mantineia |
| 35 Plataiai | 72 Pheneos | 109 Argos |
| 36 Thebes | 73 Kaphyai | 110 Berbati |
| 37 Thespiai | 74 Aigeira | 111 Kleonai |
| 38 Onchestos | 75 Sikyon | 112 Mycenae |
| 39 Askra | 76 Lechaion | 113 Nemea |
| 40 Haliartos | 77 Kenchreai | 114 Phlius |
| 41 Koroneia | 78 Isthmia | 115 Heraia |
| 42 Thisbe | 79 Corinth | 116 Samikon |
| 43 Chorsiai | 80 Epidauros | 117 Olympia |
| 44 Bulis | 81 Methana | 118 Elis |
| 45 Antikyrrha | 82 Kalaureia | 119 Zakynthos |
| 46 Medeon | 83 Troizen | 120 Dyme |
| 47 Lebadeia | 84 Hermione | 121 Patrai |
| 48 Alalkomenai | 85 Halieis | 122 Kephallenia |
| 49 Orchomenos | 86 Zarax | 123 Leukas |
| 50 Tegyra | 87 Epidauros Limera | 124 Actium |
| 51 Kopai | 88 Boiai | 125 Nikopolis |
| 52 Hyettos | 89 Kythera | 126 Kassope |
| 53 Larymna | 90 Asopos | 127 Ambrakia |
| 54 Akraiphia | 91 Helos | 128 Buthrotum |
| 55 Ptoon | 92 Therapnai | 129 Krannon |
| 56 Halai | 93 Sparta | 130 Demetrias |
| 57 Aidepsos | 94 Gytheion | 131 Gonnoi |
| 58 Chaironeia | 95 Oitylos | 132 Pydna |
| 59 Panopeus | 96 Thouria | 133 Pella |
| 60 Tithorea | 97 Nichoria | 134 Thessalonike |
| 61 Elateia | 98 Korone | 135 Kassandreia |

| | | | | | |
|---|---|---|---|---|---|
| Ambrakia | 127 | Hypata | 65 | Nikopolis | 125 |
| Amphissa | 64 | Ioulis | 7 | Oitylos | 95 |
| Andros | 10 | Isthmia | 78 | Olympia | 117 |
| Anthedon | 25 | Kalaureia | 82 | Onchestos | 38 |
| Antikyrrha | 45 | Kalydon | 66 | Orchomenos | 49 |
| Argos | 109 | Kaphyai | 73 | Oropos | 22 |
| Askra | 39 | Karthaia | 5 | Pagai | 33 |
| Asopos | 90 | Karystos | 11 | Pallanteion | 106 |
| Atene | 15 | Kassandreia | 135 | Panakton | 30 |
| Athens | 18 | Kassope | 126 | Panopeus | 59 |
| Aulis | 26 | Kenchreai | 77 | Patrai | 121 |
| Bassae | 104 | Kephallenia | 122 | Pella | 133 |
| Berbati | 110 | Kleonai | 111 | Pheneos | 72 |
| Boiai | 88 | Kopai | 51 | Phigaleia | 102 |
| Bulis | 44 | Koressos | 8 | Phlius | 114 |
| Bura | 69 | Korone | 98 | Piraeus | 17 |
| Buthrotum | 128 | Koroneia | 41 | Plataiai | 35 |
| Chaironeia | 58 | Krannon | 129 | Poiessa | 6 |
| Chalkis | 24 | Kynaitha | 70 | Ptoon | 55 |
| Chorsiai | 43 | Kythera | 89 | Pydna | 132 |
| Corinth | 79 | Larymna | 53 | Pylos | 100 |
| Delos | 1 | Laurion | 13 | Rhamnous | 21 |
| Delphi | 63 | Lebadeia | 47 | Salamis | 34 |
| Demetrias | 130 | Lechaion | 76 | Samikon | 116 |
| Dyme | 120 | Ledon | 62 | Sikyon | 75 |
| Elateia | 61 | Leukas | 123 | Sounion | 14 |
| Eleusis | 31 | Lykosoura | 103 | Sparta | 93 |
| Elis | 118 | Mantineia | 108 | Tanagra | 29 |
| Epidauros | 80 | Marathon | 20 | Tegea | 107 |
| Epidauros Limera | 87 | Medeon | 46 | Tegyra | 50 |
| Eretria | 23 | Megalopolis | 105 | Tenos | 3 |
| Gonnoi | 131 | Megara | 32 | Thebes | 36 |
| Gyaros | 4 | Melos | 9 | Therapnai | 92 |
| Gytheion | 94 | Messene | 101 | Thespiai | 37 |
| Halai | 56 | Methana | 81 | Thessalonike | 134 |
| Haliartos | 40 | Methone | 99 | Thisbe | 42 |
| Halieis | 85 | Mycenae | 112 | Thorikos | 12 |
| Harma | 27 | Mykalessos | 28 | Thouria | 96 |
| Helos | 91 | Mykonos | 2 | Tithorea | 60 |
| Heraia | 115 | Naupaktos | 67 | Troizen | 83 |
| Hermione | 84 | Nemea | 113 | Zakynthos | 119 |
| Hyettos | 52 | Nichoria | 97 | Zarax | 86 |

these various conflicts also faced the likelihood of booty taken by victorious troops, and of indemnities levied by Roman authorities.

Apart from this periodic military presence, Roman generals and ambassadors continued to intervene in internal Greek concerns. J. A. O. Larsen asked the question, "Was Greece free between 196 and 146 BC?" and concluded that she was not. In that latter year an overt case of interference – the demands of a Roman embassy that certain cities (including Sparta) be detached from the Achaean League – provoked the outbreak of the Achaean War. Military hostilities directly affected the Peloponnese and parts of central Greece. Indisputably the most famous event of this short-lived but vicious conflict was the sacking of Corinth by Mummius, a destruction famous in later memory both for its ruthlessness and for the despoiling of the city's artworks. Precisely what took place in the aftermath of the Achaean War is very confused from the scanty evidence available, although the dispatch of ten commissioners to help Mummius with the final settlement indicates that a major reorganization of the region took place. Certainly it appears to be the case that, after 146 BC, the parties hostile to Rome in the conflict now became technically subordinate to the Roman governor of Macedon; the repercussions for these areas (e.g. Corinth, Boeotia, Euboea, Phokis), in terms of their liability to taxation, will be discussed below. The remaining Greek polities would have continued to be subject to periodic Roman interference, until their formal incorporation under Augustus.

Warfare of the first century BC undoubtedly brought down the greatest misery upon the Greek population at large. With the outbreak of the war with Mithridates in 88 BC, the Greek peninsula again became a major battleground for powerful opposing forces. Different cities took different sides, with Athens and much of Boeotia supporting Mithridates, at the ultimate cost of a bitter siege of Athens and the destruction of several Boeotian towns. While in Greece, Sulla demanded men and support for his troops and was notorious for other depredations upon Greek territory. Piratical activity in the Mediterranean, most notoriously the sack of Delos in 69 BC, touched mainland Greece as well as the Aegean islands, with resulting troubles for several Greek communities. In their turn, the Civil Wars, conflicts in which Greeks had few advantages to gain and much to lose, raged across the Balkan peninsula. Both Pompey and Caesar, and later Octavian and Antony, commandeered supplies and aid from the Greek cities. Throughout the first century BC, Roman troops were almost completely dependent upon local economies for their support, placing unremitting pressure upon many parts of Greece. In 49 BC, Cicero wrote to Atticus: "I fear Epirus may be harassed, but do you suppose there is any part of Greece that will not be robbed?" (*Ad Atticum*

9.9). Troops from local communities were also drawn into these struggles, and several cities (e.g. Athens, Megara) were besieged or destroyed. Many important battles of the Civil Wars took place on Greek soil, including the final and decisive encounter at Actium, off the coast of Epirus in 31 BC. The meeting took place, however, only after the forces of both sides had been in the area for a substantial period of time, forcing a massive drain of available monies and provisions to the numerous foreign troops.[16] Plutarch, a resident of Chaironeia in Boeotia, presents a harrowing anecdote of his great-grandfather's experience at this time.

Caesar sailed to Athens, and after making a settlement with the Greeks, he distributed the grain which remained over after the war among their cities; these were in a wretched plight, and had been stripped of money, slaves, and beasts of burden. At any rate, my great-grandfather Nicarchus used to tell how all his fellow citizens were compelled to carry on their shoulders a stipulated measure of wheat down to the sea at Antikyrrha, and how their pace was quickened by the whip; they had carried one load in this way, he said, the second was already measured out, and they were just about to set forth, when word was brought that Antony had been defeated, and this was the salvation of the city; for immediately the stewards and soldiers of Antony took flight, and the citizens divided the grain among themselves. (Plutarch, *Antony* 68.4–5)

The situation in Greece at the end of the first century BC must, in many regions, have been equally grim. Some caution, however, is required before envisioning such scenes across the whole country: a uniform military presence, and uniformly dire conditions, have been taken as read in many previous studies of this period, but I shall argue at various points in this work that the negative impact of warfare was both more localized and less long-lasting than is often accepted. Even so, the harsh treatment of Greece, particularly in the first century BC can hardly be denied, and must certainly be taken into account in assessing conditions under the reign of Augustus.

Following Actium (and probably after a brief spell when Macedonia and Greece were administered together), a separate province of Achaia was demarcated. The geographical boundaries of the new province remain somewhat unclear in detail, but it would be fair to equate Achaia roughly with modern Greece, with the exception of Crete, Macedonia and Thessaly. A separate province of Epirus was later carved out (fig. 3).[17] Thereafter, from the reign of Augustus to the Herulian invasion of AD 267, Achaia was a recipient of the *pax Romana*, experiencing the benefits of long-term peaceful coexistence, both internally and with its provincial neighbors. The former days of Greek independence had never known such a prolonged spell of peace, but it was an enforced blessing. The magnitude of the transformation resulting in the creation of

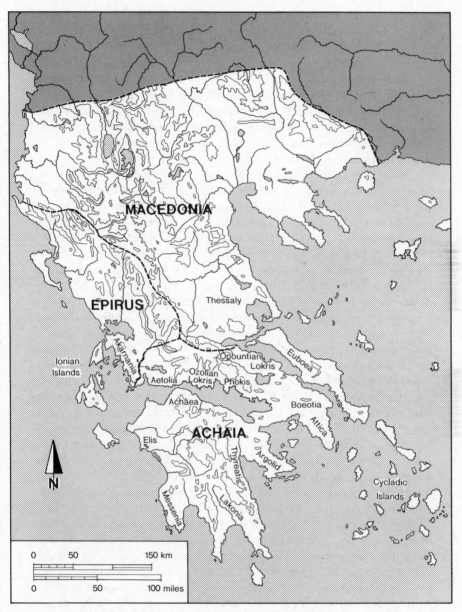

3 Boundaries of the provinces of Achaia, Macedonia and Epirus

Achaia should not be underestimated: for the first time, all of the autonomous, or largely autonomous, Greek political units were formally and forcibly brought together under an external power.[18] This transformation into a satellite territory, initiated by the Romans and maintained by their successors the Byzantines, Franks, Venetians and Turks, was not reversed until the nineteenth-century War of Independence.

Originally Achaia was a senatorial province, although in AD 15 it was transferred, together with the province of Macedonia, to the imperial province of Moesia. Tacitus stated: "Since Achaia and Macedonia protested against the heavy taxation, it was decided to relieve them of the proconsular government for the time and transfer them to the emperor" (Tacitus, *Annals* 1.76). The transfer, probably designed to allow a more efficient administration of the province, lasted for only twenty-nine years, with Claudius returning Achaia to its former state in AD 44. Other episodes of unrest and civil resistance, too, are reported from the early years of Achaia's existence, notably in Athens itself. The next major change in status occurred under Nero, who spent fifteen months in Greece participating in panhellenic and civic festivals, and finally declared the freedom of the province in AD 67. Nero's proclamation of freedom and tax immunity (*libertas, immunitas*) took place under the aegis of the Isthmian Games, in apparent emulation of Flamininus' action over 200 years before. Often considered the act of a lunatic, this grant should actually be considered as part of a wider Neronian political strategy; certainly some compensation for revenue loss was made, for Pausanias says that Nero "gave to the Roman people the very prosperous island of Sardinia in exchange for Greece, and then bestowed upon the latter complete freedom . . . The Greeks, however, were not to profit by the gift" (7.17.3–4). With Nero's death, and after only two years of freedom, Achaia was returned to the provincial flock: "in the reign of Vespasian, the next emperor after Nero, they became embroiled in a civic war; Vespasian ordered that they should again pay tribute and be subject to a governor, saying that the Greek people had forgotten how to be free" (Pausanias 7.17.4).[19] Apollonius of Tyana was said to have rebuked the emperor, saying: "Nero freed the Hellenes in play, but you have enslaved them in all seriousness" (Philostratus, *VA* 5.41).

During the Principate, Achaia acted a magnet for well-born and wealthy Romans, many of whom traveled to Greece, and especially to Athens, for a kind of educational "Grand Tour" (pp. 224–7). A revival of Greek culture coupled with a fascination with the past, resulting in a conscious archaism in literature and rhetoric, were characteristics of the movement known as the Second Sophistic, which marked Greek intellectual life in the second and early third centuries AD. In part, this

4 Sestertius of Hadrian (ca. AD 135). *Restitutori Achaiae S. C.* A personification of
the province of Achaia is raised from the ground by the emperor. Before her, a
jug with a palm-branch (symbol of the *agones* of the province).

development was generated by Roman cultural expectations, yet it also
grew from the need of the Greeks to redefine themselves and their
achievements under Roman rule. The philhellenic emperor Hadrian,
who visited the province personally on more than one occasion, raised this
interest to a new height in the second century AD (fig. 4). Apart from his
numerous benefactions to Greek cities, in AD 131/2 he founded the
Panhellenion, an organization of Greek cities drawn from around the
eastern Mediterranean, establishing its center at Athens. Such a deed
deliberately enhanced the prestige of "Old Greece" in the eastern
empire, perhaps in order to foster its traditions and values in the more
wealthy and luxurious climate of provinces such as Asia. This imperial
respect and favor continued under the Antonines, lasting well into the
third century AD.[20]

Three areas require particular discussion as major structural components in Greece's response to the imperial takeover: (a) the question of a
military presence or absence, (b) the character of provincial administration and (c) the nature of imperial and local taxation.

### Military presence

After the turbulence of the Republican era, Achaia's geographical
location, physically placed near the heart of the empire and always
buffered from the imperial frontiers (fig. 1), ensured it a largely non-
military role during the Principate. Achaia in the Early Roman period
was technically a *provincia inermis* (an unarmed province), holding on a

regular basis only a small contingent of soldiers attached to the provincial governor and perhaps troops to oversee the management of the imperial marble quarries (p. 111). No regular military levies are known to have been raised in Achaia, although a few special recruitments are reported under Marcus Aurelius and Caracalla. Trajan employed Achaia as one embarkation point in his eastern progress to the Parthian Wars in the early second century AD, but the province's role in that campaign must have been very short-lived.[21] This sheltered position had serious repercussions for Achaia's imperial development. Other garrisoned provinces experienced a stimulus to local production, responding to the need to accommodate to the presence of troops. Frontier provinces also were ensured a constant flow of taxes and supplies from elsewhere in the empire, an economic influx of a sort denied to Achaia. At the same time, Greek provincials were for the most part insulated from the influence of the Roman army. Without the immediate instruments of coercive force, other ways of representing the imperial will in Achaia were required.

## Administration

One key element in the Roman imperial plan was a preference for urban units as the basis for provincial administration. Being already an urbanized zone, Achaia did not require the overall restructuring to which other conquered areas were subjected, although changes in provincial organization did take place. These alterations, and the role of the probable provincial capital, the Roman colony of Corinth, will be discussed in chapter 4. Throughout the period under study, however, pre-existing cities remained the chief units in the organization of the province, and most aspects of provincial administration were carried out within the cellular structure they provided. The federal leagues characteristic of the Hellenistic period endured under the empire, but in general they played a role secondary to that of the cities.

The Roman empire's lack of a formal bureaucracy – with, according to one estimate, a ratio of only one official for every 350–400,000 provincials – is well known.[22] While Achaia possessed a governor and his staff, the scope of his activities would have been relatively circumscribed. For the day-to-day operation of provincial affairs, civic leaders served as the main agents, just as the cities remained the chief administrative units. As elsewhere in the empire, Roman authorities here followed a policy of promoting the rule of local *possidentes*, encouraging these individuals to identify their own personal good with that of the new ruling power. Situations are known under the Republic where property qualifications were enforced by Roman authorities as a basis for citizenship; in other cases, the encouragement of "the better sort" was more informal, if equally effective. The fostering of what Galtung has termed a "harmony of interest" between imperial and local élite groups, generally to the exclusion of other members of the provincial population, is a common enough tactic among expansionist powers everywhere. In any case, increasing domination of public affairs by a more limited number of individuals was not new with Roman formal control, having begun earlier in the Hellenistic period proper; the influence of Rome itself in part provoked this, as did the interaction of the Greeks with Hellenistic monarchs, who likewise supported and allied themselves with civic notables.[23] Given the deeply entrenched civic loyalties and traditions of the Greek east, the encouragement there of oligarchic regimes may have been a more complex process when compared to other regions, but it would be idle to deny that this "harmony of interest" was not a factor in Greek provincial life. The absence of the army, a potent reminder of Roman rule, also left the Achaian local élites as the primary representatives and arbiters of the imperial authority — a fact with important consequences for the actions and attitudes of both conqueror and conquered.

### Taxation

Among the chief tasks facing the administration of any city would have been the collection of external levies, as well as the day-to-day running of internal civic finances. Economic exploitation provides one of the chief engines of change to explore in any imperial context, particularly as a backdrop to the economic behavior of the province as a whole.

*Poleis* of the Classical era tended to avoid direct taxation and did not amass large financial reserves, preferring instead to respond on an *ad hoc* basis to demands, and relying strongly on the intervention of the wealthy; regular and uniform impositions upon all citizens or upon their land were by and large lacking. For the Hellenistic period, as many cities of Greece joined together in league associations, higher demands must have been periodically experienced, especially in times of war. Only those few parts of Greece brought under the direct suzerainty of a Hellenistic monarch would have owed regular financial subsidies to an outside power. For the most part, however, the cities of the Hellenistic period also managed to avoid consistent direct taxation, relying more and more on wealthy *euergetai* to cover unforeseen or unmanageable expenses.

While it is clear that the encroachment of Rome in the east irrevocably altered that situation, the precise course of events by which Greece was drawn into regular and enduring tax demands remains somewhat uncertain. After describing the sack of Corinth during the Achaean War, Pausanias stated:

The walls of all the cities that had made war against Rome, Mummius demolished, disarming the inhabitants, even before assistant commissioners were dispatched from Rome, and when these did arrive, he proceeded to put down democracies and to establish governments based on a property qualification. Tribute [*phoros*] was imposed on Greece. (Pausanias 7.16.9)

Such a universal imposition of taxes upon the area, many parts of which were still technically "free," has been doubted by some scholars, who have preferred to argue that taxes were laid only on the losers in the Achaean War. The few fragments of evidence for official taxation in Greece between 146 BC and the creation of the province do indeed appear to apply only to areas hostile to Rome and thus under the jurisdiction of the Macedonian governor; other regions in Greece are then assumed to have been pulled into a tribute-paying relationship, either during the first century BC or at latest under Augustus. Whether one agrees or not with this reconstruction largely depends on the view taken of the economic motivations of Roman expansion. Those who downplay such factors would argue that regular taxation began only after the watershed year of 27 BC, presupposing a Rome uninterested in systematic revenue extraction until that time. Other scholars recognize that, even by the mid-second century BC, "the Roman state was quite clear that as a collectivity it was entitled to use the resources of the Empire," and are even willing to accept Pausanias' account at face value.[24] Given the paucity of direct evidence, a moderate course is probably advisable, and I have assumed here that those areas defeated in the Achaean War were indeed taxed following 146 BC, and that they represent the *minimum* area involved in regular payments; the formal constitution of Achaia would mark the passage of the rest of Greece into a tributary relationship.

Somewhat more clear are the differences between the Republic and the Principate in forms of tax levying and collection. Under the Republic, *publicani* are known to have operated in some portions of Greece (their activity being attested most clearly in Boeotia). Given the many disruptions of the period, the actual predictability and regularity of levies is uncertain. There is reason to believe that more extraordinary impositions outweighed those burdens and provoked more severe suffering. Chief among these were the effects of the military requisitions and hostilities of the last centuries BC (see pp. 9–14). Peculation by avaricious generals and governors is another likely possibility, especially if Cicero's venomous attack upon L. Calpurnius Piso, proconsul of Macedon in 57–55 BC, can be accepted as at all factual.[25]

For the Principate, diversity has been identified as the keynote of provincial taxation systems, and unfortunately little evidence specific to the Achaian situation is known. By analogy with other provinces, however, a rough reconstruction can be offered. Under the early empire, it is clear that taxes in Achaia for the most part were taken in cash rather than kind. That situation would alter in the later empire (roughly the third century AD onward), at a time when taxation levels are also agreed to have risen significantly. The *tributum soli*, levied upon landholdings, would have been the most important tax; the *tributum capitis*, either a simple head tax or perhaps including other assets, is also attested. These formed the greatest regular burden on the provincials of Achaia; neither of these taxes was graduated or progressive in nature. Apart from these two direct taxes, other indirect impositions (*vectigalia*) would have been in effect, such as customs dues (*portoria*) or sales taxes. Beyond these charges, further levies could be raised in time of need. One especially well-documented example of such an exaction comes from Messene, where a 100,000 denarii tax was imposed on the town. The occasion for the levy, the *octobolos eisphora*, is not known; interestingly enough, *xenoi*, including Roman citizens, were liable to it. As was normal in provincial taxation, the central authorities declared the amount of money desired, leaving the local authorities (*decuriones*) to assess the worth of all property, to set the rate of taxation, and to collect the dues.[26] The opportunities for peculation or unfair distribution inherent in such a system are obvious: "it does not require a great deal of imagination to argue that the upper classes of the cities of the East . . . relieved the burdens on themselves rather than those on the lower classes." On the other hand, communal liability could take more equitable courses. Examples are known where wealthy benefactors assisted their poorer fellow citizens or allowed other public forms of income to cover outstanding debts.[27] Euergetism was very much still an option if a community or region proved too hard pressed by the weight of taxation.

On the whole, it is agreed that taxation rates for the early empire were kept consistently low; Hopkins suggests "the effective tax rate was significantly less than 10 percent of gross product." How onerous taxes were *perceived* to be by the provincials, however, is not a question the extant documentary sources can answer.[28] Even such a relatively low demand would not preclude periodic difficulties for the majority of poorer tax-payers, those with only a limited annual surplus, especially given the climatic variability common to the Mediterranean basin. An anecdote told of Tiberius indicates that at least some thought was given to this: "To the governors who recommended burdensome taxes for his provinces, he wrote in answer that it was the part of a good shepherd to shear his flock, not skin it" (Suetonius, *Tiberius* 32). It was under Tiberius that Achaia and Macedonia were transferred to Moesia, apparently in protest against heavy taxation. Whatever else is indicated by this transfer, it is clear that the pressure of regular taxation, as felt by the provincials themselves, should not be underestimated. Moreover, the potential ability of taxation to accentuate inequalities within cities, particularly between civic leaders and the rest of the population, demonstrates that suffering would not be equally shared or fairly reported.

Inequalities between cities must be considered as well. Apart from Nero's short-lived declaration of Achaia as "free and immune," certain individual cities, too, were granted their freedom, and thus lay outside the technical jurisdiction of the provincial governor and were spared regular tribute demands (fig. 5). Oliver has observed that the province boasted a high proportion of such states, who "maintained their natural rights by their courage, merits and friendly relationships, and finally by treaty and sanction of religion," according to Pliny (*Epistles* 8.24.2–3). Cities revered for their Classical past, or those who earned Roman approbation in some fashion (pp. 163–4), are numbered among these; some of the more sizeable *poleis* (Athens, Sparta) are also included. The exact date of inception and the duration of the special status of these *poleis* can often only be guessed at. Immunity was at best a precarious gift and one less and less commonly granted as time passed, but it is generally agreed that such privileges did not survive the Diocletianic reforms of the late third century. Yet although they may have been spared regular exactions, Bernhardt has argued that most of these "free cities" would nonetheless have been liable to extraordinary payments and obligations; it is known, for example, that even the free and immune community of Sparta was expected to make "friendly contributions" on demand (Strabo 8.5.5).[29] Even free cities, then, could hardly remain insensible to the pressures of the Roman presence. Unexpected, "one-off" requisitions could touch all parts of Greece, and these – sporadic and localized in their effect – may have been most debilitating of all, especially to those living close to the level of subsistence. Extraordinary levies or confiscations are mentioned in the sources, and appear to have been particularly resented as unjust. In a fictional account, Apuleius' *Metamorphoses*, the random requisition of the donkey Lucius to transport the governor's baggage is merely one example of how the unlucky provincial stood in perennial danger of casual but imperious demands. Even the honor paid to a community by a visiting emperor or lesser Roman dignitary could create problems in the scramble to provide suitable food, lodging, dedications and entertainment.[30] On the more positive side, however, Achaia was

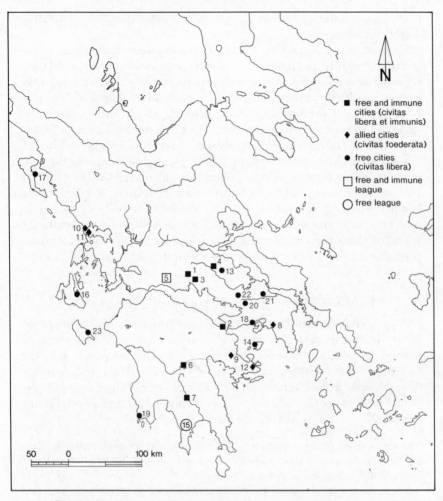

5  Distribution of cities and leagues with special status in Achaia

| | | |
|---|---|---|
| 1 Amphissa | 9 Epidauros | 17 Kerkyra |
| 2 Corinth | 10 Nikopolis | 18 Minoa |
| 3 Delphi | 11 Thyrreion | 19 Methone |
| 4 Elateia | 12 Troizen | 20 Plataiai |
| 5 Ozolian Lokrians | 13 Abai | 21 Tanagra |
| 6 Pallanteion | 14 Aigina | 22 Thespiai |
| 7 Sparta | 15 Eleutherolakones | 23 Zakynthos |
| 8 Athens | 16 Kephallenia | |

largely spared the immediate costs of military transport, troop billeting or provisioning.

To sum up, it would be fair to conclude that the regularity, the systematic nature and the directness of Roman tax demands would have required new responses from Greek provincials at all levels. Even if the tax rates under the early empire were not particularly crippling, the need now existed to produce an added surplus, above and beyond that necessary to meet local requirements. The ultimate destination of the tax flow must also be remembered. If revenues had previously been collected and disbursed in roughly the same vicinity, and generally in the interests of contributors, income now to a great extent drained away from the province, benefiting either the "core" zone of Italy or the demanding frontier provinces. Achaia, on the other hand, can be fairly characterized as a tax-exporting province.[31] What little was returned to circulation would not have been evenly redistributed across the province, but aimed primarily at already prominent cities and individuals.

### THE ANCIENT SOURCES: "REALITY" OR "RHETORIC"?

Modern perceptions of Roman Greece have unmistakably been molded by the judgments passed by ancient literary authorities. In any imperial setting, this should be enough to cause concern: if history is written by the "winners," then most testimony is bound to come either from Romans themselves or from satisfied converts to their rule. What, for example, should we make of the following eulogy composed by the second century AD rhetorician Aelius Aristides, a Greek from Mysia?

> Now all the Greek cities rise up under your leadership and the monuments which are dedicated in them and all their embellishments and comforts redound to your honor like beautiful suburbs. The coasts and interiors are filled with cities, some newly founded, others increased under and by you . . . Taking good care of the Hellenes as of your foster parents, you constantly hold your hand over them, and when they are prostrate, you raise them up. (Aelius Aristides, *Roman Oration* ¶¶94, 96)

Also to be remembered is the overwhelmingly élite and urban bias of these sources, written by men ignorant of, or not interested in, the latter-day concerns of the social or economic historian.[32] These factors inevitably leave the textual evidence an inadequate foundation upon which to base a comprehensive study of provincial life.

In the specific case of Roman Greece, matters are further complicated by the sheer variety of perspectives available (table 1). Authors range in date from the Republic (Polybius) to the High Empire (Pausanias, Philostratus), and the genres encompass narrative histories, travel

Table 1. *Chief literary sources cited in the text*

| Author | Approximate floruit (century) |
| --- | --- |
| *Greek* | |
| Polybius | second BC |
| Strabo | late first BC/early first AD |
| Plutarch | late first/early second AD |
| Dio Chrysostom | later first AD |
| Aelius Aristides | mid-second AD |
| Pausanias | mid-second AD |
| Philostratus | late second AD |
| Dio Cassius | late second AD |
| Lucian | second AD |
| *Roman* | |
| Cicero | later first BC |
| Horace | later first BC |
| Ovid | late first BC/early first AD |
| Seneca | early first AD |
| Pliny the Elder | mid-first AD |
| Pliny the Younger | later first AD |
| Apuleius | mid-second AD |

writings, personal letters and oratorical displays. Perhaps most important, both Romans (e.g. Cicero, Pliny) and Greeks, from Achaia and
elsewhere in the east (e.g. Plutarch, Dio Chrysostom), are represented.
Yet this complex web of discourses has often been reduced to provide a
single, synthetic and universally applicable account of conditions in
Greece. The resulting story has been swallowed wholesale – unfortunately, not least by survey archaeologists.[33] As with any such miscellaneous
collection of textual evidence, however, a heavy dose of source criticism is
a *sine qua non* for its acceptance as useful historical material.

The picture presented by these literary sources is almost entirely
negative. The keynote text, probably one of the most oft-cited passages in
Hellenistic history, comes from Polybius 36.17.5–9:

In our time the whole of Greece has been subject to a low birth rate and a general
decrease of the population, owing to which cities have become deserted and the land
has ceased to yield fruit, although there have neither been continuous wars nor
epidemics. If, then, any one had advised us to send and ask the gods about this, and
find out what we ought to say or do, to increase in number and make our cities more
populous, would it not seem absurd, the cause of the evil being evident and the
remedy being in our hands? For as men had fallen into such a state of pretentiousness,
avarice and indolence that they did not wish to marry, or if they married to rear the

25

children born to them, or at most as a rule but one or two of them, so as to leave these in affluence and bring them up to waste their substance, the evil rapidly and insensibly grew. For in cases where of one or two children the one was carried off by war and the other by sickness, it is evident that the houses must have been left unoccupied, and as in the case of swarms of bees, so by small degrees cities became resourceless and feeble.

This text forms the foundation for the general belief in a massive population decline in Greece during the Hellenistic and Roman era, a downturn well under way by the mid-second century BC. While more recent examinations point to the fact that Polybius here probably comments upon a geographically restricted phenomenon, affecting chiefly the wealthier elements within the citizen body, the general impression he gives of depopulation (*oliganthropia*) and disorder has undoubtedly lingered. *Oliganthropia* appears as a common theme among both Greek and Roman authors of the era. Strabo, in his *Geography*, often comments upon the presence of deserted cities, for example saying dolefully of Megalopolis: "The Great City is a great desert" (Strabo 8.8.1). Plutarch, in trying to account for the abandonment of oracular sanctuaries, remarked:

Now moderation, adequacy, excess in nothing, and complete self-sufficiency are above all else the essential characteristics of everything done by the gods; and if anyone should take this fact as a starting point, and assert that Greece has far more than its share of the general depopulation which the earlier discords and wars have wrought throughout practically the whole inhabited earth, and that today the whole of Greece would hardly muster three thousand men-at-arms which is the number that the one city of the Megarians sent forth to Plataiai (for the god's abandoning of many oracles is nothing other than his way of substantiating the desolation of Greece) . . . For who would profit if there were an oracle in Tegyra, as there used to be, or at Ptoon, where during some part of the day one might possibly meet a human being pasturing his flocks? (Plutarch, *De defectu oraculorum* 413F–414A)

Accusations of civic and moral decline frequently crop up side by side with *oliganthropia*. Dio Chrysostom, who claimed to have traveled in Greece while in exile from Domitian's court, used the land in an incisive attack upon wantonness and moral decay: "Does not the Peneus flow through a Thessaly that is desolate? Does not the Ladon flow through an Arcadia whose people have been driven from their homes?" (Dio Chrysostom, *Oration* 33.25). Several Roman authors – Cicero, Horace, Ovid – all make brief references to similar gloomy conditions during the late Republic and early Principate.[34] From Seneca, for example: "Do you not see how, in Achaia, the foundations of the most famous cities have already crumbled to nothing so that no trace is left to show that they had even existed" (Seneca, *Epistles* 14.3(91).10).

Impressively uniform as this picture may seem, it is nonetheless surprisingly easy to undermine such testimony. Most simply (and as is the case with some of the early European writers about Greece in the seventeenth to early nineteenth centuries), it is quite clear that many of these authors often utilize second-hand material, reporting sights and conditions they did not themselves experience. Indeed, several specific claims about the degraded state of certain cities or regions are flatly contradicted by archaeological data, as we shall see from time to time in the course of this book. Much more disturbing, however, is the obvious presence of entrenched literary *topoi*, conventions common to these sources. Two particularly potent tropes are easily identified: ancient perceptions of *oliganthropia*, and an obsession with past glory compared to present obscurity. These rhetorical stances emerge from the altered state and status of Greece, and from the response of both Greeks and Romans to that change.

Prevalent attitudes to population and depopulation in the Greco-Roman world have been comprehensively studied by Luigi Gallo. In brief, he argues that abundance of population (*polyandria*) was considered desirable, scarcity of people (*oliganthropia*) an unmitigated evil; *polyandria* represented prosperity and strength, *oliganthropia* the sad reverse of military weakness and political insignificance. This bipolar division of "good" and "bad" states of being developed into a frequent literary device; for example, the emphasis in Plutarch's *De defectu oraculorum* (quoted above) upon the loss of "men at arms" is telling. Read in this manner, the reiteration here of population decline becomes increasingly problematic. How often is genuine depopulation actually intended in these sources? Or how often is it merely a rhetorical device, highlighting a moral point or accentuating perceived military and political decline? Gallo also observed that a turn to pastoral activity, away from farming, often accompanies ancient descriptions of population loss, representing a retrograde step in a people's social and economic development. This development also surfaces in certain sources for Roman Greece, notably in Strabo, and will be discussed in the next chapter.[35]

A sense of decline and fall from a noble past also pervades our sources, especially those written after Greece finally passed under formal imperial control. The loss of *eleutheria* (freedom) was perceived by the Greeks themselves as the "end of an era," with significant consequences for their historical self-appraisal. In his oration to the Rhodians, for instance, Dio Chrysostom declared "it is rather the stones which reveal the grandeur and greatness of Hellas, and the ruins of her buildings"; "looking at the *men* of the present time" gives no sense at all of that former glory (*Oration*

31.159–60). Greek authors of the Principate, notably Plutarch and other members of the Second Sophistic, to some extent ignore contemporary and relatively recent history and personalities, preferring to engage with the more distant, more glowing past. In his *Guide* to Achaian cities and cult centers, the second-century AD traveler Pausanias also tends to neglect events and monuments dating after about the mid-second century BC. Such "archaism," conscious celebrations of the independent Classical past, before the fall, only threw the imperial present deeper into shadow.[36] Roman authors felt this nostalgia as well, if from the victor's perspective. Up to a point it inspired a desire to honor and cherish the Greeks for their past greatness. In a letter to a colleague on his way to serve as *corrector* (overseer) to the free cities of Achaia, Pliny cautioned:

Remember that you are sent to the province of Achaia, to the pure and genuine Greece, where civilization and literature, and agriculture too are believed to have originated . . . Pay regard to their antiquity, their heroic deeds, and the legends of their past. Do not detract from anyone's dignity, independence, or even pride, but always bear in mind that this is the land which provided us with justice and gave us laws, not after conquering us but at our request; that it is Athens you go to and Sparta you rule. (*Epistles* 8.24.1–4)

On the other hand, the defeated Greeks were also prime targets for Roman invective. *Volubilitas, ineptia, levitas*, a tendency to mendacity and effeminacy: all were charges slung at the *Graeculi*. Against this model, the antithetic, characteristic Roman virtues of *gravitas, dignitas, pietas*, military valor and so on could be compared and validated; the Greek downfall offered Roman moralists a splendid opportunity to celebrate the triumph of the *mos maiorum*.[37] More than that, however, this construction of Greek character allowed the Romans to define themselves in opposition to their defeated rivals, to distinguish themselves from a fallen power. A very similar presentation is to be found in the accounts of early modern travelers to Greece, who generally found the "descendants of Pericles" to be ignorant, superstitious, vain, perfidious, and cunning – a people who at best deserved pity from the visiting Europeans.[38]

Disillusionment with the condition of Greece, frequently voiced by visitors, must also be attributed in part to the mistaken expectations of these external viewers. Greece's reputation sometimes left it better in the telling than in the actual viewing, as the victorious general of the Third Macedonian War, Aemilius Paullus, may have found: "Paullus decided to employ the beginning of this season travelling about Greece and seeing the sights which are made so famous by repute that they are greater by hearsay than by visual acquaintance" (Livy 45.27.5). Even Greeks from

6 Panopeus in Phokis. The community boasted a fine set of fourth-century fortifications, an asset that Pausanias does not acknowledge in his harsh assessment of this *polis*.

elsewhere in the empire could be troubled. From time to time in his journey through Achaia, Pausanias (a Greek from Lydia in Asia Minor) is clearly disappointed by what he discovers; his most notable outburst is recorded at the community of Panopeus in Phokis (fig. 6):

. . . a city of the Phokians, if one can give the name of city to those who possess no government offices, no gymnasium, no theatre, no marketplace, no water descending to a fountain, but live in bare shelters just like mountain cabins, right on a ravine. (10.4.1)

Even in their Classical heyday, however, many cities would have offered little more; the title *polis* held no guarantee of an elaborate, "urban" appearance. The disappointment of élite tourists could originate in their misapprehension of what a city should look like, rather than reflecting any process of actual civic decline.[39] Under the empire, this problem would become exacerbated as larger cities outside Achaia, notably Rome itself, came to serve as conscious or unconscious models and standards of comparison.

Lastly, a special word should be said about Dio Chrysostom's *Euboean*

*Discourse* (*Oration* 7), a work that there will be occasion to mention several times in the following discussion. Dating from about AD 100, the oration purports to tell of an encounter between the shipwrecked narrator and a family of self-sufficient, isolated farmers. Set in Southern Euboea, the city nearest to their small but happy holding (probably Karystos) is described in sharply negative terms, with two-thirds of its territory said to be abandoned through neglect and underpopulation. As one of very few apparently realistic ancient treatments of rustic life, the speech has often been held to provide a valuable glimpse of city–country relationships under the empire. The oration's main theme, however, celebrates the way in which virtue is at home with poverty (*penia*); country living in an ideal community is lauded, and luxury denounced. Other sources of evidence for Euboea during this period fail to confirm Dio's grim account, while at the same time it must be admitted that the *Euboean Discourse* at many points parallels other literary idylls. On the other hand, the speech may be related to a general trend in the province – namely, the growth of large estates – and how that development was viewed by the imperial power; if so, it may reflect not actual contemporary conditions but rather (and equally importantly) contemporary perceptions and concerns.[40]

The purpose of this discussion is not to dismiss the literary sources as unimportant or unenlightening; obviously, they act as essential complements to the archaeological data and can scarcely be ignored. It is necessary, however, to assess their strengths and limitations, and – for this study of Roman Greece at least – they are found more wanting than has generally been acknowledged. In part, this is owing to their omissions: notably, the general lack of information about the countryside or about economic or demographic behavior. More devastating, however, is their frequent use of common literary *topoi*. The general concurrence of the sources in their negative presentation of Roman Greece does not necessarily prove its truth, but rather the degree to which a rhetoric was shared: depopulation and decline had become natural ingredients for representations of a defeated, inglorious Greece. The picture presented by the literary texts clearly requires either substantiation or rebuttal from other types of evidence; now that archaeology is beginning to provide such evidence, the ancient sources should no longer be allowed to dictate and shape our entire understanding of Achaian provincial life.

For all that, it would be extreme to deny any validity to these accounts of early imperial Greece; the warfare of the first century BC especially proved a terrible depressant in certain parts of the country. Servius Sulpicius Rufus wrote to Cicero in 45 BC:

There is an incident which brought me no slight consolation, and I should like to tell you about it, in case it may be able to assuage your sorrow. On my return from Asia, as I was sailing from Aigina towards Megara, I began to survey the regions round about. Behind me was Aigina, before me Megara, on my right the Piraeus, on my left Corinth, towns at one time most flourishing, now lying prostrate and demolished before one's very eyes. I began to think to myself "So! we puny mortals resent it, do we, if one of us, whose lives are naturally shorter, has died in his bed or been slain in battle, when 'in this one land alone there lie flung down before us the corpses of so many towns?' Pray control yourself, Servius, and remember that you were born a human being." (Cicero, *Ad Familiares* 4.5.4)

Unquestionably, the towns mentioned here had all been recently sacked or attacked.[41] Even here, however, the context of his letter (a consolatory note on the death of Cicero's daughter) affects its contents and tone; its elegiac flavor inspired Lord Byron in "Childe Harold's Pilgrimage":

> Wandering in youth, I traced the path of him,
> The Roman friend of Tully: as my bark did skim
> The bright blue waters with a fanning wind,
> Came Megara before me, and behind
> Aegina lay, Piraeus on the right,
> And Corinth on the left; I lay reclined
> Along the prow, and saw all these unite
> In ruin, even as he had seen the desolate sight;
>
> For Time hath not rebuilt them, but uprear'd
> Barbaric dwellings on their shatter'd site,
> Which only make more mournful and more endear'd
> The few last rays of their far-scatter'd light,
> And the crush'd relics of their vanish'd might.
> The Roman saw these tombs in his own age,
> These sepulchres of cities, which excite
> Sad wonder, and his yet surviving page
> The moral lesson bears, drawn from such pilgrimage.
>
> That page is now before me.
>          (Byron, "Childe Harold's Pilgrimage," iv.xliv–xlvi)

The similarity of response on the part of the Roman and the Romantic is more than merely amusing. Roman Greece only witnessed the beginning of this nostalgia, and of attempts to account for the fate of a once-great land. Michael Herzfeld has commented on their subsequent history:

In Greece, as well as amongst its nominal admirers, the Turkish (and some would add the Byzantine) influence on its cultural heritage constitutes a deep-veined imperfection in the marmoreal Hellenic image. European writings of the nineteenth century are full of attempts to explain why the Classical culture collapsed, what fatal flaws doomed it to such a humiliating twilight: its lack of internal debate and differentiation, the effete Greeks' supposed inability to withstand the might of sundry (European) empires that consequently succeeded to their cultural heritage . . . There is something profoundly self-serving in all these justificatory formulae, and it is reflected in the complacent self-congratulation with which the West expropriated the Classical antiquities, an orgy of acquisition that continued – with serious conse-quences for the current international relations of Greece – into the age of Lord Elgin, and it has since resurfaced in some no less unpleasant modern guises.[42]

The "taint of Turkish culture" proved the most major stumbling block for later European sensibilities, constituting as it did "a deep-veined imperfection in the marmoreal Hellenic image." Internal weakness, passive populations and innate decadence all typify western discourse on "Oriental" societies, the histories of which have been defined chiefly in terms of their contact with and eventual submission to European powers.[43] Yet ambivalent attitudes to "captive Greece," and a similarly biased historical treatment, manifestly begin well before the Ottoman period. A different approach to the study of Roman Greece, one emphasizing the conditions of life and active responses of the provincial society at large, is one way to ameliorate the unfortunate consequences of past approaches (troublesome though these will continue to be).

# 2

# The rural landscape

Conditions in the countryside – the distribution of agricultural resources, the organization of agricultural production – lie at the very heart of pre-industrial societies. Yet, as ancient historians have long known, to reconstruct the rural landscape of antiquity is no straightforward task. Neglect of the subject in the extant documentary sources is one general difficulty to be faced. Even where relevant source materials do exist, their problematic presentation of a desolate, depopulated Greece, and the need to assess how far these accounts constitute merely rhetorical exercises rather than reliable descriptions, further complicate the situation. Those few studies which have dealt with the Greek countryside of this period of necessity began (and finished) with such evidence, since nothing else was available. Thanks to the introduction and proliferation of archaeological surface survey (a development only of the 1970s and 1980s in Greece), that dependency has been broken, as we have seen. Survey elsewhere in the classical lands has already demonstrated its ability to overturn accepted opinions based on literary testimonia, not least about levels of rural habitation in antiquity: for instance, the use of purely archaeological data has seriously challenged the image of imperial Italy as a land "ruined" by *latifundia*, a reconstruction which had been based upon a limited range of documentary sources rather similar to that available for Roman Greece.[1] This analysis, then, differs from its predecessors by relying heavily in the first instance on survey evidence to evoke rural conditions. Interpretation and analysis of that landscape follow in turn, drawing upon all sources of evidence – textual as well as archaeological.

## SURVEYING ROMAN GREECE

The aim of archaeological surface survey is to locate and relate in a diachronic perspective all remains of human activity across a landscape; it thus operates on a broad temporal and regional scale. The nature of the

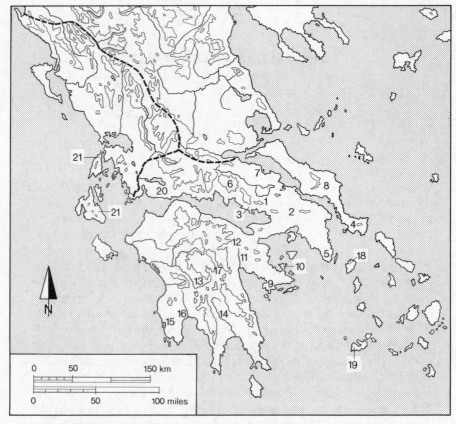

7 Distribution of archaeological survey projects mentioned in the text. (The numbers are those listed for each project in table 2.)

technique makes it well adapted to examine change in the long term – a perspective beyond the capacity of most non-archaeological sources. Another strength is its ability to encompass the material results of a wide range of human behavior, directly countering the inbuilt biases of most documentary evidence. Disadvantages, of course, include the fact that survey is a coarse-grained mode of investigation, unsuitable for the "individual event, the unique place, the particular relationship."[2] Instead, it excels in revealing general and long-term trends in residential preferences, agricultural activity and demographic behavior.

This investigation draws on the results of several regional survey projects, conducted in different parts of Greece. A comparative approach will be taken, concentrating not so much on the results from any one region as on the broader picture of conditions throughout the province, and emphasizing comprehensive spatial coverage. Figure 7 and table 2

Table 2. *Principal survey projects mentioned in the text*

| Survey project | Category[1] | Approximate area covered | Principal publication |
|---|---|---|---|
| *Central Greece* | | | |
| 1 Southwest Boeotia | A | 55 km² | Bintliff and Snodgrass (1985) |
| 2 Skourta Plain | A | 44 km² | Munn and Munn (1989); (1990) |
| 3 Khostia | B | 4.5 km² | Fossey and Morin (1989) |
| 4 Southern Euboea | B | 41 km² | Keller (1985); Keller and Wallace (1986); (1987) |
| 5 Attica | B | 25 km² | Lohmann (1983); (1985) |
| 6 Eastern Phokis | C | 1800 km² | Fossey (1986) |
| 7 Opountian Lokris | C | 1500 km² | Fossey (1990) |
| 8 Euboea | C | 3570 km² | Sackett *et al.* (1966) |
| *Corinthia/Argolid* | | | |
| 9 Southern Argolid | A | 44 km² | van Andel and Runnels (1987) |
| 10 Methana | A | 10.5 km² | Mee *et al.* (1991) |
| 11 Berbati | A | 4.5 km² | Wells *et al.* (1990) |
| 12 Nemea Valley | A | 50 km² | Wright *et al.* (1990) |
| *Central and southern Peloponnese* | | | |
| 13 Megalopolis | A | 60 km² | Roy *et al.* (1988); Lloyd (1991a) |
| 14 Lakonia | A | 70 km² | Cavanagh and Crouwel (1988) |
| 15 Messenia | B | 3800 km² | McDonald and Hope Simpson (1972) |
| 16 Five Rivers | B | 192 km² | Lukermann and Moody (1978) |
| 17 Eastern Arcadia | C | 5000 km² | Howell (1970) |
| *Cycladic islands* | | | |
| 18 Keos | A | 20 km² | Cherry *et al.* (1991) |
| 19 Melos | A | 30 km² | Renfrew and Wagstaff (1982) |
| *Northwest Greece* | | | |
| 20 Aetolian Studies Project | B | 4500 km² | Bommeljé and Doorn (1987) |
| 21 Leukas/Kephallenia | B | 2.1/2.1 km² | Gallant (1982); (1986) |

[1] For explanation of these categories, see pp. 36–7.

*Photocopy ?*

present the principal survey projects utilized in this discussion. The regions selected for analysis have been chosen not only on the highly pragmatic grounds that survey results are available, but also to ensure a representative sample of the environmental and topographical variety of Greece. Both relatively fertile regions (e.g. Boeotia, Messenia) and more rugged and arid zones (e.g. Aetolia, Southern Argolid) are included, as well as mainland and island, coastal and inland environments. Inclusion of the *ethnos*-based territory of Aetolia lends political variability to the sample as well.

Table 3. *Standard chronology for the Archaic to Late Roman periods*

| Period | Abbreviation | Approximate time span |
| --- | --- | --- |
| Archaic | A | Seventh century to early fifth century BC |
| Classical | C | Second quarter of the fifth to later fourth century BC |
| Early Hellenistic | EHL | Last quarter of fourth to late third century BC |
| Late Hellenistic | LHL | Late third century through first century BC (often to 31 BC) |
| Hellenistic | HL | Last quarter of fourth through first century BC (often to 31 BC) |
| Early Roman | ER | First to third century AD |
| Late Roman | LR | Fourth to early seventh century AD |
| Roman | R | First to early seventh century AD |
| Byzantine | Byz | Seventh to early thirteenth century AD |

In the chronological frameworks of all these projects, the Hellenistic and Early Roman epochs represent our period of interest, but their detailed subdivision does vary significantly from one project to another. Table 3 shows a "standard" system that approximates what the majority of surveys have actually used. On the other hand, absolute dates indicated here are naturally somewhat arbitrary, being based on the ceramics actually found and their probable history of use; and, obviously, the more sensitive the chronology employed, the better defined are the trends detectable in rural settlement and land use. Other difficulties in correlating and comparing survey results should not be underestimated, since research goals and field methodologies varied considerably among these various projects. Site densities, for example, have been shown empirically to vary directly with the intensity and thoroughness of survey coverage – in other words, the nature of each investigation (often linked to the date at which the work was initiated) directly affects the quality and reliability of the data retrieved. Obvious though the point may seem, comparing the results of a recent, intensive systematic survey with an older, extensive and unsystematic investigation is not to compare like with like.[3] Thus, to make this variability explicit, each survey used here has been placed within one of three broad categories reflecting their intensity of coverage and general reliability (table 2), as follows:

A: These data generally stem from the more recent and intensive of projects. Surveys of this type are designed to record systematically the density and distribution of artifacts across a clearly predefined study region, with the avowed goal of recovering the full range of past *loci* of human activity. Rigorous field methodologies include quantified in-field observation of material, controlled artifact collections and regular spacing of fieldwalkers (usually at ca. 10–20 meter intervals). In most cases, some consideration has been given to the impact of post-depositional factors (in particular geomorphological processes) on the resulting patterns of artifact distribution.

B: Two types of surveys fall within this category. The first includes explorations that are relatively systematic, but conducted on a very small scale, sometimes even single-handedly. Such minimal resources call into question the ultimate intensity of coverage, as well as the project's ability to identify and date the necessary range of artifact types. The second type comprises projects which, rather than attempting high-intensity coverage, were designed to cover a specific, usually quite large, region in a more extensive fashion; not surprisingly, a tendency to discover only the bigger sites within the study area is often demonstrable, as well as a concentration on specific categories of site location (e.g. hilltops, coastal promontories). In some cases, the investigations were not fully diachronic in intent (a preference for prehistory being especially notable).

C: Least reliance should be placed upon surveys in this category, which for the most part are both extensive and non-systematic in coverage. "Survey" is, strictly speaking, not an appropriate term to apply to this kind of reconnaissance, which normally involves the collection of sites haphazardly discovered, often over a very large area, as well as being limited, more often than not, only to the upper segment of the settlement hierarchy. Despite these drawbacks, surveys in category C can still provide useful information paralleling or supporting that from categories A and B.

This categorization allows some control over how much confidence to place in the findings of each survey and upon comparisons between the different projects. Surveys in category A, for instance, may be compared to one another with a fair degree of assurance, the others much less so.

We may now turn to a brief region-by-region review of overall developments in survey patterns from the Classical to the Late Roman period, for the most part discussing data from surveys of category A, before reviewing that from other projects. It should be emphasized that several of these projects are still awaiting full publication, while some are even now in progress. Despite the preliminary nature of parts of this study, however, we will see that some distinctive general patterns have already begun to emerge. In the following discussion, only broad trends in rural settlement and activity will be noted, since it is necessary to evaluate the relative reliability of these results before being in a position to attempt their interpretation and assess their implications later in the chapter.

### Central Greece and Attica

Pride of place must go to the Boeotia survey (1), among the first major intensive surface surveys undertaken in Greece (beginning in 1979), and also among the most fully published to date (figs. 8–10). Very briefly, this

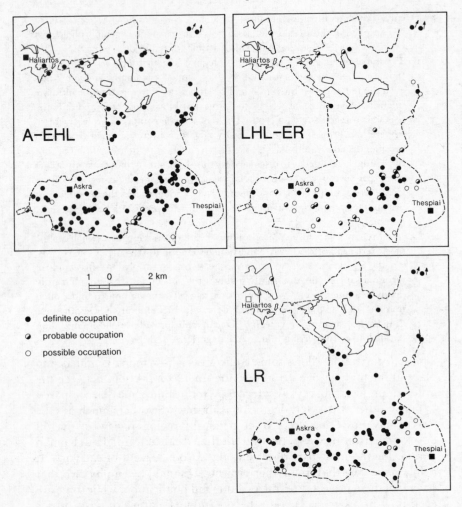

8 Southwest Boeotia, distribution of Archaic to Early Hellenistic sites

9 Southwest Boeotia, distribution of Late Hellenistic/Early Roman sites

10 Southwest Boeotia, distribution of Late Roman sites

area in the Archaic to Early Hellenistic period witnessed a very heavy level of rural occupation, most *loci* of which have been identified as small farm sites; rural hamlets and large town sites complete the regional settlement hierarchy. By far the densest occupation of the landscape dates to the Classical and Early Hellenistic period, especially the fourth century BC. The Late Hellenistic and Early Roman period (ca. 200 BC–AD 300) not only experienced a very significant drop in site numbers, but reveals markedly fewer signs of activity at some of the remaining sites. Contraction in the occupied area of urban sites has likewise been attested at this time. A "dramatic recovery" marked the Late Roman period (ca. AD 300–650), in both the rural and urban sectors.[4]

To the southeast of the study region of the Boeotia survey, the Stanford Skourta Plain Project (2) between 1985 and 1989 has examined a small upland plain lying in the frontier area between Attica and Boeotia; the survey territory probably includes the disputed border town of Panakton. Classical and Hellenistic occupation is recorded at a settlement believed to be Panakton itself, and a proliferation of sites identified as farmsteads has been noted for the Late Classical era, reaching its height at the turn of the fourth to the third century BC. At some time early in the second century BC, however, occupation at Panakton appears to come to an end; the numerous small sites disappear as well. Between approximately 200 BC and the Late Roman period, use of this remote upland area was limited to a few small hamlets along the northern edge of the plain. New sites (farmsteads and hamlets), dispersed across the study region, reappear only in the fourth to sixth century AD.[5]

Also in the vicinity of the Boeotia survey, but to the southwest, a Canadian team in the 1980s carried out a small-scale survey in the environs of Khostia (ancient Chorsiai, 3), a small town or *polisma* destroyed at the end of the Hellenistic period and not reoccupied till the second or third century AD. For the imperial period, only one *locus* of activity was discovered by this survey, perhaps contemporaneous with the resettlement of the town. It was admitted, however, that geomorphological factors may have badly skewed these results.[6]

Further east, on the island of Euboea, archaeological survey work has been undertaken at the southern tip, around the ancient town of Karystos (4), by Canadian and American scholars – first in a single-handed diachronic survey of the early 1980s and, more recently, in collaborative work aimed at studying the Classical period. A Classical high point in site numbers, possibly related to the presence of Athenian cleruchic settlement, was noted, with a sharp fall-off in the Hellenistic and Roman era. (Karystos, incidentally, is the town most often identified with the urban center described in Dio Chrysostom's *Euboean Discourse*.) A very extensive survey of the island of Euboea as a whole (8), carried out thirty years ago and aimed primarily at the discovery of prehistoric locations, also reported a gradual decline in site numbers through the Hellenistic and Roman periods.[7]

Unfortunately, little systematic survey work has been conducted in Attica. German investigations of the early 1980s in the vicinity of the rural deme of Atene (5) revealed a florescence of archaeological finds in the fifth and fourth centuries BC, followed by a decline in settlement in the area. For the third to first centuries BC, it was suggested that a greater number of deme members now resided in Athens itself.[8] At another possible deme site, Markopoulo (Pousi Kaloyerou), occupation was noted between the Late Geometric and Late Hellenistic periods, then Late Roman occupation, and perhaps Byzantine material; again, activity in the early imperial period appears to be lacking.[9]

One of the principal investigators of the Khostia project conducted two large-scale extensive surveys during the 1960s, focusing primarily on the upper end of the settlement hierarchy, in Eastern Phokis (6) and Opountian Lokris (7). In Phokis, the latter half of the Classical period (i.e. the fourth century BC) saw the maximum peak of settlement numbers; a "gentle decline" set in during subsequent centuries, with 16 Classical sites reduced to 13 definite Hellenistic and 10 definite Roman (fig. 11a). The results from Opountian Lokris suggest that settlement density likewise attained its maximum height in later Classical times, with only a slight reduction in Hellenistic and imperial times, and an essentially similar pattern of habitation is argued to continue in Late Roman times as well.[10]

### Corinthia/Argolid

No fewer than four systematic and intensive survey projects have been launched in this area, a density at least partially explained by the attraction of several major Mycenaean sites and numerous other prehistoric locations. This review will begin with the most southern portion of the region, the Akte peninsula of the Argolid, before moving to the north.

The Argolid Exploration Project (AEP, 9), an American undertaking of the early 1980s in the Southern Argolid, was one of the first surveys to record the florescence of small rural sites, noted here especially in marginal agricultural areas, in the Classical and Early Hellenistic periods (figs. 12–14). Overall site numbers increased through the fifth and early fourth centuries, with the peak of settlement dispersal (up to 110 possible sites, 78 definite) apparently falling within a short period from the late fourth to mid-third century BC. At the end of this era (which the AEP terms the "Classical/Hellenistic" period, ca. 323–250 BC), however, a sharp decline in the number of such sites was observed, with only ten sites certainly belonging to the Early and Middle Roman periods. Occupation at more substantial centers too was affected; the *polis* center of Halieis seems to have been abandoned in the third century BC. Some additional rural activity took place in the Early Roman epoch,

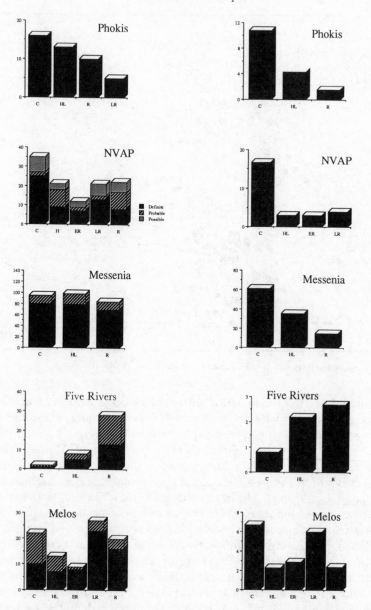

11  On left, histogram of site numbers; on right, histogram of site numbers weighted
by the length of each chronological period: (a) Eastern Phokis (b) Nemea
Valley (c) Messenia (d) Five Rivers (e) Melos. Shaded areas indicate *possible*
sites of each period.

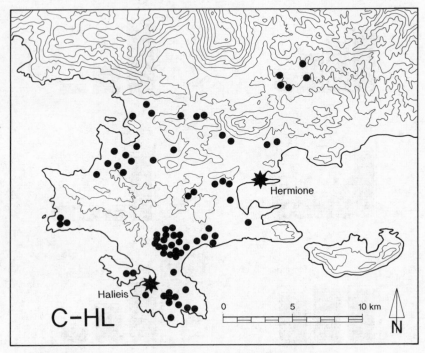

Hermione

Halieis

C–HL

0      5      10 km

N

12  Southern Argolid, distribution of Classical/Early Hellenistic sites

but only the Late Roman period witnessed a more general reoccupation of the countryside (with up to 98 possible sites, 69 definite) and the re-emergence of a developed regional settlement hierarchy.[11]

   The rugged and precipitous volcanic peninsula of Methana was explored in the 1980s by a British team (10); final publication of the project is still in progress, but useful preliminary analyses are already available (figs. 15–17). The initial phases of the Hellenistic epoch saw an increase in site numbers, with the locations of probable farmsteads suggesting that marginal agricultural land was being more intensively exploited. In the third century BC two of the three main settlements of the peninsula, Magoula and Oga, were abandoned: "a development evidently linked, perhaps towards the end of the century, with a reduction in the number of smaller, rural sites." Apart from the town site of ancient Methana itself, only a handful of sites was definitely occupied in the Late Hellenistic and Early Roman periods. From this first-century BC nadir, however, the number of sites began slowly to increase again, notably with nine sites occupied for the first time in the Middle Roman

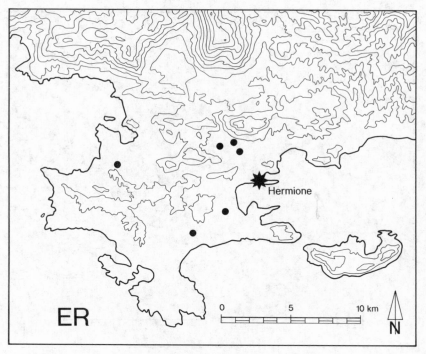

Hermione

ER

0          5          10 km

N

13 Southern Argolid, distribution of Early Roman sites

period (here defined as the second and third centuries AD). Site numbers then continued to rise throughout the fourth and fifth centuries AD.[12]

The Berbati-Limnes project (11) is a collaborative Swedish/American project whose first season of fieldwork in 1988 surveyed an area on the slopes enclosing the Berbati valley immediately to the east of Mycenae. A string of small farmsteads datable to the Classical period was found to lie scattered on these slopes, and there is a drop in the number of findspots between the Classical/Hellenistic and the Roman era (from six sites to two). Conclusions from the small sample available so far must remain preliminary, but the investigators already suggest that "it seems obvious that in Roman times people had generally moved onto the valley bottoms" (where a Roman bath, identified from earlier work, is known to be located) and "cultivated only the lower fields on the slopes of the mountains."[13]

Results from the Nemea Valley Archaeological Project (12) – a large-scale American-Greek-British venture carried out in 1984-9 – await final publication, but the chief patterns of settlement during this period have

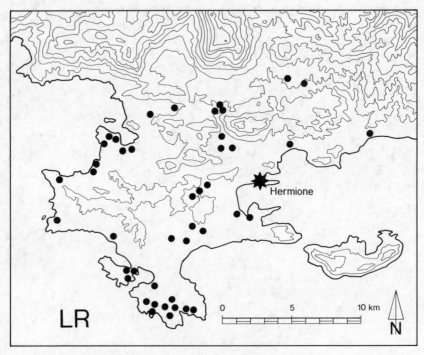

14 Southern Argolid, distribution of Late Roman sites

been established with some confidence (fig. 11b). As in most of the other data sets examined so far, the Archaic–Hellenistic period dominates the rural landscape, many sites being identified as probable farmhouses or other small-scale rural agricultural installations. Later Hellenistic and Early Roman material, on the other hand, is much more rare, except on larger sites (such as the *polis* site of Phlius), while pottery of Late Roman date is again more widely distributed. It is worth noting that these patterns "are reflected in tract collections (taken in the course of regular fieldwalking) as well as in collections taken on site, inspiring confidence in their reality."[14]

### Central and southern Peloponnese

In the land-locked, highland region of Arcadia, two study areas were explored in the territory of Megalopolis by a British team between 1981 and 1984 (13). Early results suggest that traces of the Classical and Early Hellenistic era predominated in the Megalopolitan landscape, the majority of Classical sites consisting of moderate scatters taken to

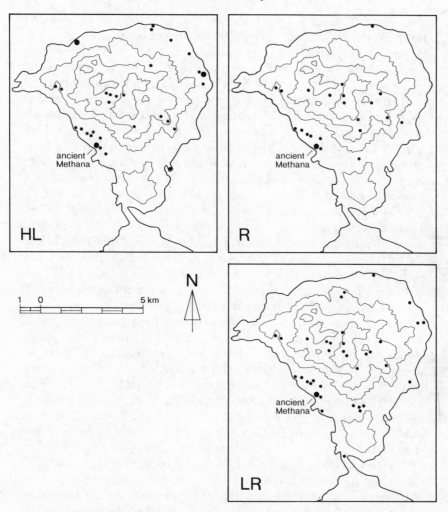

15 Methana peninsula, distribution of Hellenistic sites. The larger circles mark the locations of Ancient Methana, Magoula and Oga.

16 Methana peninsula, distribution of Roman sites

17 Methana peninsula, distribution of Late Roman sites

represent farmsteads. In the Hellenistic period, alongside such modest finds, larger sites were seen to emerge, considered by the investigators to be large and dominant rural homesteads. Many of these large farmsteads, as well as smaller sites, disappear in the first and second century AD. No significant new foundations appear during this time, and a decline of about 80 percent in site numbers from the Archaic to Hellenistic period has been hypothesized. By contrast, the Late Roman epoch (beginning in the third century AD) witnessed an increasing number of rural sites. An earlier exploration of Eastern Arcadia (17), primarily for prehistoric remains, also deserves mention; there a rough impression was registered of settlement decline from the Classical to the Roman period.[15]

Still in progress is analysis of material from the joint British-Dutch Lakonia survey near Sparta (14), on the eastern side of the Eurotas River. Preliminary indications suggest, however, that the Classical and Early Hellenistic periods (fifth to second centuries BC) witnessed a heavily occupied countryside, with a hierarchy of site types ranging widely from humble to more elaborate dwellings (but the majority identified as small agricultural sites). A significant drop in site numbers appears to occur between the Early and Late Hellenistic period; the Early Roman period may see a slight rise in site numbers (which then remain fairly stable throughout the Roman period), but many farmsteads and villages of the preceding Classical phase remain uninhabited. One particular pattern that has been observed is a clustering of small Roman farms in valley bottoms and along natural lines of communication. But the dating of Roman material is still especially problematic in this area, so final publication of the survey finds is a prerequisite for more definitive conclusions.[16]

The University of Minnesota Messenia Expedition (15) is generally considered the first relatively "systematic" survey conducted in Greece, although survey methodologies have changed so rapidly in Greece that its data (from the 1950s and 1960s) already appear quite coarse and the project has been subjected to a certain amount of criticism (fig. 11c). Primarily interested in reconstructing the Bronze Age environment of the Palace of Nestor at Pylos, the project's treatment of post-prehistoric material demands special caution. At first glance, site numbers appear to remain fairly constant from Classical through Roman times, but when these numbers are weighted by the length of period involved, a marked decline can be observed.[17] A local and somewhat more intensive survey of the 1970s within this larger region, the so-called "Five Rivers" area around the excavated site of Nichoria (16), yielded a quite different pattern, with an *increase* in site numbers for the Roman era (fig. 11d).[18]

## Cycladic islands

A collaborative British, American and Greek survey was undertaken in 1983/4 in the northwest portion of the island of Keos (18), in the hinterland of the Classical *polis* of Koressos and the Bronze Age settlement of Ayia Irini (figs. 32–5). A survey of the city of Koressos itself, with results reflecting the community's Hellenistic synoecism with the neighboring town of Ioulis, was undertaken as part of this project. A busy Classical rural landscape was observed, with numerous widely distributed sites, the majority of which have been identified as small family farmsteads. Hellenistic material is rarer in this area, with Early Roman finds even more so. The Late Roman period, on the other hand, witnessed an increase in the quantity and distribution of finds, testifying to a reoccupation of the land. Further to the south of the island, the hinterlands of the *poleis* Poiessa and Karthaia have recently been investigated by scholars from the University of Athens; in the more fertile agricultural zones around Poiessa they reported "systematic and extended habitation" in Roman times.[19]

A systematic intensive survey by a British team took place on the Cycladic island of Melos in 1976/7 (19), in conjunction with the excavation of the Bronze Age settlement of Phylakopi (fig. 11e). Hellenistic settlement on the island declined from its Classical level, in association with increasing aggregation of the remaining sites around the urban center of Ancient Melos. The Roman period, taken as a whole, saw a very substantial increase in site numbers. Yet wherever the material from individual sites can be broken down into "Early" and "Late" components, it emerges that this development was primarily a later Roman phenomenon, characterized in at least some regions by the appearance of apparently "commercial" or "industrial" sites; sites dated specifically to the Early Roman era (first to third centuries AD) remain relatively rare. The Melian evidence provides a particularly good illustration of the need to isolate – whenever possible – individual phases within the Roman epoch.[20]

## Northwest Greece

Except for a long tradition of extensive topographical reconnaissance, the northwestern part of Greece has remained relatively unexplored by comparison with other parts of Greece. To remedy that situation, a Dutch team, since the early 1980s the Aetolian Studies Project (20), has undertaken a more systematic and multidisciplinary study of a large part of Central Aetolia (figs. 49 and 50). Unusually, it was the Hellenistic era that here produced the most abundant ceramic evidence, followed by the new familiar drop in site numbers in Roman times. This decline is especially marked if these numbers are weighted by the length of chronological periods involved. It is freely admitted, however, that ceramic typologies remain extremely problematic in this area.[21]

From the Ionian islands of Leukas and Kephallenia, the results of two intensive, single-person surveys (dating to the early 1980s) of small samples of territory are worth noting (21), although the detailed analysis of ceramic finds did not extend beyond the Classical period. A relatively stable pattern of settlement from the fifth century through the Hellenistic period seems to have been in operation; by contrast, Early Roman sites appear to be totally absent, though some Late Roman material was reported.[22]

*Summary*

On the whole, these data from survey come together to form a remarkably uniform picture. The rural landscape of the Classical and Early Hellenistic era appears exceptionally active, characterized especially by the presence of numerous, dispersed, small sites. Such *loci* have generally been identified as rural farmsteads. Throughout the course of the Hellenistic and Roman periods, a drop – often a severe drop – in the number of sites was experienced in almost all regions for which detailed information is available. Traces of rural activity for the Late Hellenistic and Early Roman era are everywhere relatively scarce, giving the distinct impression of a deserted, "empty" landscape. In several regions, the starting point for this decline appears to lie within the second half of the third century BC, but it may well be later in other areas. The crudity of survey dating prevents the identification of any more specific "horizon" for the downturn, but its effects were virtually ubiquitous by the first century AD. After the initial drop-off, the level of site numbers remains broadly unchanged throughout the next five centuries or more (ca. 200 BC–AD 300) – i.e. from the period of the Republic throughout the duration of the early empire. Some regions do record a slight revival in the second or third century AD (e.g. Lakonia, Methana). A much more clearly defined increase in site numbers characterizes the subsequent Late Roman era, with patterns of rural activity once again resembling the "full" landscape of the Classical epoch.

Minor variations in this overall pattern of change and development certainly exist from region to region. Cases such as the Roman settlement boom in the Five Rivers area of Messenia, or the Hellenistic zenith in site numbers in Central Aetolia are anomalous, indicating particular regional trajectories. Yet such aberrant patterns are surprisingly few – at least at this stage of our knowledge – and it is the otherwise uniform character of this phenomenon that is so striking: in general, all the regions studied seem to change in concert and, cumulatively, they present a very similar picture, particularly if we rely most heavily on the evidence from surveys in category A. It is perhaps worth stressing that such uniformity need by no means necessarily have been expected: for example, in Italy at roughly this time, comparative analyses of survey data have revealed very different settlement and land use patterns in regions no further apart and no more environmentally variable than the areas explored here.[23] In early imperial Achaia, however, there seems now to have been established a uniform archaeological pattern that points to a considerable degree of rural abandonment.

### ARCHAEOLOGICAL SOURCE CRITICISM

To what extent can these neatly convergent results automatically be taken as "real"? Just as a naive and uncritical acceptance of documentary sources is to be avoided, so too these data must be examined to ensure that the patterns detected are not simply an artifact of the state of our archaeological knowledge – or ignorance. Most pressing for the study of the early imperial period are potential problems with survey chronologies, and with the identification, dating and interpretation of the ceramic material.

The varying chronological schemes used by these projects (in some cases, unfortunately, never made explicit) pose undeniable obstacles to a synthesis of the results. The inability of some projects to subdivide the Hellenistic and Roman periods is significant, given the obvious and important distinction between the early and late phases of both epochs in many other regions. In addition, non-compatible periodizations – for example, the Hellenistic period has been variably defined as lasting between 150 or 300 years – can adversely affect the comparison and interpretation of different survey data sets. "Weighting" the representation of site numbers by the actual duration of each period to some extent allows a more valid comparison of the data, and enough correspondence does exist between the various chronological schemes employed to permit the basic level of comparison attempted here.[24] For further refinement in such comparative studies, however, more comprehensive publication and specific description of the diagnostic ceramics for individual periods will be a *sine qua non*, as well as greater standardization in the chronological frameworks utilized.

More disturbing questions revolve around the empirically observed fall in site numbers. Is this a genuine pattern representative of behavior in the past, or is it a function of the relative "visibility" of certain periods, and of our taxonomic schemes? The greatest worry for the Hellenistic and Early Roman era in Greece is the somewhat inconsistent state of the ceramic studies of this period. On the one hand, the fine wares, from Hellenistic West Slope Ware to the Late Roman Red Wares, are well placed in chronological sequence. At certain major sites (for example, Athens, Corinth, or Delos) material of these periods has been stratigraphically recovered, and several specific classes of material (e.g. Megarian bowls, lamps, unguentaria) have received very detailed attention. Unfortunately, however, survey for the most part picks up coarse and common local wares, material of a sort which, until very recently, has not been of much interest to the classical archaeologist. The coarse wares of the early imperial period, judged to be particularly "late" and "dull," have been especially poorly served. Amphorae form one exception to this rule, but these do not appear consistently enough in the survey record to act as the chief chronological marker for site history. As a result, typologies and chronologies for the sorts of pottery most often found in surface collections offer cause for some concern.[25]

Publications of earlier or less intensive surveys (i.e. categories B and C) leave the distinct impression (albeit one rarely stated explicitly) that the dating of sites rested on fine wares alone – that is, the painted, decorated and imported material. While a firm date can usually be given to settlement occupation on the basis of such finds, this reliance on fine pottery brings into question the visibility of all relevant sites. To accept that such surveys have successfully identified the full range of rural occupation requires the assumption that residents of all rural sites would have had equal access to all pottery types; yet it seems obvious that different sites would use and discard different types of ceramics at different rates, depending on the nature of the site and the social and economic status of its inhabitants, and no uniform pattern or rate of acquisition and utilization of fine pottery can be assumed. Furthermore, for some inland regions (Nemea Valley, Arcadia, Boeotia) it has been specifically suggested that standard types of imported fine wares reached the countryside only in relatively limited quantities, being found primarily in urban or other large sites. Conversely, Keos and the Southern Argolid, "whose extensive coastlines provided direct access to maritime commerce," demonstrate patterns of more widespread distribution of imported wares (see fig. 7). Clearly, location, and access to trade networks, directly affected the quantities of the readily datable and highly visible wares entering a region, just as the function and status of individual sites would affect the types of ceramics required or affordable.

Identifying sites on the basis of imports alone obviously presents the danger of taking only a partial sample of activity in the countryside and, in particular, of missing sites at the base of the social hierarchy. The "dissemination" time of specific types of high-quality ceramics must be considered as well: there is some evidence, for example, of a time-lag in the importation and impact of western sigillata to the east, even at the provincial center of Corinth. Due allowance must be made for "trickle-down time" to other cities, let alone to the more isolated of rural settlements.[26]

Apart from differential access to pottery at different sites, Martin Millett has also warned of the effects of variations in the supply rate of ceramics. Quantified analyses of excavated finds demonstrate that the quantity of some pottery types in circulation does vary through time, with obvious implications for the total amount of pottery potentially used and discarded. In one attempt to obviate this potential source of bias in the generation of settlement pattern maps, the Ager Tarraconensis survey in Spain compared, not the absolute number of sherds discovered, but a range of density values for each period. This strategy automatically reduces the risk that periods with a plentiful pottery flow will dominate eras less well endowed. Without careful proof of actual supply patterns (which require detailed and comprehensive excavation data), however, this approach does run the risk of circularity and perhaps of unduly depressing genuine differences in the number and distribution of settlements between periods. Yet even if this particular method is not necessarily the best or only way forward, Millett is correct in demanding that survey data "be presented with full supporting evidence rather than simply as dots on a map."[27]

Variability in ceramic access and supply poses two legitimate challenges to any survey-based historical reconstruction, as well as salutary warnings about overly facile uses of the evidence. But some response can be made to both problems. More recent surveys (generally those of category A) have collected a wide variety of material, relying far less upon fine wares and other imports as the sole chronological indicators for the Hellenistic and Roman periods. The necessity of mastering local sequences of coarse pottery – wares more readily available to the whole population and less subject to production variability, if not wholly immune from it – has been acknowledged and, in several areas, acted upon. The rigorous studies necessary to monitor pottery supply rates are thus far lacking for Greece, and without such a check, purely artificial "massaging" of the presently available data hardly seems warranted. These problems, it can be concluded, do not unduly disturb the overall patterns so far established.

A further important concern arises from recent suggestions that the early imperial decline in site numbers has been exaggerated as a consequence of the increased use of alternatives to pottery, such as glass and precious metals. Such materials obviously would not survive well, especially on the surface, and – unlike pottery – they are suitable for recycling. Even a partial replacement of ceramic vessels by these other materials would result in sparser and more nondescript surface assemblages, making the identification of early imperial sites so much the harder. Glass indeed has been claimed to have been "as popular and widespread as were pottery and metalwork" in the Early Roman period; an "appreciable" amount was found at Corinth during excavations in the Forum area.[28] However, types of glass vessels (chiefly used for drinking purposes) form only a fraction of the full range of domestic wares, and glass is not a viable fabric for the functional shapes that dominate most surface assemblages (lekanai, pithoi, amphorae, cooking wares). As for precious metal as a "replacement" material, surely only a restricted élite would have possessed such objects: were that not so, fictile imitations would have been unnecessary.[29] While it is true that even a partial replacement of ceramics would result in some reduction in archaeologically retrievable material, this is a potential source of bias that applies with most force in urban or sanctuary contexts.

Lastly, we must address two other basic, and widely voiced, fears about the validity of survey evidence. The first is the issue of the relationship of surface and subsurface remains. Few ancient historians and classical archaeologists today would openly adopt the line of Kent Flannery's fictional "Real Mesoamerican Archaeologist": "surface remains are just that – the junk you find on the surface – and nothing more. And I say, screw them." On the other hand, if survey sites are but the surface signs of buried archaeological deposits, just how representative are such finds of what may actually lie below? No systematic study of this problem has been undertaken in the Mediterranean, though various individual studies comparing the results of intensive survey and excavation have discovered that they largely agreed in their reconstruction of site history. Other archaeologists, however, feel there is "less cause for optimism in our understanding of the relationship between surface archaeology and buried archaeology," for other cases are known where surface finds have failed either to reveal all periods of occupation or the precise nature of particular settlements.[30] The history of individual sites, however, has never been the study of survey; at the *regional* level of analysis, the overall impression of trends in human activity that survey produces suffices.

The second general concern lies with the ability of survey to detect *all* strata of society in the archaeological landscape: would the very poor leave any traces at all to be discovered centuries later by surface investigation? This has been doubted by some, who fear that "the remains of even the smallest 'farmsteads' discovered by archaeological survey are probably too grand for the poorest peasants."[31] The logical conclusion would be that survey cannot claim to make general statements about the rural activities of the population at large, and this should perhaps be admitted for certain less intensive surveys which have tended to report only relatively large sites, presumably missing many smaller *loci* of human activity. Yet in recent intensive surveys (category A) sites as small as 0.01 hectares (i.e. 10 × 10m), or even less, have been reported – indeed, for the Greco-Roman period small sites are by far the most commonly found. One good example of survey's ability to locate apparently undistinguished rural sites can be seen at PP17, a Late Hellenistic/Early Roman site discovered in the course of routine surface investigation by the Boeotia survey; later subsurface geophysical prospection and soil analysis confirmed the presence there of what was most probably a small habitation (ca. 5 × 7m) with an attached wall, perhaps enclosing a farmyard (12 × 8m).[32] Between the extremely modest size and material finds of so many rural sites, coupled with more definite evidence from locations such as PP17, it is not difficult to construct a defense of survey as a technique well capable of retrieving data relevant to the lowest ranks of the society. In any case, I shall argue later that the poorest of the poor are unlikely to have chosen, or been able, to live in the countryside.

"Source criticism" of the archaeological data for early imperial Greece, therefore, goes some way toward establishing the relative reliability of currently available survey results, while at the same time warning us not to take the evidence of absolute site numbers entirely at face value. Some refinement of these patterns may well occur as further period-specific ceramic analysis is completed.[33] On present evidence, however, nothing suggests that the overall observed trends in rural activity will be reversed, nor that they are the simple by-product of archaeological ignorance. Difficulties in the interpretation of survey data must be kept in perspective: in truth, they are neither more nor less intractable and opaque than any other source of evidence for the ancient world. So we are faced with a clear and cumulative pattern that demands explanation.

## SITE DECLINE = POPULATION DECLINE?

Would that I had been able to provide this gift when Greece was flourishing, so that more people might have enjoyed my grace, for that I blame the passage of time for having reduced in advance the magnitude of my favor. (*IG* VII 2713)

With these regretful words, the emperor Nero granted freedom and tax immunity to the province of Achaia. On the face of it, the image of a desolate, depopulated Greece presented by the literary testimonia reviewed in chapter 1 would seem vindicated by archaeological survey's revelation of a desolate early imperial landscape.

As we have already seen, understanding the literary sources is not a simple matter, and the interpretation of the survey data is not straightforward either, especially with regard to demographic trends. Several barriers stand in the way of the direct correlation of these two types of evidence. First, the decline in site numbers must be kept in some kind of perspective: Boeotia, for example, actually maintains a higher density of settlement throughout this time than the well-explored Italian region of the Ager Veientanus close to Rome itself.[34] Second, the evidence reviewed so far deals only with human activity in the countryside, the *chora*. The possibility of demographic movement from countryside to town must be recognized: the behavior of the city centers therefore also has to be considered before major demographic collapse is accepted as historical fact. Third, some account must be taken of the *size* of the individual sites lost. The apparently grim picture is somewhat mitigated by the fact that the majority of the abandoned sites (at least those from surveys of category A) are very small – rural farmsteads, perhaps, or even seasonally used sheds or shelters. It is significant that in the more extensive surveys, focusing primarily on the top of the settlement hierarchy, the drop in settlement numbers seems to be much less dramatic (e.g. compare Messenia and Phokis with the Southern Argolid and Boeotia; figs. 11a, 11c with 8–9, 12–13). In attempting population calculations for antiquity, classical scholars have usually taken the "typical" farmstead, somewhat arbitrarily, as having about five inhabitants per site. The loss of numerous sites of this small size looks worse in maps and histograms than its significance in terms of absolute population numbers would in fact be; and the demographic impact is minimized still further if these were only seasonal shelters for owners permanently residing elsewhere, most likely in the town. The abandonment of a site thus need not indicate the extinction of its inhabitants, but instead may point to altered social and economic priorities.

This opens up a more promising line to develop. The relative "visibility" of any individual period in the diachronic survey record may well depend more upon the particular agricultural regimes and relations of production in operation at that time than it necessarily does upon relative population levels. The Classical and Early Hellenistic period is distinctive for the prevalence at that time of dispersed rural residence, a type of settlement and land use both encouraged and allowed by prevailing social and economic conditions (notably widespread private ownership of land). On the island of Keos, a reverse correlation has been observed. When fewer and larger landholdings were dominant (as, for instance, in the Ottoman period), tightly nucleated residence and "commuting farmers" became the norm. Conversely, in the nineteenth century, after the land reforms of the post-Revolutionary period, agricultural facilities and residential structures returned to the country-side. This increase in rural capital and labor investment has been perceived as "probably a consequence of the division and redistribution of lands formerly held by large-scale landholders, such as the traditional archons and the monasteries."[35] The configuration of the countryside in the early imperial period now similarly requires this kind of broad-based, contextual analysis. The likelihood and degree of population change at this time is discussed further at the end of this chapter. What must be stressed at this stage of the argument is that our survey evidence does not *a priori* prove demographic decline, or certainly not to the extreme degree that has often been claimed: while population collapse may be the easiest way to explain the observed patterns, other factors arguably played an even greater part in determining the appearance of the rural landscape.

## THE ORGANIZATION OF THE AGRICULTURAL LANDSCAPE

The rural landscape in a pre-industrial society is formed above all by the conditions governing the division and exploitation of the land. These factors dictate the appearance of the countryside, set the level and nature of its utilization, and underlie demographic change. Given the problema-tic testimony of the documentary sources, in this discussion we will approach from a different direction, beginning with the information garnered from the survey evidence that has been reviewed, before attempting a synthesis of all other forms of evidence.

If analyzing landholding patterns is taken to entail the recovery of specific details of ownership or the relation and interaction of labor and management systems, then the material record may seem an odd place to begin. The inability of archaeology to respond precisely to these basic historical issues has long been a matter for some complaint.[36] What labor systems were in operation? Did landowners work their own holdings? How was property transferred? Such questions surely lie outside the ambit of archaeological evidence. Survey results can prove particularly frustrating, providing as they do only very basic categories of data – site size, location and function – presented in static "snapshots" in some cases representing centuries of rural activity. To ascertain with confidence the nationality or juridical status of the owner (or perhaps mere operator) of any individual settlement inevitably remains almost impossible. Yet instead of despairing of survey data, which by any reckoning constitutes our most comprehensive evidence about the ancient countryside, we ought rather to look for more appropriate uses for the distinctive type of evidence which survey provides. Tracing long-term, cumulative trends in systems of land tenure is feasible, and they can be teased out of good survey data if a rigorous and explicit methodology is employed. Monitoring variability in rural activity along several different dimensions reveals, with careful interpretation, changes in the organization of the agricultural landscape. The number of sites observed provides one such dimension (see pp. 37–49, fig. 11), and three other types of evidence will now be reviewed: continuity in site occupation, variations in site sizes, and the character and probable function of the sites themselves. The results of these separate investigations can then be pulled together to determine the nature of change across the rural landscape.

## Site continuity

We can begin with two very basic questions. Throughout the course of the early imperial period were landholding patterns affected at all? And were there shifts in the distribution of the remaining rural population, suggesting changes in patterns of settlement and perhaps land ownership? Disruption in the countryside has already been signaled by the virtually ubiquitous decline in site numbers in the Hellenistic and Roman (especially the Late Hellenistic and Early Roman) epochs, but continuity/discontinuity in site occupation between periods offers another potential index. Occupation of the same site through time (high levels of continuity) can be interpreted as reflecting some measure of stability in established landholding patterns, and, conversely, low continuity – especially if coupled with a high proportion of newly inhabited sites – can be taken to signal variability in land ownership and exploitation. These equations (continuity = stability; discontinuity = disruption in tenure) are not to be rigorously pressed. Decisions taken by individual families in particular circumstances can radically rewrite patterns of rural settlement, yet the motivations for such decisions need not always revolve around the acquisition or loss of land; and the very coarse chronological framework involved here also necessitates a cautious approach. Nonetheless, if a region experiences low continuity in rural settlement, then the possibility must be entertained that widespread disruption in the ownership of land is one of the factors responsible.

Not all surveys discussed here offer suitable data. In table 4, the first

Table 4. *Percentage of continuously occupied and new sites, by period*

| Survey project | % Continuity | % New |
|---|---|---|
| *NVAP* | | |
| Hellenistic | 67 | 33 |
| Early Roman | 29 | 71 |
| Late Roman | 38 | 62 |
| *Melos* | | |
| Hellenistic | 71 | 29 |
| Early Roman | 25 | 75 |
| Late Roman | 27 | 73 |
| *Keos* | | |
| Hellenistic | 25 | 75 |
| Early Roman | 25 | 75 |
| Late Roman | 10 | 90 |
| *Southwest Boeotia* | | |
| Late Hellenistic | 60(22)[1] | 40(78)[1] |
| Early Roman | 73 | 27 |
| Late Roman | 38 | 62 |

[1] Numbers in brackets are percentages
calculated for those sites dating specifically
from the Early Hellenistic period (rather than
Classical/Early Hellenistic period).

figure indicates the percentage of sites which continued in use from the
previous period (that is, from the Classical to the Hellenistic, and so on);
the second figure is the percentage of fresh settlements found. At Nemea
and on Melos, a hiatus in occupation continuity can be observed in Early
Roman settlement, compared to the more stable pattern in the preceding
Hellenistic era; a higher percentage of new sites accompanies this trend.
To some extent, of course, the decline in continuity simply reflects the
observed drop in overall site numbers, but the appearance of fresh sites
demonstrates the pattern is somewhat more complicated. In these areas,
a higher proportion of shifts in site occupation, and thus possibly in
landholding patterns, is therefore detectable between the Hellenistic and
Early Roman periods. The traditional chronological "break" between
these two epochs is 31 BC, but these changes could have taken place over a
longer time span and may well have been a continuous process occurring
throughout both periods. The pattern is different on Keos, where the
Hellenistic synoecism of Koressos with the neighboring city of Ioulis

clearly disrupted rural settlement. For Southwest Boeotia, levels of continuity appear higher until the Late Roman period. It is worth noting, however, that for those sites which were specifically known to have been occupied from the Early to the Late Hellenistic periods (rather than from the broader Classical/Early Hellenistic categorization), the percentage of continuous sites was only 22 (with 78 percent new), suggesting greater discontinuity in the last centuries BC (table 4). It is also worth noting, for all these surveys, that those sites occupied in the Early Roman period tend to remain in operation through Late Roman times.

At this point and for the regions which can be studied, the evidence of site continuity points tentatively toward some instability in rural settlement in the last centuries BC, before the emergence of a new configuration under the empire. Modifications in landholding patterns, including new owners or new residents on the land, provide one plausible explanation. These results suggest, if in an indirect and crude manner, that the inception of Roman influence and control led to the disruption – perhaps redistribution? – of economic resources.

### *Site sizes*

Assessments of the relative size of artifact scatters, and the intelligent interpretation of them, challenge survey archaeologists everywhere. Surface sites are notoriously subject to numerous post-depositional processes which can either diminish or "smear" them, making it difficult for the original extent of a site to be estimated with any accuracy. Only detailed geomorphological work, and repeated on-site examinations, can offer some control over this process. On the other hand, post-depositional interference strikes with little temporal bias, allowing at least rough period-by-period comparisons to be made with relative confidence. More troubling is the fact that the sites discovered and analyzed upon the basis of surface finds alone often constitute a palimpsest of material; in the Greek survey record especially, the overwhelming proportion of sites discovered are in fact multiperiod in occupation. Defining site sizes at any *particular* period in the past becomes highly problematic, and only a very few recent and highly intensive site collections allow such distinctions to be attempted.[37] Regrettably, some survey reports fail to present site size data at all, apparently considering it too tentative to be of any analytical use. Despite the numerous inherent problems, this is an unnecessarily negative attitude. Most recorded site sizes, including those used here, of necessity deal with the extent of the entire surface palimpsest, and while this level of resolution remains undesirably coarse, change *relative* to different periods can nonetheless allow useful information about settlement variability through time to be established. It is also the case that very small sites, the behavior of which bulks large in this particular study, suffer less from the "palimpsest" effect than larger surface scatters.

To recover the nature of ancient landholdings from survey evidence, the areal extent of surface scatters must somehow be related to the overall size of properties and the nature of their operation. Site sizes, it must be made clear, refer *only* to the artifact spread created by the use of habitations or other structures at the individual settlement. The size of this spread is thus a proxy measure for the size of these residences or these productive units, and depends on their longevity and intensity of use. Any estimation of the total extent of the land attached to these structures, from the evidence of site size alone, is risky in the extreme – although clearly this would be a much sharper index of the economic status of the site's inhabitants. One alternative way in which survey data can indicate property sizes may be through the relative *spacing* of sites in the landscape. Jameson, for example, discusses evidence from near the *polis* of Halieis in the Southern Argolid; there, fourth-century farm sites were regularly located in such a way as to suggest attached contiguous holdings of between 5.5 and 22.5 hectares (mean = 13.8ha; 153 *plethra*). Used cautiously, this seems a reasonable procedure, though the possibilities must also be acknowledged that these sites may not be wholly contemporaneous, and that others yet lie undiscovered. Also, as Jameson and others point out, such estimations only relate to the *minimum* amount of land held by the site's proprietor.[38] Such regular distributional patterns are rare, however, and elsewhere we need other inferences to bridge the gap between the size of the archaeological surface scatters and the probable character of the landholdings represented.

The available evidence for site sizes in these various sets of survey data reveals a general upward trend, which can even, in some instances, be quantified (fig. 18). At Megalopolis investigators suggest that Hellenistic and Roman farmsteads "though much rarer, were large compared with those of the 5th and 4th centuries BC." In Boeotia, Early and Late Roman rural sites "are certainly almost invariably several times larger than the average classical farm, ranging from estate centres around 2,500m$^2$ upwards to a minority of smallish villages of 1 or more ha in size."[39] In some areas this development had already manifested itself within the Hellenistic period proper, but overall it is more clearly marked – if nowhere very dramatic – by Roman times. What is most evident (at least in surveys of category A) is the loss of the very small sites typical of Classical and Early Hellenistic times; this downward spiral begins during the Hellenistic period in some areas, but again is noticeable almost everywhere by the earlier phases of the Roman era. In many regions, a

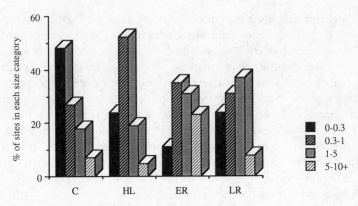

18 Histogram of site sizes (data from the Argolid Exploration Project, Nemea
Valley Archaeological Project, Melos Survey and Northwest Keos Survey)

higher rate of occupation at these tiny sites returns in the Late Roman
period, one significant feature of the very different rural conditions then
obtaining.

How are these small sites (defined here as 0.3ha or less in extent) to be
interpreted? They have usually been taken as rural farmsteads, and the
contents of the surface assemblages go some way toward supporting this
identification, with the presence of domestic wares, tile (indicating a
roofed structure), spindle whorls or loomweights, and often also more
substantial agricultural processing equipment (e.g. querns and oil- or
olive-presses). Independent small-scale proprietors have generally been
considered the most likely inhabitants, and their year-round occupancy
has often been taken for granted. But in fact, many of them could well be
field-shelters, sheds and outbuildings for use on a seasonal or occasional
basis. In truth, many of these sites probably shifted in their precise
function through time, as a family's size, needs and aspirations varied.
Such distinctions cannot be made on surface evidence alone; indeed it is
doubtful whether even excavation would be able to distinguish evidence
for full- versus part-time residence. Certainly, ethnoarchaeological work
on related structures in modern Greece found it impossible to make that
judgment from the material remains alone.[40]

Dispersed settlement on the land (full- or part-time) has recently been
argued to be the chosen agricultural and residential strategy of farmers
wishing to cultivate their holdings intensively, where these holdings are
largely consolidated in location. Intensification would demand higher
labor inputs expressed in several ways (e.g. cereal/pulse rotation, close
symbiosis of animal husbandry and arable cultivation), all of which

necessitate a significantly greater amount of time and effort invested in the land. Rural habitations (or at least seasonal shelters) would be one economically rational response to these demands. This scenario has been presented by Halstead as an "alternative" strategy to the more "traditional" model of Greek settlement and land use. By contrast, the traditional pattern involves the spatial separation of a farmer and his land, which would usually be scattered in dispersed holdings; nucleated residence, "commuting" farmers, and more extensive modes of cultivation characterize this model, all of which reduce the need for rural outbuildings. The greater investment of time and capital in the countryside possible under the "alternative" scenario allowed the chance for greater returns on property, but the necessary trade-off was diminished contact with regional centers. The choice of one or the other of these overall strategies affected more than economic goals – it reflects the ranking of social priorities as well.[41] Far from being mutually exclusive, these two strategies operated in conjunction, and different households adopted whichever was most suitable to their means and their needs. Despite this complementarity, it is clear that even in the Classical and Early Hellenistic epoch, with its abundant survey evidence for dispersed rural activity, the traditional model of man–land relations predominated, with the majority of the ancient population opting for nucleated, and preferably urban, residence. Even so, the *relative* popularity of the alternative option is a useful measure of economic goals and social values within the Greek city.

What can we infer about the socioeconomic status of the owners or operators of these dispersed farmsteads? The capacity and desire to maintain an isolated structure in the countryside, whether seasonally or permanently used, is perhaps more characteristic of proprietors of at least moderate means, for if these sites are seasonal work shelters, they represent additional capital investment in the countryside, at a level well beyond the means of the poorest in society. On the other hand, if they were permanent family homes, the amount of consolidated property necessary to make dispersed residence worthwhile, and the ability to forgo the possible economic benefits of proximity to the city, likewise make it unlikely that these sites were the houses of those just at or below the subsistence level of farming. Indeed, individuals at both extremes of the economic spectrum (either very rich or very poor) would probably opt for an urban base for their activities – if for very different reasons. (The further possibility that these small sites were owned by larger landowners and leased by tenants will be discussed in the next chapter.) One immediate conclusion is possible. If tiny sites can, with some confidence, be correlated with the existence of small-scale or modest proprietors, then the loss of these sites may be assumed to indicate the disappearance of such households. From this observation, it might be concluded that the widespread landholding and intensive cultivation identified in the settlement patterns of the Classical and Early Hellenistic epoch had vanished from the scene by early imperial times, during which a concomitant growth in larger estates, at the expense of these missing families, could be hypothesized for the early imperial period.

Before this verdict is accepted outright, however, some alternative factors must be considered. First, this evidence – by itself – tells us nothing of the fate of individual and unremarkable smallholders who lived, and had always lived, in the local city centers or in nucleated villages. Second, we should allow for some fluidity in residential decision-making. The abandonment of rural sites may reveal a household's altered agricultural strategy, but it need not indicate a major change in the organization of its property rights: a shift from isolated to nucleated settlement may be related to a wide variety of factors, both economic and social and working at the level both of the family and of the community. Third, the disappearance of some structures in the countryside could reveal new priorities in the investment of capital and labor, leading to a shift in emphasis away from rural development, even though the agricultural exploitation of a property could well continue, albeit at a lower level of intensity. All these factors warn against too simple an interpretation of the decline in the number of small sites, and therefore possibly of independent "peasant" proprietors. On the other hand, the degree to which this landscape was transformed makes it unlikely in the extreme that existing patterns of land tenure were left unscathed, or that the potential vulnerability of such smallholders went unexploited. The best reconstruction fitting the archaeological pattern so far generated takes account of two trends – a real decline in the number of moderate to small-scale farmers, and an increasing separation of the remaining landowners from their land. That "divorce" may not seem as dramatic as the outright dispossession of farmers, but it too has major implications for the redistribution of economic resources and for changes in prevailing social mores.

It has already been noted that site sizes increased during this period (fig. 18), but, given our inability to monitor period-by-period variability in size, this observation can really be taken only as implying either that larger sites endure better, or that sites newly founded in early imperial times are larger. On that basis, one can envisage two possible developments, neither exclusive of the other. One possibility is a trend toward increasing rural nucleation in larger rural communities. Surface sites marked by a sizeable and dense accumulation of debris scatter (and thus presumably sizeable in their original area and population) have most often been identified as "hamlets," "small settlements," or "villages."[42] In this scenario, individual farmers give up their isolated lifestyle in favor of residence in a larger rural settlement. This would presuppose a direct relationship between the loss of very small sites and the growth of larger ones, and thus a redisposition of people across the landscape. This hypothesis is difficult to prove one way or the other, with the available site size data. On the one hand, the very survival of these larger settlements in several regions, while individual farmsteads are abandoned, offers some measure of support; yet in Boeotia, the disappearance or attrition of such second-order centers seems to have proceeded *pari passu* with the loss of smaller sites. Regional differences are evident here, as they also are in the case of the urban sites themselves. A second possibility involves the identification of these larger surface scatters as the remains of a larger estate. An increase in property size might logically entail a growth in the estate center to accommodate necessary additional labor and agricultural processing facilities. The potential architectural elaboration of a wealthy owner's dwelling similarly would affect the extent of surface remains. Even if, as is likely, large landholdings under the empire remained fragmented entities, it is doubtful that the creation of a more impressive *fundus* would not be accompanied, at least in many instances, by a more substantial rural establishment.[43] What the development of such estate centers would signal, of course, is the concentration of greater amounts of property in fewer individual hands.

The observed general increase in site size is commensurate with either of these potential developments. To distinguish between these two different, although perhaps ultimately related, scenarios, another category of survey evidence is required.

### Site features

Defining a site's function on the basis of survey finds alone frequently proves a problematic exercise, but surface assemblages undoubtedly can yield useful information about the nature of an individual site. If wealthy landowners indeed became a more dominant feature of the early imperial landscape, reflections of this development are to be sought in the specific artifactual content, as well as in the overall size, of the surface scatter. For the Southern Argolid, it was noted that the sites which survived the mid-third century BC "break" in rural occupation tended to be both larger and more solidly constructed than was the norm, suggesting it was the "comparatively well-to-do" landowner who maintained a rural presence.[44] But what features may safely be taken to denote the presence of a wealthy and important individual at a site? The precise social implications of using certain pottery types (Megarian bowls, imported sigillata) remain unclear, and it is wisest not to take such wares as sensitive socioeconomic indicators. More trustworthy are features such as valuable agricultural equipment, architectural members (e.g. column fragments), and standing remains such as ashlar walling or perhaps a tower complex.

A significant minority of the sites discovered possess features which elevate them above the level of simple rural farmsteads. Usually, though not always, these are sites larger than the normal small farm (over 0.3ha) (table 5; figs. 19–20). The existence of such sites, in what was clearly a period of general rural abandonment, is compelling, implying as it does that often it was the "comparatively well-to-do" landowners who were willing or able either to establish or maintain a rural establishment, be it for themselves or for tenants. One probable corollary to this development is the consolidation, and quite possibly the expansion, of the landed properties associated with these rural bases.

The most clear-cut argument for identifying rural settlements with large, individually owned estates is associated with that class of site frequently dubbed "villa" in survey reports. Little systematic work has been done on the phenomenon of villas in Achaia, or indeed in the Roman east generally. In some contexts, stringent criteria for this identification have been utilized (e.g. the presence or absence of baths, marbles or mosaics, impressive size, favorable location), but in Greece the term has more often been applied in a rather vague fashion.[45] For specific questions pertaining to estate management or production systems, this vagueness would be an impediment, but for the purposes of this study, a villa can be defined simply as a large establishment, with signs of accessories indicating an affluent, even luxurious, lifestyle. Mosaics and baths are two common, and archaeologically visible, features. These complexes can occupy an urban, peri-urban or rural position; variability in location is of secondary importance on this point. A rural working establishment, a *villa rustica*, may testify more directly to the existence of a sizable landed estate, but a town house or *villa suburbana* likewise demonstrates the presence of a substantial individual, one just as likely to possess considerable holdings. The generally urban orientation of the Achaian villas noted to date could be partially related to the longstanding investigatory bias of classical archaeology, but on the whole, the pattern is probably genuine, emerging from the continuing identification of local élite families with the affairs of their home communities. Even for such rural villas as do exist, comparative evidence

Table 5. *Rural sites with possible "élite" features*

| Survey | Date range | Size | Characteristics |
|---|---|---|---|
| *Argolid* | | | |
| A53 | (C–HL),[1] HL | 0.01 ha | Tower complex; 4 × 6m |
| B86 | C–HL, (HL) | 0.14 ha | Ashlar wall |
| B89 | C–HL, HL, (ER) | 0.3 ha | Structure; ashlar-lined pit |
| E57 | C–HL, HL, (ER), (MR) | 0.9 ha | Limestone blocks; column base |
| F3 | (HL), (ER), (MR), (LR) | 0.65 ha | Tower complex; 9 × 11m |
| *Berbati* | | | |
| Findspot 8 | R | — | Marble drum; limestone blocks |
| Findspot 15 | C, R | 1.1 ha | Fragment of *lapis lacedaemonius* |
| *Southern Euboea* | | | |
| 37 | C, HL, R, Byz | 0.17 ha | Long wall; rock-cut basin/press |
| 50 | C, HL, R | — | Structure; 200m estate wall |
| 69 | HL–R | 0.15 ha | Blocks; marble column fragment |
| 74 | C (?), HL–R | 0.3 ha | Marble/sandstone blocks |
| *Keos* | | | |
| 15 | (HL), (ER), LR, MByz | 0.25 ha | Probable tower; olive presses |
| 18 | (A), (HL), (MByz) | 0.35 ha | Tower, possible forecourt |
| 26 | (A), (C), HL, ER, (LR) | 0.32 ha | Rock-cut terraces; fluted column |
| 43 | (C), (ER), LR, (MByz) | 0.6 ha | Tower (10.5 × 12.5m) |
| 45 | (C), (ER), LR, (MByz) | 1.4 ha | Possible tower; column drum |
| 48 | A, (C), (HL), (ER), MByz | 0.8 ha | Tower, probable forecourt |
| *Melos* | | | |
| 48 | (C), ER | 0.8 ha | Structure; imported ceramics |
| *Nemea Valley* | | | |
| 7 | A–C, HL, ER, LR, MByz | 1.2 ha | Masonry; cut stone, drainpipes |
| 501 | (A–C), HL, Byz | 3.6 ha | Paving tile?; imported ceramics |
| 512 | A–C, ER, LR | 6 ha | Column drum, worked blocks |
| 600 | A–C, ER, R–Byz | 20 ha | Cut blocks; opus sectile fragments |
| 904 | (A–C), HL(–ER?), (R–Byz) | — | Circular tower |

[1] Brackets indicate periods with less material represented on site.

from other early Roman provinces makes it clear that owners would be at least part-time absentee landlords; prosperous men moved frequently from estate to estate, from estate to city, and often to centers beyond. Here, the most vital point is that villas represent the possessions of wealthy men, and thus a strong élite presence in the countryside.

Sites tentatively identified as villa complexes are found in many of the regions surveyed, or have been noted in their immediate environs (table 6). Elsewhere, wealthy urban or peri-urban structures, whether strictly

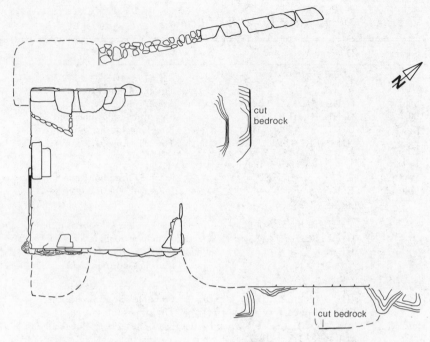

19 Northwest Keos, Site 48, a tower complex occupied in Classical, Hellenistic and Early Roman times. Scale approx. 1:200

"villas" or not, are known in Corinth, Patrai, Nikopolis, Athens, Argos, Sparta and numerous other cities. The distribution of specifically *rural* villas is not uniform, however: impressive rural sites have yet to be found in the Lakonian plain, for example, despite intensive survey of the region and the indisputable existence of large estates.[46] A major difficulty remains the exceptional coarseness of many of the current datings for these structures. With the label "Roman" applying to the entire span from 31 BC to AD 600 or so, changes specific to the early empire are often necessarily obscure. Yet such distinctions are very desirable, given the markedly different patterns of rural activity – and thus quite probably of land tenure and exploitation – in the later empire. The chronological horizon when villas first appear, or when they first become regular features in the rural landscape, remains somewhat obscure.

Nevertheless, through survey, excavation and the stylistic analysis of mosaics, indications do exist to place some villa structures firmly within the early imperial period. These include urban and peri-urban establishments, as well as rural complexes. Rural villas of definite first- to third-century AD date, for example, are known near Marathon in Attica and in

20  Northwest Keos, rock-cut olive presses near the tower at Site 15, possibly of
Hellenistic–Roman date

Argive Thyreatis in modern northeast Lakonia (both belonging to
Herodes Atticus) and Messenia (a Trajanic complex near Korone), as
well as a handful of other villas dated roughly to the second century AD on
the basis of their mosaics. At the villa of Herodes Atticus in Thyreatis
there have been found aqueducts, baths and numerous finds of marble
statuary (figs. 21–2). "Country homes" in Akarnania and a possible *villa
rustica* found in Achaean Dymaia in the northwestern Peloponnese could
also be mentioned as dating to the early imperial period.[47] The number of
securely dated rural villas remains relatively limited; a greater proliferation of such complexes in the Late Roman period could be hypothesized
on the basis of the evidence available, but only very tentatively.

What is indisputably demonstrated by the existence of these various
"élite" sites (tables 5 and 6) is the increasing presence and expenditure of
well-to-do families in the countryside. Other signposts of wealth and
status now occur in a specifically rural context. Ornate mausolea, clearly
the family burial places of substantial landowners, appear in the Roman
period. While most such monuments are placed in the traditional peri-
urban location (most famously, the monument of Philopappos in Athens,
located on the Mouseion Hill some 600m from the acropolis), some are
moved out to the countryside. In the territory of the Lakonia survey

Table 6. *Rural sites identified as "villas" by survey projects*

| Survey | Date range | Size | Characteristics |
|---|---|---|---|
| *Argolid* | | | |
| Halieis | LR | — | *villa rustica* with bath |
| *Berbati* | | | |
| — | R | — | Bath |
| *Southern Euboea* | | | |
| 55 | R–Byz | 0.5 ha | Architectural members |
| 67 | R(–Byz?)[1] | 0.1 ha | Hypocaust tiles; column drums |
| *Megalopolis* | | | |
| Rapsommati | LHL–ER | "large" | Column drum; concrete |
| *Melos* | | | |
| 56 | ER–MR | 0.8 ha | Pebble mosaics; cistern |
| 81 | R | 7.0 ha | Mosaic floor; revetments |
| 95 | R (mostly LR) | 10 ha | Architectural members |
| 100 | (HL?), R | 0.5 ha | Structure; painted plaster |
| 108 | HL, R | 2.0 ha | Structure; pebble mosaics |
| *Messenia* | | | |
| 21, 109, 408, 417, 421, 508, 515, 519, 607 | R | — | Baths |
| 546 | R | — | "Villa" |
| 107, 148, 401, 412, 505, 609 | R | — | Mosaics |
| *Messenia: Five Rivers area* | | | |
| 40, 131, 502, 503, 519 | R | — | Baths |
| 33, 40, 131, 503, 519 | R | — | Reported villas |
| 15 | R | 9 ha | Walls; sculpture |
| 31 | R | 4 ha | Apsidal wall |
| Korone | 1st century AD | — | Mosaics |
| *Methana* | | | |
| MS 109, MS209, MS211 | LHL–MR | — | *villae rusticae* |
| *Nemea Valley* | | | |
| 704 | C, (HL), ER, LR, Byz | 35 ha | Marble revetments; piping; statuary |

[1] Brackets indicate periods with less material represented on site.

21 Thyreatis, partial view of the villa complex of Herodes Atticus at Eua/Loukou

22 Thyreatis, view of the aqueduct associated with the villa of Herodes Atticus at Eua/Loukou

23  Corinthia, Roman tomb monument of the first or second century AD

project, three such cases are known, including a built chamber tomb with a colonnaded façade and sculpted marble frieze discovered at Ktirakia near ancient Therapnai. In the Corinthia, a concrete and brick constructed tomb monument of first- or second-century AD date was noted, though admittedly this lay near the road between Kenchreai and Corinth (fig. 23). Similar structures have been reported for northern Greece. Another recent discovery has been a decagonal brick nymphaeum in Epirus, dated to the third century AD (fig. 24)[48] Nymphaea, mausolea, and indeed the elaborate villas themselves have very few precedents in the Greek landscape. To the contemporary population, these monuments would have stood out in the landscape, as a visible claim to ownership and prestige. The combination of the elaboration and the location of such structures asserted the owner's dominance over the countryside.

Buildings visible in the rural landscape thus began to display signs of an increasing social and economic differentiation. Rooted in the Hellenistic era, this differentiation became increasingly blatant in the Roman epoch proper. The relatively empty countryside now held a variety of sites, ranging from very small and insignificant structures to sumptuous villa estates. Inequalities in wealth were not new in Greek society, but a lack of restraint in expressing them became a new feature of the countryside.[49] These developments may be taken not only to reveal a

24  Epirus, nymphaeum of probable third-century AD date

shift in attitudes to wealth and its display, but also to some extent a restructuring of landholding patterns – to the advantage of the wealthy. We should qualify that observation, however, by reiterating that such "élite" sites remain in the minority, and most sites (of whatever size) lack any clear signs of distinction in their surface assemblages; the larger of these are perhaps best identified as aggregations of population in the countryside, such as hamlets or villages. Again, processes of rural nucleation and of land concentration no doubt were in operation concurrently and, as we will see, were structurally interrelated as well.

### ARCHAEOLOGICAL INDICATORS FOR LANDHOLDING PATTERNS: A SUMMARY

Through the evidence of overall site numbers, site continuity, site sizes and site features, a striking transformation in rural settlement patterns has been traced for the early imperial period. These archaeological indices suggesting general trends in patterns of land ownership at this time can be summarized as follows:

71

1 A widespread and significant drop in rural site numbers was evident, most commonly beginning around the second century BC and lasting well into the early empire. Not until the third or fourth century AD do site numbers increase significantly again.

2 Instability in site occupation, and arguably in systems of land tenure, has been observed during the Hellenistic and Early Roman periods.

3 An overall loss of very small sites, most frequently associated with the holdings of small-scale independent cultivators, has been noted, particularly in the earlier phases of the Roman era.

4 Site sizes tend to increase, beginning in the last century BC but with the development most marked within the Roman era proper.

5 Survival or foundations of these larger sites, at a time when most rural sites disappear, can be hypothesized to represent *either* an increasing preference for nucleated settlement *or* the dominant presence of an élite landowning stratum in the countryside.

6 Detailed examination of surface assemblages and surviving structural remains has revealed, in a minority of cases, signs of material affluence or outright ostentation. This development is taken to demonstrate the new or continued presence of wealthy proprietors in the countryside. An expansion of their landed properties is one possible corollary of this trend.

7 The appearance of villa establishments (and other types of monumental structures) in particular signals an increasingly visible social stratification in the countryside.

These points effectively summarize what can be said about change in landholding systems in early imperial Greece, on the basis of the archaeological evidence currently available. Now, at last, we may turn to the more traditional starting point for this investigation – namely, what the documentary sources can tell us.

HISTORICAL EVIDENCE FOR CHANGES IN LANDHOLDING

What textual evidence can be employed either to support or to undermine this archaeologically derived scenario? The discussion can most usefully be organized around three major trends so far suggested: instability and discontinuity in landholding, the loss of smaller proprietors and the rise of the larger landowner.

To begin within the Hellenistic period proper, the economic history of "Old Greece" in this epoch remains somewhat enigmatic, and basic issues of land ownership and agricultural conditions have received only limited attention. One development which some scholars have thought they could detect, however, is a growth in the size of individual landed estates, although the evidence is drawn to a large degree from inferences about other trends in society, notably the growing importance of individuals and of individual wealth in civic life.[50] More direct evidence for the reorganization of landholding to the advantage of the few has been seen in the periodic episodes of "social revolution," in which calls were made for the redistribution of land (*ges anadasmos*) and the cancellation of debts (*chreon apokope*); such outbursts are known from the Aegean islands in the mid-third century BC, and from parts of central and northern Greece in the early second century. Long considered as a universal and catastrophic process in Hellenistic Greece, these occurrences are now being placed in perspective and attempts are being made to account for their genesis in specific cases. One recent theory, for example, has related some of these outbreaks to liquidity crises, sparked off by the Roman removal of booty or demands for reparation in the early second century BC. A former reluctance to distrain upon agricultural debtors appears to have given way at this time, exacerbating the risk of land expropriation for smallholders. Whatever complex of circumstances may have led to these incidents, they do – at least for certain places at certain times – imply the existence of individuals who had somehow lost all, or a significant proportion, of their property to other men.[51]

This mixture of evidence and inference at one time used to encourage a very harsh assessment of the situation in the Hellenistic countryside, where an impression of chaos and the universal dispossession of smallholders once reigned. Re-evaluation of the situation has somewhat modified the picture; for example, broadly based participation in civic life can still be observed in many Hellenistic *poleis*. Nor is it accepted that alterations in the political order necessarily reflect a parallel restructuring of economic relationships. Modern reconsideration of Hellenistic social and political disorder is nicely exemplified by the case of the disorder in third-century BC Boeotia, described with disgust by Polybius: "for many years Boeotia had been in a morbid condition very different from the former sound health and renown of that state" (20.4.1, 20.6). Once constantly cited as evidence for the supposed disarray of Hellenistic civic life and agricultural conditions, the dimensions of that disruption have been challenged and considerably reduced.[52] If the case for political instability and the marked concentration of land is thus sometimes plausible, the documentary sources by themselves fail to prove these to have been universal or deep-rooted phenomena.

From the earliest days of Roman influence in Greece, in the late third and second century BC, the imperial presence made its mark upon the conditions which underlie patterns of land tenure. Consequences of warfare included the escalation of public and private debt and the disruption of agricultural activity. Instability in land ownership also resulted from the capture or death of men in battle, as well as the proscription of citizens in bouts of civic *stasis* which often followed in the wake of the Roman presence.[53] More overt interference, involving Roman confiscation and reallocation of civic or private property, did not really begin until after the Achaean War, when Corinthian territory and the land of rebellious leaders were absorbed. Military hostilities and accompanying confiscations reached their peak in the first century BC, Sulla being a particularly notorious violator of established territorial rights. After that crisis, and with formal incorporation of the province within the imperial system, such forced redistribution of land is scarcely attested.[54]

When the disruption of tenure systems and the potential rise of dominant landowners are being considered, one vital point to establish is the amount of land that might have passed into the alien hands of either newly resident or absentee landlords. Members of the Roman aristocracy who managed to inherit, purchase, marry or coerce their way into property are well attested in the eastern provinces. Roman appropriation of the coveted right of *enktesis* (the right of a foreigner to hold property in a city's territory) was resented, and occasionally resisted – though with little success.[55] The extent of such holdings offers some clue to the degree of dispossession experienced by the indigenous population (who may well have leased the land back as tenants), as well as to the level of rent monies flowing either into the pockets of an intrusive proprietorial class or out of the province altogether.

One obvious powerful absentee landowner would, of course, be the emperor. Very little direct evidence exists, however, for the presence of Achaian imperial estates. In fact, the confiscated property of Hipparchus, the grandfather of Herodes Atticus, presents the only certain example, and even then the imperial fisc did not retain control for very long.[56] But some further level of imperial possession of land may in fact be imagined; for instance, according to Pausanias, oil from Phokian Tithorea was sent to the emperor (10.32.19). Pausanias also relates that "there was a certain law whereby provincials who were themselves of Roman citizenship, while their children were considered of Greek nationality, were forced either to leave their property to strangers or let it increase the wealth of the emperor." Antoninus Pius repealed this law, "choosing rather to show himself benevolent than to retain a law that swelled his riches" (8.43.5). More dubious is a reference in the *Euboean Discourse* to the imperial confiscation of land.[57] On the whole, large imperial *fundi* did not play a significant role in the agricultural structure of the province (imperial control of other natural resources, however, will be discussed in the next chapter). To reinforce the point, the lack of attested estates in Achaia can be placed in relation to the fifteen examples known from Africa or the eighteen in Asia – a telling comparison, even if we allow for the different sizes of these provinces relative to Achaia.

Interest and investment on the part of the Roman aristocracy (i.e. individuals of senatorial or equestrian status) likewise appear to be a relatively limited phenomenon when compared to other, more fertile provinces. The extensive estates of Atticus and the *Synepirotae* in Epirus offer practically the only directly documented examples. Of Atticus it was said that "all his income came from his possessions in Epirus and in the city of Rome" (Nepos, *Atticus* 14.3). An anecdote about C. Antonius is more difficult to interpret: after his exile he was said to have settled in Kephallenia, where he "held the whole island in subjection as though it were his private estate" (Strabo 10.2.13). The location of these undoubtedly extensive holdings is significant. These northwestern regions had already been much disrupted through military activity, especially the devastating attack upon Epirus in 167 BC by Aemilius Paullus, and in addition they lay closest to the Italian peninsula. Other parts of Greece, treated on the whole less violently and characterized by a sophisticated indigenous system of land ownership, proved more impervious to such large-scale infiltration. As with imperial holdings, however, indirect evidence may augment this picture to some extent. Particular interest paid to an area or to a city by important Roman families may well relate to actual properties held in the region: the Statilii Tauri at Thespiai in Boeotia is a good example, one member of this family even being thought to have been the recipient of a public cult as a civic benefactor.[58]

At a lower social level, it is known that foreign *negotiatores* (in Greek *pragmateuomenoi*) came to Greece in some numbers. These "men of business" first appear in the second century BC, their numbers increasing in the following century. Isolated individuals, or more usually small groups of *Rhomaioi* (as they were known), settled in many parts of the mainland and the islands (fig. 25). Commercial considerations first attracted such people eastward and determined their initial choice of settlement, but in many cases land became an additional investment – for social as well as for economic reasons. *Negotiatores* are known from the more fertile zones of Greece, such as Boeotia and Messenia. At Messene, such individuals are probably to be identified in the *octobolos eisphora* tax inscription of the early first century AD (p. 21). The *Rhomaioi* here were late in paying their share of the tax; the amount owed suggests they owned a substantial amount of land in the area. On a localized scale,

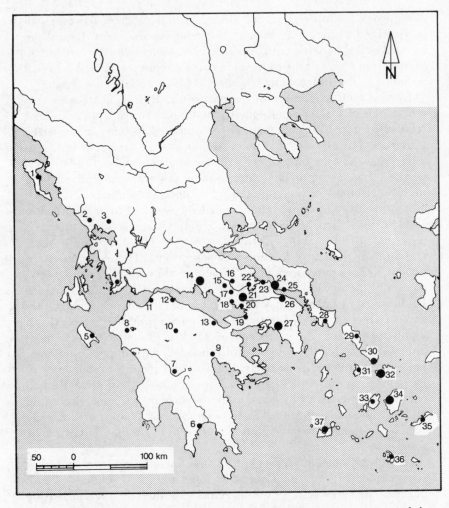

25 Distribution of *negotiatores* in Achaia. Small circle indicates 1–3 names recorded in a community, medium circle 3–10, large circle more than 10.

| | | |
|---|---|---|
| 1 Kerkyra | 10 Kleitor | 19 Pagai |
| 2 Epirus | 11 Patrai | 20 Kreusis |
| 3 Ambrakia | 12 Aigion | 21 Thespiai |
| 4 Akarnania | 13 Sikyon | 22 Akraiphia |
| 5 Zakynthos | 14 Delphi | 23 Anthedon |
| 6 Gytheion | 15 Lebadeia | 24 Chalkis |
| 7 Megalopolis | 16 Orchomenos | 25 Eretria |
| 8 Elis | 17 Koroneia | 26 Oropos |
| 9 Argos | 18 Thisbe | 27 Athens *continued* |

| 28 Karystos | 32 Delos | 36 Thera |
|-------------|----------|----------|
| 29 Andros | 33 Paros | 37 Melos |
| 30 Tenos | 34 Naxos | |
| 31 Syros | 35 Amorgos | |

therefore, these men played some part in determining and reshaping landholding patterns, but they should not be thought of as having had an overwhelming impact throughout the province as a whole. In addition, families of *Rhomaioi* stock are often seen to have settled permanently in their new homes, ploughing their wealth back into their adopted communities rather than provoking a long-term drain of local revenues.[59] Apart from *negotiatores*, other potential classes of outside landowners include colonists or discharged veterans. At this point, it will simply be noted that the relatively few formal colonies in Achaia were located where the structure of landholdings had already been severely disrupted, and in some cases even placed where territory was already possessed by Rome. Nor is there much evidence to suggest that Achaia was a popular area for discharged veterans to settle and buy land.[60]

In short, if no quantified estimate of the amount of land which passed to these various new owners can be made, it is still possible to assert that, unlike other Roman provinces, no massive alienation of property into foreign hands took place in Achaia. Yet such a conclusion does not exhaust the discussion of the effects of imperial conquest upon Greek landholding patterns. Altered social and political relationships within provincial society generated more indirect, but equally far-reaching, responses. Encouragement of rule by the "better sort," and a sharper juridical and political demarcation of rich and poor, are merely two of the relevant factors we should consider. Social barriers, once raised to prevent the accumulation of large properties and to preserve a broadly based landowning (and thus military) class, lost force in the face of Roman domination.

With these factors in mind, the rise of large estates under native *possidentes* would appear inevitable. The political dominance and extravagant euergetism of prominent Achaian families have been hailed as pointing to their overwhelming economic power.[61] As in the Hellenistic period, however, it has rarely been asked whether the estates of such men actually increased in size (presumably at the expense of those less fortunate) or whether it rather reflects altered social behavior, allowing for more public expression and recognition of wealth. The documentary sources, again as in the Hellenistic period, rarely cast any direct light on the subject. Some solid fare is provided by occasional pieces of epigraphic evidence which may suggest some degree of property expansion on the part of the prosperous. Despite the presence of *Rhomaioi* at Messene, the *eisphorai* of that city were primarily carried on the shoulders of substantial native Greek landowners. Epigraphic evidence (*IG* II–III² 2776) from Attica, which records parcels of properties, owners' names and certain associated amounts of money, has also been thought to suggest the concentration of landed properties in Hadrianic Attica when compared to the fourth century BC. Day believes this inscription (which is in very fragmentary condition and thus is highly problematic in interpretation) may be the record of an *obligatio praediorum* for an alimentation project; the individuals involved appear to be moderately prosperous.[62]

Under the empire, it became increasingly possible for citizens of one *polis* to possess holdings in several regions of the province and beyond. A supra-civic landowning class began to be formed at the élite level, as wealthy families held office (for example as *proxenos*) in other cities, intermarried and inherited from each other. More widespread patronage networks and euergetism also allowed and encouraged individuals from one city to purchase or receive land in other communities. Examples of such processes include the agricultural interests of L. Licinius Anteros, a Corinthian notable, in the peninsula of Methana, or the presence of prominent Lakonian families, the Voluseni and the Euryclids, in Arcadia. Spectacular illustrations of this development include Achaian luminaries such as Eurycles of Sparta, whose extensive holdings were enlarged by the gift of the entire island of Kythera from Augustus, and Herodes Atticus, who owned land in at least eight localities in Greece, and in three provinces.[63] Such cases are not to be taken as typical, but rather as the extreme end of the landowning spectrum, which was undoubtedly narrower now than in the preceding Classical epoch. This is a trend for which the documentary evidence argues consistently, if rarely directly; nor does it allow any reliable assessment of the geographical extent and scale of the phenomenon.

In summary, the documentary sources indicate instability in the countryside in the last centuries BC, owing to warfare and the disruptive political influence of Rome. A move away from "citizen estates" and toward fewer and larger landholdings also seems probable, rooted in the Hellenistic era but more marked under Roman suzerainty. Foreign investment in Greek territory played a secondary role in this development, since the driving force behind the reordering of land tenure systems seems to have been the local élite families, fostered and encouraged by their contact with imperial authority. It must be admitted, however, that the fate of smaller landowners here remains largely conjectural: little documentary evidence testifies *specifically* to their existence or their particular response to changing circumstances.

This historical review can now be reconciled with our earlier (and entirely independent) archaeological analysis. By and large, the different sources dovetail nicely. The documentary evidence provides specific examples of certain processes at work (e.g. confiscations, foreign landowners) which could never be accessible through archaeological data alone, and makes possible a more precise chronology for such events. In its turn, the survey data supplement the written testimony in two fundamental ways: first, by presenting more direct information about the behavior of small-scale landowners, and second, by establishing the geographical scope of this impressive transformation of the rural landscape, and of the accompanying social and economic transformation it represents. The resultant scenario – one of increasing social stratification and growing economic polarization within provincial society – is neat and plausible. Certainly, parallels can be found in many other imperial studies, not least within the Roman empire itself, where the redistribution of political and social power was accompanied by the substantial reallocation of economic resources.

Convincing as these overall trends may be, the magnitude of the process remains elusive. Was all of Greece parceled out only among Roman aristocrats, foreign immigrants and indigenous élite families? Was the large estate *the* basic unit of landownership in the province? Does this expansion of individual landholdings satisfactorily explain all aspects of the altered landscape of early imperial Greece? On the evidence so far available, we can provide no clear-cut answers. Such a reconstruction ignores the possible continued efforts of cultivators residing in the urban centers; no evidence has yet testified to their general demise. Even if all small rural sites and their residents were indeed swallowed up into the maw of acquisitive estate owners, as long as all other elements in the system remained constant, the overall system of land tenure still would not have been catastrophically disrupted. Nor was unrestrained land-grabbing on the part of the rich ever truly condoned under the empire. Also complicating the proposed reconstruction is the continued existence of nucleated rural settlements which lacked all signs of "high living."

Perhaps the most insidious reason for accepting the disappearance of small landowners is the very emptiness of the early imperial landscape. But other explanations could well be advanced for that development. In contrast to the standard hypothesis of provincial depopulation, a quite different argument, centering on population movement and an increasing preference for nucleated residence, is possible and will be considered in the next chapter. Before returning to the question of Achaian demography, however, another major issue must first be addressed: changing strategies in the exploitation of the land.

### THE EXPLOITATION OF THE AGRICULTURAL LANDSCAPE

Changes in settlement patterns and in systems of land ownership inevitably create knock-on effects for the economic utilization of land. What is the evidence for the cultivation of land at this time? Can any further insights into the new landholding pattern be gained from it? Can agricultural production in the province be seen to respond to the imperial incorporation of Greece? Two related developments might be predicted as responses to the escalation of external demands on the land: agricultural *intensification* (the maximization of returns on traditional crops through a greater investment of labor) and agricultural *specialization* (the concentration on a restricted but valuable range of crops). Either could provide the necessary additional resources required to meet taxation demands, rents or other levies.[64]

To begin with the documentary evidence for the period, some signs of production for export are certainly visible for Late Hellenistic and Early Roman Achaia. Thessalian grain shipments were sent to Rome; Hadrianic legislation regulated the export of Athenian olive oil; Pausanias twice mentions the manufacture, possibly for export, of unguents. The strongest case for agricultural specialization comes from the western Peloponnese, where *byssos* (a kind of flax) was grown specifically for processing in Patrai. Pausanias claimed this industry was significant enough to affect the gender balance of the city's population.[65] Yet examples such as these remain relatively few and far between, and all can easily be paralleled from earlier periods. Far from emphasizing intensification or specialization, the literary sources, of course, reiterate the theme of widespread abandonment of the land, of desolation and of waste. To be fair, such negative reports can be countered with other passages referring to fertile and well-tilled land, to irrigation dykes or to other forms of agricultural investment in Greece. A prominent benefactor of Boeotian Akraiphia, Epaminondas, and the emperor Hadrian a century later, took an interest in the control and drainage of the Kopaic Basin.[66] Given the built-in bias of the literary sources, coupled with these more positive statements, one may question how far the documentary evidence can be trusted as representing an *uncultivated* – rather than simply *unsettled* – landscape.

Before turning to the archaeological data, palynological and geomorphological evidence offer two independent means with which to explore broadly based anthropogenic change in the environment. Only one region, the Southern Argolid, can presently provide any detailed data relevant specifically to the early imperial period. An increase in maquis (scrub) pollen and an episode of severe gully erosion have been reported there in the course of the later Hellenistic and Early Roman periods. Interpretation of these results points to a contraction in the cultivated area of the region, to a possible increase in the territory given over to pastoral, rather than arable, purposes, and to a lessening in the area's overall agricultural productivity.[67] Another geomorphological observation about the apparently undercultivated Achaian landscape is given by Pausanias – of all people – speaking of islands offshore from the Aetolian coast.

That the Echinades islands have not yet been made mainland by the Achelous is due to the Aetolian people, who have been driven from their homes and all their land has been laid waste. Accordingly, as Aetolia remains untilled, the Achelous does not bring as much mud upon the Echinades as it would otherwise do. (Pausanias 8.24.11)

As more archaeological survey projects reach completion, more ancillary geomorphological and palynological studies will become available to help judge just how representative such observations are for conditions throughout Greece. At this point, however, our chief evidence for land use must remain the density and distribution of artifacts across the landscape.

Evidence for agricultural specialization by farmers is extremely difficult to recover with such data. The firm correlation of certain locations or certain types of soil with cultivation of specific crop types (an unwise procedure in Greek agriculture) is required. Such specialization, however, has been identified (chiefly in the Southern Argolid and in Attica) through the survey record – or so it is claimed. In these cases, intensive Classical/Early Hellenistic use of marginal land has been assumed to indicate cash cropping (particularly of olive oil) for export purposes, and the argument is that the loss of external commercial markets during Hellenistic and Roman times acted as the force behind the abandonment of numerous dispersed farmsteads, and a consequent population decline. This cycle of "boom and bust" is believed to be repeated several times in the history of the Southern Argolid. The validity of this "dependency model" is disputable, primarily on the basis of its overtly formalist economic assumptions, which include the likelihood of economically "rational" cultivators and a widespread and constant outside market for imported oil. The centrality of trade and of external contacts, so essential to this formulation, is difficult to reconcile with most current reconstructions of the ancient economy. At very least, the model cannot be readily applied to all parts of Greece in all periods; factors such as the nature of land tenure and labor systems, the size of a region, its geographical diversity and population density would first have to be assessed.[68] Setting aside the question of agricultural specialization, one is left with the related, and even more significant, issue of agricultural intensification. Is the land less intensively worked at this time, suggesting at the least a declining interest in agricultural production, at most perhaps a depression in population numbers?

The real difficulty of making such an assessment has already been intimated. One widely accepted rule of thumb declares that it "seems extremely likely that, the more numerous the traces of human activity in the landscape, the more intensively the land was exploited."[69] Since by "traces of human activity" it is most often the distribution of sites that is meant, it would be impossible to deny that the greatly diminished number of sites in the early imperial period denotes an equivalent slackening in agricultural intensity and a reduction in the cultivated area. Yet just how reliable is that equation? Increasingly sophisticated analysis of survey data suggests it can be applied only in a rather crude fashion. The absence of rural habitations or even seasonal shelters need not necessarily indicate a total lack of agricultural activity in the area. Individual proprietors in most cases would always have worked a variety of holdings, by no means all of which would have boasted a standing structure. That wealthier landowners at this time maintained some kind of permanent presence in the countryside is significant. Lesser proprietors may not have been able to afford to do so, while nonetheless still continuing to work their plots – if from some distance and less intensively. The willingness of farmers to travel significant – sometimes astonishing – distances to their fields has been observed by anthropologists in many present-day contexts, including Greece, and this is no less likely in the ancient world, even in periods of maximum settlement dispersion.[70] The distribution of population and of economic resources thus take their place as important factors governing the distribution of rural sites. Any shift in residence and investment from countryside to town would contribute to the apparent neglect of the rural landscape, making matters appear worse than they actually were. In a discussion of the evidence for land leasing and Polybius' description of Hellenistic Boeotia, Osborne observed:

There may well have been plenty of ruined structures in the countryside. To a casual observer this might look like a withdrawal from agriculture and a sign that sons were not able to succeed to their father's estates. In fact the land leases from late third century Thespiai show that although a great deal of land was in the hands of public bodies there was an active demand for that land which came from men of high status who were already farming land in that area.[71]

Measuring the total amount of land under cultivation through *site* distribution alone is a dubious operation, one that is bound to be underrepresentative. Such evidence does allow, however, a somewhat more reliable measure of the *intensity* of cultivation (the amount of time and energy invested), and on this index the early imperial landscape ranks significantly lower than the preceding period.

Before the magnitude and consequences of this disintensification can be assessed, certain ameliorating factors should be mentioned. The position of the remaining rural sites demonstrates that the province's more productive soils continued to receive regular attention: new or continuing settlements tended to be located on the best land, offering reliable returns, while marginal terrain (usually the land most recently taken under cultivation) was consistently given up. If the Classical and Early Hellenistic proliferation of small sites suggested that formerly untended, less desirable land was pressed into service, the Late Hellenistic and Early Roman period witnessed by contrast a preference for soils and terrain promising easier and more dependable yields. The Southern Argolid provides the clearest evidence of these trends, although the same general picture is visible in Southern Euboea, the Berbati valley, Melos and possibly Keos and Messenia. In some cases, the retraction of settlements simultaneously involved a move closer to the region's central place (as on Keos, figs. 32–4, and Melos); an emphasis on the farming of land more accessible to routes of external communication can also be noted. In the Lakonia survey, for example, a clustering of farms on valley bottoms and along natural routes of communication suggested both a concentration on good land and a greater need to be linked with the urban center. Early imperial sites do survive in relatively inaccessible areas, for example in the mountainous interior of Methana, but even there a preference for rich soils is apparent.[72]

To judge by the distribution of archaeological sites, then, the regular exploitation of inconvenient or marginal land was not common in early imperial times, though the more profitable, better quality soils were indeed farmed intensively. From settlement evidence alone, of course, more extensive uses of arable land (optimal or marginal) may remain archaeologically invisible. But fortunately these are not the only "traces of human activity" that survey archaeologists can use. A more refined measurement of human activity in the countryside can be provided by the use of "off-site" data, i.e. surface scatters across the landscape which fail to meet the criteria of artifact density and discreteness generally agreed as necessary for an artifact scatter to achieve site status. Sometimes referred to as "background noise," the phenomenon has been noted by most of the intensive surveys of category A, varying in different regions from a heavy and continuous blanket of artifacts to more discontinuous scatters. Transportation of such artifacts (normally pottery, but tile and lithics are also found) can often be attributed to geomorphological processes, but human agency also must have been involved. Off-site distributions thus form another index of rural, and therefore to a great extent agricultural, activity.[73]

The recording and collection of off-site material are a very recent development in Greek survey archaeology, and only a few quantified and controlled data sets are presently available. Results from the Berbati survey claim a background scatter of "Roman" pottery on slopes where Classical farmsteads had once been located, suggesting the subsequent utilization, if not habitation, of the area. Data from both the northwest Keos survey and the Nemea Valley project indicate that the Late Hellenistic and Early Roman decline in site numbers was matched by a reduction in the number of off-site finds: in other words, off-site distributions in those regions echo the sparse settlement pattern. How far does this clinch the argument for a much reduced level of agricultural production? To some extent, the answer depends on the mechanisms by which one envisions the transport of these artifacts out to the countryside (setting aside the undoubted contribution of non-human agencies such as geomorphological activity). The spreading on fields of animal manure, into which cultural debris has been introduced, has been the most popular way to account for off-site finds. Apart from areas peripheral to major settlements, such an explanation works most effectively for a pattern of landholding where cultivators keep animals in proximity to their residence, thus allowing the admixture of dung with cultural debris. The "alternative" model of dispersed settlement, notably seen in the Classical and Early Hellenistic epoch (see pp. 37–49, 60–1), provides these necessary conditions. But the very different nature of rural residence and animal husbandry in the early imperial period (the latter to be discussed further below) makes this intensive agro-pastoral symbiosis much less likely. Any lack of manuring scatter may thus reflect changed arable and pastoral strategies, and not necessarily a substantial decline in agricultural activity. If one assigns manuring the chief role in creating these scatters, therefore, the evidence remains somewhat ambiguous. More recent approaches to the problem of off-site data, however, argue that a much wider range of causes must be held responsible for these scatters, including dumping, pastoral activity, use of short-term *loci* for agricultural practices and random artifact loss; and such a range of behavior obviously signals a human presence and interest in the landscape.[74] Thus a lower level of background noise, such as seems apparent in early imperial Greece, would on this basis be indicative of some reduction in the amount of time and energy spent in the countryside.

This discussion makes clear the complexity of attempts to assess the nature and intensity of land use from survey data. Changes in the countryside must first be traced to changes in systems of land ownership and management, rather than correlated directly and uncritically with agricultural and demographic decline. In short, a shift to the less intensive cultivation of the early imperial rural landscape can certainly be accepted on the basis of the cumulative evidence – literary, palynological, geomorphological, archaeological; but the degree to which it was "abandoned" was probably not as pronounced as a superficial reading of these sources at first suggested.

### OWNERSHIP AND EXPLOITATION

Dio Chrysostom's *Euboean Discourse* paints one of the more powerful literary images of rural desolation in the early empire. Yet at the same time the oration may contain an important clue to the factors underlying the countryside's apparent abandonment. In defense of Dio's simple rustics, a member of the civic élite spoke thus in assembly:

"At this moment, sirs," he said, "almost two thirds of our land is a wilderness because of neglect and lack of population. I too own many acres, as I imagine some others do, not only in the mountains but also on the plains, and if anybody would till them, I should not only give him the chance for nothing but gladly pay money besides. For it is plain that they become more valuable to me, and at the same time the sight of land occupied and under cultivation is a very pleasing one, while waste lands are not only a useless possession to those who hold them, but very distressing evidence of some misfortune to their owners." (*Oration* 7.34–6)

"I too own many acres": from a combination of archaeological and literary evidence, a growth in estate size and a greater concentration of land ownership, at least in part at the expense of smaller proprietors, has been posited. What role might that particular development have had upon agricultural exploitation and upon rural settlement?

In terms of rural settlement, while sizable landholdings could prompt the appearance of larger, higher status sites in the countryside, a preference for full-time urban residence must be assumed for many élite proprietors. The unlikelihood of dispersed small-scale settlements within this altered system of land ownership has already been suggested, and will be further argued in the next chapter. Tenants of larger-scale landowners may have resided on the land, but even this appears a limited development.[75] A nucleated pattern of residence thus emerges as one natural consequence of the period's refashioned socioeconomic regime.

As for modes of agricultural exploitation, a close relationship has long been observed between land tenure and agricultural intensity; the size of a landholding, as well as the status of its owner, directly affects decisions about the nature of its use. Smallholders tend to diversify crop production and farm the land intensively, hence their occasional decision to reside upon their holdings. Such families work with a very limited margin of surplus, and an even smaller margin of error. On the other hand, large-scale proprietors not only operate with different residential options and priorities, but can adopt very different exploitative strategies. Rather than an intensive level of cultivation, more extensive treatment of the land, even downright neglect, can occur. Such behavior has been noted in a variety of cultural and historical contexts. Why should this be so? In some cases, the sheer extent of the property may limit the degree of agricultural attention paid to its remoter parts, especially when the labor force resides in a nucleated settlement (as would generally seem to be the case here), rather than living dispersed throughout the countryside. One basic tenet of economic geography is a negative correlation between input and returns, on the one hand, and distance from residential base, on the other – the "law of minimum effort." While this affects agricultural holdings of any size, farmers with limited holdings must resist this pressure as far as possible; larger proprietors may give way to it more gracefully. In a rich man's estate, some pattern of differential land use could be expected, with distant holdings devoted to increasingly less labor-intensive activities, such as pastoralism; total abandonment of land on the outskirts, as is suggested in the *Euboean Discourse*, represents an extreme possibility. No doubt treatment of holdings varied through time; census years would have been a particularly tempting time to leave land fallow or turned over to pasture – a tax-relief strategy only the wealthy could afford. Pliny's remarks about the negative impact of *latifundia* in imperial Italy are apt in this context; he pinpoints not only the dangers of large estates, but also the evils of undercultivation. The modern Italian term *latifondo*, too, implies unproductive utilization of land under absentee ownership.[76]

More extensive modes of cultivation are possible on large estates for the simple reason that returns of a more marginal nature can be accepted. Wealthy landowners do not risk hunger in a bad year; in fact, years of food shortage may actually prove a profitable time to release stored surplus. It is also more than likely that many élite landowners would possess a variety of sources of income, with non-agricultural forms of property investment. If they so chose, large-scale proprietors were thus in a position to accept lower returns, or even none at all, rather than adopt radical means to put land to work. In the Greco-Roman world, where the dominant social imperative tended toward conspicuous consumption, rather than productive reinvestment and maximization of income, behavior such as this would be perfectly acceptable.[77] This is by no means to deny a real concern for sufficient profits to maintain status and to provide the wherewithal for a benefactor's generosity; villas in other provinces most certainly functioned as major productive centers, and further research no doubt will prove this true in some Achaian cases too. Nevertheless, extensive holdings utilized in an extensive fashion constitute one significant contributory factor in the explanation of the apparently empty landscape of this period.

### PASTORAL ACTIVITY AND THE ACHAIAN ELITE

A related development is a possible increase in the role of animal husbandry, in the form of large flocks or specialty herds of horses or cattle, in the economic agenda of the Achaian élite. Hints of such an interest appear in a variety of literary sources, although (as so often) it is difficult to tell whether or not these references reflect a genuine increase in the scale of investment over earlier periods. Remarks by some authors (such as Strabo), who viewed pastoralism as a lower form of social behavior and thus peculiarly fitting for decadent Greece, must be taken with a large pinch of salt. What seems most reliable is the apparent upturn of interest in herding and breeding in Aetolia and Epirus – areas where wealthy, often foreign, landlords are known to have lived.[78] Independent confirmation of this trend, for instance via zooarchaeological analyses or archaeological studies of the remains of animal shelters or pens, is only now beginning to be sought. Some of the archaeological surveys considered here do report a human presence in areas traditionally considered most suitable for pastoralism. In the Southern Argolid, for example, prehistoric cave sites reused in the Early Roman era are associated with herding activities; the Megalopolis survey, too, suspects an increased pastoral activity, as has also been inferred on Methana, though there the evidence relates especially to the Late Roman period.[79]

However thin the direct evidence may be, the development is nonetheless not inherently unlikely. Pastoral activity in Greece had previously been constrained by the limited size of individual properties, as well as by the difficulties of moving large flocks across *polis* boundaries. Animal husbandry in Classical and Early Hellenistic Greece was, by and large, small in scale, with relatively few animals kept closely and carefully, near the homestead farm; agro-pastoral symbiosis, with animals providing dung for the fields and the fields providing fodder for the animals, was the predominant pattern of animal husbandry. While this level of pastoral activity undoubtedly continued for some proprietors in Late Hellenistic and Early Roman times, wealthy landlords were now free of many of these constraints. The development of larger landholdings and of élite relationships between cities facilitated more extended transhumant movements. A willingness to farm more extensively also reduced the need for a tight symbiosis of animals and arable land, allowing herds to be deployed more freely on distant holdings. Pastoralism became one pragmatic means of ensuring some measure of economic return with relatively little effort, becoming for certain proprietors a viable supplementary source of income. It has even been suggested as a possible "tax dodge," on the grounds that it is difficult to assess mobile and fluctuating herds of animals.[80]

This heightened interest in the profits of pastoralism, long accepted as a feature of life in Roman Greece, is easily exaggerated. Although certain regions of Achaia would have been in a good position to supply markets in the province or even further afield, a relatively inelastic demand for pastoral products would have gone some way to cap this trend. On the other hand, we ought not to downplay the very real importance of noneconomic motivations as well. For numerous reasons, not least initial capital costs and the amount of space required, specialist stock-raising was a rich man's hobby, and such breeding, particularly of horses and cattle, had always served as something of a status marker in Greek society.[81] Elite display in the rural landscape could take this form, as well as the building of villas and other monumental structures. In other agrarian societies, ruling élites have been known to emphasize pastoral production, not merely in order to enjoy its direct economic benefits but also to dominate marginal resources, leading in turn to a "relatively cheap form of control over the subordinate population."[82] Pasturing animals on land that owners were either unable or unwilling to cultivate kept the land securely in their hands, preventing its use by others for illicit farming or grazing. Smaller landowners, hoping for access to additional land (*incolto, saltus*) for grazing their own small flocks or for foraging, would be deprived of needed additional resources. The *voles* system of the Ottoman period (as witnessed on the island of Keos), where a few families or institutions controlled all grazing within extensive tracts of land cultivated by smaller farmers, is one excellent demonstration of this strategy.[83] Whether or not this was ever a consciously articulated élite aim, the scope of such activity in the Roman period would always have remained geographically circumscribed. Nevertheless, an increased interest in specialized pastoral production agrees with more general trends at work in Achaian society at this time, and forms another factor lying behind the formation of the rural landscape.

## POPULATION AND THE LAND

If "empty" is taken as synonymous with depopulated, then such alternative explanations for the appearance of this landscape may seem otiose. In view of the evidence for ownership and management of the land, however, it seems that a population decline less devastating than is normally accepted can legitimately be argued. The ancient literary authors have already been discussed; most secondary literature on the subject echoes their teleological view of Greek decline, likewise automatically associating population loss with military defeat and political subservience. The Greek situation has also been claimed as the natural forerunner of the population decline that later struck (or may have struck?) the entire Roman empire.[84] Such a gradualist non-explanation sheds no light on actual conditions in Greece. As for the apparent confirmation of decline in the data from surface survey, the mechanistic equation of demographic trends with site numbers and artifact densities reveals naive and simplistic analysis of a kind we should now reject.

If the catastrophic nature of the demographic collapse may be repudiated, however, some degree of population attrition in the early imperial era cannot be denied. Explaining this phenomenon necessarily involves a wide variety of factors, working on both the local and more general levels. Local events and conditions, for example, would include the eruption of the Kaimeno Vouno volcano on Methana in the early third century BC; or in the Nemea Valley, the abandonment of the panhellenic sanctuary, or for Boeotia, the potential effects of malaria owing to the proximity of the Kopaic Basin. More often cited, however, are widespread and general conditions, such as population movements following in the wake of Alexander's conquests. Such emigration (in the form of mercenaries or colonists to Alexander's new cities in the east) is indisputable, but its scale is unclear; and in any case, some measure of compensation (with people moving into Greece) was also experienced, if not at a sufficient level to balance the losses.[85]

The most oft-cited *deus ex machina* to account for population loss, however, has been warfare. Military activity, and the misery it undoubtedly caused, are inescapable aspects of early imperial Greece, and in particular certain regions such as Epirus in the second century BC and Attica and Boeotia in the first century BC. The negative impact of warfare could range from men killed outright in war, to the taking of booty, food shortages, the breakdown of security and hygienic measures, and the capture and enslavement of entire communities. All of these are certainly known in Greece during the last three centuries BC. Nevertheless, the question remains to what extent they can be blamed for the general and long-lasting demographic reduction witnessed there. If warfare is accepted as a demographic depressant, then the geographical distribution and chronology of these incidents take on a special importance. Certain areas clearly suffered more than others, yet the entirety of Greece tends to be treated as a single and undifferentiated war zone. Would the destruction of Haliartos in Boeotia have had a *direct* impact upon communities in the Peloponnese? Psychologically one might answer in the affirmative, but in demographic or economic terms the answer would be otherwise. Modern abhorrence of warfare also tends to mask our relative unfamiliarity with its implications for past communities: "remarkably little is known about problems of supply and logistics and of the economy generally in wartime or of morale unless a crisis occurred."[86] What does seem clear is that warfare did not always herald deep-seated depression or decline; nor can such negative conditions be explained purely as the result of military hostilities. Apart from anything else, between the battle of Actium and the Herulian invasions of the mid-third century AD the history of Achaia (cushioned as it was by its internal position well within the empire's frontiers) was relatively untraumatic – yet there is apparent continuity in its low population levels. So even if warfare served in some regions as a trigger for population change, it can be rejected as the sole explanation of demographic variability. Instead, a variety of factors come into play, many of which respond to the redistribution of economic and political power within Greek society.

It has been established that this period witnessed a significant transformation in the division and exploitation of agricultural land. How might this be integrated with a discussion of population change? Obviously, population decline can act to facilitate the formation of larger landholdings, as the self-evident consequence of the occupation of a constant amount of territory by fewer and fewer people. From this perspective, the process of estate growth could be taken as a development naturally following in the wake of the general depopulation of this period. If that population loss is downplayed, however, then the image of such easy and "painless" expansion rapidly recedes. Furthermore, in some cases the order of events would have been inverted, with large estates *preceding* demographic decline. The Hellenistic outbreaks of "social revolution" (p. 73), with their demands for the redistribution of land, are of some significance in this regard, for they demonstrate that the tensions lay not in a lack of men, but in their lack of land.[87] Turning the question around: what effect would the formation of large estates have had upon population numbers?

Increased pressures on family units, as must have been felt to some extent under Roman control, can be met by a variety of demographic responses. One possible reaction would be to increase family size, creating a larger labor pool to meet external demands. Such a strategy can only work, however, when there is a sufficient amount of land to justify the labor invested. Household units, particularly those operating at subsistence or near subsistence level, adapt to fit land availability and to fill labor needs; the more limited the land, the more limited the family.[88] Land scarcity could come about through high and competitive population densities or through élite monopolization of the land. For the early imperial period, the latter is clearly the dominant force at work. Despite the extra burdens created by Roman exactions, if larger estates were exerting pressures on smaller proprietors, then regulation of household sizes, and a slow and gradual process of population limitation, is to be expected.

Population decline or the formation of large estates: the chicken or the egg? Which came first or was the more powerful force affecting the Achaian landscape? No simple answer is possible, or perhaps should even be sought. To envision a dynamic relationship between demography and land tenure systems, in which the two processes interact and constantly modify each other, is a more satisfactory solution.[89] Demographic decline could facilitate the formation of large estates, but equally (and with more painful repercussions) the formation of large estates could facilitate demographic loss.

### ROMAN IMPERIALISM IN THE RURAL LANDSCAPE

What seems strangest about Achaia's relative lack of agricultural intensification is that it is precisely the opposite of what has often been predicted (and observed in practice) in newly incorporated imperial peripheries. Rather than receiving a stimulus to production and exchange, the rural landscape of Achaia – if anything – appears to have been in a period of relative decline. Additional external pressures can act, of course, as an economic depressant. Some marginal, less productive land, for example, may have become *agri deserti*, formerly cultivated territory now shed as a potential tax liability. A very few cases of emphyteutic legislation in Achaia are known, offering farmers virgin or abandoned land to cultivate and treat as their own; an initial period of tax exemption accompanied the grant.[90] These cases attest to imperial and civic awareness of the problem of undercultivation, if only sporadic attempts were made to counteract it. The effects of imperial taxation thus join the various other explanations advanced to account for the "empty" early imperial landscape: a changing agricultural regime, a preference for nucleated residence, extensive farming of large estates, an increase in pastoral activity, and lower population levels. In one way or another, all are linked to the direct or indirect impact of the Roman presence. To explore in further detail, however, the economic and social responses of the Achaian population to that presence, this rural picture must be expanded.

# 3

# The civic landscape

One possible way to expand this discussion would be to turn to urban landscapes – the architectural and spatial design of cities. Built environments serve as a "teaching medium," capable of clarifying individual and collective social roles and relationships; a changing society reconstructs itself through its building. Unfortunately, few cities in Greece have been dug extensively enough, or with enough attention paid to their Roman levels, to allow much analysis in this vein, though interesting work has been possible at Argos, Corinth, and, most productively, Athens. Hadrianic development of the latter city has received most attention – for example, the identification of an extensive civic complex (composed of the Roman agora, Hadrian's Library, a basilica and possible Pantheon), aligned to relate to each other and to link the traditional center of Athens, the Classical agora, with a newly developed area to the southeast, "New Athens" and the area of the Olympieion. A comparison of the Classical agora itself in the fourth century BC with its second-century AD manifestation is striking in the amount of construction related to the imperial presence (for example, the Odeion of Agrippa and the Temple of Ares) and the resultant loss of open, "public" space (figs. 26–7). If the agora, to quote the geographer J. B. Jackson, was "a manifestation of the local social order, of the relationship between citizens and between citizens and the authority of the state . . . where the role of the individual in the community is made visible," then, as the classical archaeologist T. Leslie Shear, Jr., remarked, these changes are "as clear a statement of the new ordering of the world as can be made through the medium of architecture."[1]

A different approach, however, is adopted in this chapter, one that allows a substantially wider variety of Greek cities to be considered. The civic landscape, as defined here, centers on the interaction of town *and* countryside: in other words, to our picture of the nature of rural activity and the social and economic implications derived from it (chapter 2), we now add the town (*astu*) itself. In the Classical period, the basic pattern

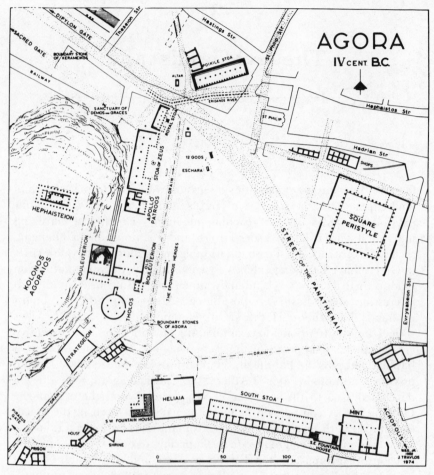

26 The Athenian agora in the fourth century BC

uniting the town and its associated hinterland was a simple one, constituting a "primate" *astu* that directly dominated smaller settlements in the landscape (i.e. in central place theory, the "administrative," or "solar," marketing model). That the altered status of Roman cities, now placed within a wider provincial framework, affected this standard Classical pattern is a possibility which this chapter explores in some detail. To do so, individual *poleis* will be treated as self-contained entities, and each city center considered in its regional context – that is, as the chief settlement and focus of activities within a wide and differentiated landscape. Redistribution of population and resources within the civic

94

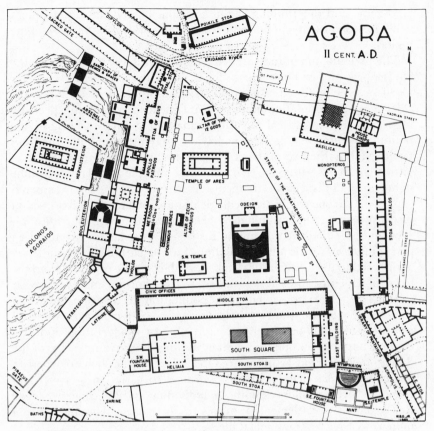

27 The Athenian agora in the second century AD

landscape can be read as a reflection of the network of economic and social relations that underlay the early imperial *polis*.

Chapter 2 discussed in detail the empirical evidence for a radical transformation of the countryside in the Early Roman period, and the various possible explanations for such a development already put forward include demographic decline and a concentration of landholding. A third factor, also already mentioned, is the seeming trend toward increasingly nucleated habitation. Nucleation is defined here as a preference for residence in larger, more populous settlements; this entails the rejection of isolated rural occupation and of Halstead's "alternative" mode of agricultural production that in part characterized Classical settlement patterns (pp. 60–1). Such a change in residential priorities will be argued here as an important force in the transformation of the Greek landscape, and determining the motivations behind this development will serve to illustrate numerous pressures at work within the *polis* of the period.

The potential magnitude of such a redistribution of people across the landscape must first be weighed. Life in nucleated settlements was, after all, always the preferred choice in Classical antiquity, with the *astu* as the chief center of population in most *poleis*. The discovery of unexpectedly numerous small Classical farmsteads may have once encouraged the notion of numerous people widely scattered throughout the *polis* territory; but that reconstruction fails to take sufficient account of settlement trends within the *polis* as a whole, and the actual demographic significance of dispersed settlement has now been somewhat tempered (pp. 44–5). In one recent archaeological study, of the *polis* of Koressos on Keos, survey and epigraphic evidence combined to demonstrate that, even in the period of maximally dispersed settlement, only some 25 percent (at *most*) of the total population chose to live full-time in the *chora*, as opposed to the *astu*. Classical and Early Hellenistic evidence from the town of Hyettos, intensively studied by the Boeotia survey, likewise suggests that some 70 percent of its population lived within the urban center itself.[2] So the trend to nucleation proposed for the early imperial period would thus be merely a heightening or exaggeration of a pre-existent pattern, yet one that neither diminishes the significance of the development, nor rids us of the need to analyze it. The choice of where to live is a complex decision, highly sensitive to variation in social and economic circumstances at both the individual and the collective level. Reassessment of settlement priorities results from a reorganization of numerous aspects of provincial life.

### THE EVIDENCE FOR NUCLEATION

Increased levels of nucleated residence, in villages or other larger rural settlements, have already been argued on the basis of the survey data for later Hellenistic and Early Roman Greece (pp. 62–3, 72). That communal residence was preferred is suggested by the fact that such larger communities survived instead of (or at the expense of) small farmsteads at this time. It is more difficult, however, to amass hard data about behavior in the towns themselves. The literary sources, urban-biased as they are, actually offer little help in judging the demographic ratio between town and country. Urban excavations begin, and usually end, with the public center of the community and rarely reach the city limits, making it impossible to measure overall changes in settlement size. Measuring urban populations through other standard archaeological indices (e.g.

theater sizes, wall perimeters, water supplies) is a dubious exercise even in the best of circumstances, and particularly where period-by-period comparison is involved. A more reliable means of noting variations in site size on a diachronic basis is, however, offered by urban or "large site" survey, a technique only recently adopted in Greece. In such investigations, the tactics of archaeological survey are applied to the *entire* human landscape – that is to say, to its urban, as well as to its rural, components. Artifact density distributions resulting from fieldwork of this kind can provide a vivid sequence of images of the rise, florescence and decline of an urban center, while at the same time permitting the city to be related directly to its rural hinterland. Urban survey, of course, can serve only as a rough demographic indicator: change in site size need not correlate directly with change in urban population levels, and the absolute number of people within a given area can vary through time depending on a wide range of cultural factors. Nevertheless, as a crude guide to city size and civic "health," urban survey is fast becoming recognized as indispensable, especially for assessing trends in settlement nucleation and dispersion.

Because this kind of survey is relatively new to Greece, only a handful of results are so far available for use here. In Boeotia, the large *kome* of Askra, and the *polis* centers of Haliartos, Hyettos and Thespiai have been intensively surveyed by the Boeotia survey. Haliartos was sacked by the Romans in the Third Macedonian War and its territory given to the Athenians; the survey evidence confirms the city's destruction and subsequent prolonged abandonment. The site identified as Askra, the home of the poet Hesiod, declined in size in Hellenistic times, and evidently disappeared completely in the Early Roman period, seemingly in confirmation of the testimony of Pausanias: "Of Askra in my day nothing memorable was left except one tower" (9.29.2). Hyettos, too, markedly contracts in size during later Hellenistic and Roman times, although a vigorous life is said to continue within the urban nucleus. Most interesting of all is the large city of Thespiai, over 100 hectares in extent in its Classical manifestation: there too a Late Hellenistic and Early Roman contraction in site size (to very approximately 72 hectares by the Early Roman period) has been observed (figs. 28–9). Considering also the overall decline in rural site numbers for the Boeotian landscape as a whole and, more tenuously, the sorry reports of Polybius, Strabo and Pausanias, it seems an inescapable conclusion that the region at large experienced a serious demographic collapse.[3] From the Boeotian perspective then, the explanation of settlement nucleation is more than a little far-fetched.

That this trajectory was not universal, however, is demonstrated by

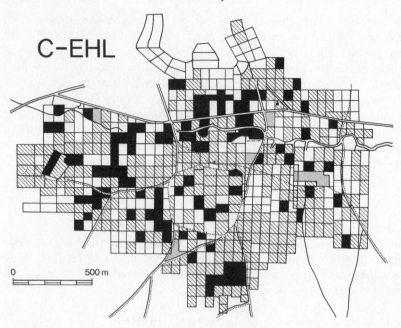

28 Thespiai in the Classical/Early Hellenistic period. Number of artifacts in each
collection unit datable to the period: blank = 0; hatched = 1–5; black = > 5.
Solid gray areas were inaccessible, or outside the city area.

another urban survey, this time in the northeastern Peloponnese at the
*polis* of Phlius. A strong Hellenistic and Early Roman presence has been
detected at that site, suggesting if anything (on the basis of artifact
numbers and distribution) *growth* in the town's size over that of the
Classical period (figs. 30–1). Excavation at the site has also yielded
evidence for considerable building activity in the agora area in the Early
Roman period. Phlius then appears to flourish at this time, as Pausanias'
approving account would suggest. Yet the Nemea Valley survey,
conducted in the valley systems immediately to the east and southeast of
the Phliasian plain, revealed the typical decline in rural settlement
numbers, opening at least the possibility of in-migration from countryside to urban center in this case. Supporting evidence is provided by the
city site of Ancient Methana, which surface exploration suggests
expanded during the Hellenistic and Roman periods – a development
the survey organizers believe to be explicitly associated with the decline
of village sites elsewhere in the peninsula.[4]

From this exceedingly small sample of urban surveys alone, it is
impossible to determine which response – urban growth or urban decline

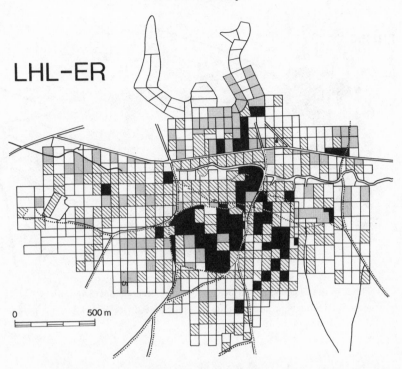

LHL-ER

0    500 m

29 Thespiai in the Late Hellenistic/Early Roman period. Number of artifacts in
   each collection unit datable to the period: blank = 0; hatched = 1–5; black = > 5.
   Solid gray areas were inaccessible, or outside the city area.

– was the more typical of civic behavior in early imperial Greece. What is
more significant is the realization that, while the rural landscape may
present a uniform appearance, different explanations may be required to
account for that pattern in different regions. In Boeotia, for example,
claims of grave demographic loss can scarcely be contested, yet in other
areas nucleation may offer a viable alternative solution. A great deal of
regional variability is to be expected in the urban history of the province,
as the next chapter will argue at length.

   To explore the process of nucleation, some further, rather less reliable
indicators must be employed. In the first instance, we can turn to regions
for which the available surface survey results reveal a distinct drop in
rural site numbers, yet where other forms of evidence (excavation,
literary sources or epigraphic information) suggest that the urban center
apparently endured in good condition. From the Southern Argolid, the
rural settlement evidence is quite clear; yet Pausanias reported the town

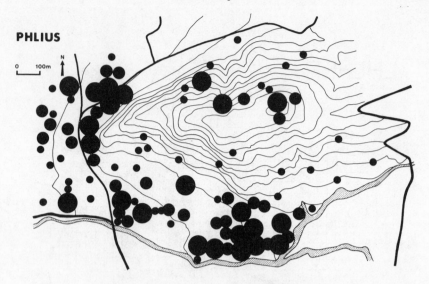

30  Phlius in the Classical period. Relative size of circles indicates density of material definitely or possibly datable to the period (see Alcock [1991], 447 for details of computation).

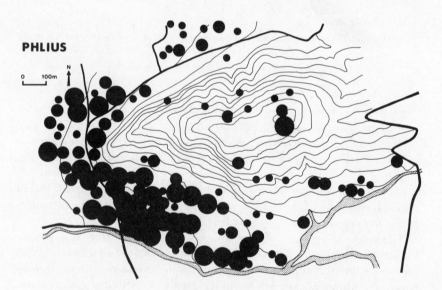

31  Phlius in the Early Roman period. Relative size of circles indicates density of material definitely or possibly datable to the period (see Alcock [1991], 447 for details of computation).

of Hermione as a "city which I found afforded much to write about" (2.34.11), recording seven functioning temples and notable cult practices. Signs of dedicatory and building activity have indeed been traced throughout the early imperial period. Pausanias does mention an "old" and "new" city, which has sometimes been taken to indicate a shrinking urban area in Roman times, but that interpretation rests on very weak foundations. Such apparent prosperity is especially compelling when it is remembered that only a dozen or so rural sites were found in the city's hinterland. Karystos in Southern Euboea is another case in point. Although rural settlement declined, new civic and religious buildings have been assigned to the Hellenistic and Roman era, and an expansion of city size in Roman times has been suggested on the basis of archaeological investigation. The exploitation of the nearby *cipollino* marble quarries, capitalizing on the vital imperial market for colored marbles, is often credited with generating this civic vitality – which, in any case, is a far cry from Karystos' possible identification as the decayed city of the *Euboean Discourse*, with "men farming the gymnasium and grazing cattle in the market place" (Dio Chrysostom, *Oration* 7.38–9). Ancient Melos, the city center of the island of Melos, has not been intensively explored, but signs of building or other activity for the Roman period are not lacking, such as imperial portrait statuary, a refurbishment of the theater, a bath, an aqueduct serving the gymnasium and a Roman necropolis. The mineral resources of Melos, exploited in the Roman era (if chiefly in the Late Roman period) are thought to have generated a degree of economic prosperity in the town; certainly the presence of *negotiatores* on the island is attested. Elsewhere, in Attica, the disappearance of rural sites in the deme of Atene has been thought to reflect the local population's preference for residence in Athens itself. Although no survey evidence is available for its immediate hinterland, the Boeotian town of Tanagra is also worth mentioning: described by its investigator as "peaceful and prosperous" under Roman rule, Tanagra underwent a radical urban renewal, with the imposition of an essentially new orthogonal plan, dating largely to Late Hellenistic and Early Roman times. Finally, in Messenia and Phokis too, it has been suggested that the observed contraction in Roman settlement numbers was related to the concentration of population in fewer towns, but no specific evidence for such a development has been adduced.[5]

Evaluating the robustness of urban life through evidence such as new buildings or dedicatory inscriptions is admittedly an indirect and problematic procedure. Do many honorific statues correlate with general civic well-being? Are temple repairs a sign of overall vitality, or simply the product of largesse on the part of a single individual? Does a lack of such signs unambiguously point to decline? Civic grandeur can easily reflect increasing exploitation of the population, rather than a rise in *per capita* income, general prosperity or higher urban population levels. Still, monumental benefactions and building activity testify at least to a continued élite interest and expenditure in a city.[6] This, above all, formed an important prerequisite for a viable urban life, as we will see.

An emphasis upon life in the urban center can also be monitored in a somewhat different fashion by the use of the rural survey evidence. Abandonment of the countryside was not a random process, but rather displays some measure of patterning. One interesting development, albeit only clear in some regions, is an increased tendency for early imperial sites to concentrate in proximity to the urban center. In the Southern Argolid, for example, sites endured better in the Ermioni drainage, near to Hermione (fig. 13); Ancient Melos and Karystos likewise served as something of a settlement magnet. On Keos, the urban center of Koressos underwent a synoecism with the inland city of Ioulis in the second century BC, and the subsequent spatial distribution of later Hellenistic and Roman finds reflects Ioulis' new centrality and attraction. Keian sites also cluster nearer to the harbor of Ioulis at Otzias, north of the city, where a mole of Roman construction once existed; this shift stands out especially sharply, given the former concentration of sites around the city of Koressos and the general evacuation of the rest of the countryside (figs. 32–5). For the Lakonia survey, the location of smaller Roman farms along natural lines of communication provides a comparable pattern. Alternatively, the more or less total abandonment of remote zones lacking a nearby urban center (such as the Skourta plain on the Attic/Boeotian border) could be noted. Overall, a desire for increasing proximity to the town center on the part of those individuals remaining in the countryside seems reasonably well established, if more distinctly so in some areas than in others.[7]

This locational choice is intriguing, for the closer second-order settlements are to major regional centers, the fewer distinctive functions they are likely to retain. Proximity to the *astu* would discourage the social and economic independence of secondary settlements, suggesting a greater reliance on the town for craft production, agricultural processing facilities, and opportunities for employment and exchange. Of course, the *astu* had always been the dominant resource center for the *polis*, so what seems to be witnessed here is again the intensification of a pre-existent pattern. Allied to this phenomenon is the relative scarcity of special-purpose sites (e.g. kilns, commercial sites, rural cemeteries) in the early imperial countryside. Survey evidence for such rural activities is never very abundant, but their avoidance of the countryside now appears

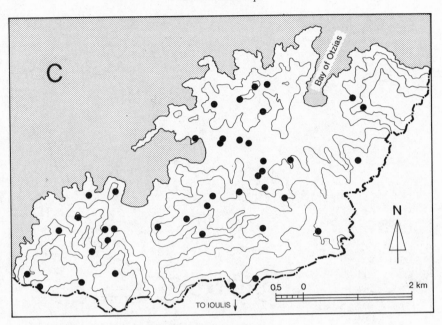

32 Northwest Keos, distribution of Classical sites

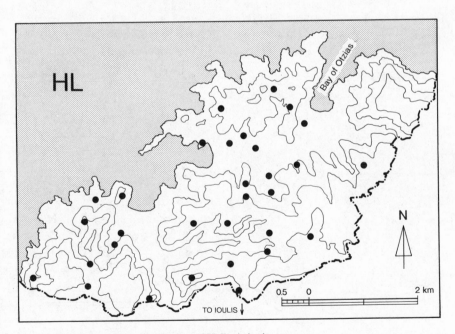

33 Northwest Keos, distribution of Hellenistic sites

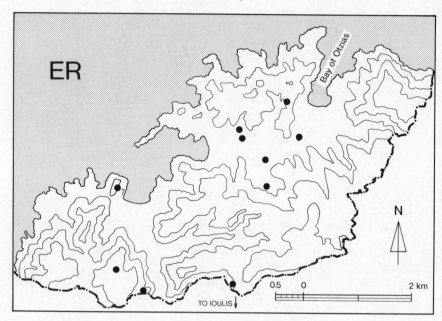

34 Northwest Keos, distribution of Early Roman sites

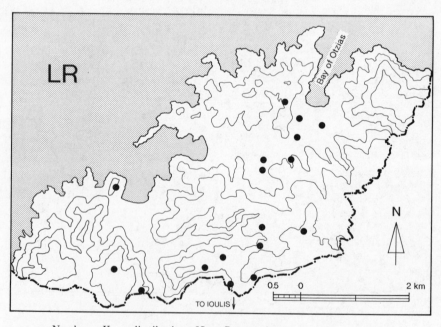

35 Northwest Keos, distribution of Late Roman sites

especially marked.[8] This, too, points in the direction of increased dependence, both economic and social, upon the urban center. The evidence of rural sanctuaries, a very important but much neglected class of survey site, will be considered separately in chapter 5.

Apart from this range of archaeological evidence (admittedly of varying quality) for greater nucleated settlement, some arguments from probability are also possible. If the abandonment of the countryside is taken at face value and massive demographic collapse accepted, then the ultimate repercussions on the civic structure of Greece would have been devastating. Some cities do indeed decline, as will be seen, yet throughout the period of Roman domination Achaia remained one of the most highly urbanized regions of the entire empire. In many areas, demographic levels sufficient to enable a high degree of civic continuity must have been maintained; the archaeological data make a strong case that urban residence must have been the preferred choice of the provincial population. This argument has been increasingly taken up by ancient historians and archaeologists seeking to account for rural conditions in early imperial Achaia.[9]

### THE ATTRACTIONS OF NUCLEATION

Why might people choose to change their place of residence, in many cases necessitating a change in their agricultural strategies? What forces would encourage a transfer to a larger community, even to the *astu* itself? Why does the central place appear increasingly to dominate its hinterland? No single answer can do justice to these questions. Deciding where to live is a complicated process, the final outcome a product of a wide range of factors.[10] The large time-scale involved here adds a special incentive for stressing the multivariate character of decision-making about residence. A span of approximately 400 years, some dozen or so generations, is being analyzed largely on the evidence of essentially static survey "snapshots," each representing long periods of time. Given this lack of chronological refinement, we ought to consider a range of motivations which, gradually or abruptly, could have engendered the new civic landscape.

One popular explanation for a shift to agglomerated residence is the perceived need for defense – in times of external threat, personal safety lies in numbers. While this response to danger is indeed often seen, cases are also known where historically well-documented episodes of warfare, piracy or raiding leave no trace in the overall distribution of settlement, and it would certainly be an over-simplification to identify defensive considerations as the *sole* force behind any major settlement shift.

Nevertheless, the periodically intense outbursts of warfare during the later Hellenistic period may well have triggered population mobility in certain regions. Military conflict and its accompanying evils could easily have encouraged a narrowing of residential options, forcing the abandonment of small, isolated sites in the countryside. This explanation is especially apposite in the more war-torn areas of Greece, such as Boeotia. Brigandage would contribute as well; outbreaks are reported, for example, in second-century BC inscriptions from the town of Hyettos, which lies within the survey territory of the Boeotia survey, and the fact that many of the small Classical/Hellenistic sites discovered by this survey disappear rapidly between the second and first centuries BC supports this argument.[11] Yet even if the need for defense did provide an initial stimulus for nucleation, the persistence of the pattern in the era of the *pax Romana* demands that its continuity be explained through the introduction of further, more structural factors.

First, it has been suggested that dispersed residence is often the result of smallholders concentrating their holdings so as to work them efficiently from a single rural base (pp. 60–2). Such arrangements of necessity require complicated negotiation and would be achieved through intermarriage, rentals and purchases. If such carefully engineered plans were imperiled or disrupted, for example by conditions of local instability or the encroachments of large landowners, then we would expect in response some increase in the attractive power of the urban center. The argument can perhaps be taken a step further. If powerful landlords were expanding their domains (as the archaeological and documentary evidence agree), then some smaller primary producers would have been squeezed out of a portion, or perhaps even all, of their land. In such cases, urban residence becomes a strategy of survival, the town offering economic opportunities lacking in the countryside. For the Classical period in Attica, Osborne observed how those elements of the population lacking land (in his study, freed slaves) were overwhelmingly attracted to urban centers. Those with skills to market did best; others who gravitated to the town could wind up as parasites upon it. In early imperial Italy, the urban presence of dispossessed rural dwellers is well documented; less outright evidence exists for the trend in Greece. Apuleius does provide one chilling fictional vignette of the Achaian urban poor when in Boeotian Plataiai the *vulgus ignobile* gorge on the corpses of bears meant for the games that were found in the streets: "Then the common people, who are forced by ignorant poverty with no taste in their choice of food to seek the filthiest supplements and free meals for their shrunken bellies, came running up to these banquets lying strewn about" (*Metamorphoses* 4.14).[12] A positive correlation has already been noted in other epochs between the dominance of extensive rural landholdings and a preference for nucleated settlement (p. 55). On one level then, disruption of land ownership patterns could make urban residence a safer choice, or even the last resort of those with nowhere else to go.

A second line to explore begins with the assumption that most elements of the Greek population were now subject to increased demands for cash payments, levied through both imperial taxation and private rents. If intensification of agricultural activity was not an option generally pursued at this time, one alternative response would be increasing crop specialization. The rather limited direct archaeological and literary evidence for this development has already been reviewed (pp. 80–2). Specialization "in response to markets frees large stretches of time for other employment in or beyond the community. But a major restraint in turning to specialization . . . was diminution of *autarkeia*."[13] Such a strategy could raise cash income, as well as improving an individual's chances of being seasonally available for other kinds of wage labor. For most households, however, any development along these lines would be constrained by the basic first need to feed themselves. Only relatively stable and well-endowed landowners could attempt such a tactic on any scale, and even for them cash-cropping, or any concentration of effort and resources on a smaller range of crops would be a risky option to adopt; in addition, it can foster a more active land market, a competition the wealthy would inevitably win.[14] To whatever extent agricultural specialization took place, certain consequences are predictable: specialization could potentially lead to the loss of land, to an added reliance upon other forms of supplementary income, and to an interest in fostering a strong support network – all of which point to a preference for urban residence.

The desire to supplement income and raise necessary revenue would have led individual households to a more general economic diversification. If opportunities to seek additional and alternative employment were to be seized, these chances were possible only through the town. In addition to farming their own land, individuals could work for wages, sharecrop, take on tenancies, or pursue non-agricultural employment (this last possibility to be discussed further below). Urban residence would facilitate this mixture of tenures and options. There certainly exist ancient references to peasants looking for work in cities on a seasonal or permanent basis. For what it is worth, the protagonists of the *Euboean Discourse* only adopted their isolated lifestyle after unsuccessfully seeking employment in the town, while from Apuleius' *Metamorphoses* Fergus Millar extracted the observation that "the towns are represented as providing real concentrations of activity both by way of exchange and in the hire of labour."[15] Occupational diversification of this kind could be relied upon to generate income in place of agricultural intensification, though such a course of action generally leads to a lower standard of living. The price exacted by this strategy was a shift to more extensive farming practices. Moreover, available surplus, perhaps once spent on investment in the countryside, was also diminished by imperial and local taxation. The abandonment of small rural agricultural sites, and the turn to centralized residence, would be one result of these related developments.

If this reconstruction is at all correct, it is likely that numerous families would now have sought to work land apart from their own individual holdings, either for subsistence or to increase their cultivation of cash crops. Such opportunities would, of course, have been greatly expanded by the growth of larger estates. Although slave labor was undoubtedly used in Greek agriculture during this period, tenancy would also have been a common phenomenon in the early imperial period. In general, recent scholarship has argued that land leasing was a much more significant economic and social strategy in Classical and Hellenistic times than has been credited in the past; households would take up or relinquish land depending on the family's changing composition and requirements through its "life cycle." Roman historians have long assumed that the proportion of individuals involved in tenancy relationships increased under the early empire. Tenancy is a very broad category, and a wide variety of dependency relationships must be included within the term. Tenants would also be drawn from a variety of backgrounds: the completely dispossessed, small farmers seeking additional income or additional types of land to farm, wealthy men adding to their existent holdings.[16] At this juncture, the important point to pursue is how the status of tenant would affect the hypothesized preference for centralized residence.

The size of the holding and the nature of the contract matters a great deal in answering this question. Foxhall has recently argued that smaller tenants probably lived chiefly in "more or less" nucleated settlements, with perhaps seasonal occupation in temporary (and thus less archaeologically visible) shelters. The presence of larger-scale tenants, however, has been detected at a few rural sites on Methana which combine sturdy buildings and impressive agricultural facilities with impoverished surface assemblages. Foxhall's equation of these relatively inaccessible, but well-endowed, Roman farms with tenant holdings demands considerable caution, given the obvious difficulties involved in identifying an owner or occupier's legal status on the basis of archaeological remains alone. Nonetheless, her working assumption – that only tenants on sizable

properties adopt a rural residence – does seem more than likely.[17] Those
leasing smaller parcels of land may well have chosen to live in the city,
both to maximize social benefits and to minimize travel times to scattered
holdings, the same pressures felt by small-scale independent proprietors.
As for the nature of individual contracts, short-term leases with little
security on the land would encourage less intensive working and thus an
urban, economically diversified lifestyle. Longer-term leases might
encourage more rural investment of time and labor, and thus a more
dispersed pattern of residence. For Achaia, direct evidence one way or
the other is very slight, and no doubt leasing arrangements varied
greatly. Some fourth-century evidence, however, has been interpreted to
suggest that at least some private leasing was short-term, perhaps lacking
a written contract, and subject to the whim of the landlord. Relatively
short-term leases (five years perhaps the norm), let for a fixed annual
rental in cash, seem to have been the most common pattern for private
farm tenancies in Italy during the early empire, and similar arrangements may be suggested for Achaia as well.[18]

The nature of the payment required (cash or labor dues, sharecropping) also directly affects the dependent farmer's behavior, not least in
the mobility of the individuals involved. Cash obligations, for example,
are more liable to permit elements of an individual household to move
about, either on a permanent or seasonal basis. Sharecropping too allows
some mobility, certainly more so than tenancies with labor obligations
attached. Cash rents and sharecropping probably predominated in the
early imperial period, allowing some flexibility in a tenant's choice of
residence. For the Classical/Hellenistic era, Osborne notes that rents in
cash were much more common than rents in kind, leading to a large
circulation of money within the city, strongly implying "that there was a
lively market for agricultural goods which could absorb home produce in
sufficient quantities to make it possible to pay off rents that were in some
cases very large."[19] A similar conclusion seems appropriate for the early
imperial era as well. This circulation of cash would in turn encourage,
and make possible, higher levels of urban occupation and residence.

Agricultural production must always have constituted the lion's share
of ancient economic activity, but other options were open to households
interested in diversifying their income. Possibilities included working at
craft production, in service industries, or at short-term jobs such as
building projects. Although it is very hard to judge from the extant
information, there are signs that at least some of those areas endowed
with natural resources (marbles, minerals, metal ores) utilized them
more fully in Roman times. This development is most apparent in the
case of marble quarrying and the marble trade. In the east lay the

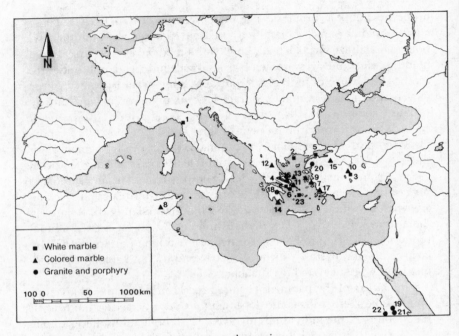

36 Distribution of marble sources across the empire

| | | |
|---|---|---|
| 1 Carrara | 9 Chios | 17 Iasos |
| 2 Thasos | 10 Docimium | 18 Krokeai |
| 3 Docimium | 11 Karystos | 19 Gebel Dokhan |
| 4 Mount Pentelikon | 12 Thessaly | 20 Troad |
| 5 Proconnesos | 13 Skyros | 21 Gebel Fatireh |
| 6 Hymettos | 14 Cape Tainaron | 22 Aswan |
| 7 Teos | 15 Verzirken | 23 Paros |
| 8 Chemtou | 16 Chalkis | |

majority of the empire's sources of white and colored marbles, the demand for which grew greatly from the second century BC. From Achaia, green-veined *cipollino* from Karystos in Euboea was reaching Rome already by the first century BC; until late in that century Attic quarries provided Rome with most of its white marble. Under the early Principate, quarrying activity is recorded from several other regions of Greece and the Aegean islands (fig. 36).[20] Mining evidence is more problematic. Roman iron-working is attested in some regions, for example Boeotia and on the island of Gyaros, but it is unsure whether or not this truly indicates an increase over previous levels of exploitation. The most important Classical mines of Greece, the silver mines of Laurion, appear to have been gradually exhausted, with activity ceasing around the end of the second century BC. In the time of Augustus, dumps were said to be worked over, before the mines were abandoned again until the fourth century AD.[21]

Other non-agricultural economic activities reported in Achaia include flax weaving at Patrai, ceramic manufacturing in Aulis, unguent production at Chaironeia and at Tithorea, and mineral exploitation on Melos. Exploitation of shellfish for purple dye is also attested for the Roman period in several areas of Greece: Lakonia, Euboea, the island of Gyaros, Bulis in Phokis and the city of Hermione. Increasing demand for building materials (bricks and tiles, as well as decorative stone) would also have been generated by growth in public and private building activity, at least in the more flourishing cities. Such seems to have been the case, for example, at Sparta.[22]

Obviously the owners or controllers of such resources would benefit from their exploitation and consumption, as would the local labor force – arguably now more interested than ever in generating additional income. Countering at least some positive developments in these areas, however, was the imperial annexation of certain resources, in Achaia primarily the marble quarries. Quarry inscriptions reveal definite imperial ownership of some, if not all, Greek sources; for example, Mount Pentelikon and the quarries of the Peloponnese do not preserve any clear indications one way or the other, but it is generally agreed that most quarries (such as Karystos) would have been under imperial control by the early Principate. The operation and workforce at these quarries probably varied from case to case, ranging from leasing to direct imperial supervision; military personnel are known to have been involved in the Karystian *cipollino* quarries on Euboea (fig. 37). Although it has been argued that imperially owned and operated production units would have largely been segregated from neighboring communities, they nonetheless still required local servicing and feeding, so that some overall positive stimulus to local economies seems undeniable. The city of Karystos, despite the undoubted imperial ownership of the nearby quarries, is still assumed to have benefited from its proximity to valuable natural resources.[23]

Such cases of non-agricultural exploitation are known chiefly through documentary evidence, and so we have a very incomplete and unbalanced record of them. Nor is it meant to suggest that all these industries ranked equally in economic weight and importance; the scale of their local or regional economic impact would have varied greatly. Places such as Bulis, where "more than half its inhabitants are fishers of the shellfish that gives the purple dye" (Pausanias 10.37.3) or Aulis, where "there are but few inhabitants . . . and these are potters"

37 View of column within the *cipollino* quarries at Karystos on Euboea

(Pausanias 9.19.8), were obviously very unusual. Yet even minor developments along these lines could, directly or indirectly, improve a household's scope for supplementing its income or a community's chances of prosperity. The presence of a popular sanctuary in a city's neighborhood could likewise serve as a significant economic stimulus (p. 211).

The scenario envisioned thus far suggests that people were now working for a variety of incomes, holding a diversity of agricultural tenures from an urban base of operations. Paradoxically, this development can lead to the stabilization of a class of smallholders, albeit one at a relatively low level of existence. The net transfer of land to larger estates simultaneously stimulates a market for agricultural labor and for land-leasing, providing supplementary income opportunities for the peasant farmer. This additional income, further bolstered by whatever non-agricultural employment was available, would, with luck, allow such households to survive.[24] This potential stability is worth bearing in mind as a check on the assumption that large landholdings would inexorably grow until they completely controlled the Greek countryside. Fragmentation of income, diversity of agricultural tenures and a preference for urban living were not, of course, new strategies in early imperial times: in the *poleis* of the Classical world, these had been valid options for the landless, or for those whose landed holdings were not sufficient to meet all their obligations.[25] What is argued here is that the number of people falling into those categories *increased* under Roman domination.

### THE BENEFITS OF NUCLEATION

If the provincial population was economically more vulnerable under the empire, then the formation of new social ties, designed to ward off potential disaster, is to be expected. One traditional and well-established safety valve was the creation of extensive patronage networks, both horizontal and vertical. Membership in such a network would tend to militate against isolated residence in the countryside; life in a larger and more broadly based community, on the other hand, facilitated the formation of social obligations and linkages. While horizontal relationships of mutual support would always have remained vital, with the increasing power of élite families under the empire, vertical ties of patronage would have become ever more important. Access to power networks, for example, has been suggested as one additional motivation to tenancy at this time. Ties between urban-based patrons and rural clients were entirely possible, but the predominantly urban location of the wealthy and powerful must have proved literally an attractive force to many.[26]

Apart from individual patron/client relationships, more widespread benefactions, such as food distributions to the civic population, could be considered. The city alone offered opportunities for such provisioning, either through its own institutions, the largesse of an emperor or – and probably most reliably – the gift of a wealthy *euergetes*. Although civic *sitoneia* schemes became more common in Greece during the Hellenistic period, their practice was always limited. Nor were great strides in this direction taken under the empire. Athens and Corinth appear to have boasted the most developed schemes. Some type of Hadrianic corn dole and a possible alimentary program is recorded at Athens; for at least part of its history, Corinth possessed a *curator annonae*.[27] For the most part, however, the participation of local élites remained vital in this capacity, and acts of town-based euergetism provided the chief bulwark against food shortages and consequent social disruption. Banquets for city-dwellers were popular outlets for liberality in the Hellenistic and Early Roman era, with examples recorded from the Greek mainland, the Aegean islands and Asia Minor. Decrees honor local *euergetai* who revived such celebrations, which had lapsed through civic weakness (*asthenia*); Epaminondas of Akraiphia in Boeotia is perhaps the most famous example from the mainland. Such gestures also served to promote and to perpetuate the role of the wealthy in city life, contributing to the acceptance of a new social order within the community. Such benefactions, only periodically offered, can hardly have provided the primary reason for moving into the city; for instance, they could never be relied upon as a family's chief source of sustenance. But a town-based system of euergetism, "which ensured that even the less well-off had access to some of the pleasures and benefits of city-life," adds another strong incentive to the other motivations already enumerated.[28]

### THE CONSEQUENCES OF NUCLEATION

In other cultures, such a concentration of resources has been turned to the advantage of élite families, with their monopolization of facilities, such as agricultural processing equipment, needed by all. Restricting access to strategic resources increased dependence upon the urban élite, a control augmented by their role in the collection of imperial and civic taxes.[29] The domination of the wealthy already observed in the rural landscape (pp. 63–71) is echoed in the town, in their dedications, monuments, houses and tombs. Yet this flow of expenditure (on buildings, services, luxuries, and other signs of conspicuous consumption) generated in turn the economic activity on which the population at large increasingly relied. It was essential that élite families respond to local needs and maintain their civic pride; the consequences of its lack will be discussed in the next chapter.

An undertone of conflict may well have entered into this new residential patterning, as the goals of different elements of the population came into collision. Proprietors or tenants of limited means might prefer an urban and economically diversified lifestyle, but its inevitable consequence was less intensive, less productive land use. Some large-scale landowners, and the imperial authorities, might well view this with vexation, as the evidence of emphyteutic legislation suggests (p. 91). The desire of tenants to live in the city, instead of on their leaseholds, in the majority of cases must reflect their own wishes, not those of the landlord. The contrasting Late Roman situation could be considered. The more oppressive tax burden of the later empire, coupled with the erosion of the social and legal status of the population at large, meant that people could be forced to live on the land, with the *coloni* physically affixed to their tenancies. Studies by human geographers of the medieval world have noted that feudal modes of exploitation tend to locate peasants within an explicit spatial framework, leading to a process of increasing immobilization.[30] The Late Roman rural landscape, with its return to dispersed settlement, often in small farmsteads, reflects major socioeconomic transformations within the later empire. If social status directly affects the decision where to live, then the nucleated settlement characteristic of the early imperial period appears as the choice of those who could still choose.

In some ways, this development seems somewhat counter-intuitive. It rejects the intensive agricultural production more predictable in an imperial periphery faced with increasing tax demands (pp. 91–2). The loss of political independence and of overtly democratic forms of government might likewise be expected to diminish the appeal of centralized residence, formerly associated with active popular involvement. Population concentration at Hellenistic Thespiai, for example, has been attributed to the sheer intensity of civic affairs, serving as a "magnet" for urban in-migration. With more restricted political participation, a less town-based society and a resultant "flight to the countryside" becomes a strong possibility.[31] But such a course of action, although it is actually the one presented in the tale of the isolated and happy rustics of the *Euboean Discourse*, does not reflect the realities of the early imperial landscape as a whole. Instead, the encroachment of larger landowners, additional economic pressures, the need to diversify incomes, and the pull of the local élite together outweighed all other motivations and dictated the residential and economic responses of the majority of the Achaian population.

It is impossible to say which of these obviously interrelated factors was primarily responsible for this centrifugal movement of population. Their relative importance undoubtedly varied from household to household, city to city, and region to region; free cities, for example, would feel certain pressures less than those directly taxed. All are, however, profoundly indicative of broad trends in provincial society at this time: a more pronounced economic imbalance, greater polarities in the quality of life, more emphatic social stratification. In a period requiring innovative responses, nucleated settlement reveals the impact of imperial incorporation.

## THE SUCCESS OF NUCLEATION

So far it has been assumed that this strategy of heightened nucleation "worked" in the early imperial period. Yet how accommodating would most urban centers have been to influxes of population? Did the necessary economic flexibility for this proposed development actually exist?

Nucleated settlements possess "contagious" properties: the more people living together, the more needs and services are generated, the greater the division of labor, the wider the range of available functions. Competition and expenditure on the part of local élites also fueled economic activity. In other words, the bigger a town became, the bigger it could become. The wealth-creating potential of some centers was recognized by Dio Chrysostom; commenting on provincial assize centers he remarked "And this contributes not a little to prosperity; for wherever the greatest throng of people comes together, there necessarily we find money in greatest abundance, and it stands to reason that the place should thrive" (*Oration* 35.16). Yet given the economic and technological limitations of the ancient economy, this could not be an uncontrolled, let alone exponential development. Even with a mixture of agricultural and non-agricultural sources of income, an inelasticity of overall demand for goods and services on the part of the urban poor and rural peasantry might be expected to be in effect, imposing a ceiling on the development of most urban centers.[32] Elite spending or patronage likewise could stretch only so far; food grants or building projects would prove only short-term boosts.

Recent investigations suggest that such primitivist reconstructions have underplayed the level of internal economic exchange taking place within the cities, and that under certain conditions cash taxation can prove a stimulus to production and trade. To some extent, then, *poleis* may have been more able to accommodate the shift toward nucleation than has been allowed.[33] This would be more true, however, of larger than smaller towns. For the majority of small *poleis*, the total number of people who could productively take up predominantly urban residence would be limited, although the existence of a minority sunk in genuine unemployment and misery can also be reckoned into the equation. Such smaller cities then must have had an upper limit, beyond which the urban center could not expand – physically or economically. Any "excess" population would have to flee or "disappear."

The likelihood of some degree of population "disappearance" has already been discussed (pp. 89–91). In some cases nucleation could well have acted as another form of demographic constraint. The need to maintain an urban presence led to the slackening of agricultural production; mixed and possibly irregular forms of income would encourage voluntary family limitation. Urban-based economic strategies might ensure civic survival, but they would not guarantee civic growth. And indeed some *poleis* failed to survive under the changing conditions of the early imperial period; others declined. Paradoxically, however, others flourished. That observation is closely related to the second suggestion: that individuals could flee a potentially unhappy lot in their original home city. Not all Achaian cities were small and economically limited; larger urban centers, with the necessary advantages and "critical mass" to attract and support a more substantial population, did exist. The possibility of movement from smaller to larger centers, as need or ambition pressed, opens up the question of the distribution and relationship of cities across the province, topics which belong properly to the next chapter. Before leaving the civic for the provincial landscape, however, we can reconsider the evidence for the bond between town and country in the early imperial period.

### TOWN AND COUNTRY

Classical *poleis* were composed of a unity of *astu* and *chora*, with no juridical or social distinctions drawn between the two: citizen-farmers formed the backbone of the city. Any conceptual division of town and country can be rejected outright, in favor of speaking of a "variously peopled landscape."[34] What of the early imperial situation, however, when farmers no longer formed the community's military force and when the nature and scope of citizenship was drastically revised? With such dramatic changes in the political and social make-up of the *polis*, it is fair to ask if the traditional bonds of the Classical city had been severed. From the available historical evidence, the answer is negative. The *polis* module endured in Hellenistic and Roman times, with the agricultural hinterland acknowledged as part of the city for tax purposes and without the creation of new institutions which excluded the countryside.[35] Does the archaeological evidence of settlement and land use, however, cast any different light on this question?

Even a cursory glance at regional settlement patterns at this time demolishes any possibility of the development of an "independent" countryside. The point is worth establishing, because it distinguishes early imperial Achaia from other areas of the eastern empire, where village life flourished in the substantially larger civic units of provinces such as Asia. By the fourth century AD, Libanius (*Oration* 11.230) stated that Antiochene villages had "little need for the town, thanks to the exchange among themselves," but Antioch was vast when compared to the scale of Achaian *poleis*.[36] The scenario of a separate rural life must be reconsidered in Late Roman Achaia, however, when settlement returns to the countryside in a configuration very different from the early imperial era. For the early imperial period, the town obviously emerges as the dominant partner.

Was this dominance exerted at the expense of the countryside? Increasing nucleation of population and resources can lead to the increasing alienation of man and land, as seems to be the case, for example, in the agro-town of the modern Mediterranean. Several factors suggest, however, that such alienation was not the rule in early imperial times. The established acceptance of a high degree of nucleated settlement, coupled with the remaining level of rural settlement, argues that the period did not herald a traumatic break with the preceding era. Elite interests may have been focused firmly on the town, but rural villas indicate that the countryside formed part of their social perspective as well. An ongoing concern for border demarcation (to be considered below) suggests continued efforts on the part of individual *poleis* to retain their territorial integrity. Other symbolic means of declaring the mutual commitment of the town and its surrounding countryside will be discussed in chapter 5.

If urban and rural ties were not dissolved, this does not mean that they were not rewritten and perhaps weakened at this time. Given the undeniable alterations in land tenure and residential patterns, the relationship of men to the land was undoubtedly affected to some degree. The equality of town and country would be less of a certainty, especially given the growth of power charted here for the urban-based élite. The pragmatic preference for urban residence may offer some proof that country-dwellers, once located securely within the political structure, would now have been more vulnerable, and in need of patronage. Watching for signs of the possible transformation of the *polis* "module" reveals undoubted strains upon the Classical harmony of town and country, yet without any decisive break – at least until the later empire. Regional analyses suggest the early imperial period was a transitional time, preceding the more likely divisions of the Late Roman epoch, and they reveal a more complex internal dynamic to the question of town and country relationships.

### THE BOUNDARIES OF THE *POLIS*

As a territorial unit, the Classical *polis* had placed great emphasis on its boundaries, marking them in various ways and punishing any transgression of them. The forcible unification of Greek cities within a provincial structure might be expected to affect attitudes to these all-important borders, breaking down formerly impermeable barriers. Yet substantial evidence shows that this does not seem to be the case: the cities of Hellenistic and Early Roman Greece in fact preserved a great interest in their borders, an interest often resulting in litigation and appeals to higher authority. Indeed, the recorded number of border disputes increases in the Hellenistic period. If this is owing in part to the survival

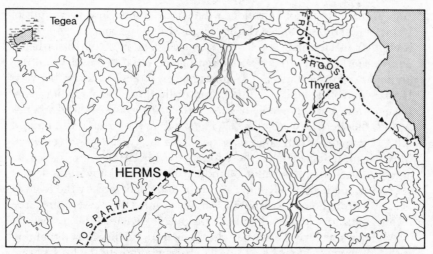

38 Map illustrating part of Pausanias' route in Book 2 (2.38.7), and the location of the "Herms," stone figures on the boundary between Lakedaimonian, Argive and Tegean territory

rate of documents, another explanation is that the cities now were "more and more solicitous to safeguard their interest and those of their citizens in a period of serious economic difficulties."[37] Boundary maintenance (or even territorial expansion) was one tactic by which a city could survive (or even flourish) under the changing conditions of the early empire (pp. 152–4). At very least, these disputes indicate that frontiers and boundaries were still essential in preserving the integrity of the city. Even of Panopeus, that small Phokian community derided by Pausanias for its lack of civic amenities, it was admitted that "nevertheless, they have boundaries with their neighbors" (10.4.1).

Pausanias' narrative emphasizes the continuing role of sanctuaries, shrines and other sacred places in locating and defining territorial boundaries. As he passes from the sphere of one *polis* unit to the next, the traveler often enumerates associated cult places, most often dedicated to Hermes, as god of travelers and thresholds (fig. 38). In Arcadia, for example:

About fifteen stades distant from Phaedrias is an Hermaeum called "by the Mistress"; it too forms a boundary between Messenia and Megalopolis. There are small images of the Mistress and Demeter; likewise of Hermes and Heracles. I am of the opinion that the wooden image also, made for Heracles by Daedalus, stood here on the borders of Messenia and Arcadia. (Pausanias 2.35.2)

And in the territory of Hermione, "Sanctuaries have also been built of Demeter Thermasia, one at the border towards Troizenia ... while there is another in Hermione itself" (2.34.12; cf. 2.34.6–7). Far from being passive sentinels, revered places often played an active part in border arguments. For instance, Pausanias reports "the boundary between Heraia and the land of Elis is according to the Arcadians the Erymanthus, but the people of Elis say that the grave of the Koroebus bounds their territory" (8.26.3–4). The sanctuary of Artemis Limnatis in the Taygetos mountain range was one focal point for the tension between Messene and Sparta over the *ager Dentheliatis*. At least six separate arbitrations in this particular boundary dispute are known, the last of which was made by the Roman governor and confirmed by the Roman Senate. Throughout this dispute, both sides argued their case, citing "the records of history and the hymns of the poets" (Tacitus, *Annals* 4.43).[38]

While on one level Pausanias clearly signals the divisions remaining within Achaia – remarking on border crossings, and ending his separate "books" as he departs from individual districts – at the same time his *periegesis* encompasses and relates all of Greece within a single narrative structure. As Elsner has noted:

> The very conflicts of the *hellenika* as tirelessly repeated in the myths and histories of internecine war become a cohesive factor, a shared myth that brings them together against the Other of non-Greece, which is to say Rome. The divisions of Greece themselves become the definition of a unified identity, a past when it was possible to be divided before the present of integration within a larger and more dominant whole.[39]

This observation gently raises the point that, however successful individual cities may have appeared in their pursuit of continued independence, such a quest was now essentially fruitless, as *polis* units were linked together, first within the provincial structure of Achaia and then within the empire as a whole. The broader implications of this imposed unity will be explored in the next chapter, but first we should consider certain phenomena capable of transgressing individual civic boundaries.

Chief among these are transhumant pastoralism, road networks and aqueducts. None of these are necessarily new in the Roman period, of course, but their development in the Roman period signals a growing permeability of political borders. A rise in large-scale pastoral activity, requiring more extensive movement of flocks, has already been argued, at least for some regions in Achaia (pp. 87–8). Elite-level friendships and other inter-*poleis* links would smooth territorial crossings more often avoided in the earlier Classical period. Roads are somewhat more problematic, since so little systematic work has been done on the Roman road network in Achaia. The main route in the Balkan region at large was obviously the *Via Egnatia*, running from Apollonia to Thessalonike in Macedonia, first built in the mid-second century BC to service the frontier zone to the north. In Achaia proper, no real imperial interest in road building or repairs seems to be indicated until the time of Trajan. In part, this must be due to the province's broken and dissected topography (encouraging maritime transport), in part to its military unimportance. Construction of at least one major route in the Peloponnese, probably accompanied by the repair of others, has been linked to Trajan's use of Achaia on his Parthian campaign route (ca. AD 114/15). The road in question lay in the western Peloponnese, in the Elis/Triphylia area where a milestone was recently found (fig. 39); the port of Hermione in the Southern Argolid may have been the specific embarkation point to the east. This Peloponnesian activity was probably tied in with a much broader program of road work, including a renewal of the *Via Egnatia*, for the Parthian Wars. A road network designed to connect the northwest and the Corinthian Gulf area (including the important imperial foundations of Corinth, Patrai and Nikopolis), although first begun in the first century BC, was also fully established, complete with milestones, during the reign of Trajan (fig. 40). Hadrian too had a care to link major centers, for example in his improvement of the Skironian road between Corinth and Athens, as reported by Pausanias (1.44.6):

The road called Skironian to this day and named after Skiron, was made by him when he was minister of the Megarians, and originally they say was constructed for the use of active men. But the emperor Hadrian broadened it, and made it suitable even for chariots to pass each other in opposite directions.

Corinth formed one major transportation hub of the province, with routes running out northeast to Athens, Boeotia and beyond, west to Patrai and Elis, south to Argos, Mantineia and Sparta, and southeast to Epidauros and Troizen.[40] Pausanias makes it clear that besides such central arteries, a variety of viable secondary roads and paths existed throughout the province.

Although the road network system that developed in the province remained relatively simple, nonetheless any imperial activity in this area stresses the need for – and the central authority to ensure – closer communication between different parts of Achaia, as well as further afield: "in a sense, then, all roads lead from Rome, all are built to extend and consolidate the imperial power."[41] That the province was from an early stage integrated within the empire's communication system is also demonstrated by the activity of the *cursus publicus*, the official information

39 Milestone of Trajanic date (probably AD 114/15) found at Epitalion in the Elis/
Triphylia area. The inscription reads:
Imp(erator) Caisar, di-/vi Nervai f(ilius),
Nerva/Traianus optumus/Aug(ustus) Ger(manicus), Dacic(us),
Pon-/tif(ex) max(imus), Trib(unicia) Pote(state)/XVIIII,
Imp(erator) VIIII, Cos(ul) VI,/P(ater) P(atriae),
mensuris viarum/actis poni iussit/VIIII.
The milestone can be associated with Trajanic road construction linked to the
Parthian campaigns.

network of the empire. A Claudian edict regulating its demands has been
found at Tegea, a city centrally located within the Peloponnese (fig. 2).
While placing not inconsiderable demands on the community in
question, the *cursus publicus* could act also as a local stimulant, with other
traffic and commerce likely to follow in its wake.[42] With the establishment of certain imperially defined communication routes, conditions for

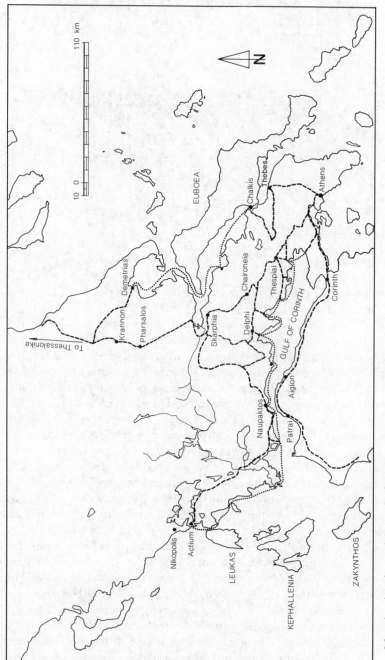

40  Map showing the road network of northern Achaia in the first century AD

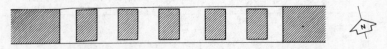

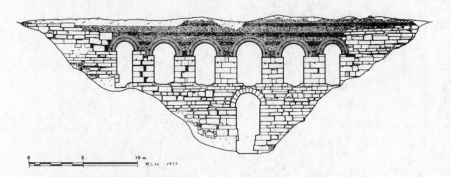

41 Elevation of one section of the aqueduct connecting Stymphalos and Corinth

the well-being or even the very survival of towns altered, as some areas were benefited and others by-passed (p. 162).

One clearly novel development of imperial times was the construction of long-distance, above-ground aqueducts. Previously, Greek cities had been eminently cautious about such structures, since water-supply systems which entailed crossing *polis* boundaries were impossible to secure. Coulton has compared the building of massive fortifications, necessary in Greece's earlier fragmented and divided state, to the aqueducts of the *pax Romana*: "the absence of earlier Greek parallels for the aqueducts of Rome was not due to poverty, ignorance or inefficiency, but to the very obvious dangers of dependence on a visible and vulnerable lifeline from outside."[43] As with roads, aqueducts in Achaia have received only sporadic attention, especially when compared, for example, to work undertaken in the province of Asia. The most famous Achaian aqueduct was that built by Hadrian to bring "water from Stymphalos" to Corinth. The route followed was long and difficult, running from Stymphalos, skirting the Phliasian plain to the south (at one point passing through the survey area of the Nemea Valley Archaeological Project) before turning north to Corinth (figs. 41–2). In the nineteenth century, Puillon Boblaye estimated its length at some 100 kilometers; the aqueduct's ultimate course remains uncertain, although its engineers clearly contended successfully with a remarkable number of mountains and valleys. The important point here is that the Hadrianic aqueduct, built to supply the probable provincial capital, must have

42 View of part of the aqueduct connecting Stymphalos and Corinth

passed through the territories of several *poleis* – at least those of Pheneos, Phlius, Kleonai, and Argos – before reaching Corinth itself. The security necessary for such a route was now guaranteed.[44]

Violation of territorial boundaries was not always necessary; if local resources were sufficient they would be utilized. The Hadrianic improvement to the water supply of Athens, for example, ran a conduit from Mount Parnes to a reservoir on Mount Lykabettos. The reservoir (of some 500m³ capacity) was ornamented with an Ionic portico inscribed at the time of its completion by Antoninus Pius (fig. 81). All major centers (e.g. Corinth, Nikopolis, Athens, Argos) acquired an ample supply of running water (fig. 43). Nymphaea and baths multiplied in these cities: twenty-four baths, as well as a new, centrally located and highly decorative nymphaeum, are attested in Athens alone (fig. 44). Major sanctuaries also benefited, most notably Olympia with the gift of a monumental nymphaeum by Herodes Atticus (figs. 70–1); the healing sanctuary of Epidauros enjoyed the gift of a rainwater reservoir by a "Roman senator," Antoninus, probably Sextus Iulius Maior Antoninus Pythodorus, not the emperor Antoninus Pius. Smaller towns too, such as Hermione and Ancient Melos, could boast advances in civic amenities. Indeed, by the early third century most cities in the Greek east probably had acquired more elaborate water-supply systems; "among monuments

43  Aqueduct running across the Louros River in Epirus to service Nikopolis

of material prosperity which made the status of the city visible, those connected with water occupied a special place."[45] Certainly by the time of Pausanias, the lack of "water descending to a fountain" was another complaint that could be made against the community of Panopeus (10.4.1).

As for the agency behind these aqueducts, in Asia Minor it was observed that imperial involvement, rather than local euergetism, was most often responsible for their construction. As far as can be determined, this seems true for Achaia as well, although in both provinces private benefactions are visible (and more visibly displayed) in the building and decoration of water delivery points such as fountains and nymphaea.[46] As well as indicating a level of civic prosperity and population, improved water supplies increased the attractiveness of the towns by improving their sanitation. Yet the gift of water from afar signals more than a concern for civic health. A more confident control of the physical environment is implied, the harnessing and channeling of natural resources to serve human needs, as well as the ability to transgress individual political boundaries by imperial mandate.

The *polis* as a territorial and political entity endured in the early imperial period, if subject to new tensions and pressures. Certain phenomena, however, make clear that boundaries – however well-

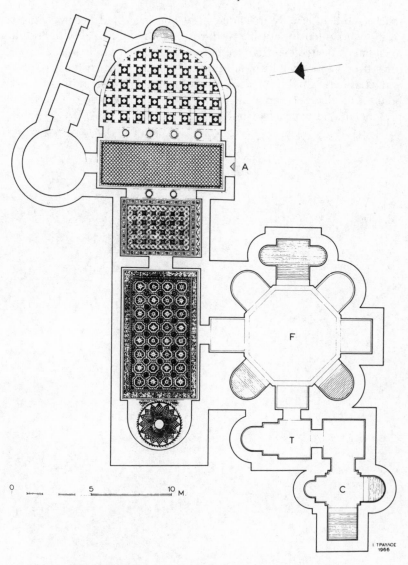

44 Athens, Hadrianic baths north of the Olympieion (ca. AD 124–31).
A = entrance, F = frigidarium, T = tepidarium, C = caldarium. This bath was
apparently in use until the seventh century AD.

marked and internally defended – on one level had become illusory, easily overridden by outside authority. An awareness of vulnerability must have affected external perceptions of the civic landscape, as well as the self-perceptions of its inhabitants. Discussing the existence of routes and channels capable of disrupting the integrity of individual civic boundaries thus sets the scene for a different conception of Greece, the provincial landscape as a whole.

# 4

# The provincial landscape

The triumph of Rome led to the creation of Greece. The history of the land before the Roman conquest, in ideological if not always in practical terms, had been the individual histories of independent *poleis*, or at most of regional leagues. Unity came only with subservience to an outside power. This chapter explores how this change affected the administrative and political structure of the province as a whole, as well as the social and economic priorities of its various inhabitants. The concept of the provincial landscape requires that Achaia be seen as a totality, with an emphasis placed on the relationships between its constituent elements. Since Greece was predominantly a land of cities, both before and after conquest, this investigation can be framed around questions of civic numbers and distribution, their relative importance, and the manner in which they interacted and affected one another.

Within peripheries of imperial territories, restructuring frequently, if not invariably, accompanies expansion. A more efficient provincial infrastructure is often developed, either through the *addition* of certain elements (e.g. compulsory urbanization, politico-administrative foundations, population relocation) or through their *subtraction* (e.g. a simplification or streamlining of the existing settlement hierarchy). On the other hand, if the conquered territory's existing organization was deemed acceptable, it could be left intact.[1] A spectrum of strategies, ranging from the dramatic to the subtle, has thus been employed in different empires, the basic goal of the new ruling authority being always to ensure the presence of an administrative framework receptive to their needs.

For the Roman empire, the best known and most ubiquitous intervention was the promotion of new centers within either non-urbanized or poorly urbanized indigenous zones. Such cities (*poleis* or *civitates*) were regarded as useful self-governing communities, capable of undertaking duties such as tax collection and the maintenance of internal order. Compulsory urbanization, which took place in many parts of the empire, is associated with a preference for indirect

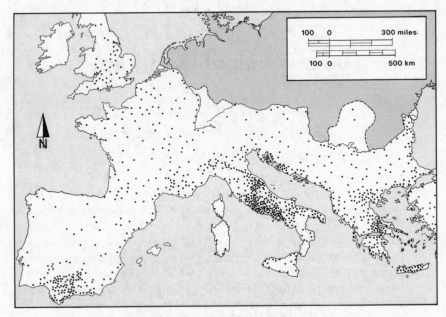

45  The distribution of cities within the Roman empire

administration, with key members of native ruling groups persuaded to serve as agents of the imperial interest. A civic framework was considered most normal for the operation of such individuals; Rome itself, after all, had begun its career as an individual city-state. In the eyes of the Greco-Roman élite, the city inculcated civilized and peaceful values; Aelius Aristides' idealized view of the empire, for example, saw Rome as the glorious *astu koinon*, surrounded by a constellation of civic entities (fig. 45).[2] So the encouragement of urban development as a tool of imperial policy places Rome well within the tradition of other imperial systems, both ancient and modern.

The transformation of previously nonurbanized territory into a world of cities has received a disproportionate amount of attention from both ancient historians and archaeologists. But what of the impact of Roman incorporation on landscapes that were *already* highly urbanized, already neatly divided into a mosaic of civic territories? The eastern Mediterranean as a whole was developed in this fashion to a great degree by the time of the Roman conquest; "Old Greece" in particular was one of the most urbanized zones ever incorporated. Literally hundreds of *poleis* are known in pre-conquest Greece, spread in a remarkably dense distribution across the landscape (fig. 45). In fact, given the total geographical area and population involved, an overabundance of cities must have existed, as measured in terms of sheer economic rationality (i.e. the functional services they provided, or the marketing needs they served). Many of these cities were indisputably small and unimpressive, such as Panopeus in Phokis. Yet whatever their size, all *poleis* were technically on the same political footing, with independence and self-sufficiency their avowed goals. The changed sociopolitical conditions of the Hellenistic age, with pressures exerted by neighboring monarchs, left such circumscribed units at a real disadvantage in regional politics and war-making. One response was the rise of federal league structures – that is, associations of cities responsible for diplomacy and foreign policy. Nonetheless, apart from the military organization of the leagues, the *poleis* remained the primary political and economic entities with which the Roman conquerors had to contend and come to terms.

What then was the Roman response to this complex, highly fragmented landscape? Compared to the dramatic changes witnessed elsewhere, the eastern Mediterranean might be distinguished as a relatively quiet backwater. Certainly, it is on conservatism in the treatment of the region that most stress has generally been placed, with only "minor adjustments" made to a basically fixed political structure: by and large the Romans took what they found and left well enough alone.[3] But is that a fair assessment of the situation in Achaia? A propensity to overestimate the static character of life in the province leads to a tendency to underestimate the potential impact of Rome. Rather than accepting without question the notion of an unchanged provincial landscape, we need to re-evaluate the whole question by assessing change in Achaian political geography from the perspective of Achaia itself.

The precise strategies employed in ensuring provincial control emerge from the complex interrelationship of two factors: the requirements of the ruling power and the conditions of the subordinate population. Understanding the position of the vanquished not only involves reconstructing their indigenous political system, but also the geographical location of their territory, its ecological constraints and environmental potential, and their past history of interaction with the enemy. The goals of the imperial power too must be established; overtly interventionist strategies might be applied only if the province was a target for systematic exploitation, or lay in a sensitive frontier zone. Specific systems of taxation or tribute – for example cash dues versus labor corvées – obviously carry with them different consequences for an administrative structure. A final variable would be the relative size and coercive strength of the imperial core in relation to the periphery in question, as well as the distance between the two. The "weaker" the core, and the further from the periphery, the less active meddling with local provincial affairs might be expected.[4]

Strategies of provincial consolidation, and particularly the issue of territorial reorganization, must therefore be appreciated as the product of a dynamic interaction between the winners and losers. In imperial studies, most attention is lavished on cases of direct *external* interventions: city foundations, forced population movements, large-scale labor projects. *Internal* adaptations, however, can play a parallel, and perhaps even more pervasive, role in reordering administrative geography. Modifications in the provincial landscape need not be attributed solely to explicit directives from on high, but may instead be generated from within – yet both represent the by-products of imperial activity. Furthermore, minor local changes are just as revealing as the ruling power's generally better documented, more spectacular actions. For the Achaian provincial landscape, these two strands will be examined: the effects of overt external intervention and the evidence for local, internal adaptation to Roman rule. Moses Finley once declared that a large part of the history of Greece is a question of tracing "the history of the complex transformations" undergone by her cities "as variables are introduced, internally as well as externally."[5] His statement remains true even as "Greece" passed under Roman control.

### IMPERIAL ACTIVITY: ALIENATION AND FOUNDATION

Roman interference in Greek settlement and demographic patterns did not have to wait for the area's official annexation. Apart from the disruptions caused by military action, reward and punishment are known to have been doled out through transfers of land from one city to another. The land of Haliartos, destroyed in the Third Macedonian War, was turned over to the Athenians – at their own request, much to Polybius' disgust. To this example could be added gifts from Antony to Athens, or Sulla's grant of Theban territory to various sanctuaries. The Romans comfortably asserted rights over the spoils of victory, as well as their ultimate distribution. New inhabitants, too, were foisted upon the region at Roman convenience: for example, Pompey the Great settled "most" of 20,000 Cilician pirates at Dyme in the northwestern Peloponnese. It had been claimed that Dyme was "bereft of men and had much good land" (Plutarch, *Pompey* 28.4), but how far that statement might reflect "an official line which excused much Roman practice" remains unclear.[6] Behavior of this sort amply demonstrates the *de facto* subjugation of the Greek cities to Roman wishes long before 27 BC.

More radical were the colonial foundations of Julius Caesar, quite probably located at Dyme and definitely at Buthrotum and at Corinth (fig. 46). The most important of these events proved to be the refoundation of Corinth, on the strategically located isthmus between the Peloponnese and central Greece. Mummius had sacked the city during the Achaean War, a deed resulting in, among other things, a famous pillaging of "artworks." Corinthian territory was largely given over to the neighboring town of Sikyon, though some land is also known to have been *ager publicus* in 63 BC. Rhetorical exaggeration may well color descriptions of this destruction, perhaps in order to match the violence of the annihilation of Carthage in the same year. Archaeological evidence actually suggests some degree of settlement at the site during the subsequent hundred or more years. This "interregnum" was brought to a close by the foundation of *Colonia Laus Julia Corinthiensis*, established by Caesar shortly before his assassination in 44 BC – ironically, the year Carthage too was refounded. According to Apuleius, "Corinth est totius Achaiae provinciae caput" (*Metamorphoses* 10.18); while no incontrovertible evidence exists to seal this identification, the colony is generally agreed to have served as the provincial capital of Achaia.[7]

Further manipulations of population and territorial boundaries were engineered by Caesar's successor, Octavian, resulting in the creation of two cities: the Roman colony of Patrai (*Colonia Aroe Augusta Patrensis*), and the *civitas libera* of Nikopolis (fig. 46). Patrai, established by 14 BC, was a colonial foundation composed of both veterans and members of the indigenous population; the precise political and juridical situation of the latter remains unclear.[8] The "Victory City," established near the site of Octavian's camp at Actium and founded soon after the battle, carried with it, of course, immense propaganda value (fig. 47). The precise institutional and political status of Nikopolis (as free Greek city or as "double community"), while exercising many scholars, will not be debated here. More central to the present investigation is the encouragement the city received from the emperor, including significant representation in the Delphic Amphiktyony and possession of major festivals, the Sebasta and Aktia.[9] Such celebrations brought revenues, as well as great prestige, to their host city.

Imperial support for these two centers is best seen, however, in the upheavals leading to the creation of their hinterlands. Territorial domains (larger by several orders of magnitude than the average *polis*) were attached by imperial mandate to the new foundations, regardless of previous local ties or affiliations. Nikopolis, for instance, was given the land of Ambrakia, Akarnania and part of Aetolia. Some independent cities subsumed within this grant continued to be inhabited, and to

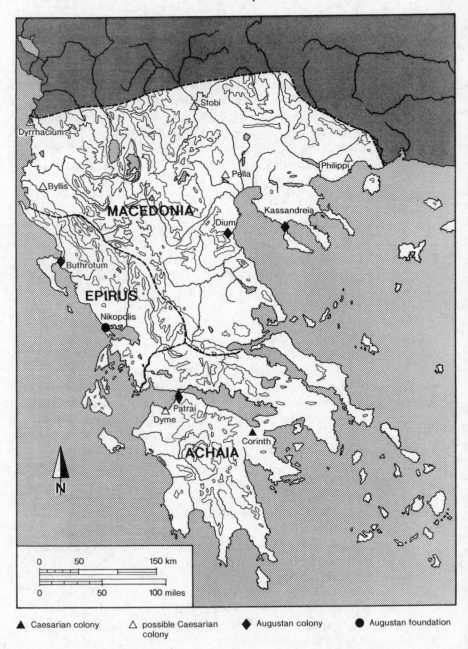

▲ Caesarian colony    △ possible Caesarian colony    ◆ Augustan colony    ● Augustan foundation

46 Location of Roman colonies and foundations in Achaia and Macedonia

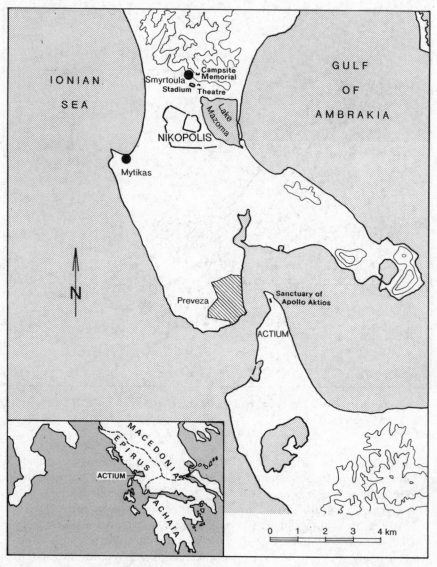

47 Nikopolis in its regional setting

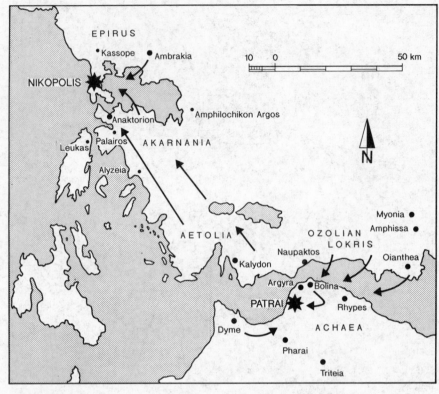

48 Regions and communities involved in the Augustan foundations of Nikopolis
and Patrai

function after a fashion (as *perioikides*). Palairos, Alyzeia, Leukas,
Ambrakia and Amphilochian Argos are numbered by Strabo among the
communities which became subordinate to, and dependent upon, the
new center (fig. 48). Other towns or villages, however, were clearly
destroyed outright, and their populations transplanted wholesale to
Nikopolis, thus contributing to the city's demographic strength. One
recent study goes so far as to argue that Octavian ordered the destruction
of fortification circuits in order to discourage any attempts to return to
ancestral homes. Archaeological evidence suggests that formerly prominent regional centers, such as Ambrakia and Kassope, were now
deliberately supplanted.[10] As for Patrai, the colony was assigned large
tracts of land on both sides of the Corinthian Gulf. Expansion of the city's
*chora* has been traced through the epigraphic evidence by the presence of
veterans or Roman citizens, and other desirable economic resources also

appear to have been transferred to the pampered foundation, or at least to some of its inhabitants. Strabo, for example, mentions a well-stocked lake near the dispossessed city of Kalydon in Aetolia, now "held by the Romans who live in Patrai" (10.2.21). As with Nikopolis, formerly independent settlements in the region were either brought under the new center's sway, or in several cases evacuated and their populations transplanted to boost the size of the colony. Previously, population in the area had been dispersed in several towns:

> Augustus, for some reason, perhaps because he thought that Patrai was a convenient port of call, brought back again to Patrai the men from the other towns, and united with them the Achaeans also from Rhypes, which town he razed to the ground. He granted freedom to the Patraians and to no other Achaeans; and he granted also all the other privileges that the Romans were accustomed to bestow on their colonists. (Pausanias 7.18.7)

Pausanias also mentions how two former *poleis*, Pharai and Triteia, now "belong to" Patrai (7.22.1, 6).[11]

The imperial design apparently met with some opposition:

> One hundred and twenty stades away from Delphi is Amphissa, the largest and most renowned city of Lokris. The people hold that they are Aetolians, being ashamed of the name of Ozolians. Support is given to this view by the fact that, when the Roman emperor drove the Aetolians from their homes in order to found the new city of Nikopolis, the greater part of the people went away to Amphissa. (Pausanias 10.38.4)

Archaeological confirmation of the magnitude of these territorial realignments is beginning to accumulate. Apart from excavation data from various abandoned towns (Kassope, Kalydon), preliminary survey results from an extensive portion of Aetolia reveal a significant drop in site numbers between the Hellenistic and Roman eras, emphasizing the severity of regional disruption (figs. 49 and 50). Somewhat sketchier evidence comes from a survey near Patrai, where some Hellenistic settlements in the *chora* of ancient Dyme go into decline and are abandoned in the Roman period.[12]

Apart from the redrawing of territorial boundaries, other signs have been detected of the dominance of these centers. For a long time, little recognition was given to the possibility of cadastral organization in Achaia. More recently, however, inspection of aerial photographs has resulted in various hypothesized field systems. While such systems are admittedly hard to identify with absolute certainty, their proposed Achaian locations are intriguing, for they correlate with these self-same foundations. Faint traces have been claimed for Corinth, though this particular evidence is highly problematic. The territory at Dyme, on the other hand, is said to boast excellent evidence for such a Roman plan;

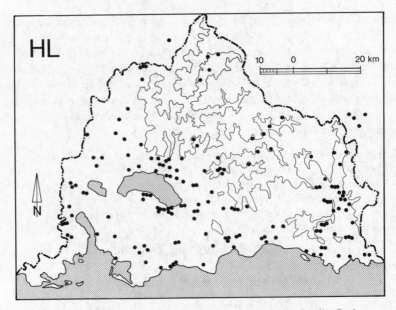

49 Distribution of Hellenistic sites discovered by the Aetolian Studies Project

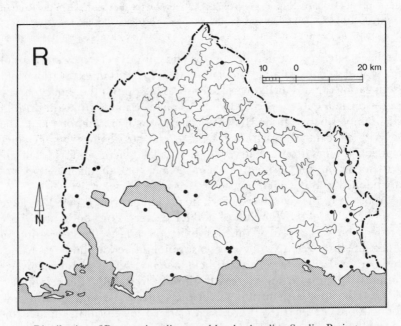

50 Distribution of Roman sites discovered by the Aetolian Studies Project

51 Traces of cadastral organization at the site of Nikopolis

traces of a similar network have been observed at Patrai as well. The most intriguing evidence, however, comes from the northwest, at Nikopolis and at Arta (ancient Ambrakia). The foundation of Nikopolis was accompanied by a cadastral organization of its territory, or at least of the peninsula south of the town; the module of the resulting centuries (identified as 20 × 40 *actus* or 707 × 1414m) and the network's orientation (identical to that of the urban plan) have been distinguished (fig. 51). Land divisions observed here dictated for centuries the subsequent organization of the Nikopolitan peninsula. As for Ambrakia, the city's decline has already been noted, but signs of a centuriated pattern, most likely dating to the years just after the foundation of Nikopolis, demonstrate that its territory was not abandoned. Drainage of marshy

52 Coins representing the chryselephantine cult image of Artemis Laphria. The
goddess, armed with a bow, wears a short chiton, and is accompanied by a dog.

areas accompanied this particular systematization of the cultivated
landscape.[13] Cadastral organization established new farmers on the land,
an important prerequisite for the flourishing of regional centers. Yet
pragmatic as such acts were, they bore a symbolic weight as well,
signaling the appropriation and mastery of new imperial holdings.

Other aspects of Roman intervention likewise reached well beyond the
purely material plane. Cult objects taken from defunct centers were
divided up and redistributed among other communities. Their destina-
tions are significant.

On the acropolis of Patrai is a sanctuary of Artemis Laphria. The surname of the
goddess is a foreign one, and her image too was brought in from elsewhere. For after
Kalydon with the rest of Aetolia had been laid waste by the Emperor Augustus in
order that the Aetolian people might be incorporated into Nikopolis above Actium,
the people of Patrai thus secured the image of Laphria. Most of the images out of
Aetolia and from Akarnania were brought by Augustus' orders to Nikopolis, but to
Patrai he gave, with other spoils from Kalydon, the image of Laphria, which even in
my time was still worshipped on the acropolis of Patrai . . . Every year too the people of
Patrai celebrate the festival Laphria in honour of their Artemis . . . the festival is not
only a state function, but also quite a popular general holiday. (Pausanias 7.18. 8–9,
11–12)

The cult of Augustus is known to have been associated with Artemis
Laphria, sharing an annual priestess (fig. 52). Also in Patrai there was "a
sanctuary of Dionysos surnamed Kalydonian, for the image of Dionysos
too was brought from Kalydon" (7.21.1). Cult objects were removed
from settlements newly dependent upon Patrai as well: at Pharai,
Pausanias saw "neither temple nor images, the latter, according to the
natives, having been carried away to Rome," and a similar fate overtook
an image of Athena from Triteia (7.22.5, 9).[14] More is conveyed by such
acts than the simple seizure of war booty. Removing a patron god or

goddess demonstrates the absolute power of the conqueror, at the same time enacting a community's symbolic destruction. Transferal of cult images also served to undercut former territorial loyalties and to foster new ties, as the destination chosen for these Aetolian deities proclaims. The implications of such ideological manipulation will be further discussed in the next chapter.

Contemplating the *location* of Corinth, Patrai and Nikopolis, and of their hinterlands, helps us divine some specific concerns behind direct Roman intervention in the provincial landscape (fig. 46). All share a westward position or orientation, indicating a greater emphasis upon communications and contact with Italy, the new core zone of the Mediterranean. If Greek interests and activities could formerly be said to incline to the east, absorption within the wider Roman world soon altered that bias. Various attempts to cut a trans-Isthmian canal quite near Corinth, thus avoiding the dangerous sea voyage round the Peloponnese, also testify to a genuine interest in facilitating an east–west flow of information and goods. The most flamboyant attempt was made by Nero, who "took a mattock himself and, at a trumpet blast, broke the ground and carried off the first basket of earth on his back" (Suetonius, *Nero* 19). Traces of Nero's efforts were still visible at the time the present canal was dug in the nineteenth century (fig. 53).[15] The specific zones selected for territorial reworking, especially Southern Epirus, Aetolia and the north coast of the Peloponnese, also share certain fundamental characteristics:

1 These areas had represented long-standing antagonism to Rome, encompassing the heartlands of the Aetolian and the Achaean Leagues, the political and military alliances which, at one point or another, had offered stubborn opposition to Roman aggression. These territories could therefore be perceived as potential centers for future resistance. With the benefit of hindsight, it is easy to disregard the likelihood of Roman anxiety on this score, yet discontent and even episodes of rebellious activity are certainly recorded in Achaia during the early years of Roman rule. In the first stages of imperial consolidation, the breaking up of formerly hostile zones would have been a reasonable imperial policy.

2 Often as a result of opposition to Rome, these areas had been severely disrupted by military activity. Epirus suffered dreadfully from the merciless assault of Aemilius Paullus in 167 BC, when seventy cities were said to have been destroyed and 150,000 people taken captive. While this event predated the Augustan synoecisms by a wide margin, over a century later its devastating effect – and the consequent loss of manpower – was still mentioned as a drain on the region's productivity. Indeed,

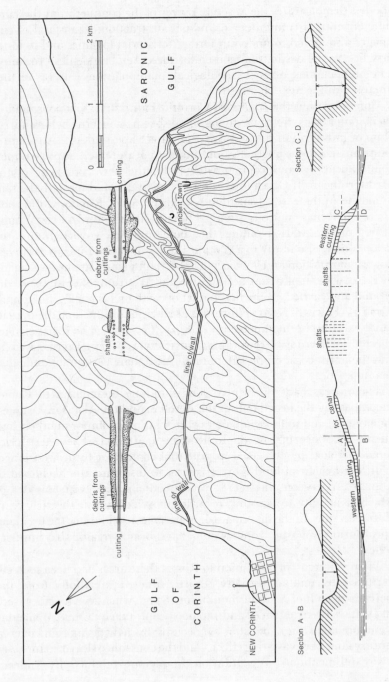

53 Archaeological remains of Nero's attempted canal across the Isthmus of Corinth

when speaking of Ambrakia's former prosperity, Strabo stated: "In later times, however, the Macedonians and the Romans, by their continuous wars, so completely reduced both this and the other Epirote cities because of their disobedience that finally Augustus, seeing that the cities had utterly failed, settled what inhabitants were left in one city together" (7.7.6). Corinth itself, of course, had been destroyed in the mid-second century BC; the situation in the region around Patrai is also believed to have been particularly grim at the time of the Civil Wars. Abuses by Roman administrators in these areas prior to the Augustan reorganizations may have taken an added toll.[16]

3 Partly as a result of these devastations, but also partly because of their own particular regional history, to any observer at about the time of Actium these areas would have appeared as marginal zones – under-urbanized, inefficiently administered, inadequately exploited. The northwestern Greek mainland especially had long been proverbially "backward" compared to the rest of the country, slow to adopt a strongly *polis*-oriented way of life.

4 This generally unhappy state of affairs could not go disregarded, for it was perceived that various imperial interests would be served by the imposition of a stronger organizational framework. Military and economic concerns both figured in this assessment. The importance of Epirus, and the *Via Egnatia*, in the empire's communication network demanded stabilization of the northwestern region. Corinth and Patrai were strategically located for east–west trade and communications. According to Pausanias, Augustus perhaps selected Patrai because he found it a "convenient port of call" (7.18.7); Corinth was restored "because of its favorable position" (Strabo 8.6.23). Between the Caesarian and Augustan colonies (including Buthrotum, Byllis and Dyrrhachium in Macedonia), a chain of urban centers was created running down the western coast of the Balkan peninsula, conveniently close to Italy (fig. 46). The presence of influential Roman landowners along that side of the peninsula is attested from before the time of the new foundations (p. 75), and these individuals were deeply involved in the politics behind these settlements. The economic interests of individual proprietors, as well as of the state, could thus be served. Developing a "special relationship" between the two coasts of the Adriatic appears a particular objective; Augustan propaganda promoted a legendary connection between western Greece and Italy.[17]

No doubt some combination of circumstances prompted specific acts of Roman interference. What must be recognized is the fact that imperial attention to these particular zones was not fortuitous, nor can any of these sites be considered in isolation: they appear as related elements within a wider imperial scheme. As both pragmatic and symbolic acts, these state settlements represented the imperial power, while simultaneously fashioning the infrastructure necessary to perpetuate its rule. Obliteration of indigenous, potentially hostile power networks would follow from compulsory resettlement, especially when accompanied by acts of "symbolic violence." Finally, while no colony ever carried with it an overtly Romanizing *mission civilisatrice* (indeed, in time both Corinth and Patrai took on an increasingly "Hellenic" aspect), the allegiance of these centers to Rome cannot be discounted.[18] All in all, these interventions are to be taken as deliberate efforts to render the control of potential "trouble spots" more efficient, economical and stable.

Roman responses to the problems of conquest and consolidation in Achaia led to a forcible recasting of the provincial landscape. That conclusion flies in the face, of course, of the more usual image of a relatively "static" situation. But the issue of scale may clarify that apparent contradiction. Within the context of the Roman empire as a whole, these new settlements indeed appear as relatively unimportant. Within the context of Achaia proper, however, the potential repercussions escalate; from the point of view of the communities involved, the lives of thousands of individuals were severely disrupted. From that vantage point, Roman interference in the political landscape appears far from inconsequential. Admittedly, such overt cases are comparatively few in number, nor did they directly affect the entirety of the province. On the whole, the continued existence of numerous small political units was reconcilable with the Roman reliance upon the capabilities of local élite groups. From the point of view of administrative efficiency, a multiplicity of such lowest-order centers might not be desirable, but it was acceptable. A "hands-off" policy would also be encouraged by the insulated position and relative unimportance – economic, political and military – of the province within the empire as a whole. The likelihood of imperial "meddling" grows more remote given that particular combination of external expectations and local conditions. Yet the notion of complete imperial indifference to Achaian political geography is no longer credible; nor is the *direct* impact of such meddling the only point to consider.

Two final points about these interventions are worth making. Where the Roman authorities did undertake the overhaul of an area's administrative structure, a preference for fewer and larger units – rather than the perpetuation of numerous individual polities – is patently obvious. The goal was to provide populous and economically viable centerpoints for regions where Roman interest, for whatever reason, ran particularly high. As for the chronology of these events, activity clearly concentrates in the early stages of Achaia's history. The assumption of formal control offered an opportunity, as it were, to reset the provincial chessboard. It is interesting that one of the rare administrative changes documented from later in the empire also centered upon the north-western quadrant of the province. A separate procuratorial province of Epirus was carved out, at latest in Antonine times and possibly in conjunction with the first-century AD freeing of Achaia, which embraced Epirus, Akarnania and the Ionian islands; Nikopolis served as capital (fig. 3).[19] Apart from this radical development, after Augustus the province was largely left to its own devices, with carefully fostered civic élites managing this small corner of the empire.

## INTERNAL REORGANIZATION: PRESSURES

In the formation of the provincial landscape, the objectives of the subordinate society play as active a part as any external initiatives; internal strategies might prove less extravagant, but are just as profound in effect. To uncover internal processes of change, we can begin with a very simple question: how many cities were operative in Achaia during the course of Roman rule? One general pattern – the presence of fewer functioning cities – emerges distinctly: "The multiplicity of independent cities, which had once brought glory and disaster, was rapidly disappearing."[20] Of necessity, realization of this decline has been based primarily on literary testimony, with the bulk of evidence furnished by the accounts of Strabo, Pausanias and Hierocles (of the late first century BC, second century AD and early sixth century AD, respectively). Despite various major shortcomings in such sources, their résumés of provincial cities, both active and defunct, remain helpful in uncovering Greece's changing political geography.

In the course of their travels, Strabo and Pausanias periodically report the "ruins" (*ereipia*) of cities (table 7). The problematic representation of a defeated and inglorious Greece colors both these texts; other factors contribute to the ambiguity of these lists of "dead cities." For Strabo, besides his limited first-hand experience in Greece and his fascination with Homeric topography, an especial difficulty is his equation of existence and political independence. "Extinct" – to Strabo – could mean one of two things: either a people have vanished "or else merely their ethnic name no longer exists and their political organization no longer remains what it was" (9.5.12). In the changed political environment of Roman Achaia, that equation becomes particularly doubtful. Pausanias' personal autopsy of the province, and his accep-tance (however unwilling) of undistinguished towns such as Panopeus as

Table 7. *Communities described as abandoned or*
*"in ruins" by Pausanias*

*Book 2*

| | | | |
|---|---|---|---|
| Mycenae[1] | 2.16.6 | Halice | 2.36.1 |
| Orneai[1] | 2.25.6 | Asine[1] | 2.36.4 |
| Tiryns[1] | 2.25.8 | Nauplion | 2.38.2 |
| Midea | 2.25.9 | | |

*Book 3*

| | | | |
|---|---|---|---|
| Sellasia | 3.10.7 | Pellana | 3.21.2 |
| Pharis | 3.20.3 | Etis | 3.22.13 |
| Bryseai | 3.20.4 | Zarax | 3.24.1 |
| Helos | 3.20.6 | Hippola | 3.25.4 |

*Book 4*

| | | | |
|---|---|---|---|
| Andania | 4.33.6 | Dorion | 4.33.6 |

*Book 5*

| | | | |
|---|---|---|---|
| Arene | 5.6.2–3 | Skillous | 5.6.4 |

*Book 6*

| | | | |
|---|---|---|---|
| Phrixa | 6.21.6 | Pyle | 6.22.5 |
| Harpina | 6.21.8 | Letrini | 6.22.8 |
| Pisa | 6.22.2 | | |

*Book 7*

| | | | |
|---|---|---|---|
| Olenus | 7.18.1, 7.22.1 | Rhypes | 7.23.4 |
| Argyra | 7.23.1 | Helike | 7.24.5 |
| Bolina | 7.23.4 | Aegae | 7.25.12 |

*Book 8*

| | | | |
|---|---|---|---|
| Nestane | 8.8.1 | Acacesion[1] | 8.36.10 |
| Maera | 8.12.7 | Haemoniai | 8.44.1 |
| Amilus | 8.13.5 | Oresthasion[1] | 8.44.2 |
| Nonacris | 8.17.6 | Asea[1] | 8.44.3 |
| Lusi | 8.18.7 | Brenthe | 8.28.7 |
| Paous | 8.23.9 | Trapezos | 8.29.1 |
| Melaeneai | 8.26.8 | Thocnia[1] | 8.29.5 |
| Thyraeon | 8.35.7 | Cromi[1] | 8.34.6 |
| Hypsos | 8.35.7 | Charisiae[1] | 8.35.5 |
| Phalanthos | 8.35.9 | Tricoloni[1] | 8.35.6 |
| Macareai[1] | 8.36.9 | Zoetia[1] | 8.35.6–7 |
| Daseai[1] | 8.36.9 | Paroria[1] | 8.35.7 |

*Book 9*

| | | | |
|---|---|---|---|
| Hysiai | 9.2.1 | Harma | 9.19.4 |
| Erythrai | 9.2.1 | Mykalessos | 9.19.4 |
| Scolus | 9.4.4 | Onchestos | 9.26.5 |
| Potniae | 9.8.1 | Aspledon | 9.38.9 |
| Glisas | 9.19.2 | | |

*Book 10*

| | | | |
|---|---|---|---|
| Ledon | 10.33.1 | Parapotamioi | 10.33.8 |

[1] Involved in the synoecisms of Argos and Megalopolis

*poleis*, combine to make him a more reliable witness, but problems still remain. For both authors, dates of civic abandonment remain vague in the extreme: "of old," "they say once," "in course of time." In some cases, ruined cities are singled out on the basis of their appearance in Homer, with few or no details of the settlement's subsequent history. This hints at a desertion predating the early imperial epoch by a substantial margin. In other cases, the falsity of certain descriptions can be demonstrated outright. Strabo (9.2.25) asserted: "Now in earlier times travellers would go up to Thespiai, a city otherwise not worth seeing, to see the Eros; and at present it and Tanagra are the only Boeotian cities that still endure; but of all the rest only ruins and names are left." Archaeological and epigraphic evidence disprove that claim, leaving us with the intriguing fact that Strabo here names the two *civitates liberae* of Boeotia.[21] The need is obvious for greater archaeological knowledge about a wider spectrum of Greek cities, for until such data are available, our understanding of the phenomenon of civic desertion will necessarily remain crude, as well as vulnerable to the distorting influences of rhetorical treatment.

To attribute all these episodes of abandonment automatically to the time at which they are *reported* would be foolhardy. On the other hand, it is equally unwise to deny that the early imperial period did witness the loss of some *poleis*. As for the scale of this phenomenon, only one comparatively clear-cut development can be wrested from the literary documentation. If we compare city numbers in Pausanias to the total in the sixth-century AD *Synekdemos* (The Fellow Traveller) of Hierocles, it emerges that the latter reports only seventy or eighty cities, roughly half the number given by the former in a discussion of approximately the same area. Admittedly, Hierocles may be only an epitome of a more detailed original, and while it is not easy to test it for completeness, comparisons with other texts "do not inspire great confidence in Hierocles' accuracy." On the other hand, archaeological evidence confirms a Late Roman presence on all Hierocles' named cities, as well as others he fails to mention, arguing that the absence of a former *polis* from this list indicates a loss of civic status, not necessarily the settlement's abandonment.[22] On this evidence, the later imperial period, between the second and fifth/sixth century AD, witnessed a relatively greater collapse in city numbers, but the process of civic decline in the early imperial period requires explanation as well.

The drop in city numbers has not, of course, passed unnoticed, but compounds the general impression of a desolate and unhappy Greece. Perhaps more remarked by ancient historians, however, has been the converse case, the relative *survival* of tiny political units and the continued density of city distribution. Even if we allow the testimony of Hierocles, Achaia retained its position as one of the most urbanized parts of the eastern Mediterranean, and thus of the empire as a whole. Persistence of civic life is a subject worthy of attention, not least because of the light it sheds on the transition between the Roman and Byzantine empires, yet the disappearance of cities from the Achaian landscape deserves equal treatment.[23] Three standard lines of argument have normally been advanced, with varying emphases: depopulation, alterations in land-holding patterns and the impact of warfare. All three factors, as we have seen, appear relevant to the rural countryside, and no doubt they played some part in creating the provincial landscape as well. Nonetheless, the degree to which these forces *alone* can be held responsible remains open to debate.

While the magnitude of Achaian depopulation has been somewhat revised, the later Hellenistic and Early Roman periods are agreed to have experienced some level of population loss (pp. 89–91). Lack of a viable demographic base would be a predominant cause of civic *asthenia* (weakness) and potential abandonment of cities. Pausanias, for example, comments on one vulnerable settlement in Phokis: "Once Ledon also was considered a city, and the dwellers on the Kephisos were about seventy people. Still the name of Ledon is given to their dwellings, and the citizens, like the Panopeans, have the right to be represented at the general assembly of the Phokians" (Pausanias 10.33.1). When accounting for a decline in Lakonia from one hundred down to thirty extant towns (*polichnai*), Strabo invokes this same factor: "Lakonia is now short of population as compared with its large population in olden time" (8.4.11). The familiar *topos* of *oliganthropia* recurs in this passage (pp. 26–7). Moreover, a simple explanation of population decline avoids alternative interpretations, such as the changing distribution of towns through synoecism. Indeed, to take depopulation as that development's primary cause begs several questions. Why do most cities (on the evidence of Hierocles) seem to disappear *after* the second century AD? The rural settlement evidence for the later Roman period suggests an upsurge in site numbers and agricultural intensity, possibly intimating a population on the rise. Yet during a period of apparent demographic decline, a considerable number of cities (on the evidence of Pausanias) remained in operation. Simple population change also fails to answer important questions such as why certain cities survive while others do not, or how to account for the resulting disposition of towns across the landscape.

As for patterns of landholding, a shift in favor of larger proprietors has been identified with some confidence (pp. 63–72). Other scholars have correlated pressure on primary producers with the potential shrinking of citizen bodies, precipitating the subsequent attenuation and disappearance of communities. This argument undoubtedly carries a certain amount of weight. Yet those scholars who have argued it most vehemently, notably Kahrstedt, clearly envision enormous estates (*latifundia*) crowding out or swallowing vulnerable cities, which in turn dwindle into dependent *komai* or even give way to villa estates. No direct archaeological confirmation for this last hypothesized development has yet emerged. Only three securely attested examples of villas established on former urban centers are known, and all are of Late Roman date – in two cases on a site abandoned centuries before.[24] Nor has the concentration of landholdings required by the extreme version of this scenario been established. "Strangulation" by large estates alone cannot account for the loss of cities, although its indirect consequences, such as the increasing wealth and dominance of prominent landowners, will be seen to play some part in the process.

Warfare, which itself plays a part in demographic and agricultural change, is the third element most commonly invoked, and it is again one that has a certain validity. The outright destruction of certain cities has been recorded for the various conflicts of the last two centuries BC, particularly in hard-hit regions such as Epirus or Boeotia. In Boeotia, for example, Haliartos was lost in 167 BC, during the Third Macedonian War, and intensive urban survey there has confirmed the destruction and subsequent abandonment of the site. Koroneia, which also backed the Macedonian cause, likewise suffered at this time. Some twenty years later, during the Achaean War, inhabitants of Thebes fled their city and its walls were dismantled. In the Mithridatic wars, sixty years later still, Boeotia served as the battlefield for two major confrontations (Chaironeia and Orchomenos); Lebadeia and Anthedon, as well as neighboring Larymna and Halai, were destroyed and Thespiai besieged. Ancient Chorsiai (Khostia) also seems to have met a violent end, although only archaeology testifies to this loss. The harsh treatment of Plutarch's great-grandfather and his compatriots during the Actian campaign is also worth remembering. This is only a partial résumé of the troubles brought upon Boeotia through military activity, but it renders the high proportion of "dead cities" in Strabo's and Pausanias' accounts of this region less surprising.[25] Even if such "war zones" can be identified, however, not all regions were equally affected by military brutality. Instead of treating war as a *general* explanation for provincial troubles, a more balanced appraisal localizes its impact in both time and space. Moreover, it is perplexing that the most marked civic losses apparently occurred while Greece still largely enjoyed the benefits of the *pax Romana*. In frontier provinces more exposed to hostile activity, warfare might play a more constant role in the question of city survival; for Achaia, the longer-term consequences of military activity, rather than the actual campaigns and sieges themselves, played a more significant part in this process.[26]

Although the serious involvement of these three factors is not to be denied, they do not themselves suffice to explain the problem of civic decline and survival. To seek other forces at work, however, means abandoning certain ways of looking at the province. Past suggestions have tended to emanate from a narrow appreciation of Greece's plight, with endogenous developments much emphasized: *Greece* was war-torn, *Greece* was depopulated, and so on. Such a conception of Greece as an isolated economic and social unit, following some private downward trajectory, should be rejected in favor of stressing the province's new relationship to an external power. In this view, explanations for the loss of cities must take full account of Achaia's peripheral location within a larger imperial system.

From this perspective, the altered status of the *polis*, with a debasement in the meaning of *eleutheria*, and its eventual loss, immediately becomes an issue to consider. Civic self-government continued with Roman approval, and many former political institutions, such as public assemblies, did indeed survive under the empire. Yet the formal existence of such institutions can never be confused with the persistence of their actual power. Independent political life, once channeled through the *polis*, had ended. Plutarch, for one, grasped this point, spelling it out in an essay to a young man considering political life, the *Praecepta*.

. . . when entering upon any office whatsoever, you must not only call to mind those considerations of which Pericles reminded himself when he assumed the cloak of a general: "Take care, Pericles, you are ruling free men, you are ruling Greeks, Athenian citizens," but you must also say to yourself, "You who rule are a subject, ruling a State controlled by proconsuls, the agents of Caesar . . . You should arrange your cloak more carefully and from the office of the generals keep your eyes upon the orators' platform, and not have great pride and confidence in your crown, since you see the boots of Roman soldiers [or, better, 'the senatorial shoes of the proconsul'] just above your head . . ." [The statesman] will instruct his people both individually and collectively and will call attention to the weak condition of Greek affairs, in which it is best for wise men to accept one advantage – a life of harmony and quiet – since fortune has left us no prize open for competition. For what dominion, what glory is there for those who are victorious? What sort of power is it which a small edict of a proconsul may annul or transfer to another man and which, even if it last, has nothing in it seriously worth while? (Plutarch, *Praecepta gerendae reipublicae* 813D–F, 824E–F)

From autonomous political corporations, *poleis* were now transformed into dependent administrative districts.[27] Overriding civic concerns now became the meeting of tax demands, the provision of an efficient market

location, the support of a healthy and viable population, the maintenance of a *chora* adequate for its needs, and Plutarch's "life of harmony and
quiet." Whereas city location and distribution previously reflected
political (rather than primarily economic) needs and priorities, the
development of a new arrangement could now be predicted.

Facilitating this development would be the increasing burden of
financial pressures upon the Greek cities under the empire. With the
imposition of regular taxation and other provincial duties, obligations
placed upon the cities of Achaia escalated rapidly under the early empire,
if not as severely as in the later period of Roman domination. As well as
such external liabilities, cities were expected to attend to their own
internal affairs. Compared to pre-conquest conditions, achieving a
viable economic base for the Greek city – from adequate civic income or
the presence of sympathetic and wealthy benefactors – became a more
formidable task. To maintain the necessary levels of civic affluence often
did become a problem; we can see that many cities were in debt, both to
individuals and to other *poleis*, during the Hellenistic and Early Roman
era. From various parts of the province, examples are known of towns
incapable of meeting tax dues, of supplying necessary magistrates or of
financing local festivals. Involvement in warfare or the mere proximity of
troops, especially, worked to undermine the solvency of certain towns.
Epigraphic evidence from Akraiphia in Boeotia presents one of the best
documented of all such cases of civic *asthenia*; but Akraiphia is hardly
unique in the troubles faced in the early imperial period.[28]

A wide variety of pressures can thus be identified as contributing to the
potential decline in the vitality of the communities of Roman Achaia.
What can be ruled out, however, are explanations which hinge on the
acceptance of moral and political decay. No supposedly "normal"
Classical pattern ever existed to which the situation under the empire can
be disparagingly compared. Even before the Roman conquest, the
distribution of cities was not immutable: warfare or population
movement led to the abandonment, temporarily or permanently, of some
cities and the establishment of others; territorial boundaries underwent a
constant process of adjustment.[29] If greater dynamism is accepted in pre-
conquest political geography, it becomes harder to dismiss subsequent
changes as a sign of weakness and decadence. Instead they represent
modifications commanded by new collective needs and priorities,
constituting part of the long-term history of the Greek city. Rather than a
process of straightforward urban degeneration, transformations in the
provincial landscape can be credited to the active response of the
province's inhabitants.

### INTERNAL REORGANIZATION: RESPONSE

The pattern of city survival emerged as the product of decisions taken both by individuals and by civic administrations; some of these decisions contributed to the demise of cities, but more often they worked to oppose that trend. Many strategies existed to compensate for increasing pressures, some of which were successful, others not. If independent existence could not be maintained, alternative options included synoecism, league associations or dependence upon larger and more flourishing centers. Through such designs, means were deliberately pursued to withstand the forces undercutting a community's chance of survival.

One material possibility for a city faced with an immediate or potential threat was to increase its territory, thus acquiring a larger catchment area upon which to draw in raising necessary revenues. This is one rationale underlying the extensive zones made over to Patrai and Nikopolis, as well as other imperial gifts periodically made over to cities currently in favor. Athens, for example, received Aigina, Keos, Eretria and three other small islands from Mark Antony, and later the island of Kephallenia from Hadrian; Sparta was rewarded by Hadrian with Kythera, and possibly the island of Gaudos and the Messenian city of Koroneia at the same time. What attracted imperial largesse to these particular cities will be further detailed below (pp. 162–4). Removal of such "bonus" land was also used as a punishment, an effective form of economic sanction. To demonstrate his displeasure with the obstreperous city of Athens, Augustus stripped away Antony's grants, thereby undoubtedly doing damage to the city's economic well-being, still fragile after the conflicts of the first century BC.[30]

If a city failed to capture imperial notice and benevolence (or sometimes even if it succeeded), other self-engineered expansionary strategies were available. With escalating external demands, higher levels of competition for rural hinterland become one predictable development. Rivalry over precise boundary lines had been a constant feature of inter-city relations, and such struggles continued under Roman rule, sometimes explicitly "propter exigenda tributa." Boundary maintenance, it has been suggested, played a major role in sustaining the social cohesion of a *polis* (pp. 118–20). These wrangles can also now be credited with some part in the preservation of cities. Given the impossibility of outright fighting between *poleis*, such initiatives offered the only "independent" means to realize territorial ambitions. As Pausanias remarked in his account of Athens' treatment of its subject area, Oropos, in the second century BC: "the Athenian populace sacked Oropos, a state

Table 8. *Provincial leagues (*koina*) extant in Achaia under the empire*[1]

Achaean League
Akarnanian/Aetolian Leagues
Amphiktyonic League (based at Delphi)
Arcadian League
Argolid League
Boeotian League
Commonalty of Achaeans, Boeotians, Lokrians, Phokians and Euboeans
  ("Panhellenes"; "Achaeans and Panhellenes")
Eleutherolakones
*Koinon* of Boeotians, Phokians, Euboeans, Lokrians and Dorians
Lokrian League
Panhellenic *synhedrion* (based at Plataiai)
Phokian League

[1]Drawn from Deininger (1965); Larsen (1938); (1955); Bowersock (1965a)

subject to them. The act was one of necessity rather than of free-will, as the Athenians at the time suffered the direst poverty, because the Macedonian war had crushed them more than any other Greeks. So the Oropians appealed to the Roman Senate" (7.11.4). The frequent arbitration in these disputes of the provincial governor, or even the emperor, demonstrates, however, the extent to which such enterprises were monitored by the external authorities.[31]

The theme of inter-*polis* rivalry, manifested in many ways, recurs increasingly throughout this period. Closely related to border aggression stands rivalry for imperial acknowledgment of claims to status, a phenomenon familiar from a number of provinces, notably Asia. Serious motivations underlay the fierce demand for titles of ever-increasing grandeur and the civic tugs-of-war that frequently ensued. Of course, border disputes and status quarrels in part provided local élites with an arena for display, now they were denied former outlets such as warfare, but the recognition had also dawned that status was a shield against attempted aggression by neighbors – neighbors themselves eager to expand their own holdings and promote their own standing.[32]

If economic pressures continued to mount, and territorial and status quarrels proved ineffectual, other tactics could be adopted. Membership in provincial leagues allowed some sharing of financial and diplomatic burdens, and several regional league organizations (*koina*) are known from Achaia (p. 18; table 8). Actual amalgamation of *poleis* presented another feasible, if more drastic, option. Formal synoecism, combining two or more *poleis*, created a new and more powerful political entity, if at the cost of their independent existence. Its virtues had long been appreciated in Greece. Argos and Megalopolis offer two examples:

The Arcadians united into it [Megalopolis] to gain strength, realizing that the Argives also were in earlier times in almost daily danger of being subjected by war to the Lakedaimonians, but when they had increased the population of Argos by reducing Tiryns, Hysiai, Orneai, Mycenae, Mideia, along with other towns of little importance in Argolis, the Argives had less to fear from the Lakedaimonians, while they were in a stronger position to deal with their vassal neighbors. It was with this policy in view that the Arcadians united. (Pausanias 8.27.1–2)

The early imperial period witnessed this process in action, for example in a first-century BC *sympoliteia* of Medeon and Stiris in Phokis, and in various unions within the Aegean islands, including a Late Hellenistic/Early Roman synoecism within the Keian tetrapolis.[33] That other synoecisms have been lost from the documentary record must be considered. Such unions, or perhaps simply the informal movement of one city's population to another, may be indirectly preserved in reports of neighbors cultivating an abandoned city's land or of one or more defunct towns in proximity to a more flourishing one. For example, in Boeotia Pausanias visited Aulis and noted: "There are but few inhabitants of Aulis, and these are potters. This land, and that about Mykalessos and Harma [two cities 'in ruins'] is tilled by the people of Tanagra" (a more flourishing center) (9.19.8). Or Strabo in Achaea: "Aega (for Aegae is also called thus) is now uninhabited, and the city is in the possession of the people of Aigion. But Aigion has a considerable population" (8.7.5). Finally, and perhaps ultimately least desirable, smaller towns or villages could become formally subordinate, dependent satellites, to a larger center; an example of this phenomenon is the attachment of Lykosoura, with its important sanctuary of Despoina, to Megalopolis (fig. 80). The existence of such dependent communities, known from elsewhere in the empire, offers an important indication of the host city's prestige and prosperity.[34]

### PEOPLE ON THE MOVE

What made these various shifts and strategies feasible at all, of course, was the devotion and economic support of local élite families. With the timely intercession of euergetism, even cities faced with significant hardships, such as Akraiphia in Boeotia, could survive. To such communities, the most devastating blow possible would be a lack of interest on the part of those endowed with the necessary financial surplus to bear civic burdens. But is there any evidence that the allegiance of civic leaders could be diverted from their "home towns," leaving them vulnerable to potential disaster? In other states and empires, incorporation frequently results in the formation of an increasingly united aristocratic network forged through intermarriage and other close social bonds. Such networks extend throughout individual provinces and beyond, in many cases encompassing members of the imperial élite, and even the emperor himself. A frequent corollary is a diminishing sense of local identity by the indigenous ruling classes and a concomitant alienation from the remainder of the subject population. New forms of social behavior and new allegiances become more central to élite self-definition, as old ones are abandoned.[35]

Signs of a cosmopolitan and cohesive élite network are certainly legion throughout the eastern empire, including the province of Achaia. Intermarriage, political affiliations, and guest friendships, often stretching over long distances, bound distinguished families together. Prosopographical studies, with the complex interconnected stemmata of prominent Achaian clans, have gone a long way toward marking out these relationships in some detail. Plutarch's writings everywhere display the nature of this high-ranking society, his dialogues recounting their meetings, their conversation, their concerns. The *Metamorphoses* of Apuleius likewise reveals a network of relationships connecting the families of local aristocrats; its Corinthian hero, Lucius, possesses various relatives in other towns – including Plutarch himself in Chaironeia. Apart from families and friendships extending over the eastern empire, alliances or patronage links with members of the Roman ruling élite were deliberately sought as well. In the *Praecepta gerendae reipublicae*, Plutarch noted: "not only should the statesman show himself and his native state blameless towards our rulers, but he should also have always a friend among the men of high station who have the greatest power as a firm bulwark, so to speak, of his administration; for the Romans themselves are most eager to promote the political interests of their friends" (814C).[36] But if notable Achaian families undoubtedly became more cosmopolitan in their friendships, allegiances and outlook, did they actually lose their sense of local loyalty as a result? The evidence for that particular development is more mixed.

The loss of *eleutheria*, coupled with the growth of this supra-local aristocracy, might well be expected to loosen ties of local obligation – for instance, some shift in élite goodwill away from home communities, making more prominent "alien" cities their new arena for benefaction and display. Patterson has defined "élite mobility" as a "transferral of activities by existing élites to new (and more prestigious) locations"; in his Italian case study, such individuals shifted their attention away from *vici* and *pagi* to the newly developing *municipia*.[37] In Achaia, obvious targets for potential upper-class "refugees" would be larger urban centers, endowed with the magnetic combination of attractive amenities and the presence of other wealthy and cultured families, but to assess the scale on which any such movement occurs is extremely difficult. What literary and epigraphic evidence exists not surprisingly reveals the provincial capital of Corinth as one major node in the overarching élite network; links are attested between major Corinthian families and those in other cities (e.g. Sparta, Athens, Epidauros). Prosperous citizens of other towns can be traced to Corinth, where they are known to have held important magistracies. One particularly spectacular example, Cn. Cornelius Pulcher (helladarch of the Achaean League, high priest of Greece, priest of Hadrian Panhellenius, panhellenic archon, procurator of Epirus, military tribune and juridicus of Egypt and Alexandria, friend of Plutarch), was from Epidauros, yet he served in Corinth as *duovir quinquennalis* and *agonothete* of the Isthmian Games. The Euryclid C. Iulius Spartiaticus, a citizen of both Sparta *and* Corinth, became the first high priest of the Achaean League's imperial cult. The provincial capital has rightly been described as "the centre of *Romanitas* in Greece, a city with a strong gravitational pull for the province's magnates."[38] Signs of a similar concentration of notables are witnessed in Athens, where an increased number of foreign residents has been observed, drawn always by the city's reputation, the Eleusinian mysteries and, after Hadrian, by the Panhellenion; these included wealthy and prestigious men from Achaia itself and beyond. Outsiders held liturgies and acted as *euergetai* in other cities as well. Much traveling and visiting, utilizing the far-flung web of aristocratic friendships, is also well attested.[39] The absolute number of people involved in these activities would, of course, be insignificant, but the impact of their desertion upon the fate of a community cannot be calculated in demographic terms alone; indifference or loss of civic benefactors would strike hard at any city's economic and political viability and puny and obscure *poleis* were clearly the most vulnerable.

This potentially grim scenario needs, however, to be qualified sharply. Movement by members of the provincial élite from one city to another was clearly not always permanent, and certainly did not automatically herald the abandonment of their place of origin. Wealthy men acted as *euergetai* to many communities, including their own *patris*. In numerous cases in Achaia, repudiation of local interests can be disproven outright; the families of both Cornelius Pulcher and Iulius Spartiaticus, for example, were major local benefactors as well. The continued *philotimia* of patriotic élites, steeped in their own civic traditions and passionately concerned with home-town affairs, emerges from many different contexts, not least in the sheer volume of epigraphic evidence for civic euergetism. In the *Metamorphoses*, Byrrhaena of Hypata entertains Lucius, asking: "How are you enjoying our native city? To my knowledge we far excel all other cities in temples, baths and other public works ... At any rate there is freedom for anyone at leisure, and for the stranger coming on business a crowd of people like that at Rome" (2.19, translation Millar [1981], 72). Plutarch, who is known to have traveled widely (including a visit to Rome), nonetheless always returned to Chaironeia: "But as for me, I live in a small city, and I prefer to dwell there that it may not become smaller still" (*Demosthenes* 2.2). Moreover, while noting that the Romans "are most eager to promote the political interests of their friends," Plutarch went on to remark "and it is a fine thing also, when we gain advantage from the friendship of great men, to turn it to the welfare of our community" (*Praecepta gerendae reipublicae* 814C).[40] Undoubtedly, such pride and devotion accounts for a number of the small and relatively insignificant cities that – despite everything – survived.

But to limit this discussion to upper-class activity alone is not satisfactory, for others were on the move too. In chapter 3, I argued that the attraction of urban centers was a major factor in recasting the rural landscape of Greece, and that the increasing marginality of certain elements within Achaian society led to population instability (pp. 115–17). In these movements, small and economically limited towns must in general have been by-passed in favor of larger and more flourishing centers; the promotion of certain places at the expense of others would inevitably result. Successful candidates might well be found outside Achaia proper, since some migration beyond provincial boundaries is more than likely. The ultimate "winner," of course, was Rome itself, the pre-industrial "super-city," fed and cosseted at the empire's expense, which acted as a demographic magnet for outside populations. Levels of urbanization throughout Italy as a whole must also have demanded some external supply of population (though to estimate how much of this was drained specifically from Achaia is impossible). Dismissive references to "Graeculi" in Rome, or assertions that Greeks, "most of them clever and educated men, emigrated in masses to countries which offered better opportunities," say more of biased attitudes to Greeks under the empire than of ancient demographic behavior.[41] On the other hand, the proximity of Greece to Italy, and the bonds between the two coasts of the Adriatic, may indeed have fostered a strong westward demographic pull.

Even so, it is still fair to assume that most such relocations would have taken place within Achaia itself, and the rise of anomalously large and successful cities among the rank and file of Greek *poleis* seems to offer some support for that argument. While this proposition is difficult to verify in absolute terms, there exists a variety of convergent evidence. The prominence and positive descriptions of certain cities in the literary sources can be mentioned first: most frequently named are the imperial foundations, though eminent older towns (notably Athens) also appear.[42] Although civic prestige must obviously not be confused with civic size, nonetheless a significant population density in these centers does not seem unlikely. In the case of Patrai, for instance, Strabo claimed the city to be "exceptionally populous at present, since it is a Roman colony" (8.7.5). An odd demographic imbalance is recorded here by Pausanias, who stated that women outnumbered men in the colony by two to one; as well as being "amongst the most charming in the world" (7.21.14), they earned their living weaving the flax grown in the region. More tangibly, archaeological investigation suggests that the city was enlarged at the time of the colonial foundation, as well as laid out on a Hippodamian-like plan (fig. 54). Nikopolis too, Strabo writes, is "populous [*euandrei*], and its numbers are increasing daily, since it has not only a considerable territory and the adornment taken from the spoils of the battle, but also, in its suburbs, the thoroughly equipped sacred precinct" (7.7.6). No archaeological evidence can yet be cited to confirm the growth of this city beyond its original number of settlers, but the extent of the site's known remains make this more than likely (figs. 47, 51). In the case of Athens, apart from the presence of wealthy individuals attracted by the city's reputation, the development of a "new city" of Hadrian, in the district to the southwest of the agora and acropolis, may be taken as evidence for an expansion in urban size, and possibly in population as well.[43]

Turning lastly to Corinth, Strabo presented the city as "great and wealthy . . . and well equipped with men skilled both in the affairs of state and in the craftsmen's arts" (8.6.23). Aristides called Corinth the "common city" of the Greeks:

. . . and this is the strangest and at the same time most pleasant of all the spectacles on the earth – people on each side sail in and sail out at the same instant with favorable breezes and men put out to sea and into port with the same winds in this land and sea alone of all, and this is the reason why the land even from earliest times was praised as "rich" by the poets, both because of the multitude of the advantages which are at hand and the felicity which is embodied in it. For it is, as it were, a kind of market place, and at that common to all the Greeks, and a national festival, not like this present one which the Greek race celebrates here every two years, but one which is celebrated every year and daily. If just as men enjoy the official status of being public friends with foreign cities, so too did cities enter into this relationship with one another, the city would have this title and honor everywhere. For it receives all cities

54 Town plan of modern Patrai, with the regular grid plan showing the city's
   enlargement to the northwest in Roman times

and sends them off again and is a common refuge for all, like a kind of route and
passage for all mankind, no matter where one would travel, and it is a common city
for all the Greeks, indeed, as it were, a kind of metropolis and mother in this respect.
(Aelius Aristides, *Oration* 46 [The Isthmian Oration: Regarding Poseidon] 22–4;
translation Behr 1981: 273)

The appeal of the city, with its numerous religious, economic, educational, and recreational attractions, is illustrated by the wealth and
variety of its physical remains; and in another way, the activity of the
apostle Paul and the Corinthian church emphasizes the city's role as one
important crossroads of the early empire.[44]
    Several different strands of archaeological evidence combine to
indicate a substantial growth in this city's population during the early

imperial period. Improvements in water supply systems, such as the Hadrianic aqueduct (figs. 41–2), when coupled with great building activity, are suggestive, if not conclusive. Extensive surface examination of the site points to an occupation area of some 725 hectares (including Lechaion) in the second century AD, so that, as Engels recently commented: "Few would argue that Roman Corinth was not a large city" adding from his calculations that "an urban population of 80,000 and a rural population of 20,000 does not seem unreasonable" (fig. 55).[45] Measures taken to guarantee a food supply for such numbers could provide another index of demographic change: for instance, extensive investigation of the area around the city hints at a significant density of settlement, with – hypothetically – a considerable suburban zone of villas, gardens, and farmsteads surrounding the hungry city. That an increasing supply of local goods was finding its way into Corinth is also provisionally suggested by one analysis of the early imperial ceramic evidence from the city. Even with these responses, however, Corinth's demands almost certainly outstripped the productive capacity of the city's immediate hinterland.[46]

It is entirely conceivable that Corinth attracted some of its additional residents from beyond the borders of Achaia. Nonetheless, it is equally probable that Greek cities forfeited elements of their population to Corinth, a city with the capacity to accommodate landless newcomers. The burgeoning of Corinth, coupled with the potential growth of the other major centers referred to, paralleled the process of *polis* decline witnessed elsewhere. It is interesting that the two cities nearest to Corinth, Megara and Sikyon, are reported to be in a weakened state under the empire: the Megarians "are the only Greeks that not even the emperor Hadrian could make prosperous" (Pausanias 1.36.4), and "the reason why the Sikyonians grew weak it would be wrong to seek" (Pausanias 2.7.1). One reason is a close connection between successful and unsuccessful cities.

## WINNERS AND LOSERS

If the competition between cities during the early imperial era saw both winners and losers, what determined the fate of an individual community? Why did some cities win through while other died out? On the credit side, imperial promotion and protection, and the presence of a vital civic élite, must rank high. City size too is an important element; asking "How big is it?" in this context is no mere antiquarian question, as Finley once suggested, for smaller cities consistently proved more vulnerable to synoecism, incorporation or desertion.[47] Despite the numerous problems

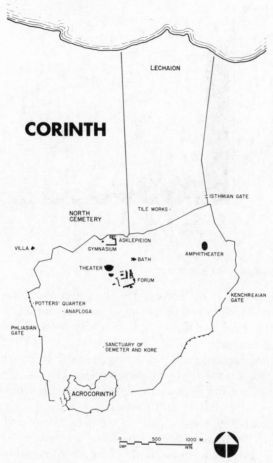

55 City area of Corinth

of determining site size, figure 56 attempts to compare the magnitude of various cities in the province of Achaia (generally on the unsatisfactory basis of city wall perimeters). The extent (and monumentality) of some cities, notably the provincial capital, when juxtaposed with more "normal" *poleis*, proclaims an increasing differentiation in the spectrum of Greek civic wealth and power under the empire: in other words, the gulf between a Corinth and a Panopeus widened significantly, and once this imbalance was established, it became self-perpetuating. Individuals or families (both rich and poor) could move to the more successful centers, draining the "losers" of financial backing and manpower and

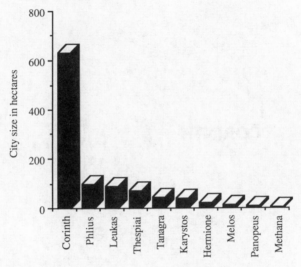

56  Histogram of city sizes in the province of Achaia

further encouraging (or forcing) the desertion and disappearance of smaller *poleis*. As with the results of imperial intervention, a trend toward the creation of fewer and bigger administrative units within the province is clearly discernible.

Spatial considerations also played a part in this winnowing process. A city's geographical position had always molded its particular historical development, but in the Roman period what constituted a desirable location was somewhat transformed. The westward orientation of the imperial foundations, located with an eye to exchange and communication, has just been mentioned. Coastal cities performed consistently better than inland locations, both along the Corinthian Gulf (e.g. Naupaktos) and in the Peloponnese (e.g. Gytheion); relatively greater deterioration in civic conditions in Arcadia and inland Phokis bears witness to this. Internal road networks too played a role in galvanizing some cities and not others. For instance, Tegea's role as a relay point on the *cursus publicus* may in part have been a trying duty, but *ipso facto* signaled the town's importance, even acting as a potential stimulant, and certainly Tegea appears as one of the more vibrant towns of the central Peloponnese at this time.[48] A position convenient for access to the outside world, and to the major centers of Achaia itself would prove a boon to any city.

Despite these various considerations, no simple rules for predicting winners and losers could ever be formulated for Achaia, for the patterns of civic survival are immensely variable and often unpredictable. In many individual cases, precise explanations for success or failure will surely never be known – for example, in trying to reconcile the very different histories of Phlius and Thespiai, or even of Thespiai and its Boeotian neighbor Tanagra (pp. 97–101; figs. 28–9, 30–1). What is evident is that "rational" economic considerations cannot in all cases account for historically observed patterns of development or decline, and we must also take into account another potent ingredient – the Greek past, the myths, legends, cults and deeds of the individual *poleis* themselves.

Benefactions by Roman generals and emperors, apart from the short-lived grant of freedom by Nero, were not given indiscriminately: they had to be earned. In some cases, prominent individual citizens – sophists, philosophers, doctors – were responsible for bringing good fortune to their home town by attracting the attention of the emperor.[49] A city's contemporary bearing in its conduct toward Rome could also count, as for example in the case of the grant of freedom to Elateia, in return for its opposition to Mithridates. More often, however, benefits were won on the strength of a city's past history – a task obviously far easier for some *poleis* than for others. Athens, despite repeatedly joining anti-Roman alliances, was "forgiven" again and again, by Caesar with the words: "How often will the glory of your ancestors save you from self-destruction?" (Appian, *Bella Civilia* 2.88). Apart from the punishment of Augustus, Athens was a perennial recipient of imperial encouragement, most spectacularly the largesse of the philhellene emperor Hadrian, who selected Athens as the headquarters of the Panhellenion, thus designating the city as one center of the eastern empire. Hadrian concerned himself with the fate of other cities as well, being honored with the title "savior and founder" in the cities of Aidepsos, Sparta, Tegea, Megalopolis, Megara, Thespiai and Thasos. A personal incentive for his interest in the Arcadian city of Mantineia was its connection with the emperor's favorite, Antinoos. The ancestral practices of Sparta, especially the Lykurgan customs, fascinated the Greco-Roman élite, permitting "this otherwise fairly typical provincial Greek city to maintain a place in the world and allowing the Spartans to feel that they were still 'special.' "[50] An apparently humble present, moreover, in no way prevented cities from cashing in on an illustrious past. Formerly sovereign cities became moralizing tales of greatness come to ruin: "Boeotian Thebes, once deemed worthy to be the head of the Greek people, why, its name includes only the acropolis and its few inhabitants" (Pausanias 8.33.1); "Thebes today does not preserve the character even of a respectable village" (Strabo 9.2.5). Archaeological evidence does indeed support these assertions of a much diminished settlement, but Thebes remained a functioning *polis* throughout the Roman period.[51]

So, despite contemporary pressures, past greatness could act in such

ways to keep a city alive. In some cases, it could even do more. While less
fortunate *poleis* descended to the level of *komai*, well-pedigreed *komai* could
be raised to the status of *poleis* – reversing every trend discussed so far in
Achaian political geography:

My story next requires me to describe whatever is notable at Pallanteion, and the
reason why the emperor Antoninus the first turned it from a village to a city, giving its
inhabitants liberty and freedom from taxation. Well, the story is that the wisest man
and the best soldier among the Arcadians was one Evander . . . Sent out to establish a
colony at the head of a company of Arcadians from Pallanteion, he founded a city on
the banks of the river Tiber. (Pausanias 8.43.1–2)

"Palatine" is thus derived from "Pallanteion": "These are the reasons
why the emperor bestowed boons upon Pallanteion" (8.43.2–3).
Attention to civic origins and kinship ties (*syngeneia*), sought especially
with the most ancient and famous cities of Greece, became common
preoccupations for many communities across the eastern empire,
furthering both the upward ambitions of civic élites and local claims to
status. This is a phenomenon particularly prevalent in Hadrianic and
Antonine times.[52]

To the Greek cities, the past thus became a present source of strength,
something to be marshaled in order to attract imperial attention and to
compete in inter-city rivalries. Elite families too participated in this
discourse, demanding acknowledgment of their ancient, even divine,
descent. Genealogical claims aided in the formation of supra-local
kinship networks, as well as reinforcing the position of such families in
provincial affairs. Historicism was hardly a new feature of Greek civic or
individual self-presentation. The political uses of nostalgia had been
enjoyed before, but in the Roman world of the Second Sophistic the
invocation or invention of a glorious past reached a new height.[53] While
not denying the part played by invention, recognition of such claims
would always come more easily to some *poleis* than to others. Myths and
antiquities rewrote the history of Greece; bound up with the powerful
variables of élite support and civic size, the power of the past took a
vigorous part in reshaping the province's political geography.

A UNIFIED PROVINCE?

From the foregoing discussion, it will be plain that there is a clearly
detectable trend toward the creation of fewer and larger administrative
units in Greece, a trend stemming in part from direct imperial
interventions, in part from various internal processes of civic reorganization. The development was not insignificantly curtailed, however, by the

continued existence of many relatively small and insignificant *poleis*, supported in some cases by their history and in almost all by their local élites. This chapter began by remarking upon the novelty of a united Greece, located within a wider imperial setting. Yet to what extent did Achaia ever really become an internally integrated unit? Two potential centralizing measures to consider, from an administrative point of view, are the presence of provincial leagues and the creation of an imperial "bridgehead" community.

In the escalating scale of the administrative and economic system in which Greece now operated, individual cities conspicuously rank as small and weak units. It was in the Hellenistic period that the realization first dawned that the days of *polis* dominance in political affairs were over. Contemporary responses to the problem included territorial reorganizations (similar to those discussed above), often undertaken at the behest of monarchs, or grants of *asylia* or *isopoliteia*. A parallel development was the formation of leagues (*koina*) – that is, associations designed to place federations of cities on a somewhat more equal footing with the new gargantuan kingdoms of Alexander and his Successors. Leagues forged prior to the Roman conquest were initially dissolved after the Achaean War, presumably as a measure to disable hostile political alliances, but with the firmer establishment of Roman influence, the ban was apparently soon lifted.[54] Leagues were either restored or newly created in many parts of the province, suggesting a shared imperial and indigenous interest in fostering middle-range administrative units, designed to serve as a bridge between individual cities and the imperial authorities (table 8).

Each of these bodies possessed its own particular aims and capabilities, yet – at risk of oversimplification – they could all be described as more "convenient" territorial divisions, representing their members in a variety of functions and relieving them of all sorts of financial burdens by sharing them round. In this capacity, they received encouragement from several emperors. It is chiefly ceremonial and diplomatic duties that are attested for these *koina*: petitions, for example, or congratulatory embassies, and, eventually, imperial cult duties. Leagues also possessed the power to indict corrupt officials (although no record exists of any such prosecutions in Achaia) and they may have mediated between cities and census officials. Internal administrative responsibilities apparently differed from league to league, and probably through time as well. One provincial governor referred an early first-century BC boundary dispute to the council of the Thessalian League; on the other hand, the Phokian League was completely disregarded by Roman authorities deciding a lawsuit involving a member city. A comparatively restricted range of duties, and limited internal authority, thus seems to characterize these *koina*.[55]

Whatever their specific role, the appearance and relative longevity of these leagues (several of which endured into the third century AD) testify to administrative units working at a scale larger than that of the individual city. Yet the Achaian *koina* always remained very regional in orientation, as well as restricted in scope: no single, pan-provincial league structure ever emerged. The nearest attempt at a "provincial assembly" came with the early first-century AD Commonalty of Achaeans, Boeotians, Lokrians, Phokians and Euboeans, created (as the name implies) through an association of several smaller bodies; but, although called the "Panhellenes," this relatively short-lived association (lasting, at latest, till the time of Hadrian) never represented the entirety of Achaia. Indeed, the geographically more limited *koina* tended to be the most enduring. However useful leagues undoubtedly proved in individual regions, they singularly failed to provide an overarching, powerful administrative framework for Achaian affairs, thus leaving the city as the principal politico-administrative unit of the province. In this context, it is interesting that the Panhellenion, with its Greek members drawn from the eastern empire, may have been geographically restricted (fig. 57), reflecting "resistance on Rome's part to permit the permanent union of a large part of the Greek world within an organization administered by the Greeks themselves."[56]

Could an individual city, then, play a centralizing role? Certainly, the creation of "bridgeheads" of external authority seems to be a regular and characteristic feature of many other systems of imperial dominance. Combining symbolic with coercive elements, such communities are established to represent outside interests, and can serve as "gateway communities" in the promulgation of imperial ideology and control.[57] If *Colonia Laus Julia Corinthiensis* was the "caput" of Achaia, what effect did this designation have upon the city's wider role in provincial life? Did Corinth form, for example, a middle tier in the empire's administrative hierarchy, positioned somewhere between the core city of Rome and the mass of individual Achaian *poleis*?

In a formal bureaucratic sense, the answer must be no. Although the provincial governor and his staff based themselves in Corinth, and although provincial embassies occasionally were heard there, evidence from elsewhere in the empire suggests that most official functions would have been carried out during provincial tours. A steady bombardment of the emperor and senate with civic and league petitions and embassies can also be documented, but such appeals were not formally collected and channeled through Corinth. Nor did Corinth dominate the provincial

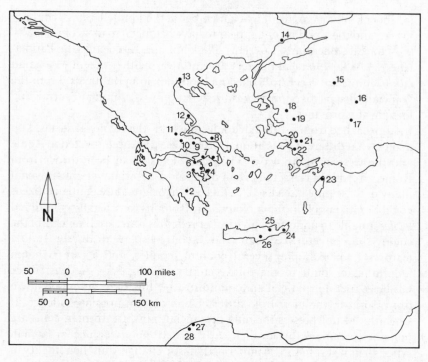

57 Distribution of city members of the Panhellenion

| | | |
|---|---|---|
| 1 | Athens | 15 Aezani |
| 2 | Sparta | 16 Synnada |
| 3 | Argos | 17 Apamea |
| 4 | Methana | 18 Thyateira |
| 5 | Epidauros | 19 Sardis |
| 6 | Corinth | 20 Tralles |
| 7 | Megara | 21 Magnesia-on-the-Maeander |
| 8 | Chalkis | 22 Miletos |
| 9 | Akraiphia | 23 Rhodes |
| 10 | Amphikleia | 24 Hierapytna |
| 11 | Hypata | 25 Lyttos |
| 12 | Demetrias | 26 Gortyn |
| 13 | Thessalonike | 27 Apollonia |
| 14 | Perinthus | 28 Cyrene |

leagues of Achaia. While it was a member of the Panhellenion, it did not host it; and the city does not appear to have belonged to the Commonalty of Achaeans, Boeotians, Lokrians, Phokians and Euboeans (the Panhellenes).[58] As for financial matters, Corinth was neither the only Achaian city to mint, nor a central collection point for imperial taxes. From the "official" perspective then, Corinth acted only as a limited centralizing force in the province.

Approached from a different angle, however, the colony's role takes on a somewhat different coloration. Corinth was tightly connected to Rome and the west in many ways. The first colonists had been drawn from Rome's freedman class, the urban poor and Caesarian veterans. Even if many of these may have been "Graeculi" in origin, only Roman citizens could be citizens of the new colony; non-Romans were legally considered *incolae*, unable to undertake political or religious liturgies. Elements of the colony's architectural design and layout display distinctly Italian features – for example, several podium temples, and a rare Achaian amphitheater built in the third century AD (fig. 55). At least three basilicas, used for judicial and administrative functions, are also known from Corinth, the most from any Achaian city on present evidence. If Corinth did not possess the only provincial mint, Corinthian coins are nonetheless remarkable for their early and strong preference for Roman types, their fast response to imperial dynastic change, and their fidelity in conforming to Augustan monetary denominations.[59] Western influences can be detected in other ways as well, notably through ceramic evidence from the city. Detailed and quantified study of excavated materials suggests that not only did Corinth come to serve as a "nexus of Aegean trade," but that in its pottery assemblages Corinth, "like contemporary Knossos and perhaps other provincial capitals, began to show greater western influence than other eastern cities."[60]

Religious and symbolic links between Rome and her provincial capital are also apparent. Though its precise location is disputed, a Capitolium – possibly one of the earliest to be founded in an overseas colony – lay somewhere in the agora. A reappraisal of Corinthian urban topography suggests that one of the most elaborate temples (Temple F, to Venus) may have been the first erected in the forum. The site's excavator, C. K. Williams, does not think this mere whimsy on the part of the colonists, nor "was there any intention in their action of evoking the Classical glories of Aphrodite Hoplismeni who had succoured the Greek city from Akrokorinthos ... The Venus of the Forum is different. She is placed at the centre of the city as the Mother of the Roman Nation, and as such as Mother of the Roman colony."[61] Another relevant monument, representing Roma on the Seven Hills of Rome, was discovered along the Lechaion Road and probably dates to the first half of the second century AD; unique in Achaia (and, indeed, practically unparalleled elsewhere) it served "to make the provincial audience in the capital city of Achaea more fully aware of the geographical and political, as well as the religious significance of the Urbs Roma Aeterna."[62] Epigraphic evidence likewise exhibits the Corinthian aristocracy's devotion to – even its obsession with – the imperial cult: for the first century or so of the colony's existence "the majority of extant dedicatory inscriptions or records of priesthoods are aimed at Roman gods and to imperial cults," though admittedly this preoccupation slackened off over time.[63]

Quite aside from the colony's size (fig. 56) and its magnetic appeal for members of the Achaian élite, Corinth's control of the Isthmian Games provided another means by which the city could act as a pro-Roman focal point in Achaian life. This patronage was returned to Corinth only some forty years after the colony's foundation; the city's first real prosperity is associated with the time of the restoration. The panhellenic celebrations at Isthmia, where *agones* in honor of the imperial family were also held, drew the attention and homage of people from all over Greece. At the main entrance to the sanctuary stood a monumental triple arch, probably dating to the second half of the first century AD and forming a significant marker on one of the major routes running from central Greece into the Peloponnese (fig. 58).[64] Both Flamininus and Nero used the Isthmian festival as their opportunity to make major public statements, their proclamations of Greek liberty. Corinth's domination of this sanctuary, granted by imperial fiat, not only yielded great prestige: it furnished an additional mechanism by which Corinthian influence could be transmitted throughout the province.

If informal and symbolic threads of influence bound Corinth and Rome, so other provincial cities may similarly have been bound to Corinth. But just as direct intervention in provincial structure was confined chiefly to the early days of incorporation, so Corinth's importance as a bridgehead community may have diminished with the passage of time. By the second century it was said that Corinth, "though Roman, has become thoroughly Hellenized" (Ps.-Dio Chrysostom [Favorinus], *Oration* 37.26); the ethnic composition and identity of the city seems to shift, as the Hadrianic change in official language, from Latin to Greek, demonstrates. Yet even with such changes in language and culture, Corinth need not have relinquished its dominant position within the province's life. As "common city of the Greeks," just as Rome was *astu koinon* to the empire, Corinth could serve as an informal clearing house for provincial affairs and, particularly in the early years of Achaia's existence, as a force that helped to promulgate Roman rule.

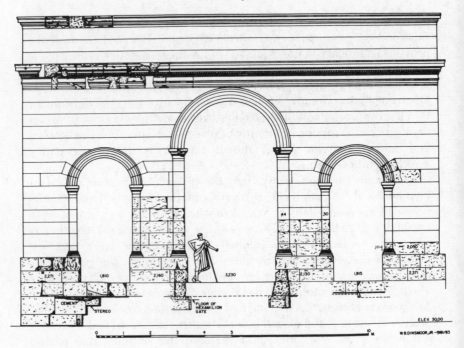

58 Actual-state and restored elevation of the Roman triple arch at Isthmia

## CREATING THE PROVINCIAL LANDSCAPE

Under that rule, Achaia experienced purposive interventions in both territorial and demographic arrangements, acts designed to serve the economic and managerial goals of outside imperial interests. For the most part, however, Roman authorities found Achaia's pre-existing political framework acceptable to their particular and limited needs in the province. Yet episodes of direct imperial interference by no means represent the full spectrum of the change within provincial geography. Further major modifications came about through local responses to incorporation within a larger and more demanding system. As formerly independent entities were transformed into cogs in the administrative machinery of empire, different processes came to dictate the necessary conditions of civic life. Some *poleis* could meet these successfully – others could not.

What characterized the cities that won out? Life was easiest for those towns with imperial support, gained either through their strategic location or by Roman respect for their glorious past. The support of local civic élites, however, was the surest guarantor of a city's continued buoyancy. High civic status and prestige might help to guarantee this interest, but fierce loyalty continued to be devoted even to undistinguished towns. The size of a city's demographic base proved another important factor, the smaller centers consistently proving more vulnerable to pressure. Population shifts, either of élite patrons or of poorer migrants, acted – in very different ways – to help some cities, while hurting others. Cities in trouble could turn to various compensating stratagems: quarreling, co-operating, even combining. Achaian political geography thus emerges as a dynamic construction, constantly modified by both external and internal agency through the years of Roman domination. For all that Roman imperialism in Greece may not have been overtly *interventionist*, it was nonetheless highly *intrusive*; the provincial landscape shows the marks of Roman conquest and control.[65]

# 5

# The sacred landscape

The sacred landscape, like all the others we have examined so far, was created through a variety of human actions: building, dedication, dramatization, procession, and ritual all marked space in certain ways, serving individual and collective needs and aspirations. The resulting patterns played a central role in articulating various human relationships, demonstrating relative status and authority, for example, or overseeing moments of social transition. A spatial context greatly enhances an understanding of ritual activity. Not surprisingly, anthropologists and archaeologists frequently ask questions such as: Where are sacred ceremonies performed? Why are temples, mounds, tombs and monuments located where they are? How are these locations related to places of human settlement or to natural features? How might integration or conflict, both social and territorial, be prescribed through the organization of sacred space?

Sacred landscapes emerge as both culturally constructed and historically sensitive, immensely variable through time and space. Far from being immune to developments in other aspects of human life, they can reflect a very wide cultural and political milieu. Yet they also provide more than a simple mirror of change by their active participation in the conditions of social reproduction.[1] In the Greco-Roman world especially, attitudes and actions were continually molded by current conceptions of mythic or cultic geography. If we admit that influence, the "landscape of the gods" becomes as informative as that of men. This chapter, then, adopts that perspective in order to shed further light on a number of issues we have already discussed: the relationship of town and country, the question of nucleated settlement, the role of the élite, and competition between cities.

In classical archaeology, excavation and study of ancient cult places have always taken pride of place, and with some justification. Sanctuaries were dominant elements in the Greek world, serving an immensely wide variety of functions: apart from providing a place for the interaction of human and numinous forces, they acted as centers for entertainment, communication and exchange, as politically neutral zones, and as arenas for competition between individuals and larger social groups. Religious behavior played an integral role in structuring and reconciling disparate elements within the life of the *polis* and the Greek world at large.[2] Two major flaws mark, however, much past archaeological work on Greek cult places. One is the general lack of interest in their *spatial* dimension, in the regional geography of cult distribution. For the most part, analyses of sanctuaries and ritual behavior ignore the issue of where they occurred, instead concentrating upon "internal" matters such as the temenos plan, sanctuary dedications and, of course, architectural monuments and their refinements. Scant attention was paid to how location might relate to other significant elements in the terrain, such as human settlement, natural features, or other sacred precincts. Synthetic works on the subject tend to classify sanctuaries by deity or cult type, or else simply move from the discussion of one individual sanctuary considered in isolation to another. Greek cult places have thus been "decontextualized," excised from their topographic setting, and more or less divorced from any wider dynamic of social and political change.[3] Secondly, the burden of meanings and functions carried by sanctuaries has been perceived as largely static, almost ahistorical. This assumption can be attributed to many factors. Among them are the conservative role generally attributed to religion in modern western civilization; the way in which classical archaeology as a discipline has impeded more diachronic and comparative studies, both in its concentration upon the Classical era and in its emphasis on architectural and artifactual description; and an overwhelming reliance upon a single literary source, namely Pausanias. An insensitivity to potential developments in cult distribution, and the meaning inherent in such developments, has inevitably resulted.

Such archaeological approaches to Greek religion in the past are under pressure from both outside and within the discipline. The possibility of change in Greek religious practice, related to developments within its larger social context, is increasingly appreciated. As for the importance of "cultic maps," the work of François de Polignac is proving highly influential in some circles. Drawing upon wider discourses in symbolic and structuralist geography, de Polignac argues that cult enacted an essential part in the rise of the *polis*, with the physical location of certain sanctuaries (notably extra-urban sanctuaries) proving a major determinant. De Polignac's analyses have been questioned on specific points, and they certainly require extension and development. Nonetheless, his assertion of cult distribution as a valid independent subject has already provoked new lines of research, establishing the geography of cult as a potent area to explore.[4]

To return to the early imperial period, significant alterations in other landscapes – rural, civic, provincial – have been observed, and in turn related to major transitions in social, economic and political behavior in Achaia. If ritual serves to reconcile people to their environment (natural and human), then it would be foolhardy to assume a static symbolic world for the Greeks of this epoch. Certainly, ideological responses, owing either to external interference or to internal adaptation, are a constant feature in other imperial studies.[5] Spatial order, as observed in the sacred landscape, will be seen to articulate social order, and be linked with shifting relations of power and influence.

The sources available make this investigation particularly appealing. Central to the discussion in this chapter will be the use of Pausanias and his mid-second century *Guide to Greece*. A pilgrim rather than a tourist, Pausanias has already been noted for his concentration upon the cult places and practices of Greece, ranging from the most major of panhellenic sanctuaries to the most minor of local cults. In the past, his single-mindedness has won him few friends among ancient historians hoping to find a far wider variety of information from this valuable "eyewitness" of Roman Greece. Long pilloried for his alleged tedious-ness, his tunnel vision, and his occasional inexactitude on matters of historical detail, Pausanias is currently experiencing a florescence of scholarly interest and approval. This re-evaluation, which recognizes at last that Pausanias is not some early and flawed version of *Baedeker* or the *Blue Guide*, has been encouraged by two developments. One is that archaeological or epigraphic investigations have proved a number of his more problematic statements to be in fact correct. More profoundly, however, the text of Pausanias is now read as a product of its age, and his *periegesis* appreciated as one individual's attempt to construct a religious identity for Greece under Roman rule, revealing something of "what it was like to be a Greek at the height of the Roman Empire."[6] Pausanias thus plays an important role in the discussion in this chapter as a self-aware observer of the sacred landscape of second-century Greece, a viewer remarkably sensitive to issues of "space" and "place" in his discussion of *panta ta Ellenika* ("all Greek matters," or "the whole of Greece"). Part of his importance for the present study lies in the fact that he actually traveled and wrote during the period which concerns us here: he is much more a man of his time than has been appreciated by those who have attempted to apply his testimony indiscriminately to more or less any period of antiquity on the dubious assumption (noted above) that cult activity was a relatively static phenomenon. For the early imperial period, in other words, he provides us with one important *contemporary* voice.

Above all, what we need is a sophisticated archaeological contribution, which is the only source of information which can provide the required diachronic and regional overview of cult activity. In this chapter I muster as much archaeological evidence as possible, but certain impediments do exist which are best acknowledged at the outset. First, it has been suggested, perhaps with some justice, that post-Classical activity at Greek sanctuaries can in some cases be difficult to identify, even at well-excavated sites. It remains undetermined how much of this difficulty may be the result of a general lack of interest in later finds on the part of excavators.[7] Second, the range of available evidence remains limited, since most archaeological attention has been confined to the major sanctuaries, either panhellenic or urban in character. Yet Greek cult activity took place in all manner of locations, both urban and rural, and on all scales, from an official temenos with temples to a simple holy place – a spring, a rock, a grove of trees, or just an open space. That we have so far studied only the tip of the iceberg is not entirely the fault of previous investigators: many such locales are obviously very difficult, if not impossible, to recover archaeologically. It is, however, helpful to admit that our knowledge of Greek cult places remains more underdeveloped, and biased toward the upper end of the spectrum, than is generally acknowledged. Some remedy for this situation can be sought through recent developments in archaeological work in Greece, notably intensive field survey, and Pausanias, who held both mighty and humble cult places in awe, can also help balance the picture. More and better archaeological evidence is vital, however, as the best means to determine independently when and where cults appear, flourish and expire.

Despite the problematic nature of these sources, I believe they provide a sufficiently sound basis for studying the spatial location and distribution of certain types of sanctuary. Three particular aspects – *displaced cult*, *centralized cult* and *rural cult* – have been selected for detailed examination. In each of these categories, examples of cult endurance, failure or transformation cast light on the changing nature of Achaian society under Roman rule.

### DISPLACED CULTS

As the name suggests, these are cults which, through the process of conquest and incorporation, were deliberately shifted from one place to another. One instance – the transfer of sacred images accompanying the synoecisms of Patrai and Nikopolis – has already been mentioned in the previous chapter as one form of "symbolic violence," reinforcing the implacable imperial will in these areas (pp. 140–1; fig. 48). Moving the Artemis Laphria from Kalydon to Patrai might simply appear to "make

59 View of the foundation of the Temple of Athena Alea at Tegea

sense" given the depopulation of the one area and the favored status of the other. Yet seemingly less straightforward examples of such symbolic reorganization can also be traced elsewhere. From the famous sanctuary of Athena Alea at Tegea in Arcadia (fig. 59), for example, Augustus removed certain of the contents to his imperial capital. Pausanias' account of this act is interesting, and worth quoting in full.

The ancient images of Athena Alea, and with it the tusks of the Kalydonian boar, were carried away by the Roman emperor Augustus after his defeat of Antonius and his allies, among whom were all the Arcadians except the Mantineans. It is clear that Augustus was not the first to carry away from the vanquished votive offerings and images of the gods, but was only following an old precedent. For when Troy was taken and the Greeks were dividing up the spoils, Sthenelus the son of Kapeneus was given the wooden image of Zeus Herkeios; and many years later, when Dorians were migrating to Sicily, Antiphemus the founder of Gela, after the sack of Omphace, a town of the Sicanians, removed to Gela an image made by Daedalus. Xerxes, too, the son of Dareius, the king of Persia, apart from the spoil he carried away from the city of Athens, took besides, as we know, from Brauron the image of Brauronian Artemis, and furthermore, accusing the Milesians of cowardice in a naval engagement against the Athenians in Greek waters, carried away from them the bronze Apollo at Branchidai. This it was to be the lot of Seleucus afterwards to restore to the Milesians, but the Argives down to the present still retain the images they took from Tiryns; one, a wooden image, is by the Hera, the other is kept in the sanctuary of Lycian Apollo. Again, the people of Cyzicus, compelling the people of Proconnesus by war to live at Cyzicus, took away from Proconnesus an image of Mother Didymene. The image is of gold, and its face is made of hippopotamus' teeth instead of ivory. So the emperor Augustus only followed a custom in vogue among the Greeks and barbarians from of old. The image of Athena Alea at Rome is as you enter the Forum made by Augustus. Here then it has been set up, made throughout of ivory, the work of Endoios. Those in charge of the curiosities say that one of the boar's tusks has broken off; the remaining one is kept in the gardens of the emperor, in a sanctuary of Dionysos, and is about half a fathom long. (Pausanias 8.46.1–5)

Concentrating on the Augustan episode mentioned at the beginning of this passage, such a deed could be viewed simply as the emperor's personal caprice or artistic fancy. Yet, of the multitude of Greek sanctuaries, what was it about Tegea that made it liable for such treatment? Civic status and recent history might provide some answers. The city's support of Antony against Octavian was unfortunate, but hardly unique – almost the entire Peloponnese (with the exception of Sparta and Mantineia) had so chosen. But Tegea's position as an influential power in the Peloponnese was *not* commonplace. The city was a major node in the region's communication network, as its part in the *cursus publicus* implies, and Athena Alea herself was much venerated throughout the Peloponnese, drawing people's loyalty to Tegea as a religious center. Removing cult objects to Rome (where they were separated and displayed in totally different, Roman contexts) struck hard and directly at the Tegeates' sense of history and of independence. In short, this was neither a random nor a whimsical gesture.[8]

Another similar example is the cult of Poseidon at Samikon in Triphylia. Strabo reported that this sanctuary received great respect and financial support from the entire regional population. Surprisingly, Pausanias does not mention this prominent local cult, but he does report seeing a statue in Elis "worshipped in ancient times at Samikon. Transferred to Elis it received still greater honour, but the Eleans call it Satrap and not Poseidon, having learned the name Satrap, which is a surname of Korybas, after the enlargement of Patrai." (6.25.6). One explanation for this state of affairs is that the image had only very recently been moved to Elis, dispossessing Samikon of its role as a regional cult center. Baladié, for one, believed this abandonment was inevitable because of the desertion of the countryside (and the relationship between the deserted countryside and the sacred landscape will be considered further below); but it is perhaps just as likely that what underlay the transfer was a desire to restructure existing territorial and personal allegiances in this district. The mention of Patrai in relation to the cult's renaming, as well as the western orientation of Triphylia, also lend support to this conclusion.[9]

The most common examples of cult displacement, however, are undoubtedly the innumerable statues removed from Greek cities and sanctuaries as "plunder" by Roman troops or by greedy emperors. Many specific cases are recorded: the depredations of Mummius at Corinth supplied Rome with its "greatest number and best of the public monuments" (Strabo 8.6.23); Sulla's snatching of the precious ivory image of Athena from Boeotian Alalkomenai led to the sanctuary's subsequent neglect; and Nero, with his "universal irreverence," appropriated no less than five hundred bronze statues, "some of gods, some of men," from Delphi (Pausanias 10.7.1) and others from Olympia (Pausanias 5.25.9; 5.26.3). Nor were cult images the only target of these "looters"; "among other Athenian treasures," Sulla removed votive shields from the stoa of Zeus Eleutherios at Athens.[10]

Two general points are worth making about such instances of "displacement." First, the objects selected – cult statues, votives related to a people's mythic or recent past – did not represent antiquities, curiosities or *objets d'art* to the Greeks, whatever the supposed Roman (or indeed modern) perception of them. As sacred things, they contained and declared the history and identity of individual civic entities, as well as of the Greeks as a whole. Emotional investment in cult objects is well attested throughout Greek history; one has only to think of the care and significance attached to the safety of the image of Athena Polias or indeed of the Trojan Palladion. In one tale told by Pausanias, the Phokians prepared to immolate their women, precious objects and divine images on a vast pyre, rather than let them fall into enemy hands (10.1.6–7). Religious expressions of pride and independence were also manifested physically in the refusal to rebuild temples destroyed by barbarians, leaving them "for all time as memorials of their hatred" (Pausanias 10.35.2).[11] Against this background, episodes such as the removal of the Eros of Thespiai emerge as events of tragic significance for the community at large:

Of the gods the Thespians have from the beginning honored Eros most, and they have a very ancient image of him, an unwrought stone . . . Later on Lysippos made a bronze Eros for the Thespians, and previously Praxiteles one of Pentelic marble . . . The first to remove the image of Eros, it is said, was Gaius the Roman emperor; Claudius, they say, sent it back to Thespiai, but Nero carried it away a second time. At Rome the image perished by fire. (Pausanias 9.27.1, 3)

The magnitude of such losses would not have been diminished in the Roman period, when the past continued to form an essential part of civic self-definition.

If Greek responses to such actions have at times been underestimated, so too the intentions of the imperial agents (whether generals or emperors) have frequently been misinterpreted. Put simply, these actions have been taken far too inconsequentially and dismissed as the behavior either of boors (Mummius) or of connoisseurs (Marcellus), men interested only in plunder or ornament. Other, more sinister motives lurk in the background: the source of Caligula's (and later Nero's) interest in the beautiful Eros from Thespiai, for instance, is all too clear. Yet while a fascination with Greek art and a lust for loot cannot be denied, Roman consciousness of exactly what they were taking from the Greeks must also be allowed.[12] Depriving one's enemy of sacred objects and possessing them yourself served two related purposes: defeating them in perpetuity and adding the power of their gods to your own symbolic arsenal. As Richard Gordon has observed, "there was a particular value in depriving a conquered city of its religious sculpture and painting, since this action 'removed' its gods, in much the same way that the traditional Roman practice of *evocatio* removed the power of a divinity from the enemy to the Romans."[13] Moreover, gifts of the gods could also be used as rewards. At the sack of Corinth, Mummius may well have skimmed off many of the best pieces, but lesser prizes were assigned to an ally, Attalus' general; these statues still stood in Pergamon in the time of Pausanias. Viewed in this light, the removal of a city's cult images forms a deliberate tactic of domination: strengthening the victorious side, weakening the losers. The Romans were far from the first to employ this strategy in the Greco-Roman world, as the catalog already quoted from Pausanias demonstrates.[14]

The strategy could backfire, however, if the gods became angered. After the taking of Tarentum in 209 BC, Fabius Maximus left well enough alone: "although he carried off the money and other valuables of the city, he allowed the statues to remain, adding this widely remembered remark: 'Let us leave these gods in their anger for the Tarentines'" (Plutarch, *Marcellus* 21). Pausanias several times associates the despoiling of sanctuaries with punishment. The impious Sulla, for example, with his "mad outrages against the Greek cities and gods of the Greeks" was eventually afflicted with "the most foul of diseases" (9.33.6). Immediately after recounting the history of the Eros of Thespiai, Pausanias proceeds to remark: "Of the pair who sinned against the god, Gaius was killed by a private soldier, just as he was giving the password . . . The other, Nero, in addition to his violence against his mother, committed hateful crimes against his wedded wives" (Pausanias 9.27.4).[15]

An appreciation grows of both the power and the danger inextricably associated with any episode of cult displacement. Such acts of symbolic violence worked effectively to undermine local loyalties, to shatter established relationships of authority and, above all, to weaken any pretense of independence. Most drastically, as in the Augustan-period synoecisms in northwest Achaia, removal of cult objects represented the deliberate symbolic destruction of a community. It is surely significant that most episodes of cult displacement occurred early in the history of the province, for the most part during the Civil Wars and the first century of Roman rule, and the subsequent waning of such behavior can be attributed only in part to factors such as increasing philhellenism or the development in Rome of a "more refined world of collecting and connoisseurship."[16] Presumably, as resistance was either quelled or became a more remote possibility, the need (as well as easy opportunities) for such actions passed.

The phenomenon of displaced cult can thus be identified as an externally motivated act, designed to disrupt or override local symbolic systems in the interests of the new political order. Two sides exist, of course, to the story of these transfers. For every town that lost out another gained; as some places suffered, certain locations (Rome itself or favored cities within Achaia) benefited from these ritual reshufflings – just as they benefited from concentrations of population and economic resources. For good or ill, then, displaced cult is something seen mainly in areas of special imperial interest or sensitivity. A westward bias is noted in the redistribution of sacred objects, an echo of which can perhaps be detected in the relative prosperity of Olympia in Roman times.

## CENTRALIZED CULTS

The term "centralized cult" is used here to refer to those types of sanctuary located almost exclusively within urban centers. In particular, attention will be focused upon recent innovations in Greek religious life, and the appearance and florescence of new or newly popular gods during the Hellenistic and Early Roman period, among them those of the Eastern mystery religions – Isis, Serapis and Attis. A clear bias toward central locations can be detected in their spatial distribution, no doubt partly on account of the cosmopolitan nature of urban centers and their population's greater willingness to experiment with new deities; these more "personal" gods also fit most naturally within populated centers, rather than in the now relatively empty countryside. "Foreign" cults also appear with particular frequency in coastal cities, or in large urban units and the smaller centers surrounding them. Serapis and Isis, for example, are known in Corinth, while Isis (with or without Serapis) also appears in the surrounding smaller communities of Megara, Methana, Hermione, Troizen and Phlius – presumably the result of the transmission of new

ideas emanating from the main center. One major exception to this
urban preference is the Isis sanctuary at Tithorea in Phokis, "the holiest
of all those made by the Greeks for the Egyptian goddess" (10.32.13),
where a festival with an important periodic market was held, ensuring
the cult still maintained a central position in the perceptions of local
residents.[17]

## The imperial cult

In any religious study of a Roman province, the institution and reception
of the imperial cult must bulk especially large, although here only the
spatial dimension of this enormous subject can be considered. The most
basic question to ask is where temples, images or altars of the imperial cult
were established. From the perspective of Achaia as a whole, all the
province's larger cities hosted the cult: Athens, Corinth, Nikopolis,
Patrai, Argos and Sparta, for example, accumulated many shrines and
monuments to the emperor. A far wider distribution across the provincial
landscape is also demonstrated, however, by the cult's additional
appearance in small and relatively undistinguished centers, such as is
shown in the distribution of altars dedicated to Augustus in the province
(fig. 60). Some more subtle variants have been suggested within this
overall pattern; for example, in Arcadian cities dedications by and large
seem directed to those emperors who had themselves visited Greece in
person. Free cities, too, have been suspected to rely especially heavily
upon this channel to maintain their privileged position. On the whole,
however, given the obvious advantages to be gained from attracting
imperial attention and favor, the cult's presence in small as well as large
Achaian cities is hardly unexpected.[18]

As for the topographic placement of cult within these individual civic
units, a strong preference for the most prominent and public of locations
springs out as one immediately compelling pattern.[19] Examples, both
from Pausanias and from the results of archaeological investigation, are
plentiful; only clear and representative cases will be cited here, beginning
with the major centers. In Athens, both the agora and the acropolis
became scenes for the imperial cult, as well as the gigantic Olympieion of
Hadrian to the southeast; this latter, though officially dedicated to Zeus,
was as much a precinct sacred to the emperor, and each Greek city was
said to have set up his image in the temenos, resulting in a veritable forest
of at least 136 Hadrians (fig. 61). On the acropolis, a small Ionic
monopteros to Roma and Augustus, modeled closely in points of detail
upon the nearby fifth-century BC Erechtheion, probably stood before the
east end of the Parthenon (fig. 62). A massive bronze inscription on the

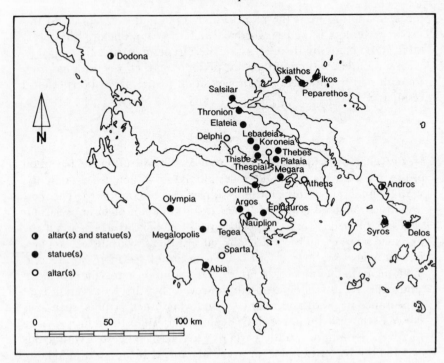

60 Distribution of altars and statues dedicated to Augustus in Achaia

Parthenon's eastern façade is a prominently placed summary of an honorific decree to the emperor Nero; at the end of the second century AD, the cult and temple of Athena Polias was assimilated to Julia Domna. As for the second center of civic life in ancient Athens, manifestations of the imperial cult in the agora will be discussed in some detail below (pp. 195–6), and here it is simply worth noting that of the fifteen public Athenian altars to Augustus, all but one were found in or near this area. The new Roman agora, begun by Julius Caesar and finished under Augustus, has also been proposed as the site of a Kaisareion.[20] For comparison, Pausanias says of Sparta: "On the market place are temples; there is one of Caesar, the first Roman to covet monarchy . . . and also one to his son Augustus, who put the empire on a firmer footing and became a more famous and a more powerful man than his father. His name 'Augustus' means in Greek 'Sebastos'" (Pausanias 3.11.4). The Spartan potentate, Eurycles, set up *naoi* to Caesar and Augustus in the agora of both Gytheion and Messene.[21]

This concentration upon the most public and accessible zones of the city is visible in other centers as well. The Sebasteion in Messene, dating

61 An early twentieth-century view of the Olympieion in Athens, with the
acropolis behind

to the Augustan period, lies at the head of a monumental staircase set
within a large precinct of Asklepios; this precinct probably bordered on
the Messenian agora (fig. 63). In Boeotian Orchomenos lay the Treasury
of Minyas, a Mycenaean tholos tomb reused in the Hellenistic period as a
heroon. Excavation revealed a large statue base inside the tomb
monument, with a partial inscription attesting to the presence of the
imperial cult – a particularly unusual setting for it, one might think, until
it is remembered that the Treasury was still visible and prominent in
Roman times, indeed being considered by Pausanias "a wonder second
to none either in Greece itself or elsewhere" (9.38.2; fig. 64). Apart from
sanctuaries proper, other public centers could be involved in the
performance of rituals connected with the cult, as for example at
Gytheion, where sacrifices were enacted within the theater as part of the
worship of emperors. Processions throughout a city could also form one
aspect of an imperial festival; at Gytheion again, ceremonial movement
symbolically linked together various key religious and political centers of
the city (sanctuaries, the agora, the theater).[22]

   In his study of the imperial cult in Asia Minor, Price observed a very
similar distributional pattern. It is also worth noting that related

183

62 The Parthenon and the Temple of Roma and Augustus. The remains of the Roma temple lie in front of the Parthenon's east façade, directly before the crowd of people.

monuments, such as triumphal arches, tend also to be in central and prominent locations. Probably the best-known Achaian example is the Arch of Hadrian in Athens. The usual assumption that this arch stood as a boundary marker between an "Old City" (of Theseus) and a "New City" (of Hadrian) has recently been challenged by the suggestion that Hadrian is celebrated here as a founder (*ktistes*), replacing Theseus and renewing the city of Athens as a whole; in this reading, the arch serves more as a propylon to the Olympieion temenos, bestriding a road leading back toward the acropolis and agora (fig. 65). Whatever the truth, the arch clearly held a definitive place in Attic civic topography. Another major triumphal monument is the victory trophy raised by Augustus after Actium. Rather than being in "downtown" Nikopolis, the monument sat upon a hill on the city's outskirts (figs. 66–7).

Here "under the open sky" on a wide terrace supported by a Roman rostra [*sic*] of grandiose proportions was a portico which focused the visitor's attention on two

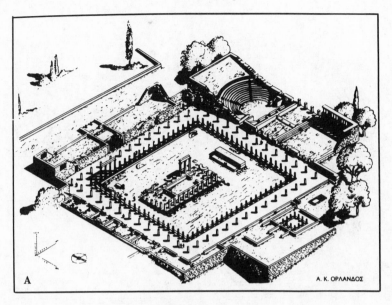

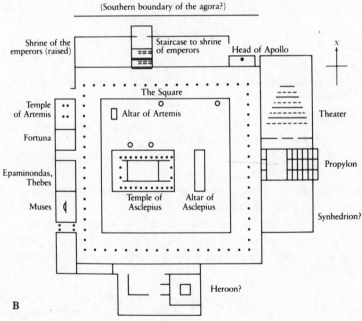

63 Messene, reconstruction and schematic plan of the Asklepieion, with the
   Sebasteion to the north

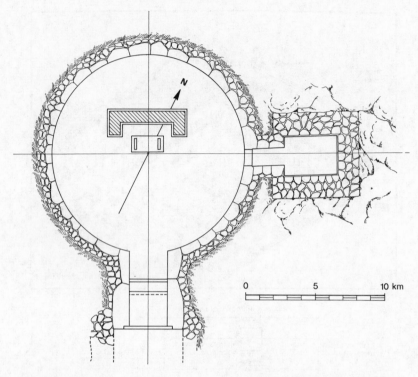

0    5    10 km

64  Orchomenos, Treasury of Minyas, the Mycenaean tholos tomb with its later
    internal altar

images. The first was near at hand: the simple consecrated place where Octavian's
tent had stood. The second was in the distance, where one could see on the horizon the
site of the glorious Battle of Actium; and in the middle ground hummed the living city
which celebrated the great victory.[23]

Even if not in the city center, the monument's link to the urban
foundation is eminently clear.

The cult of Antinoos, the favorite of the emperor Hadrian, also
deserves mention in this context. His cult proved rather popular in
Greece (fig. 68), with (according to Pausanias) worship offered especially
in Mantineia.

Antinoos too was deified by [the Mantineians]; his temple is the newest in Mantineia
. . . He has won worship in Mantineia for the following reason. Antinoos was by birth
from Bithynium beyond the river Sangarius, and the Bithynians are by descent
Arcadians of Mantineia. For this reason the Emperor established his worship in
Mantineia also; mystic rites are celebrated in his honor each year, and games every
four years. (Pausanias 8.9.7–8)

65 An early twentieth-century view of the west side of the Arch of Hadrian in Athens. The columns of the Olympieion can be glimpsed through the arch.

Other civic structures too were linked with the cult: the gymnasium, for example, held several images of the youth. The Spartan dynast C. Iulius Eurycles Herculanus L. Vibullius Pius (d. AD 136/7) erected a small shrine commemorating both Antinoos and his own benefactions; this "will have been among the most prominent structures in post-Hadrianic Mantineia" (and its erection, incidentally, provides a good example of an Achaian magnate's overt attempts to link himself with external sources of power and authority).[24] All of these edifices were in city-center locations.

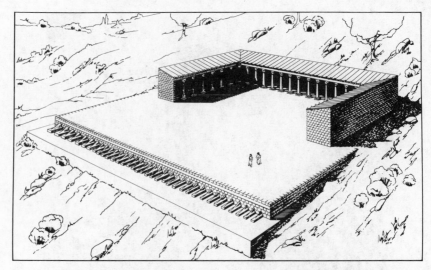

66 Nikopolis, restored general view of the Augustan victory monument from the southeast

67 Nikopolis, restored view of the Augustan victory monument

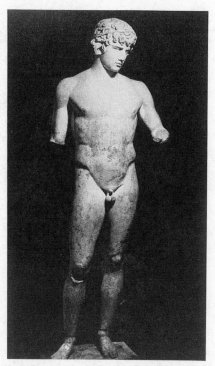

68 Delphi, statue of Antinoos now in the Delphi Museum

## *Panhellenic centers*

Panhellenic sanctuaries too hosted the imperial cult. The overall
"centralizing" pattern argued above is not disturbed by this fact, for
people from all over Greece, and further afield, continued to converge at
these centers at festival time. The four major panhellenic celebrations
(Olympia, Delphi, Isthmia, Nemea) continued throughout this period;
other festivals accorded similar status increased in number throughout
Achaia and the rest of the Greek east. These new festivals and games tend
to be found in predictable locations – Athens or Sparta, for instance, or
the site of an existing famous sanctuary. Very often they were associated
with imperial worship, as in the Boeotian festivals of the Kaisareia
Erotideia Romaia or the Megala Kaisareia Sebasteia Mouseia at
Thespiai. All such festivals drew large and cosmopolitan crowds,
providing élite families especially with a popular time to meet and
interact, celebrating success in the games or in their administration.[25]
  Of the four original panhellenic sanctuaries, it was Olympia that

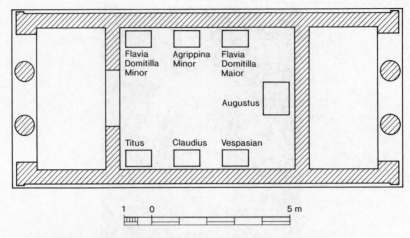

Flavia
Domitilla
Minor

Agrippina
Minor

Flavia
Domitilla
Maior

Augustus

Titus

Claudius

Vespasian

1   0                                5 m

69 Plan of the Metroon at Olympia, showing the arrangement of imperial cult
images

flourished most consistently under the empire. Several of the improved or
newly founded festivals in Greece were named after, and in some cases
fashionably modeled upon, the Olympics of Elis – for instance, the
Olympia Commodea at Sparta. Although celebrations of the Elean
festival fell into chaos during the turmoil of the Republican era, they were
rescued and restored by the benefactions of (among others) Agrippa and
Herod the Great, and Tiberius and Nero themselves competed in the
games. As a general point of fact, we should take note of the imperial or
external impetus for much of Olympia's Roman prosperity. Of the new
buildings erected in the temenos, several were related to benefactions or
visits by emperors or other notables, for example the so-called "House of
Nero," a villa to the southeast of the Altis, and a triumphal arch,
demolished after the emperor's death. The Metroon, temple to the
Mother of the Gods, became the setting for a dynastic representation of
the imperial family, with Augustus centrally enthroned as Zeus (fig. 69).
Imperial images were eventually erected within the pronaos of the
nearby temple of Zeus itself. A complex political message was also
conveyed by the hemicycle of the nymphaeum erected by Herodes
Atticus not far from the Metroon – a monument, often criticized by
modern scholars as tasteless, which promulgated dynastic claims with a
heady mixture of honors to the families of Marcus Aurelius and of Atticus
himself (figs. 70–1).[26]

The value of Olympia as a political theater was clearly still appreciated
in the Roman era. Monuments erected here would certainly be widely

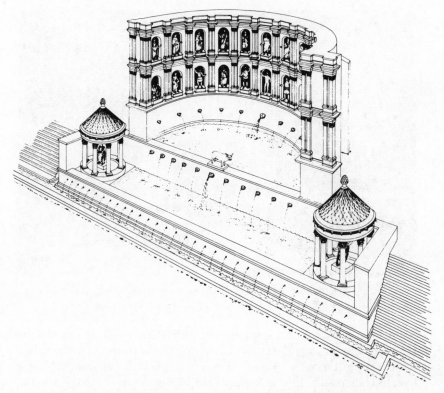

70 Reconstruction of the Nymphaeum of Herodes Atticus at Olympia

seen; gestures made here could not fail to be noticed. So at least Peregrinus, the Cynic philosopher who chose Olympia as the scene of his self-immolation in AD 165, must have reasoned. Ironically, Peregrinus complained of Herodes' gift of water to the sanctuary; and in another speech made in a festival context, he publicly encouraged the Greeks to take up arms against the Romans.[27] The prominence of Olympia no doubt in part stemmed from its immense antiquity, as well as its western location. The other panhellenic sanctuaries, if apparently less flourishing, also received imperial images and largesse, as well as playing a major role in facilitating communication among Greek cities and beyond.[28]

## Itinerant temples

The urban, centralized location of so many aspects of imperial cult activity was neither accidental nor a matter of mere convenience. In fact in Achaia, the strength of this trend can be measured by the fact that it

71 Imaginative reconstruction of the Nymphaeum of Herodes Atticus at Olympia

could even provoke cult displacement, in which outlying sanctuaries assimilated to the imperial cult could actually be transferred to the urban center. For instance, aspects of the cult of Zeus on the summit of Mount Lykaion in Arcadia appear to have been moved down into Megalopolis, probably at the time when the cult of the emperors was joined to that of Zeus. The sanctuary on the summit was not fully abandoned but, deprived of its chief festival, it seems to have been in decline by Pausanias' time: "Of old they used to hold here the Lykaion games. Here there are also bases of statues, with now no statues in them" (8.38.5).[29]

But it is the movement of fifth-century BC architectural elements, taken from rural Attic sanctuaries, into the Athenian agora that provides the most extravagant example. These elements were originally located in the demes of Acharnai, Sounion and Thorikos (12, 44 and 40 kilometers from Athens, respectively). The most dramatic transfer saw an entire temple, the Temple of Ares thought to originate in Acharnai, dismantled in its original setting and reconstructed in the agora. It lay to the east of the Temple of Apollo Patroos, with its altar on an axial alignment with the imposing Odeion of Agrippa, set toward the center of the former open area. From Sounion, portions of two temples made the trek: part of the Temple of Poseidon was utilized in the Ares temple, while columns from the Temple of Athena were employed in the façade of a small temple (now known as the Southeast Temple) which faced north and looked

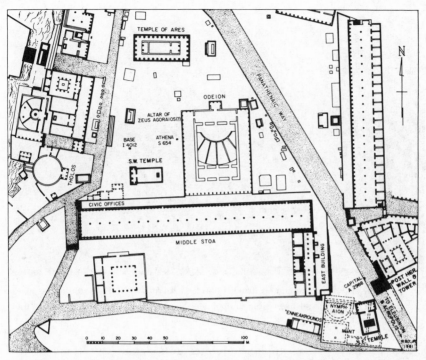

72 Plan of the Athenian agora, showing "itinerant" temples and findspots of other
   architectural members

along the Panhellenic Way. From Thorikos, columns from an unidenti-
fied, unfinished building were reused, most probably in the so-called
Southwest Temple placed to the east of the Tholos (fig. 72). Other
elements of Classical architecture found in the agora excavations were
probably recycled in a similar fashion, but their precise functions remain
uncertain. Another traveling monument, the Altar of Zeus Agoraios
which may have been transferred from the Pnyx, ended up just to the
northeast of the Eponymous Heroes and south of the Temple of Ares (fig.
73). As Shear noted, "it may not be coincidence that Zeus, whose special
task it was to govern the political assemblies of the Athenians, should
depart the Pnyx at just the time when Augustus is said to have curtailed
sharply the powers of those same assemblies."[30] The date assigned to all
this activity, on the basis of built foundations and masons' marks, is the
era of Augustus or shortly thereafter. The resultant "infilling" of the
agora radically altered the appearance and function of this public space
(p. 93; figs. 26–7).

The "itinerant temples," as Homer Thompson dubbed them, have

193

73 View of the Athenian agora from the west in August 1951. The foundations of
the Temple of Ares are visible to the lower left, the Altar of Zeus Agoraios to the
lower right, with the Odeion of Agrippa beyond.

been published in exemplary architectural detail, but the reasons
advanced for their movement demand further attention. The presumed
desertion of the countryside, a development we have explored at some
length, has served as one common explanation. While it is more than
likely that the Attic rural landscape was less widely inhabited than
formerly, it does not necessarily follow that temples in the countryside
were automatically abandoned. Indeed, there exists inscriptional
evidence from roughly this same period which proves an active civic
interest in re-establishing and maintaining Attic rural sanctuaries. For
instance, a decree, now usually dated to the very end of the last century
BC, testifies to the restoration of sacred property (shrines and sacred
precincts) and real estate (sacred and secular) which had wrongfully
fallen into private hands during the disorder of the previous decades; it
forbade any future alienation of territory, called for the cleansing of the
sanctuaries, established fresh rules for leasing of temple land, and
reinstated cult practice at the chosen centers. An accompanying list of 52
locations (of, originally, perhaps 80) reveals just how major this
undertaking was. The places mentioned were widely scattered as well,
with 19 in the Piraeus or Athens itself, 10 on Salamis, and 13 in the Attic
countryside.[31] This evidence warns us that simple parallels between
abandonment of the rural and the sacred landscape are unwise.

A more contextually sensitive interpretation sees the itinerant temples as yet another reflection of the self-conscious archaism typical of Roman Greece. Athens above all wished to surround Romans with pointed reminders of past greatness, to ensure that visitors could not fail to appreciate the presence of the Classical past. One satisfied customer was Lucius Cicero, who is said to have remarked to friends: "there is no end to it in this city; wherever you go you tread historic ground" (*De Finibus* 5.2.5). That the agora took on – as did Athens and indeed Greece as a whole – "something of the aspect of a museum" in one sense cannot be denied.[32] Artificially and artfully creating a showcase of Periclean art and architecture obviously helped to ensure due admiration and respect.

But important as such motivations may have been, another major impulse can be identified behind these wandering temples, for a plausible association can be made between the transplanted Attic structures and imperial cult activity. This link was perceived by earlier investigators, who agreed the agora was "an appropriate spot where the new cults of the Roman imperial family might plant themselves most visibly in the city," but its full significance in *promoting* the temple transfers was never explicitly stated.[33] The evidence for this suggested association is varied. Most interesting and convincing is Bowersock's correlation of the Ares temple with dynastic conflict in the Greek east, the succession struggles between Tiberius and Gaius Caesar. On a tour of the east in 2 BC, Gaius visited Athens where he was hailed as the "New Ares" – hence the appropriateness of the Acharnai temple. The itinerant temples seem to be part, therefore, of a much wider propaganda program throughout the empire, linking Gaius, the "New Mars," with the contemporaneous dedication of the Temple of Mars Ultor. Later, Athens was able in turn to honor the new "New Ares": Drusus, the son of Tiberius, the victor in the deadly dynastic squabbles.[34]

The imperial family was visible elsewhere in the agora as well. An annex to the Stoa of Zeus Eleutherios, dated to the first century BC, housed a double cult, one cella of which is known to have held images of the emperor and members of his family. Next door to the Stoa was the Temple of Apollo Patroos, a deity with whom the emperor Claudius was identified. An inscribed statue base discovered nearby revealed that Livia (in her guise as Julia Augusta) had been assimilated to Artemis Boulaia. The proximity of this find to the Southwest Temple has been used to argue that she was the dedicatee of the "new" temple; the evidence is suggestive, but also inconclusive. The choice of deities selected for such assimilation is significant for "by their epithets they emphasize the primary civic function of the Agora in the city's life," now brought within the imperial ambit.[35] In early imperial Achaia, the desire to house

74  Delphi, reconstruction of the monument of Aemilius Paullus

the imperial cult in fine fifth-century BC architecture is evident and understandable, but it must also be stressed that the imperial presence aimed to control the civic space.

### Annexing monuments

Reuse of monuments, as demonstrated by the itinerant temples, is actually part of a broader phenomenon and there exist other cases where structures or monuments were taken over and redirected to the glory of Rome. Different manifestations of such reuse can be identified. Commemorative markers, for example, were sometimes redeployed. Aemilius Paullus, after Pydna

> gave his army a chance to rest, while he himself went about to see Greece, occupying himself in ways alike honorable and human ... At Delphi, he saw a tall square pillar composed of white marble stones, on which a golden statue of Perseus was intended to stand, and gave orders that his own statue should be set there, for it was meet that the conquered should make room for their conquerors. (Plutarch, *Aemilius Paullus* 28)

Such commemoration won him, of course, a second symbolic victory over Perseus and an important memorial at a panhellenic sanctuary (fig. 74).

75 Athens, Monument of Agrippa outside the Propylaia on the acropolis

Another "second-hand" monument stood just outside the Propylaia on the Athenian acropolis. Originally an Attalid dedication, it was in turn made over to Antony and Cleopatra (as the New Dionysos and Isis), and then, fittingly enough, to their nemesis Agrippa, probably at the time of the dedication of his Odeion (fig. 75). Under the empire, a quadriga in the Athenian agora, probably dedicated originally to Attalos II in thanks for the eponymous stoa before which it stood, is known to have been rededicated to Tiberius, probably in the early years of his reign. Other forms of such ritual reuse include the annexation of pre-existing shrines to the imperial cult, in which the emperor either completely took over or "shared" the temple with the older gods. We have just seen examples of such processes at work in the Athenian agora, and other cases are numerous – from the Metroon at Olympia, to "an ancient sanctuary" in Megara where "in our day likenesses stand . . . of Roman emperors, and a bronze image is there of Artemis named Savior" (Pausanias 1.40.2). The addition of Hadrian to the line of Eponymous Heroes in the Athenian agora can be regarded as simply another aspect of this same type of activity.[36]

Reuse of monuments should not be thought of as simple "economizing," either on the part of the conquering power or of the subordinate communities. Rededication of monuments harnesses the power of the past to the purposes of the present – witness the bizarre spectacle of an emperor worshiped in a royal tomb some fifteen hundred years old. Monuments are durable objects, over time gathering new layers of meaning which subsume and subvert, without ever erasing, their original message. In the cases cited here, the new message conveyed is Rome's inevitable domination of past symbolic discourses. The impetus for this kind of re-employment came from both above and below: from the victorious side to announce its presence, from the conquered to assimilate it.

### The place of the emperor

Why was it so essential that the imperial cult be centrally located? Why, for example, were emperors not worshiped in fertile fields or on the tops of mountains? The association of the cult with various additional functions may provide one answer. Imperial sanctuaries became major landmarks within a city, offering an attractive and prestigious public setting for the display of other monuments, such as honorific statues. The use of imperial cult places, or indeed images of the emperor, as a type of legal sanctuary is also attested by one passage in the *Metamorphoses* of Apuleius. Lucius, in the form of an ass, appeals to a statue for help:

I tried to invoke the august name of Caesar; and I did actually keep crying out "O" clearly and loudly, but I could not utter the rest of the name of Caesar. (3.29)

Slaves, too, could be set free before an imperial image.[37] Apart from such functions, however, the networks of political and social relationships negotiated by the worship of emperors must be determined.

Most obvious, of course, is the connection between the external authorities and the provincial communities. Yet again, the status of Achaia as a *provincia inermis*, and its underdeveloped provincial bureaucracy, are important factors to consider. The imperial cult offered a peaceful means of representing the sovereignty of Rome to the population at large, and the effective communication of this message, especially to the increasingly urban-based provincials of Achaia, was best achieved in prominent urban locations.

This urban orientation also helped to express and foster ties between imperial and provincial governing élites – a "harmony of interest" which resulted in a local élite manifestly ready and eager to demonstrate loyalty to Rome. Association with the imperial cult proved a key element in the strategies of these urban-based groups. Imperial priesthoods were coveted offices for provincial magnates to hold. Civic festivals subsidized or revived by wealthy men often had an imperial component added to their celebration, as at the Megala Ptoia and Kaisareia in Boeotia refounded by Epaminondas of Akraiphia.[38] In addition, tendance of this "universal" cult allowed the formation of ties with élite families resident elsewhere in the province, and throughout the empire. While Price has undoubtedly demonstrated clearly that worship of the emperor was more than just an élite game, it is undeniable that provincial notables were most active, indeed highly competitive, in promoting and leading the cult. Such high-profile urban activity was important, not only to demonstrate an individual's or a city's loyalty to the emperor, but to broadcast the message to other cities as well. Price has rightly identified emperor worship as one outlet for the expression of rivalry over status and imperial largesse.

The cult became one of the major contexts in which the competitive spirit of the local élites was worked out; it formed one of a range of civic provisions by which the prestige of the city was measured; it shared in the dominance of Greek culture as a whole . . . Access to this culture was the crucial path for advancement both for individuals and for communities. Individuals could aspire to greater wealth and social standing, communities could hope to be freed from their position of financial and social dependence on a neighboring city. The existence of Roman rule intensified this dominance of Greek culture.[39]

The necessary emphasis on Greek culture also inevitably locates the imperial cult within the urban center.

Finally, the imperial cult served to articulate relationships within the provincial communities themselves. Important citizens led from the front, using the cult as one of many opportunities to bolster their position as guides to the populace at large. A strategic urban location not only ensured clarity about who was in charge, but also allowed some measure of control over the rest of the community, lest anyone prove unwilling to participate. Placing the imperial cult "downtown" guaranteed the necessary demonstrations of loyalty, while at the same time inculcating the need to respect the imperial presence.

Behind these various relationships that the cult could help to structure lie several that it could not. The imperial cult held no place in the countryside and played no part in mediating the relationships of man and nature in ensuring fertility or in defining the link between territory and city. Such concerns were left to other, more traditional deities in the sacred landscape. Instead, the orientation of the imperial cult demanded that it dominate the most populous and prominent space, the arena for civic political activity.

### RURAL CULTS

Since dramatic changes seem to have been taking place in the rural landscape of Achaia in the early imperial period, the fate of rural sanctuaries is an important topic for us to pursue. A wide variety of subjects could be addressed under this general heading: concerns about agricultural fertility, for example, or the definition of gender relationships, or the separation of "cultivated" and "wild" nature. Here, however, it is on the territorial and political implications of rural cult activity that the discussion will focus.

In the course of his travels, Pausanias periodically reports seeing abandoned sanctuaries and untended temples both in the cities and in the countryside.[40] This phenomenon has always caught the modern reader's eye; in his commentary Frazer wrote: "again and again he notices shrunken or ruined cities, deserted villages, roofless temples, shrines without images and pedestals without statues, faint vestiges of places that once had a name and played a part in history."[41] Reports of such forlorn locales readily encourage the by now familiar interpretations of Greece's parlous state under the empire, but – just as with the reports of "ruined" cities (pp. 145–7) – caution is required in accepting such testimony at face value. For instance, not all of these lost temples can be assigned unambiguously to the early imperial period. Commenting upon a burnt temple near Corinth, Pausanias himself says "there have, of course, been many wars carried on in Corinthian territory, and naturally houses and sanctuaries outside the wall have been fired" (2.5.5), before going on to attribute this particular destruction either to Pyrrhus, son of Achilles, or to lightning. Moreover, sanctuaries in all periods go in and out of use for numerous reasons, not all of which can be connected with major political or institutional change. Yet despite such uncertainties, an early imperial date for the relinquishment of at least some cult locations must be accepted as likely.

Understandably enough, abandoned temples have most often been correlated with the generally negative forces at work within the province: depopulation, warfare and the economic distress of cities. Plutarch's *De defectu oraculorum*, for example, claimed population decline as the cause for the passing of oracular sanctuaries (p. 26); but, as argued elsewhere in this book, this is a factor which provides at best only a partial explanation for developments in the Achaian landscape. Numerous individual cases of sanctuary loss can indeed be attributed to the rampant piracy or warfare of the last centuries BC, such as at Boeotian Haliartos or Alalkomenai; and as for the undoubted economic distress felt by many cities, Jost's research into Arcadian sanctuaries concluded that "the lack of regional vitality and the absence of active euergetism" was to blame. Pausanias certainly acknowledges all of these processes in the course of his travels, remarking for example that a colossal temple to Zeus Basileus was left half-finished "either because of its size or because of the long succession of wars" (9.39.4). To a very considerable extent, as Jost claims, the history of sanctuaries is indissolubly linked to each region's socioeconomic history.[42] But the formation of the Achaian sacred landscape cannot be reduced to a passive reflection of political and economic events: to concentrate exclusively on factors such as depopulation or warfare is to ignore the symbolic value holy places possessed – or, rather, came *not* to possess when pressures within Achaian society began to mount.

One way to proceed is to ask how and why certain rural sanctuaries *survived*, while others did not. It must be stressed that the number of these is quite considerable; a balanced reading of Pausanias' *Guide to Greece* reveals a dozen or more functioning rural shrines or hallowed places for every romantic ruin. In one startling comparison, for example, more rural cult places were identified by Pausanias in the area of the Southern Argolid than the total of settlement sites discovered by intensive survey (fig. 13). No simple and direct correlation exists between habitation in the countryside and levels of religious activity, or between the vitality of sanctuaries and rural population figures. Pausanias and rural survey between them build up the image of an early imperial landscape still densely inhabited by its daimons and its gods – if no longer necessarily by its people.

How can we account for the maintenance of these numerous rural cults? One underlying force at work must be the rampant archaism of Greek life under the empire, fostered as it was by Roman expectations. The notion that Greece was simply "a country learning to be a museum" has been rejected as the central fact about Roman Greece, but the conscious cultivation of the glorious past was patently in operation. With the right pedigree and suitable foundation myths, recognition and respect (as well as economic and political advantage) could be wheedled out of indulgent rulers (pp. 163–4). The readiness with which local guides (such as the Troizenians, "unrivaled glorifiers of their own country," Pausanias 2.30.5) greeted Pausanias and other "tourists" with tales of their past is another, humbler aspect of this same phenomenon. Yet the past was not simply a commodity useful to Greeks eager to pander to Roman cultural insecurities: history and myth (insofar as they were separable at all) were also used, as Pausanias himself demonstrates, to construct a present and to chart a future for Greeks within the Roman empire. Sacred places and images became crucially important in this endeavor, as a channel by which that past became immanent in the present. Preservation of revered sanctuaries would be one way to husband these resources; it is certainly true that the oldest and most venerable of Greek cults appear to survive best under the empire.[43]

Powerful as this motivation would be, it still begs too many questions to assume that cultic continuity, particularly of rural cults, was due solely to a calculated ossification of religious life, to a conscious desire to "look old." Other civic needs and ambitions too must be considered – for example, the question of territorial self-definition, which we have already identified as an important concern in early imperial Achaia (pp. 118–20, 152–4). Anthropologists and geographers have commented on processes of ritual demarcation, notably in the deliberate placement of a society's most sacred locations in peripheral positions, so as to mark both cultural and territorial claims. Active human participation, in the form of processions between the core of a community and its outlying territory, underscores this creation of a ritually defined social space. Particular manifestations of this phenomenon can take various forms; many cultures use ritual action of this sort to link local communities to the center of state power (in some cases a monarch). Skinner suggested that religious processions in the Chinese city were used to define the earthly domain of temple gods in an "annual reaffirmation of the community's territorial extent and a symbolic reinforcement of its town centred structure."[44] In all cases, the underlying intention is to bind a territory together and to instil in its inhabitants a sense of unity under the authority of a deity or monarch.

The most developed application of such a model for ancient Greece is de Polignac's study of the birth of the Greek city (p. 173). De Polignac discusses the placement of monumental extra-urban sanctuaries at notional *polis* boundaries and the accompanying "centrifugal" processions moving from *astu* to *chora*. His best-developed example is the Argive Heraion, located some 9 kilometers from the town of Argos (fig. 76). The parade of Argive citizens to and from this sanctuary fostered perceptions both of their city's territorial compass and of their own civic identity; the message conveyed to neighboring political entities is also unambiguous. If the birth of civic self-definition can thus be monitored, then rural cults and their celebration should have something to say about the later *polis* as well. Given the numerous changes in the political status and organization of the Greek city, what evidence exists for rural cults as territorial markers?

For Roman Crete, Callaghan has linked changes in cult celebration at the sanctuary of Kommos, as well as the abandonment of other Cretan

76  The Argive Heraion, with Argos in the distance across the Argive plain. This
photograph was probably taken around the time of the temple's excavation in
the 1890s.

sanctuaries, to the establishment of Gortys and Knossos as Roman
provincial centers, no longer conforming to a strict *"polis"* model.[45] In
Achaia, however, the continued presence of major rural sanctuaries
(examples from Pausanias are listed in table 9), where urban dwellers
went out to sacrifice and to hold festivals, clearly demonstrates that a
ritual "taking possession" of the land still featured significantly in civic
cult. Little can be said about the Argive Heraion, although it is worth
noting that the sanctuary received a series of impressive imperial
dedications, revealing that major rural cults could attract external
attention.[46] Clearer examples of town–country ritual interaction are
attested elsewhere. Of the *polis* of Phlius, found to be in apparent good
health in the early imperial period (p. 98, figs. 30–1), Pausanias said:
"Celeae is some five stades [1 km] distant from the city, and here they
celebrate the mysteries in honor of Demeter, not every year but every
fourth year" (2.14.1). From Lakonia, a procession linked the Helos
region to the Eleusinion at Sparta, an important civic sanctuary (albeit
some 7 kilometers from the city proper): "By the sea was a city Helos . . .
From this Helos, on stated days, they bring up to the sanctuary of the

203

Table 9. *Extra-urban sanctuaries named in Pausanias*

| Reference in Pausanias | City or kome | Distance from settlement | | God or goddess |
|---|---|---|---|---|
| | | Stades | Km | |
| 2.11.3 | Sikyon | 10 | 2 | Hera Protectress/Kore |
| 2.11.4 | Sikyon | 20 | 4 | Eumenides |
| 2.14.1 | Phlius | 5 | 1 | Demeter |
| 2.34.6–7, 12 | Hermione | ? | ? | Demeter Thermasia |
| 2.36.3 | Mases | ca. 270 | 54 | Apollo, Poseidon and Demeter |
| 3.10.7 | Karyai | ? | ? | Artemis and the Nymphs |
| 4.33.4 | Lakonia | ? | ? | Great Goddesses |
| 4.34.7 | Korone | 80 | 16 | Apollo |
| 6.26.1 | Elis | 8 | 1.6 | Dionysos |
| 7.22.5 | Pharai | 15 | 3 | Dioskouroi |
| 7.27.9 | Pellene | 60 | 12 | Mysian Demeter |
| 8.6.5 | Mantineia | 7 | 1.4 | Dionysos |
| 8.10.2 | Mantineia | 6 | 1.2 | Poseidon Hippios |
| 8.13.1 | Orchomenos/Mantineia | ? | ? | Artemis Hymnia |
| 8.15.4 | Pheneos | 15 | 3 | Demeter Thesmia |
| 8.15.5 | Pheneos | 15 | 3 | Pythian Apollo |
| 8.21.5 | Kleitor | 4 | 0.8 | Dioskouroi |
| 8.36.6 | Megalopolis | 5 | 1 | Demeter "in the Marsh" |
| 8.36.8 | Megalopolis | 40 | 8 | Despoina |
| 8.41.4–6 | Phigaleia | 12 | 2.4 | Eurynome |
| 8.41.4 | Phigaleia | 40 | 8 | Apollo |
| 8.53.11 | Tegea | 7 | 1.4 | Artemis |
| 9.19.5 | Mykalessos | ? | ? | Mykalessian Demeter |
| 9.23.6 | Akraiphia | 15 | 3 | Ptoion Apollo |
| 9.25.5 | Thebes | 32 | 6.5 | Kabeiroi |
| 9.38.6 | Orchomenos | 7 | 1.4 | Heracles |
| 10.32.12 | Tithorea | 70 | 14 | Asklepios Archagetes |
| 10.33.12 | Tithronion | ? | ? | Apollo |
| 10.34.7–8 | Elateia | 20 | 4 | Athena Kranaia |
| 10.37.1 | Antikyrrha | 2 | 0.4 | Artemis |

Eleusinion a wooden image of the Maid, daughter of Demeter" (3.20.6–7; fig. 77). The distance covered in this ceremony was some 35 kilometers. Or Phigaleia in Arcadia: "Phigaleia lies on high land that is for the most part precipitous, and the walls are built on the cliffs. But on the top the hill is level and flat. Here there is a sanctuary of Artemis Savior with a standing image of stone. From this sanctuary it is their custom to start their processions" (8.39.5). This Artemis shrine was located either in or just outside the town: the goal of these processions lay out in the chora, including the sanctuary of Apollo at Bassae (fig. 78) some 40 stades (8 km)

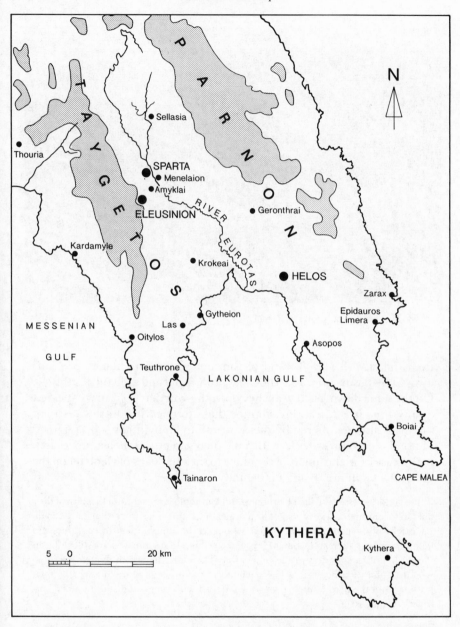

77 Map of Lakonia showing the relative positions of Sparta, the Eleusinion and Helos

78  The Temple of Apollo at Bassae

from the city (8.41.7–8), and of Eurynome, some 12 stades (2.4 km) away. This latter cult was: "a holy spot from of old and difficult of access... On the same day in each year they open the sanctuary of Eurynome, but at any time it is a transgression for them to open it. On this occasion sacrifices also are offered by the state and by individuals" (8.41.4–6).[47] Pausanias even provides us with a detailed vignette of such a procession, in this case from the town of Hermione to the sanctuary of Demeter on the Pron, the mountain rising up behind the city.

[T]he goddess herself is called Chthonia, and Chthonia is the name of the festival they hold in the summer of every year. The manner of it is this. The procession is headed by the priests of the gods and by all those who hold the annual magistracies; these are followed by both men and women. It is now a custom that some who are still children should honor the goddess in the procession. These are dressed in white, and wear wreaths upon their heads . . . Those who form the procession are followed by men leading from the herd a full-grown cow, fastened with ropes, and still untamed and frisky. (2.35.5–6)

The order of precedence followed here will be considered again below.

On one level, such behavior reveals a continuing civic commitment to rural cults, and thus to the countryside. Demeter and Dionysos, gods of fertility, together with the *kourotrophes* Artemis and Apollo, dominate

Table 10. *Active cults in defunct cities or* komai *observed by Pausanias*

| Reference | Abandoned settlement | God or goddess |
|---|---|---|
| 2.25.6 | Orneai | Artemis/all gods |
| 2.38.2 | Nauplion | Poseidon |
| 3.20.3 | Bryseai | Dionysos |
| 3.20.6–7 | Helos | Kore |
| 3.22.13 | Etis | Asklepios and Hygeia |
| 3.24.1 | Zarax | Apollo |
| 3.25.9 | Hippola | Athena Hippolaitis |
| 8.25.1 | Kaous | Asklepios Kaous |
| 8.28.1 | Gortys | unnamed |
| 8.29.1 | Trapezos | Great Goddesses |
| 8.29.5 | Basilis | Eleusinian Demeter |
| 8.35.7 | Zoetia | Demeter and Artemis |
| 8.36.7 | Peraitheos | Pan |
| 8.36.7 | Lykoa | Artemis Lykoan |
| 8.44.2 | Oresthasion | Artemis |
| 9.8.1 | Potniai | Demeter and Kore |
| 9.19.6–8 | Aulis | Artemis |
| 9.33.1,3 | Haliartos | Praxidikai |

Pausanias' account of extra-urban sanctuaries. The place of these deities in the *chora* was still considered essential to the continued functioning of *polis* society. In other words, the countryside retained its symbolic value in this period, not becoming a zone to exploit, then ignore. As far as town–country relationships were concerned, sanctuaries in the early imperial period worked to preserve the union of the *polis*, acting as a bond that endured long after many other traditional forces (e.g. widespread landholding, hoplite military service, rural residence) had weakened (pp. 117–18). Thanks in part to these ritual ties, the final disruption of that relationship, and the end of the *polis* as a coherent territorial unit, do not belong to the period studied here.

When we examine the persistence of rural cults, a separate and rather odd pattern emerges. Pausanias periodically informs his readers that a city or a village is defunct, "in ruins," yet then goes on to describe an apparently still functioning sanctuary (or sanctuaries) within it (table 10). The phenomenon of failed cities, and underlying factors for this development, have already been analyzed in chapter 4. Yet what might explain these suddenly "rural" sanctuaries – cults still working in an abandoned town? In some cases, the degree of the town's decrepitude may simply be exaggerated. Archaeological data, or contradictory testimony within the *Guide* itself, occasionally suggest that a settlement sufficient to service a shrine did exist. For example, of the "ruins" of the city of Onchestos in Boeotia, Pausanias writes, "In my day there remained a temple and image of Onchestian Poseidon, and the grove which Homer too praised" (9.26.5), yet archaeological survey evidence has shown that there existed a continued, if much attenuated, settlement there.[48] In some cases, Pausanias may well have overemphasized the decline of communities, perhaps because they were now dependent upon more successful centers. Not all examples of this phenomenon, however, can be explained away like this. As original host cities simply faded away – or were more violently destroyed – neighboring towns, one can imagine, may have taken over responsibility for their sacred places. Such annexations may have been made easier if inhabitants of the declining town moved to the successful center, but that would not be a necessary condition for this process. If this were so, one net effect would be the extension of a city's ritual ties across the landscape. Border disputes were frequent and intense in this period, and sacred places participated actively in these conflicts (pp. 119–20). Sanctuary acquisition and upkeep could also expand a city's existing boundaries by redefining the extent of its territorial sway.[49]

As with border disputes generally, this proposed "ritual expansion" may in some cases reflect actual economic pressures for growth, such as the need for additional land or for a wider tax catchment area. But land hunger cannot be the only valid explanation: survey evidence demonstrates all too clearly that land already possessed was often not utilized to its full capacity. Pragmatic explanations alone do not suffice here, any more than they fully account for the frequency of boundary quarrels. A link is clear between such disputes and continual arguments about status in the Greek east; this type of competition between cities (or between civic élites) was deemed acceptable by the imperial authorities. The adoption of rural cults forms part of this same strategy. Taking possession of an endangered sanctuary allowed an inflated claim to territory (whether it was actually exploited or not) and to prestige. Such bold moves to claim additional land and consequence offered one way to avert the evils of civic weakness or of dependence upon another community. Maintenance of rural cults can thus be deemed another strategy of civic competition and civic survival.

This interpretation, together with the role of deliberate archaism in cult maintenance, implies that the rural cults most likely to endure would be those of relatively high status. Given the list of deserted temples mentioned by Pausanias, it seems likely that only one of several cults might be chosen for preservation. Archaeology, again, can be of some help here. The sample of survey evidence is small, but there are a few

79 "Temple of Nemean Jupiter," the panhellenic sanctuary of Zeus at Nemea in a
view published in Baron Otto Magnus von Stackelberg, *La Grèce, vues pittoresques
et topographiques* (1834). Mount Phoukas (ancient Apesas) stands in the
background to the right; the ash altar of Zeus Apesios lies atop Phoukas.

cases where minor local cults (usually identified on the basis of worked
blocks, fine pottery or votive finds) sputter out of use during this period.
Two small rural shrines from the Nemea Valley Archaeological Project
are typical examples. At both Sites 204 and 306 – the latter an ash altar to
Zeus Apesios on top of Mount Apesas – Classical and Hellenistic, but not
Roman material, was discovered (fig. 79). In Attica, Fowden reviews
several minor cult sites (such as the Cave of Pan at Vari and the cult of
Zeus on Mount Hymettos) that go out of use in later Classical or
Hellenistic times, only to be "revived" in the Late Roman period.[50] The
existence of these minor, local shrines emphasizes the ubiquity of Greek
cult places, and our still limited knowledge of their distribution and
diachronic history. Sanctuaries such as these would probably have been
dependent on local people, or an individual proprietor, or perhaps a
small rural community – in other words, the very people who were now
abandoning rural residence. Although the evidence remains impression-
istic, the early imperial period seems to have been a critical period for
small cults in the countryside, and this was evidently the level of cult
activity and organization most severely affected by the thoroughgoing
changes in the rural landscape.

In Italy, agricultural and residential restructuring had an obvious
impact on the formation of the sacred landscape. Changes in cult

participants and votive practices at sanctuaries in Southern Etruria and Latium have been attributed by Blagg to the rise of villa estates and the dispossession of the peasantry. In central Italy, a loss of small rural shrines similar to that hypothesized for Achaia was noted by Frederiksen, who attributed the development to a centralization of population and financial support, in turn encouraging spending and devotion at town-based cults. Crawford linked this disappearance of rural shrines (as well as changes in funeral practices) to a radical realignment of religious practices and loyalties "in a new framework, that of urban, Roman Italy".[51] The nature of that realignment in Achaia remains to be further explored. The fact that those cults which appear to endure most consistently in the countryside are the major, "state-run" sanctuaries indicates something of the agency behind cult maintenance.

### THE CONSTRUCTION OF THE SACRED LANDSCAPE

In this landscape, urban-based élites appear as the chief arbiters of stability or change. Epigraphic evidence reveals wealthy *euergetai* paying for temple upkeep, holding priesthoods, financing festivals, reviving defunct celebrations, and restoring rural sanctuaries. Benefactions to various sanctuaries or festivals paid for by individuals such as Herodes Atticus or Epaminondas of Akraiphia spring instantly to mind, but these are only the most obvious cases. Such generosity led Jost to identify the early imperial era as an active period of sanctuary restoration in Arcadia. Other signs of élite pre-eminence in the religious sphere are apparent in the proliferation of honorific statues, greater disparity in the value of individual offerings, and seating arrangements at games or plays.[52] The construction of the sacred landscape was inevitably affected by the composition of the group financing and managing cult activity.

A strong élite impetus behind the celebration of the imperial cult has been remarked (pp. 198–9), but motives for their concern with more traditional sanctuaries can also be identified. Shared interests in a particular cult, for example, facilitated closer connections between important families (a high priority during this period), as is demonstrated clearly at Lykosoura, a sanctuary dedicated to Despoina (the "Mistress") in the *chora* of Megalopolis (fig. 80). Dedications are found here from many prominent Achaian families, probably linked to the sanctuary by the Euryclids, a Spartan family apparently holding land in the Megalopolis area; the families involved include the Voluseni of Sparta, known in turn to have ties to families in Athens and Epidauros, as well as the Athenian Philopappos. The latter's appearance as worshiper at a relatively rural Arcadian sanctuary is somewhat surprising, until we

80 Lykosoura, Sanctuary of Despoina

recall his relationship to the Euryclid family. Encouragement of, and participation in, major cults offered another link in the developing aristocratic network in the Greek east.[53]

Economic benefits must also have entered élite calculations, for large and successful sanctuaries or agonistic celebrations attracted tourists and revenues. A clustering of Roman farms found by the Lakonia survey has been related to an increased interest in transporting agricultural goods to the city of Sparta, a major agonistic center in the empire: "the regular influxes of visitors attracted by the cycle of civic festivals provided local producers with an additional market for their surplus, fluctuating but predictable."[54] For cities with more than one set of important games, or for an important panhellenic sanctuary, the impact of such temporary but recurrent markets was no doubt commensurately greater: large landowners in the area would benefit proportionately, as would the standing of the community as a whole. The wealth drawn in by festivals helped to ensure the preservation and enrichment of the sanctuaries, and the renown won by local magnates for their part in cult organization encouraged their continued interest.

Behind all such considerations, however, there often lay a basic loyalty to the interests of the native *polis* and a deep desire to sustain it. Elite families led the way in the competitive cut and thrust of inter-city relations of the period, and their support for select rural sanctuaries thus acted as one strategy to maintain civic traditions or to boost the chances of civic survival. In some instances, however, a more direct personal or familial motivation can be detected. So, for example, in the case of the Lakonian cult of Demeter and Kore at Helos (fig. 77), more than one prominent Spartan family may have owned land in the area; hereditary priests of the cult included the family of the Roman senator Brasidas.[55] Moreover, the dominance of wealthy benefactors in cult organization demands a re-evaluation of the message conveyed by such celebrations, especially the regularly held processions out to the countryside. They certainly continued to play an important role in bonding town and country, and as a communal force unifying elements within the city, but such rituals must now have taken on an added layer of significance. Pausanias' ordering of the Hermione procession – priests, magistrates, men, women, children – describes a predictable and probably standard arrangement. Yet continuity of ritual form does not guarantee continuity in content: the role played by those individuals at the head of procession, all drawn from the restricted cadre of families providing civic magistrates and priests, was transformed during the early imperial period. As with the imperial cult, the celebrations gave such individuals the opportunity to shine, leading processions they often organized to sanctuaries they had themselves in many cases subsidized. Such an overt association of élite families with territorial definition strengthened their grasp upon civic ideology. While these rituals continued to convey a range of meanings to their participants, their performance now worked to construct and to display distinctions within the community.

### THE PLACE OF CULT

Displacement or dislocation of cult symbolically violates "natural" territorial boundaries and loyalties; such interventions occurred where Rome's hand fell most heavily or its favor most freely. Centralized cult, particularly that associated with the worship of emperors, mediated relationships between external and internal authorities, as well as fostering a new social order within subordinate communities. Rural cult played many roles, not least in keeping the age-old bond of town and country from tension and disintegration. Adoption of endangered cults allowed for ritual competition between cities and the expansion of territorial claims. Although many forces were at work here, one inescapable trend is the growing influence of prominent and wealthy families, guided by their own particular goals and concerns, upon the formation of the sacred landscape.

These three broad categories of cult location express, in one form or another, the shifting distribution of social power. When taken together, there begin to emerge common or complementary patterns like those already detected in the other landscapes we have examined. The presence of the imperial authority (however supposedly "invisible") easily dominates the local scene. Competition for resources among cities, especially on the part of civic élites, is also highlighted. New social divisions and affiliations within the province as a whole, as well as within individual communities, were promoted through cult's deliberate placement. Where sanctuaries appeared and, equally, where they did not, which endured and which did not – such patterns reveal new forces at work within this province. Nor does the record of Achaian cult activity passively mirror these changes; the organization of sacred space acted to create and perpetuate the new social environment as well.

Many other opportunities exist for probing the nature of religious behavior in Roman Greece. The ritual environment of a single city could be analyzed more fully; or perhaps two very different cities (a Corinth, say, and a Panopeus) might be compared. A single sanctuary, or class of sanctuaries, has the potential to provide useful insight on developments in cult organization and variability in votive offerings. The institution or abandonment of specific rituals can also prove revealing.[56] On cultic geography specifically, the distribution of sacred places has been studied with profit in other provincial landscapes: Britain, for example, displays an intriguing mixture of native traditions and assimilation to the Roman presence. Such analyses promise a fruitful subject for cross-provincial comparisons.[57]

Another area deserving fuller exploration is that of religious resistance. In other empires, religion often becomes a field for bitter conflict, as native populations are pressed to convert or indigenous belief structures are forced "underground." In the Roman province of Africa, some scholars have claimed that resistance was significant, given the persistence of local deities and cultic continuity. On such criteria, Greece was a positive hotbed of dissatisfaction, yet considering the similar Roman pantheon and the respectful imperial treatment of Greek deities, such an argument is clearly not right. The simple equation "of survival with resistance cannot be accepted ... the Romans were on the whole tolerant of local cults as long as they did not become a focus of disturbance and rebellion." If opposition did appear in the provinces, spearheaded through religious spokesmen, severe steps were taken to root it out, as happened with the Druids in Britain or the Jewish revolts.[58] No such events in Achaia suggest that direct external intervention of this sort was necessary; indeed, given the social composition of the province's priesthoods, little opportunity existed for any such "alternative" religious authority to develop. Yet it can still be argued that symbolic means were used to express disapproval of, and resistance to, Roman rule in Achaia.

Periodic eruptions of anti-Roman feeling are known from the province (p. 16), not surprisingly mainly in the early years of the empire (although some flared up well into the second century AD). Athens especially experienced several outbursts of open antipathy to Rome, serious enough to call down the anger of Augustus.

He [Augustus] honored the Lakedaimonians by giving them Kythera and attending their public mess, because Livia, when she fled from Italy with her husband and son had spent some time there. But from the Athenians he took away Aigina and Eretria, from which they received tribute, because, as some say, they had espoused the cause of Antony; and he furthermore forbade them to make anyone a citizen for money. And it seemed to them that the thing which had happened to the statue of Athena was responsible for his misfortune; for this statue on the Acropolis, which was placed to face the east, had turned around to the west and spat blood. (Cassius Dio 54.7.2–3)

"Blood" spattered on a cult image "to give the impression that Athena, the protectress and patron goddess of Athens, had spat blood at Rome," as Hoff puts it, illustrates dramatically the only potent weapons available to the Greeks: their religion and the revered history of their culture. Other more subtle signs of disobedience or subversion of authority could be sought in odd juxtapositions of images or rituals, exploring the possibility of ambivalence or division within the society.[59]

A more deep-rooted and constant form of "resistance," however, is expressed through cultic geography. Despite extreme vulnerability to external pressures, Greek cities clearly wished to control and to shape their own territorial and social organization, as articulated through the use of sacred space. If Pausanias offers, as Elsner suggests, "a guide to the formation of Greek religious identity as a resistance to the realities of Roman rule," this tension is visible in the sacred landscape as well. Without violent measures or seeking the overthrow of Roman control, the mute endurance of certain sanctuaries guaranteed that local and traditional priorities continued to be served. On the other hand, different aspects of the sacred landscape were manifestly working to promote the transition to Roman rule, encouraging new loyalties and the acceptance of a new social order. The sacred landscape, then, was no simple construct, but a complex and dynamic reaction to imperial incorporation. What emerges with greatest clarity is the active role played by this landscape in mediating the Greek response to Roman domination, in defining that response, and in transmitting it to subsequent generations.

# 6

# Greece within the empire

Ancient of days! august Athena! where,
Where are thy men of might? thy grand in soul?
Gone – glimmering through the dream of things that were:
First in the race that led to Glory's goal,
They won, and pass'd away – is this the whole?
A schoolboy's tale, the wonder of an hour!
The warrior's weapon and the sophist's stole
Are sought in vain, and o'er each mouldering tower,
Dim with the mist of years, gray flits the shade of power.
                    (Lord Byron, "Childe Harold's Pilgrimage," II.ii)

No doubt the memories of Roman, Byzantine and Frankish rule are less pleasing than the memories of the old Athenian commonwealth. But all alike are parts of the history of Athens, of Greece, of the world. The historian can have no sympathy with the mere classical pedant who thinks only of the events of a few favoured ages. In the wider view of œcumenical history, the lessons of one age may be more attractive, more instructive than those of another: but no age is without its lesson. All are alike parts of the great whole: of none are the material witnesses to be recklessly swept away. (Edward Freeman, *Historical Essays* [1879], 285, quoted in McNeal [1991], 49)

We began this book with two images of Roman Greece: one of a people largely untouched by Roman domination, the other of a country in decline. The first can be rejected, since we have examined a variety of responses to imperial control, experienced at all levels of provincial society, each of the different sorts of "landscape" defined in this study revealing some measure of profound change. The rural landscape was transformed through the development of a new system of landholding, one that favored the wealthier elements in Achaian society, and by corresponding modifications of the nature and intensity of agricultural exploitation. Change in the countryside contributed to a redistribution of people within the civic landscape of the *polis*; a preference for nucleated residence emerged as one potential solution to the challenges posed by

215

increasing economic pressures and greater social polarities, factors which had become an entrenched part of provincial life. The number and distribution of cities across the province as a whole were also affected by Greece's newly peripheral position within the empire, and especially by the need to provide an administrative organization acceptable to external authority. The notion of population decline (once thought to be *the* characteristic feature of this period) has been examined and to a certain extent confirmed. We have argued throughout that the causes underlying this demographic trend – usually assumed to be some combination of endemic warfare and moral decadence – need expanding so as to include factors such as the redistribution of land and the preference for residence within larger communities. Moreover, re-evaluation of the magnitude of the trend serves to limit its ultimate role in dictating the course of provincial history. Finally, the sacred landscape, while mirroring many of the social and economic developments observed in other spheres of activity, worked to preserve a sense of Hellenic identity, yet at the same time sought to reconcile Greek provincials to the realities of their new state. This reinterpretation of Greek society under Roman rule emerges very much as a product of the types of data employed. Archaeological evidence, especially the results of a growing number of surface survey projects, provides an essential complement to the more usual sources for the period, and allows fresh insights into the behavior of the "people without history."

If the image of a "static" Greek society can thus be dismissed easily, it is far more difficult to treat the charge of *decline*. Of course, the accusation of "decadence" can be identified as largely an external reading, forced upon the Greeks in order to explain their "fall" from excellence and to define them in opposition to their conquerors, both ancient and modern (pp. 3, 31–2). To divide history into "good" and "bad" epochs, or periods of "prosperity" and "decline" – a surprisingly common practice among ancient historians and archaeologists – has increasingly come to be regarded as indefensible and counter-productive, given the moral baggage that inevitably accompanies such labels. Yet for all that, is there not some element of truth in the notion of Roman Greece as a "backwater"? In the Roman scheme of things, Achaia assumed the role of a minor province, redeemed only by its antique reputation and the prestige of certain of its inhabitants. With the exception of a few of its leading towns, the land did not flourish to the extent enjoyed by certain other eastern provinces such as Asia. Would it not be fair to admit that the province as a whole (if not some of her leading citizens) really did slip quietly into the background of important events and decisions taking place elsewhere?

If the terms "backwater" or "museum" might seem justified from the point of view of the conqueror and the dictates of political history, where I would disagree is in assigning responsibility for this development. Whereas internal fractiousness and spiritual exhaustion have previously been blamed, we can now see more clearly that conditions in the province were molded by the constant working of imperial influences, both direct and indirect. Decisive factors – new economic priorities, the altered social order, the Roman desire to stabilize the country – all emanated from imperial and local responses to Greece's annexation. The position of Achaia *vis-à-vis* other provinces within the empire, to be considered further below, is another key element in provincial history (pp. 220–4). Viewing the empire within a core–periphery framework emphasizes this point by stressing that a provincial, peripheral society can never be analyzed outside of the system of domination in which it is set. The direct and indirect effects of imperial incorporation reached deep within Greek society, to a degree not previously acknowledged, transforming not only the way in which people lived and interacted with each other, but also their civic image and self-perceptions, their reading of their past, and their plans for a future.

## TRADITIONAL AND ALTERNATIVE CHRONOLOGIES

The study of Greek history normally follows a course charted by the documentary sources, in which periods are defined chiefly by events and personalities – battles, regnal years, the deaths of individuals. Although such standard periodizations are widely acknowledged as being essentially arbitrary, for the practical purposes of historical analysis some divisions of this sort are necessary, and the written sources long provided the only basis available for their construction. But the new availability of archaeological survey data I suggest now makes possible, and indeed necessitates, the adoption of substantially different sorts of chronological frameworks which draw instead on the evidence of settlement and land-use patterns. Such a framework is determined by social and economic factors lying deep in society, working at what proponents of the *Annales* school would recognize as the level of *conjoncture*. The Classical, Hellenistic and Roman periods offer one very good example of the development of such an "alternative" chronology. Typically, the division between the Classical and Hellenistic epochs is recognized as the battle of Chaeronea or the death of Alexander (i.e. roughly the last quarter of the fourth century BC), while in terms of "event-oriented" history, the break between the Hellenistic and the Roman period is taken to be the battle of Actium. Yet examined from the vantage point of the survey archaeologist, such distinctions as these appear largely irrelevant. Instead, the Classical and Early Hellenistic periods (down to the third/ second century BC) clearly "belong together," as do the later Hellenistic and Early Roman epochs, while the Late Roman era appears as an entirely different matter again. It becomes awkward to speak of a unified "Hellenistic" or "Roman" period in Greece: far too many changes are masked by such a treatment. Alternative chronologies of this sort, it must be stressed, are not intended to replace more traditional periodizations; the nature of a particular historical or archaeological study must be allowed to dictate the appropriate framework. But it is necessary to recognize that a choice exists between different and equally valid ways in which to order information and structure analysis.

The focus of this book – the early imperial period – springs from just such a revisionist approach. It has been argued throughout that Roman influence left its mark upon Greek society long before Greece's official incorporation in the empire. Rome was not, however, the only external force at work in the region in the later Hellenistic era, and it is fair to ask what role might have been played by Hellenistic monarchs in the processes we have been considering. Greek interaction (as allies, as enemies, or as the recipients of royal largesse) with eastern kingdoms – the Antigonid dynasty of Macedon, the Ptolemaic of Egypt, the Seleucid of Asia – is well attested. To a considerable extent, the intervention of such powers in Greek affairs fostered many of the same trends as did the actions of Roman authorities: the bolstering of oligarchic regimes, accumulation of landed property, territorial realignments, the growth of league institutions. To distinguish exactly who precipitated which example of each particular development is an impossible task, at least at the level of analysis adopted here. In one sense, Hellenistic monarchs and the Roman state represented the same thing to the cities and leagues of Greece: they were territorially extensive, unified, and more powerful entities working their will on a vulnerable collection of smaller individual political units. Responsibility for initiating the changes visible between the Classical/Early Hellenistic and early imperial period should be assigned to a range of external influences, with Rome as the dominant element, and, of course, the ultimate victor.

A very clear disjunction also separates the early imperial period from its successor. Certainly, wherever the survey evidence is precise enough to tell, Achaia looked very different in Late Roman times. As we have seen, the Late Roman period (generally defined as beginning in the fourth and ending in the seventh century AD) witnessed a high degree of dispersed settlement in the countryside, which could be taken as evidence for a lessening interest in nucleated residence as an economic and social strategy, for an increasing involvement in intensive agricultural production, and – possibly – for demographic growth. A decline in the number of functional urban centers is another likely development of this epoch (pp. 147–8). No detailed attempt will be made to account for this transformation, but a few suggestions may be advanced here, partly on the basis of the extant documentary sources, and partly by comparing Late Roman patterns with our interpretation of conditions in the preceding era.

The third century has, of course, long been regarded as a vital turning point in the social and economic history of the Roman empire. We can begin with the nature of tribute demands, already identified as one major element in strategies of imperial control and of provincial response (pp. 19–24). In the Late Roman period, levels of taxation are assumed to have risen, increasing the financial pressures felt by provincials everywhere. In addition, it is believed that there was a turn from taxation in cash to taxation in kind (although admittedly the degree of this shift and its geographical progression remain unclear). Nonetheless, an inscription from Megara of AD 401/2 reveals something of the mechanics behind this development in Greece:

It was arranged among the Greek cities meeting with common intent in the metropolis of Corinth before the *vir clarissimus* and the most magnificent proconsul Claudius Varius, how much each city was required to release into the offices of the *horreorum praepositi* [officials in charge of the state granaries], the cities of Boeotia, Euboea and Aetolia delivering to the (granaries) at Scarphia, the Peloponnesian (cities) to those of Corinth. (*IG* VII 24, translation by Antony Spawforth)

Several implications for Achaian provincial society arguably follow from these developments. Communities would bear an increasing financial burden; any free cities that had endured until the third century would now, for the first time, feel the pressures of regular and direct taxation (p. 22, fig. 5). One strong motivation for nucleated residence (the need to generate income for cash taxes) was lost, and new economic strategies can be perceived in the repopulation of the Late Roman rural landscape. For Greece, demands in kind would for the most part, as the inscription above suggests, have to be met with agricultural goods; intensification of cultivation, and the return to marginal lands abandoned in the preceding period, becomes a predictable development. Furthermore, it is interesting that coastal site locations are seen to develop at this time (noted, for example, in Melos, Methana, Phokis and the Southern Argolid), presumably as staging points for the transport of produce or for other commercial activities.[1]

The increasing burdens of the Late Roman era likewise affected the behavior of native *decuriones*, who are thought to have shied away more and more from shouldering magistracies and liturgies; local obligations once undertaken with enthusiasm now had to be made compulsory. In order to survive, the early imperial city had relied heavily upon the willing contribution of such individuals; but with the lack of such support a decline in the number of functioning cities is hardly surprising. Even where urban units endured, the lack of élite expenditure – for instance, on building, patronage, food distributions – meant that incentives for residence within them declined even further.[2] Other alterations in the social structure of the period – the era of the *vir clarissimus* – also help to account for the very different landscapes of Late Roman Greece. Harsher distinctions emerged in social and legal privileges and power, with a widening gulf between *honestiores* and *humiliores*. Rural residence, to allow intensive cultivation and to increase agricultural production, would be the pattern preferred by local landlords, civic leaders and imperial authorities. Forcibly attaching cultivators (*coloni*) to the land, through stricter contractual agreements or even coercion, served the dominant interests of the society. In the early imperial period, it was argued that individuals retained a certain independence in their choice of residence, a flexibility which perhaps was denied to them in the later epoch. This ability to "fix" people in space is characteristic of a more authoritarian, feudal mode of exploitation (pp. 114–15).

Among other possible factors involved in the transformation between the early and late empire in Achaia there should certainly be included the selection of Constantinople as an imperial capital in the fourth century, and thus the creation of a new eastern axis of exchange and communication. Greece conceivably could have become a more important resource for the eastern Roman world than had previously been the case, though the archaeological trade studies necessary to verify such a suggestion are sadly lacking.[3] Finally, although the passage of time itself cannot effect change, the sheer duration of Roman rule in this region is worth considering. By the third century AD, Greece had been under formal (let alone informal) Roman control for some two hundred years, decades longer than the North American colonies survived under British dominion, and a century or so longer than the entire lifespan of the Aztec empire. Empires are dynamic, with continual internal shifts and readjustments inevitably calling forth change within all their constituent elements.

## ROMAN PROVINCIAL DIVERSITY

If empires are dynamic structures, they are also, in almost every case, very diverse in their make-up. Instead of viewing any imperial system as a unitary phenomenon, a more patchwork composition would be closer to the truth. A lack of uniformity in response to conquest and annexation is a recurrent feature in cross-cultural studies, which recognize the existence of "a profound gradation of conditions and policies" across an empire.[4] In the Roman empire, for example, differences between east and west are often highlighted. One attempt to go beyond such relatively crude distinctions appears in debates about the concepts of development and underdevelopment within the empire. In these arguments, some provinces (such as Gaul) are believed to have advanced, while others (such as Africa) were depressed and retarded, each region's behavior being dependent upon the specific nature of Roman exploitation and the nature of the imperial administrative infrastructure. Objections to such neo-Marxist analyses have been numerous, centering on their "over-modernizing" tone and their poor adaptation from contemporary Third World developmental theory. The quest for an understanding of provincial variability in these terms appears dubious, for in the most basic sense the entire Roman economy was underdeveloped – that is, the mass of the population lived (and had always done so) at or near subsistence level.[5]

Wrongheaded as such inquiries may be in specific details, they at least serve to stimulate the idea of provinces developing in different ways, at different speeds, and subject above all to a specific history of interaction with the ruling power. The physical character and location of each province also is a major determinant of its imperial fate. In recent years, two related conceptualizations of the Roman empire have been put forward, both with individual provinces assigned differing roles. Hopkins envisages three spheres of activity: (i) the cosseted core zone of Italy and Rome, (ii) an inner ring of relatively rich tax-exporting provinces, and (iii) an outer ring of demanding frontier provinces. Garnsey and Saller likewise propose a threefold division, based on the part each province played in supplying the empire's needs: the provision of wheat to Rome, of necessities to the army, and of cash for soldiers and officials. Achaia can be placed in that last category, within the "inner ring" of Hopkins. Both formulations stress the relationships which connected a diverse collection of provinces and their interdependent role within the imperial system.[6]

This diversity is reflected in the heterogeneity of responses to Roman domination to be seen in the local agrarian economies absorbed within the empire. As more and more detailed studies of rural conditions in different provincial societies become available, a wide range of patterns has emerged in land tenure systems and in levels of exploitation – some marked by sharp discontinuity with pre-Roman conditions, others by a relatively stable state of affairs. In those areas identified as surplus-producing regions, marked intensification of production is indeed often seen to take place with the inception of Roman control. Survey evidence testifies to just such a development, for example, in Baetica and in Tripolitania, areas that were both major olive-oil producers and exporters under the early empire. In the Guadalquivir Valley in Baetica, where subsistence agriculture had previously been the norm, villa and farm numbers increased dramatically in the early first century AD, and the size of individual estates is thought to have grown at this time as well. In Libya, semi-nomadic pastoralism of the pre-Roman era gave way to a dramatic explosion in sedentary living and agricultural activity, demanding, among other things, the evolution of sophisticated means of water control. In a sharp break with previous tradition, private land ownership was also encouraged by Roman authorities, cutting across former patterns of tribal ownership.[7]

In the northern frontier provinces, the need to supply the Roman troops stationed in the vicinity often generated a second "army" of producers. As Garnsey and Saller have noted, however, this was not always a spontaneous development. Direct imperial intervention was sometimes necessary, in order to restructure an area's rural organization to meet specific military needs. One example of this has been claimed in the forced settlement of Dobrogea in Lower Moesia during the second and third centuries AD. Other parts of this province, on the other hand, seem little affected by the Roman presence. In the neighboring, less exposed province of Dalmatia, the Roman period (100 BC–AD 400) witnessed a significant rise in agricultural exploitation, marked especially by the expansion of cultivated land, yet an underlying continuity has nonetheless been detected between pre- and post-conquest land management and settlement. By comparison, in Britain, no fundamental change in agricultural practice has been associated with the time of the Roman invasion; indigenous cultivation systems were sufficiently productive to accommodate the additional pressures of taxation. Only in the Late Roman era was there a "flowering of the countryside" with an increase in the number of villas and a diversification of agricultural production. The growth of estate sizes, the movement of *decuriones* to the countryside and the growing pressures of Late Roman taxation are thought to have underwritten this phenomenon.[8] Even this quick examination of a mere handful of regional studies emphasizes the variety of rural landscapes that could be found in different parts of the empire, each formed by the interaction of indigenous social and economic conditions with the specific demands of the imperial power.[9]

For all this heterogeneity in local adaptation and response, however, an overall trend toward increased agricultural production seems to be characteristic of many parts of the empire, a development fostered not only by tributary demands, but by the *pax Romana*.[10] While this study has raised a number of objections to the standard picture of Achaian "decline," it does not automatically follow that Greece was therefore like other parts of the Roman empire in the degree of its intensification. To account for this phenomenon, it is helpful to place Greece within its imperial context. Of foremost importance, no doubt, is the province's location and its cocooned position sheltered from the frontiers of the empire (fig. 1), while other significant factors include such physical characteristics of the province as its small size and limited agricultural potential. Achaia could never serve as an imperial "breadbasket," as comparison with more fertile provinces (such as Egypt or Baetica) makes glaringly obvious. During the Principate, therefore, underproduction in the region never became a matter for burning imperial concern. The internal structure of the province also affected its economic development: for instance, the number of early imperial "free cities" reduced external pressures upon a not inconsiderable portion of the province. Perhaps most important of all, it is clear that imperial strategies in Achaia depended upon the cooperation of local power networks. Decisions taken by the local populations, above all by indigenous élite families, appear largely to have dictated the degree and nature of land use under the empire. The maximization of economic returns from the province, which clearly would have been possible through more active and systematic intervention (as seen in Late Roman times), simply was not an objective during the early empire. Imperial priorities in this minor province were stability and acceptable taxation returns, both ensured through the encouragement of local élite groups.

While recognizing a "gradation of conditions and policies" within the Roman empire, broader categories of provincial behavior can also be identified to some purpose. One such pattern is suggested in John Patterson's study of Samnium and Lycia, two highland areas blessed with only a limited amount of fertile land and lying, for the most part, "off the beaten track" of the empire. In these regions, Patterson has identified three structurally connected phenomena: settlement change in the countryside (most notably a decline in rural settlement and the growth of large estates), élite mobility (meaning the transfer of the attention of important families to more prestigious locations), and an increase in public building and expenditure in the towns (as a means of élite competition). Urban growth is taken as one consequence of these developments, with the partial in-migration of the dispossessed rural population. Taken together, such developments radically transformed life within these territories. As Patterson points out, "the isolated mountains of Lycia and Samnium are areas we might least expect to be affected by Roman rule: the fact that the results of Roman control are so apparent even here shows the tremendous impact of the Empire on the Mediterranean basin as a whole."[11]

There exist a number of useful parallels between Patterson's model and my conclusions about Achaian conditions: the increasing dominance of large estates, the decline in rural settlement, élite interest in supra-local connections and institutions, the dominance of élite expenditure in the provincial economy, the potential growth of towns.[12] Above all, both interpretations argue in terms of the redistribution of wealth and population within a region, rather than giving credence to a simple image of decline. The model had originally been formulated to account for the development of highland regions, but it may be extended more broadly, helping to explain the development of areas found to be "relatively unimportant" to the imperial power (being agriculturally limited and lying some distance from the frontiers), yet which were dominated by the presence of active local élite groups. It must be stressed that Samnium, Lycia and Achaia are not *identical* in their response to imperial incorporation, but to identify similarities between such regions allows some control in understanding processes of imperial and native interaction. Searching for regional variation and regional similarities, drawing on individual provincial studies such as this one, becomes an attractive – and increasingly feasible – study. The Romans themselves were certainly aware of differentiation within their domains, of zones that were central or peripheral to their interests. That, after all, is implicit in the notion of Rome as *caput* to an immense imperial body.[13]

## IMAGINARY LANDSCAPES

As tourists and as students, wealthy and leisured Romans traveled to Greece in pursuit of a world of learning and of culture that they admired and longed to emulate. The interests of individuals in the province were, for the most part, extremely limited, restricted chiefly to places and events where the lessons they sought could be absorbed. Yet one additional attraction was a desire to spend time pleasurably, especially in the company of their élite provincial counterparts. As in the Greek communities of Italy itself, Greece became a place to celebrate the benefits of *otium*, a place to escape the cares of the world. Both the large cities and smaller communities could offer suitable retreats for visiting Romans and members of the native aristocracy. Plutarch tells us for example:

Aidepsos in Euboea has become a popular resort for people from all over Greece, particularly because of the place called Hot Springs, which possesses many natural resources for the worthy enjoyment of leisure, and is further embellished by villas and elegant apartment houses. Game and fowl are caught there in abundance, and the sea no less lavishly supplies the market with provisions for the table . . . This resort flourishes especially when spring is at its height, for many continue to come there all that season. They gather together, exempt from every want, and, having the leisure, engage endlessly in conversation. (*Quaestiones conviviales* 667C–D)

The thermal springs of Aidepsos had been known as early as the fourth century BC, but only in the Roman period did the community flourish; although little formal archaeological work has been done at the site, Roman remains (bathing establishments, sculptures, inscriptions) have been found scattered throughout the modern settlement (which remains a health resort today). Prominent and affluent Romans are known to have found their way to Aidepsos; in 86 BC Sulla, afflicted with gout, "used the hot waters there, taking a holiday at the same time, and passing his time pleasantly with the theatrical artists" (Plutarch, *Sulla* 26.3). In the early first century AD, the *legatus Augusti pro praetore* of the combined province of Moesia, Macedonia and Achaia (p. 16) there received a delegation from the Thessalian *koinon*. Epigraphic evidence demonstrates the presence of the families of *negotiatores* or imperial freedmen as well. Periodic donations reveal that the Roman emperors took an interest in this resort town, one locale where the aristocracy of the empire congregated to play.[14]

For those interested in leisure pursuits and relaxation, the province of Asia may have offered the visitor more flamboyant pleasures: "Old Greece" first and foremost drew men through the allure of its glorious past, and, for the most part, it was the past in the present the Romans wished to see. To achieve this, they made their way to the important sanctuaries and festivals of the province and to its major cities, above all to Athens. Athens, in welcoming and catering to Roman needs, acquired the aspect of a "college town," a transformation remarked by the classically educated poet Louis MacNeice:

> And Athens became a mere university city . . .
> And the philosopher narrowed his focus, confined
> His efforts to putting his own soul in order
> And keeping a quiet mind.
> And for a thousand years they went on talking,
> Making such apt remarks,
> A race no longer of heroes but of professors . . .
> The Glory that was Greece: put it in a syllabus, grade it
> Page by Page . . . (*Autumn Journal* IX)

Cicero's *De finibus* offers an illuminating vignette of the behavior of Roman visitors to the city. One young aristocrat remarks: "Whether it is a natural instinct or a mere illusion, I can't say; but one's emotions are more strongly aroused by seeing the places that tradition records to have been the favourite resort of men of note in former days, than by hearing their deeds or reading their writings" (5.1.2); the youths go on to compare their particular sights of interest: Plato's Academy, the beach where Demosthenes practiced voice-control, the tomb of Pericles. The thrill of being in Athens lay in the proximity of antique greatness, not in any interaction with contemporary life. Sparta likewise welcomed numerous tourists, who marveled at the revived "Lycurgan customs" practiced there. Such customs were only one aspect of a conscious civic archaism that attracted the curious, in the twentieth century earning the city (in one modern newspaper headline) the title of "World's First Theme Park."[15] In all the country's long history of tourism, the Romans were only "the first travelers to be inspired by the idea of a Greece that no longer was."[16]

In some aspects of the contemporary literature composed by members of the Greco-Roman élite, conceptions of Greece carry with them a similar air of unreality. Dio Chrysostom, for example, claimed to travel during his exile, spending some time among Greek countrypeople. "At last I arrived in the Peloponnesus, and keeping quite aloof from the cities, spent my time in the country as being quite well worth studying, mingling with herdsmen and hunters, an honest folk of simple habits" (*Oration* 1.51). In this carefully contrived setting, he meets a rustic prophetess, who recounts a tale he is one day himself to tell a great ruler: his oration (*On Kingship*) was probably delivered before Trajan. The *Euboean Discourse*, through its presentation of an idyllic rural community, extolled the virtues of a life lived in harmony with nature. For Dio, placing these episodes in Greece grounded them geographically, while at the same time permitting free use of his imagination in creating highly evocative atmospheres.[17] Arcadia is perhaps the best-known example of Roman literary idealization (and manipulation) of the Greek landscape. The land of love, shepherds, poetry and music has nothing, of course, to do with the "real" Arcadia – the landscape studied, most recently, by the Megalopolis survey – but it cannot be entirely divorced from Roman perceptions of Achaia. Arcadia has been viewed, by Snell for example, as a "spiritual landscape," "a land far distant from the sordid realities of the present . . . a far away land overlaid with the golden haze of unreality." Alternatively, Virgil's *Eclogues* can be thought of as employing "an imaginary setting in a poetic world of ideas to insulate and objectify the problems, so that the reader senses, as from a distance, the underlying realities." What emerges from such interpretations is a sense of distance, of Arcadia as a remote and imagined place. Jenkyns has recently remarked, quite rightly, that no fully developed "Arcady" is to be found in Virgil, and that the pastoral world of the *Eclogues* is "teasing, riddling, playfully elusive"; yet at the same time Arcadian allusions cannot be dismissed as simply meaningless.[18] To whatever extent Arcadia is evoked in the *Eclogues*, it appears not simply because it was the home of Pan, or because Polybius claimed its inhabitants liked music, or even because of its links to early Rome, but because Roman authors could project their desires or concerns upon that "other" land.

In the imaginations of her conquerors, Greece took whatever roles were assigned, assuming the shape and nature they desired. The ability of the Greco-Roman élite to disregard actual contemporary conditions in Greece, as they walked in (or wrote of) a land of their own imagining, presages the behavior of later visitors to the country. Eighteenth- and nineteenth-century travelers to Greece, armed with Homer, Pausanias and their own preoccupations, also saw what they wished to see. Ruins, battlefields and glorious scenery, as well as the deep pleasure of connecting ancient literary texts with physical remains, were the chief delights of these educated individuals (although the opportunity to acquire antiquities scarcely passed unnoticed). Even if some interest in the real landscape and its living people did gradually develop, especially with the growth of European sympathy for the cause of Greek independence, "this aspect hardly ever constituted the principal concern or purpose of their journey":

The travellers visited Greece full of expectations. They were to set foot in the country that could evoke past glories, to recognize a landscape described by Pausanias, to wander in the Arcadia of their dreams, or to identify long-forgotten towns from the existing ruins. In this respect Greece certainly did not disappoint them. For the travellers the country itself was more important than its inhabitants.[19]

Given the European (and indeed Roman) disdain for the Hellenes of their own time (p. 28), such a focus for these sentimental journeys is hardly surprising.

Eighteenth- and nineteenth-century artists also preferred an imaginary landscape to the actual thing, often picturing a moist and softly focused "Arcadian" countryside utterly unlike the sharp reality of the Greek terrain. Classical scenes and ruins in fabulous settings were popular images, catering to the expectations of learned buyers and viewers. If members of the indigenous population were permitted to enter these scenes, they knew their place:

The figures are appropriately small and are integrated harmoniously with the landscape as decorative elements in an aesthetic scheme; dressed in their brightly colored costumes, they either sit nonchalantly with their backs to the spectator

81 Watercolor, *Hadrian's Aqueduct* by Louis François Cassas, 1775

amongst architectural remains, or guard their flocks like Virgilian shepherds. Such pictures are generalized evocations rather than particular images: no contemporary references are appropriate in this dream world. European spectators were thus given an opportunity of escaping into a lost paradise, a happy land of classical perfection which was, nevertheless, geographically real and fairly easily accessible.[20]

It is all too easy to poke fun at the biases inherent in representations of this sort (e.g. fig. 81). Yet do not modern tourists endlessly photograph the Parthenon, little realizing that the acropolis itself is a modern construction, deliberately stripped of its post-Classical history as something of which to be ashamed? As McNeal rightly says, "Everything has been sacrificed to the age of Pheidias."[21] Although it is rarely acknowledged openly, a kind of imperialist voyeurism still endures today. And it is significant that Umberto Eco, when discussing the ideology underlying the Getty Museum in Malibu, California, evokes the "crocodile tears of the Roman patrician who reproduced the grandeurs of the very Greece that his country had humiliated."[22]

To recognize certain strong resemblances between modern, early modern and Roman perceptions of this kind returns us to the problem of Roman Greece, that strange mix of glory and despair. At some point, the power of these inherited preconceptions about the country and its people must be ended – or at least explicitly acknowledged. To achieve that, Freeman's anachronistic claim that "no age is without its lesson" (quoted at the head of this chapter) must be faced by ancient historians and archaeologists alike. Nor is this simply an external, European problem. At the time of the Greek Revolution, and with the constitution of the independent nation, legitimacy and ideological vigor were sought through a connection between Classical and modern "Hellas." Leaders of the Revolution drew explicit parallels: "Let us recollect, brave and generous Greeks, the liberty of the classic land of Greece, the battles of Marathon and Thermopylae; let us combat upon the tombs of our ancestors who, to leave us free, fought and died"; the Turks were often compared unfavorably with the barbarous Persians. The Greek uprising, as Michael Herzfeld has termed it, was "revolution as resurrection."[23] The intervening centuries, lived out under various foreign regimes, were to a large extent rejected as a shameful interregnum. This was partly a tactical device to emphasize the pure Hellenic heritage admired by those outside powers whose goodwill was so essential; moreover, it offered one means of encouraging a sense of national pride – for the reminder of defeat was a cruel and seemingly unanswerable taunt:

Respecting their ancestors their ideas are almost as absurdly inflated as those of an Oxford or Cambridge tutor. This national vanity renders a true Greek the most insufferable animal in the world, and I take great pleasure in pulling him down: I remind him of the subjugation of the Greeks by the Romans and of their degraded situation under the Turks, both of which facts I aver are positive proofs that with all their pretensions to superiority, they are really all an inferior race. To be thought inferior to the Turks, what Greek can endure? Beyond this point, the argument never proceeds.[24]

Overt arrogance of this sort may no longer be so visible and vocal, but only an acceptance of the country's history under foreign rule can completely defuse such accusations, ending the myth of the Greek "fall from grace."

In his 1843 preface to the first edition of *Greece under the Romans*, George Finlay wrote that "the same facts afford innumerable conclusions to different individuals and in different ages. History will ever remain inexhaustible."[25] Finlay's "same facts," combined with the fresh insights of archaeological evidence, make possible a new reading of Greece within the empire. The primary advantage of this study lies in its attempt to recover some measure of response to imperial incorporation on the part of the population at large, to make them active participants in their own history, rather than being imagined either as superior beings or as passive creatures. Undoubtedly these responses were more various and complex than we will ever know; signs both of accommodation and of resistance are visible in the patterns we have traced. Instead of a cultural haven, an imaginary world, or a museum locked in spiritual twilight, Greece under Roman rule must be understood as a society in the process of change, adapting and assimilating itself to a new position within an imperial system – just as countless other subordinate societies have been forced to do throughout the centuries.

# Notes

PREFACE

1 Dyson (1981a), 10.


I    THE PROBLEM OF ROMAN GREECE

1 Jones (1963), 3; Kapetanopoulos (1965); Millar (1981a), 195–6; Syme
(1979a); (1988). For studies of the Greek élite under the empire: Bowersock
(1969); Crawford (1978); Katzoff (1986). An example of the "biographical"
approach to the period, Graindor (1930).

2 The common treatment of the Byzantine empire as a "fossil" or "ghost" of the
Roman world is one result of such perceptions; see Gregory (1984), esp. 268.

3 Mahaffy (1892), 190 wrote of the "senility of the Greeks," while arguing (pp.
196–7) that Greek history is "intensely modern," "we have to deal with a
people fully developed in its mature life; nay, even in its old age and
decadence." For a discussion of evolutionary frameworks in archaeology, see
Cherry (1983a), 35–6; Cohen (1981); Dunnell (1980).

4 Bowersock (1965a), 90–1 echoing Hertzberg (1866–75), 527. For the views of
other scholars, see Mahaffy (1890), who speaks of a "fossil society"; Stobart
(1911), 261; Thirlwall (1844), 459–69; and Finlay (1857), xii, xviii, 1–106,
though this last does admit "the records of enslaved Greece are as much a
portion of her national existence as her heroic poetry and her classic history"
(p. x). Rostovtzeff too presents the familiar "picture of poverty and gradual
depopulation," though he attributes Greece's "loss of nerve" to uncertainty of
life and general impoverishment, brought about chiefly by warfare and the loss
of industry and commerce; he recognizes an improvement in the early years of
empire (1941), 604–32, 739–57; (1957), 253–4, 651–2 n. 101. Greek decay was
thought to have its roots in the Hellenistic era, when Greece made contact with
eastern luxury and lost her most ambitious men to Alexander's colonies. For a
study of the historical preconceptions attached to the Hellenistic period, see
Austin (1981); Alcock (in press, a).

5 Grote (1862), 581. Grote, of course, idealized the Athenian democracy; see
Turner (1981), 213–34. For other standard histories which ignored the
Hellenistic and Roman periods: Beloch (1927); Bury and Meiggs (1975); Glotz
(1936); Hammond (1986); Mitford (1820). Mahaffy (1892) staggers on a little

longer than most: "the history of Greece, as most historians, even of wider views, have understood it" ended with "the reeking smoke of the ruins of Corinth" (i.e. 146 BC; p. 195); cf. Cary (1951).

6 For a recent "state of the art" collection of papers, see Walker and Cameron (1989), though even there a bias toward cultural (particularly art historical) themes is evident. The situation is now beginning to improve, with notable work undertaken, for example, at the Fondation Nationale de la Recherche Scientifique Grècque in Athens.

7 Three notable exceptions must be made to this schematic presentation of past studies. The first is J. A. O. Larsen's solid and level-headed (if now of course somewhat out of date) study of "Roman Greece" (1938), forming part of Tenney Frank's *Economic Survey of Ancient Rome*. Another is Ulrich Kahrstedt's work on the economic conditions of the province (1954), essentially a review of the archaeological and epigraphic evidence that was available at the time. Ambitious for its time, the book asks interesting questions about land tenure and civic continuity, but many of Kahrstedt's ultimate conclusions appear unfounded; cf. Jones (1956). The final exception is Bowersock's excellent *Augustus and the Greek World* (1965a) which takes as its theme the Augustan consolidation of the empire. Yet even here the discussion remains largely limited to the upper reaches of provincial society, while also stressing the lack of Roman intervention in the province.

8 Syme (1988), 20; Wolf (1982). Herzfeld, commenting on Wolf, remarks that modern Greece "has a history, though this is not its own but an ancient history expropriated by the West" (1987), 213–14 n. 18.

9 Kohl (1987a), 24. For the original exposition of the world-system concept, see Wallerstein (1974); (1980); and Schneider (1977). For general discussions of the center– or core–periphery model, see Champion (1989); Ekholm and Friedman (1979); Galtung (1971); Rowlands *et al.* (1987). Some recent attempts to apply these concepts to the Roman world include Haselgrove (1987); Hedeager (1987); Woolf (1990). Specifically archaeological applications of core–periphery models, in both the Old and New World, are to be found in Kohl (1987a); (1987b); Pailes and Whitecotton (1979); Upham (1982); Small (forthcoming).

10 Recent literature on the archaeology of empires includes: Adams (1979b); Cherry (1992); Earle *et al.* (1987); Keatinge and Conrad (1983); Paynter (1981); (1982); Trinkaus (1984); Wenke (1987). See also Miller *et al.* (1989).

11 Cosgrove and Daniels (1988), 1; Cosgrove (1984). On defining "landscape": Jackson (1984), 3–8, 147–57; (1986); Cosgrove (1984), 13–38.

12 Jackson (1984), 8, 156. Relevant archaeological and geographical studies include Cosgrove (1984), 13; Kus (1989); Sack (1980); Smith (1990); Tuan (1971), 183; (1974); (1977); Wagstaff (1987). Influential archaeological investigations of landscape are still most common among prehistorians – see Barrett *et al.* (1991); Bradley (1984) – and students of the British landscape: Hoskins (1955); Reed (1984); Williamson and Bellamy (1987); Woodell (1985).

13 On issues of exchange and commerce, so little detailed ceramic analysis has

been done that it would hardly be possible to reconstruct trade patterns in the eastern Roman empire. This neglect is becoming more and more of a problem to those attempting to reconstruct supply and exchange networks throughout the empire as a whole, and the necessary work is now beginning: see, for example, Empéreur and Picon (1986); (1989); Fulford (1989); Gunneweg (1987); Hayes (1983); Riley (1979); (1981); and the work of Kathleen Slane at Corinth (1986); (1987); (1989).

14 On Caracalla's edict: Finley (1978), 2. The relationship of Braudelian history and survey archaeology is discussed in Barker (1991), Bintliff (1991a) and Knapp (1992); cf. Braudel (1973).

15 For this summary, the starting point can be Larsen (1938) and Levick (forthcoming). For studies of specific subjects, see Accame (1946); Bernhardt (1971); (1977); (1985); Crawford (1977); Larsen (1935); Owens (1976). On Athens during this period: Day (1942); Ferguson (1911); Follet (1976); Geagan (1979); Graindor (1927); (1931); Oliver (1983). The most recent political history of the "coming of Rome" to the Greek east is Gruen (1984a); he is right to emphasize Greek initiatives and responses during this time, but his dismissal of Rome's direct and indirect influences in the region goes too far; see pp. 527–8, 721–3.

16 On the first century troubles: Larsen (1938), 422–35; Millar (1984), 14–15; Will (1982), 402–5. Plutarch (*Pompey* 24) mentions difficulties with pirates in Greece; a specific example of a troubled community is Gytheion in Lakonia: see Migeotte (1984), 361.

17 For the provincial boundaries of Achaia (particularly the exclusion of Thessaly, which was most likely removed from Achaia and attached to the province of Macedonia in AD 67), see Strabo 17.3.25; Bowersock (1965b); Cherf (1987). These boundaries varied in the later empire, see Kosso (n.d.). On "Achaia": Oliver (1983), 147–53. (Note that "Achaia" is the name of the Roman province, but "Achaea" is the name of the region of the northern Peloponnese – hence "Achaean League," "Achaean War.") For the province of Epirus, see p. 145.

18 One relatively minor break in the *pax Romana* was the raid of the Costoboci during the reign of Marcus Aurelius; local and regular troops beat off the incursion, which reached as far as Delphi and Eleusis: Larsen (1938), 494. On the Herulian invasion and post-Herulian Greece: Castrén (1989); Frantz (1988); Millar (1969); Thompson (1959); Wilkes (1989). Some cities and regions of Greece had already come, for greater or lesser lengths of time, under the control of Hellenistic monarchs; these areas include the Antigonid control of Thessaly, Euboea and the "fetters" of Greece (Demetrias, Corinth, Chalkis). What distinguishes the new situation under Rome is the comprehensiveness of the annexation and its longevity.

19 Achaia's transfer to Moesia may have been connected with reported unrest in Athens during the last years of Augustus: Bowersock (1965a), 108. For other episodes of resistance among the Greeks (one of which was said to occur as late as Antoninus Pius), see Bowersock (1965a), 101–11, 147; Hoff (1989a); Syme (1979b), 199. On Nero's decree of freedom and its interpretation: Tacitus,

*Annals* (hereafter referred to as *Ann.*) 13.50; Suetonius, *Nero* 24; Pliny, *Naturalis Historia* (hereafter *HN*) 4.22; Alcock (forthcoming); Holleaux (1938); Oliver (1971). For Vespasian's action: Suetonius, *Vespasian* 8.4; Jones (1971b), 17–18.

20 For detailed studies of the Panhellenion and the cultural climate it created, excellent recent treatments are Spawforth and Walker (1985); (1986) ; see also Oliver (1951); (1970), 92–138. Several essays and an extensive bibliography on the Second Sophistic are offered in Bowersock (1974); see also Bowersock (1969). For Hadrian's visits to Greece, see Halfmann (1986), 188–210.

21 On Achaia's military status, see Gilliam (1965); Sherk (1957). Military levies: Jones (1971a); Spawforth (1984), 267–9. For the Parthian campaign, p. 121.

22 Hopkins (1980), 121.

23 On this "harmony of interest" in other systems of domination: Galtung (1971); Paynter (1982), 171–8. There is some dispute about the extent to which oligarchies were externally imposed: for example compare Bernhardt (1985) and Touloumakos (1967), who underplay this development, to de Ste. Croix (1981), 518–21, 523–9, who speaks of "the destruction of Greek democracy." Other studies of the local aristocratic response to Roman rule: Briscoe (1974); Brunt (1976); Quass (1982).

24 Those arguing a late date for the imposition of taxation include Gruen (1984a), 525–6; (1984b); Hill (1946). The possibility of earlier levies is suggested by Crawford (1977), 50–1. Arguing the middle line are Larsen (1938), 306–8; Rostovtzeff (1941), 748–9.

25 *Publicani*: Cicero, *De natura deorum* 3.49. On the supposed depredations of Cicero's enemy Piso, see his *In Pisonem*; also Brunt (1961); Nisbet (1961).

26 For general discussions of taxation, see Brunt (1981), 163–8; Jones (1974); Neesen (1980). *Tributum capitis*: *IG* XII 5 724, 946 (Andros and Tenos). *Portoria*: de Laet (1949), 295 and n. 4, 353; *Digesta* 14.2; *De lege Rhodia* 9. *Sales tax*: Jones (1974), 166; Larsen (1938), 456–7. The Messenian *octobolos eisphora* (*IG* V 1 1432–3) has recently been assigned to the early first century AD, probably between 35 and 44; see Giovannini (1978), 115–22; Hopkins (1980), 121 n. 59, but the debate about its date continues: Brunt (1981), 166; Spawforth, pers. comm.

27 On peculation: Cicero, *Ad Atticum* (hereafter referred to as *Att.*) 6.2.5; Polybius 6.56.13; Crawford (1977), 45; Corbier (1991), 231. Local benefactions to aid the tax burden: *IG* XII 5 724, 946 (Andros, Tenos); Jones (1940), 140 (Lykosoura) cf. Crawford (1975), 592. One high priest of the Macedonian League, Q. Popillius Python, paid the entire *tributum capitis* for Macedonia; *SEG* 17 315; Deininger (1965), 95; Millar (1966), 389–90.

28 On low rates of taxation: Hopkins (1980), 120. For optimistic verdicts on taxation levels, see Athenagoras, *Legatio pro Christianis* 1.2; Aelius Aristides, *Oration* 35 ("Regarding the Emperor") 16; *Roman Oration* ¶67B.

29 The most recent discussion of Achaian free cities is Bernhardt (1971); (1980); cf. Abbott and Johnson (1926), 40 and n. 4; Neesen (1980), 22, 207. On the proportion of free cities in the province: Oliver (1973), 389. Leagues could also be granted special status, as in the case of the Ozolian Lokrians (Pliny, *HN* 5.124; Pausanias 10.38.9; free and immune), and of the Eleutherolakones

(Strabo 8.5.5; Pausanias 3.21.6; free). In times of difficulty or disaster, short-term grants of tax-exemption could also be made to individual communities; examples include Aigion in the northern Peloponnese (Tacitus, *Ann.* 4.13.1) and the island of Gyaros (Strabo 10.5.3).

30 Apuleius, *Metamorphoses* (hereafter referred to as *Met.*) 9.39; Millar (1981b), 67–8. Hadrian's visits to Sparta are known to have sparked subsistence crises: Woodward (1925–6), 227–34; for other examples, Garnsey (1988), 247–8, 252–3; Jones (1940), 141, 328 n. 89.

31 Hopkins (1980), 101; cf. Corbier (1991), 235; Crawford (1977); Garnsey and Saller (1987), 95–6. From a theoretical perspective, Gall and Saxe (1977) discuss how resource flows from periphery to core can act to keep peripheries in an "immature" state.

32 Oliver (1953) offers a full analysis of Aelius Aristides, *Oration* 26 ("Regarding Rome"), hereafter referred to as *Roman Oration*. Various problems with utilizing documentary sources could be explored, for example the effect of imperial ideology, Nutton (1978), or the limitations of ancient travelers, Pédech (1971); cf. Price (1980).

33 For example, Bintliff and Snodgrass (1985), 145–7; Runnels and van Andel (1987), 318. Cf. Sallares (1991), 104–6.

34 Cicero, *Pro Flacco* 16.62–4; Horace, *Epistles* 2.2.81–6; Ovid, *Metamorphoses* 15.430.

35 Gallo (1980); (1984). A well-developed ideology underlay this hostility to pastoralism: see Gallo (1980), 1243, 1264–5; Shaw (1982/3). It is significant that pastoralism has played a role in economic interpretations of another "Dark Age" in Greek history (the period following the end of the Mycenaean palaces): Cherry (1988), 29–30; Snodgrass (1980). Epigraphic data, especially those relating to infanticide, were once heavily employed to argue a Hellenistic demographic decline: e.g. Pomeroy (1983); Rostovtzeff (1941), 623–5; Tarn and Griffith (1952), 100–2; Vatin (1970), 232. Yet inscriptions are both socially and temporally limited sources, which greatly restricts their use in a diachronic study of a complex social phenomenon; see Hopkins (1988); also Gallo (1979), 1586; Gauthier (1972), 212.

36 Bowie (1974); Habicht (1985), 104 n. 34. The Greek defeat in the Achaean War seems to have been perceived as a major turning point; according to Pausanias, "it was at this time that Greece was struck with universal and utter prostration" (7.17.1). Significantly, Walbank (1979), 680 believes that Polybius 36.17.5–9 was composed after 146 BC.

37 Petrochilos (1974) provides the most detailed collection of material about Roman attitudes to the Greeks, their perceived characteristics (pp. 35–53) and comparisons with Roman virtues (pp. 55–62). See also Wardman (1976), 1–24; Crawford (1978), 198. For Greek views of the Romans, see Forte (1972).

38 Angelomatis-Tsougarakis (1990), 85–93; Tsigakou (1981), 31.

39 Gallo (1979), 1585; (1980), 1264. For historical and archaeological information about Panopeus (a city endowed with a not inconsiderable fortification circuit), see Fossey (1986), 63–7; Jones (1956), 53. Petrochilos (1974), 63–7 assembles the evidence for Roman comparisons of Classical and contemporary Greece.

40 Day (1951); Jones (1978a), 56–61; Hodkinson (1988), 58.
41 Day (1942), 121–5 discusses conditions in the area at the time of Sulpicius'
   visit. It is also worth noting that Strabo's personal experience of Greece
   likewise dates to Greece's undoubted nadir, shortly after the battle of Actium:
   Baladié (1980), 305–6; Wallace (1979); Weller (1906).
42 Herzfeld (1987), 20. Other quotations of Roman authors are to be found in
   early modern tales of Greece. Constantine (1984), 4 observed: "Cicero's
   sentiments on the debased condition of Athens so matched those of seventeenth
   and eighteenth century travellers that they could quote him at the appropriate
   point in their accounts." See also Spencer (1954), 48–9.
43 Said (1978); see also Inden (1986); Kabbani (1986); Prakash (1990).

## 2   THE RURAL LANDSCAPE

1 The textual evidence includes Pliny, *HN* 18.35; Plutarch, *Tiberius Gracchus* 8.7;
   for the archaeological response, see Dyson (1978), 260; (1981b), 272; Potter
   (1979), 125. Another instance is Strabo's image of the abandonment of Sicily
   (6.2.6), which is increasingly called into question by archaeological evidence
   for a well-populated landscape: Wilson (1990), 194–5.
2 Snodgrass (1982), 806. On archaeological survey in the Mediterranean region
   and the relationship of survey to ancient history: Cherry (1983b); Dyson
   (1982); Snodgrass (1982); (1987), 93–131; (1990).
3 Site densities: Cherry (1983b), 390–4 and fig. 1; Bintliff and Snodgrass (1985),
   135–6; Plog *et al.* (1978). On survey comparability: Alcock (1989b), 11; Bennet
   (1986), 42–3; Hodder and Orton (1976), 134–46; Millett (1991a); (1991b).
4 Bintliff and Snodgrass (1985), 139–49; (1988a), 177–9; (1988b); (1989), 288–
   90; Bintliff (1985); (1991a), 19–26; (1991b). See also Fossey (1988).
5 Munn and Munn (1989b), 100–10, 122–3; (1990); also Munn (1988); (1989);
   Munn and Munn (1989a).
6 Fossey and Morin (1989), 166–73, esp. 169; see also Busing and Busing-Kolbe
   (1972).
7 Keller (1985), 195–230; Keller and Wallace (1986); (1987). Extensive survey
   of Euboea: Sackett *et al.* (1966).
8 Lohmann (1985), 91–2; (1983).
9 *AR* (1987/8), 13. Fowden (1988) speaks for a "late Roman intensification of
   activity" in Attica, see esp. p. 55.
10 Fossey (1986), 96–102, fig. 23; Fossey (1990), 112–15, 132–6, figs. 24, 27, 28.
   Another project, combining excavation and extensive topographical reconnaissance in north central Greece, may also be mentioned at this point: work
   by an American team along the boundary between Phokis and Doris suggested
   that the Hellenistic period itself witnessed the greatest surge in rural activity,
   but that by the Roman period decline had set in: Kase and Wilkie (1977).
11 Runnels and van Andel (1987), 317–20; van Andel and Runnels (1987), 109–
   13; van Andel *et al.* (1986), 117–20. See also Jameson *et al.* (forthcoming);
   Munn (1985).
12 Mee *et al.* (1991), 223–8, esp. 223; see also Foxhall *et al.* (1989).

13 Wells *et al.* (1990), 230–3, esp. 233. All work for the 1988 season was conducted at and above 300 m a.s.l. contour.

14 Wright *et al.* (1990), 610–17, esp. 617; Wright *et al.* (1985); for Phlius, see Alcock (1991b); Wright *et al.* (1990), 646–59.

15 Lloyd (1991a), 189–90; Roy *et al.* (1988), 181–2; (1989). Previous investigation: Howell (1970).

16 Cavanagh and Crouwel (1988), 79–81; Cavanagh (1991), 110–12.

17 Lazenby and Hope Simpson (1972); McDonald and Hope Simpson (1972). For later critiques of this work, see Cherry (1983b), 392–3; McDonald (1984).

18 Lukermann and Moody (1978).

19 Cherry *et al.* (1991), 327–47. An earlier, less intensive survey of northern Keos is reported by Georgiou and Faraklas (1985). On southern Keos: for Poiessa see Mendoni and Papageorgiadou (1989); *AR* (1986/7), 45–6; for Karthaia, Mendoni (1985/90); Mendoni and Mourtzas (1990).

20 Wagstaff and Cherry (1982a), 144–6; (1982b), table 19.1.

21 Bommeljé and Doorn (1984); (1985); (1987); see Vroom (1987) for discussion of problems in Aetolian ceramic chronology and typology. Earlier topographic reconnaissance: Athanassakis (1983); Hammond (1967); Woodhouse (1897).

22 Gallant (1982); (1986).

23 For regionally variable survey patterns in Italy, see: Barker *et al.* (1978); Barker and Hodges (1981), 10–13; Dyson (1978); Patterson (1987), 134–46; Potter (1978); (1979); Spurr (1986), 116.

24 For example, the Hellenistic era in the Southern Argolid is defined as the "third to first century BC," with a Classical–Hellenistic period preceding it (323–250 BC). In the Melos publication the Hellenistic period covers 330–146 BC, in Southern Euboea 300–1 BC, and in Messenia 369–146 BC. In Boeotia, on the other hand, the epoch has been divided into an early.(330–200 BC) and a late (200–30 BC) phase. Thus the Hellenistic period ranges between roughly two and three centuries in length, with the additional complication of regional subdivisions. Cf. Alcock (1989b), 11 n. 20. On this problem in another context: Weiss (1977).

25 Hellenistic and Roman pottery sequences as a whole: Hayes (1972); (1980); Lévêque and Morel (1980); (1987). Special classes of material: Anderson-Stojanovic (1987) (unguentaria); Empéreur and Garlan (1986) (amphorae); Perlzweig (1961) (lamps); Rotroff (1982) (moldmade bowls). For the relevant ceramic sequences at certain key sites, see, in particular, for Athens, Robinson (1959); Thompson *et al.* (1987); for Corinth, Edwards (1975); Hayes (1973); Slane (1986); Wright (1980); for Delos, Laumonier (1977). On problems of differential "visibility" in survey ceramic finds: Rutter (1983).

26 On these issues generally: Millett (1991a), 20; (1991b), 178. For Greek studies: for Boeotia, see Bintliff and Snodgrass (1988b), 69–70; for Arcadia, Lloyd (1991a), 188; for Keos, Sutton (1991); for the Southern Argolid, van Andel *et al.* (1986), 118–19; and for Nemea Valley, Wright *et al.* (1990), 610 and n. 63, 658–9. For the Corinthian evidence: Wright (1980), 174.

27 Millett (1991a), 26; also (1991b), 178–9.

28 Davidson (1952), 77, 83; Harden (1987).

29 For specific forms made in glass: Anderson-Stojanovic (1987), 113; Davidson (1952), 78–82; Harden (1987), 93; Robinson (1959). Fictile imitations: Fulford (1986), 153; Gill (1986); Vickers (1985); (1986).

30 Barker (1991), 5. The "Real Mesoamerican Archaeologist" is found in Flannery (1976), 51. Criticism of survey: e.g. Hope Simpson (1984); Isaac (1988), 240. Studies arguing a general agreement of surface and buried archaeology: Alcock (1991b), 447, 458–60; Runnels and van Andel (1987), 308; Ward-Perkins *et al.* (1986); Whallon (1979), 288–99; see also Cherry (1984). For a New World comparison, Tolstoy and Fish (1975).

31 For doubts: Foxhall (1990), 108. In an Italian survey context, the normal archaeological "small site" has been criticized as "a relatively elaborate construction inappropriate to a basic peasant cottage" (Garnsey and Saller [1987], 76).

32 On PP17: Gaffney and Gaffney (1986); Alcock *et al.* (in press).

33 This is suggested for example, in the case of the Megalopolis survey; Lloyd (1991a), 190.

34 Lloyd (1991b), 235–6.

35 Whitelaw (1991), 428. See also Alcock *et al.* (in press); Cherry *et al.* (1991), 463–70; Davis (1991); cf. Blok (1969), 129.

36 Finley (1986); Garnsey (1979), 3–4. Survey evidence can, however, provide a framework for the analysis of these historical concerns, such as the frequency of tenancy: Foxhall (1990); Osborne (1988); Wood (1988), 181–4.

37 For example in detailed grid collections, such as those conducted by the Nemea Valley project (Cherry *et al.* [1988], 162–5; Wright *et al.* [1990], 606–8) and in Boeotia (Bintliff and Snodgrass [1985], 134–6). Urban surveys are another matter; these will be discussed in the next chapter. On these problems generally, cf. Ammerman and Feldman (1978); Hirth (1978b).

38 Jameson (forthcoming, a); see also Alcock *et al.* (in press); Whitelaw (1991), 437–9.

39 Megalopolis: Roy *et al.* (1988), 182; Lloyd (1991a), 190. Boeotia: Bintliff (1991b), 126.

40 Whitelaw (1991), 412–19. On the identification of rural farmsteads: e.g. Bintliff and Snodgrass (1985), 139; Cherry *et al.* (1991), 327–47; van Andel and Runnels (1987), 158–60; Wright *et al.* (1990), 610. For the complete publication of finds from one Attic farm: Jones *et al.* (1973).

41 This schematic analytic dichotomy of "traditional" and "alternative" agricultural regimes is presented by Halstead (1987), 77–87; see also Cherry *et al.* (1991), 463–4. On the issue of whether these small sites were permanent or temporary shelters, see, above all, Osborne (1985a), 119–28; also Lloyd (1991b), 236–7.

42 Size classes of scatters representing "hamlets," "small settlements," or "villages," respectively, could range from 0.3–1, 1–5, 5–10+ha.; see Alcock (1989b), 17. But such associations of size with functional class are still largely taken for granted and remain lamentably inexplicit in most of the Greek survey literature.

43 Evidence for the fragmentation of large holdings under the empire: Day

(1942), 233; Duncan-Jones (1976), 7–33; Gregory (1984), 271; Jones (1953), 52–3, 57.

44  Munn (1985), 343.

45  On the definition of "villa" elsewhere in the empire, see, for example, Hingley (1989), 20–3; Percival (1976), 13–15. Barker expresses recent concerns about survey identifications of villas on the basis of site sizes; cf. (1991), 5 commenting on Dyson (1978); Lloyd and Barker (1981) and Potter (1979). On villa classification schemes in Greece, Lukermann and Moody (1978), 99. Other discussions of villas in Achaia: Gregory (1984), 271–2; Kahrstedt (1954); Percival (1976), 157; Ramsden (1972), 517. On the urban bias of eastern villas and the relative neglect of the phenomenon in the Roman east, see Rossiter (1989).

46  For Corinth, see S. Grobel Miller (1972); Shear (1930); Wiseman (1978), 72; (1979), 528; Williams and Zervos (1983), 18–19. For Patrai, see *AD* 26 (1971) B1: 149–75; 31 (1976) B1: 88–115. For Nikopolis, *AAA* 6 (1973), 222–4. To these archaeological identifications, one could add Kahrstedt's reports of "Ziegelbauten" in Greece. In some cases, his association of brick structures with Roman villas is plausible. On most points, however, the evidence is forced further than is advisable, with not only villas identified but specifically the residences of an area's most important landowners, e.g. (1954), 174–5 and end figure. Such unwarranted assumptions leave Kahrstedt's overall analysis unacceptable. For the absence of Roman villas in Lakonia: Cartledge and Spawforth (1989), 142.

47  For mosaic studies: Bruneau (1985); Ramsden (1972); Waywell (1979), 293–321. For villas: in Attica, see Vanderpool (1970), 43–5; in Thyreatis, Faklaris (1990), 96–104; Spawforth (1980), 210 and nn. 46–7; in Messenia, Valmin (1938), 470–3; in Akarnania, Murray (1982), 363; in Dymaia, *AR* (1986/7), 22.

48  At Ktirakia in Lakonia, four sarcophagi were discovered within the monument, one of which was dated to the early third century AD: Cartledge and Spawforth (1989), 142; Cavanagh and Crouwel (1988), 81. On tomb monuments in the Corinthia: Wiseman (1978), 69; in Epirus: *AD* 30 (1975) B1: 211–13; 32 (1977) B1: 182; 35 (1980) B2: 321; Rhomaios (1930). Monumental family burial markers have also been observed in Troizenia, though here they lie within a few hundred meters of the city wall: Welter (1941), 41–2; Faraklas (1972), fig. 30. The general elaboration of burials in Hellenistic and Roman times is a phenomenon requiring further study. On the nymphaeum in Epirus: Chrysostomou (1982).

49  Jameson (forthcoming, a), 182–3 has remarked that "it is likely that the most important exceptions to the general modesty of classical housing were to be found in the countryside, away from the physical constraints of space and perhaps the social constraints of envy," but relatively little evidence exists for such distinctions in the Classical period.

50  de Ste. Croix (1981), 518–21, 523–9; Ferguson (1911), 55–7; Migeotte (1984), 400; Préaux (1978), 412–13; Tarn (1925); Tarn and Griffith (1952), 108–9; Will (1975), 554–65.

51 On "social revolution," see Fuks (1984), especially 40–51. On the theory of a liquidity crisis: Davies (1984), 293–4 and nn. 228–30. Liquidation of debts usually came in the form of land expropriation: Davies (1984), 294; Guiraud (1893), 401–2; Will (1975), 561–2.

52 Compare, for example, Feyel (1942) with Hennig (1977); Migeotte (1984), 360 n. 17; (1985a); Osborne (1985c). On Hellenistic conditions generally, compare Guiraud (1893), 63 with the more balanced assessments of Davies (1984), 294–6 and nn. 231–4 and Walbank (1981), 170.

53 Asheri (1966), 43–60. A good example is Thisbe in Boeotia, ca. 170 BC: *IG* VII 2225; Abbott and Johnson (1926), 254–6.

54 One of the more interesting clauses of the treaty between Rome and Aetolia in the First Macedonian War agreed that Rome would be satisfied with booty, Aetolia would keep all immovable spoils of war: Livy 26.24.8–14. After the Second Macedonian War, Flamininus wrote to one defeated community: "As many of your possessions, in land and houses, as remain of those belonging to the public property of the Romans, we grant them all to your city so that ... you may know our nobility" *SIG*³ 593. On Achaean War confiscations: Strabo 8.6.23; Cicero, *De lege agraria* 1.5, 2.51; cf. Hill (1946), 38 (at Corinth); Polybius 39.4 (private properties). Sulla is known to have confiscated and given away territory in Greece (some 10,000 *plethra* to the general of Mithridates): Plutarch, *Sulla* 23.2. The best attested case of confiscation during the Principate is the seizure of the estates of Hipparchus, grandfather of Herodes Atticus: Philostratus, *Vitae Sophistarum* (hereafter *VS*) 2.547.

55 Crawford (1977), 48–9.

56 Philostratus, *VS* 2.547; Oliver (1953), 960–3. Cf. Crawford (1976), 66, Table 5.1.

57 For the *Euboean Discourse*, Dio Chrysostom, *Oration* 7.12, 27. Law of Antoninus Pius: Habicht (1985), 124; cf. Broughton (1934), 239 for parallels in Asia Minor. Kahrstedt posits the existence of imperial estates on the basis of imperial benefactions to individual cities, but there is little evidence to support such claims: (1954), e.g. 258 and *passim*.

58 Atticus and the *Synepirotae*: Cicero, *Att.* 1.5, 2.6; Varro, *De re rustica*, hereafter referred to as *Rust.* 2.1.1–2, 2.2.1; Deniaux (1987), 245–54; Horsfall (1989). On the treatment of Epirus: pp. 141–3. For the evidence from Thespiai: *SEG* XXVII 72; XXXI 514 (late first century BC and early first AD); Moretti (1981); Alcock (in press, b).

59 On *negotiatores*, see Hatzfeld (1919); Wilson (1966); Crawford (1977), 52. For the *octobolos eisphora*: *IG* V 1 1432–3; see p. 21. The benefactions of the Cloatii to Gytheion are a good example of *negotiatores* identifying with their new homes: *IG* V 1 1146. Many "oriental" senators came, ultimately, from *Rhomaioi* stock: Oliver (1983), 115–36; Walton (1929).

60 On veterans discharged in the east, especially in Crete or Macedon, see Cicero, *In Pisonem* 47.92.96; Brunt (1971), 219–20; Crawford (1977), 48.

61 Documented clearly in several cities: see, for Akraiphia, Oliver (1971); for Athens, Day (1942), 237–51; for Sparta, Cartledge and Spawforth (1989), 160–5; for Thespiai, Jones (1970); see also Thessalian Gonnoi: Helly (1973).

62 See, for Messene, Migeotte (1985b); for Athens, *IG* II–III² 2776; Day (1942), 221–35.

63 Evidence from Methana: *IG* v 2 516; Gossage (1954), 51–6; from Arcadia: Spawforth (1978); Lloyd (1991a), 191. The close networks linking Achaian élite families will be further discussed in chapter 4. For Eurycles, see Strabo 8.5.1; Baladié (1980), 329 and nn. 184–5; Bowersock (1961); Cartledge and Spawforth (1989), 104; Spawforth (1978), 251–2. As for Herodes Atticus, aside from holdings in Italy and Egypt, he owned land in (at least) five places in Attica, as well as in Kynouria, Euboea and Corinth; his family may also have owned land on Keos: *IG* XII 5 631; *SEG* XIV 542; Ameling (1983), 93; Day (1942), 235–6 and nn. 321–7; Dunant and Thomopoulos (1954); Graindor (1930).

64 For an analysis of these agricultural strategies: Jameson (1977/8), 122–45. For the possible impact of taxation: Hopkins (1980).

65 Larsen (1938), 483–6 provides a useful review of Greek agricultural exports in the Roman period. Thessalian grain shipments: Philostratus, *VS* 1.526; Garnsey *et al.* (1984). Athenian olive oil: *IG*² II 1100; Garnsey (1988), 75–6; Oliver (1953), 960–3. Unguents: Pausanias 9.41.7, 10.32.19. *Byssos*: Pausanias 5.5.2, 6.26.6, 7.21.14; Pliny, *HN* 19–21; Purcell (1987), 80–1 and n. 47.

66 On drainage and other agricultural improvement schemes, see, for Kaphyai, Arcadia, Pausanias 8.23.2, for Tegea, 8.44.1, for the Kopaic Basin, 9.24.1, for Thisbe, 9.28.1, 9.32.3. For the Kopaic Basin: *IG* VII 2712; Oliver (1971) (Epaminondas); Fossey (1979); Knauss *et al.* (1984), 53 (Hadrian). Cf. Argoud (1987), 31–6.

67 Sheehan and Whitehead (1981); van Andel and Runnels (1987), 112, 141; van Andel *et al.* (1986), 118–20. Other palynological evidence: Athanasiadis (1975); Bottema (1982); Greig and Turner (1974). Detailed pollen evidence from cores taken by the Nemea Valley survey project will soon become available: Wright *et al.* (1990), 593. For geomorphological work on Melos: Davidson and Tasker (1982), 82–94; in Berbati valley, Wells *et al.* (1990), 212–14.

68 For the Southern Argolid, see van Andel and Runnels (1987), 105; van Andel *et al.* (1986) 117; Runnels and van Andel (1987). For the Attic evidence, Lohmann (1983); (1985). Critiques of this model: Cherry *et al.* (1991), 461–2; Dickson (1989); Gallant (1991); Sallares (1991), 103–5.

69 Osborne (1987a), 69–70.

70 Modern Greek parallels: Bentley (1987); Forbes (1976); Friedl (1962), 14–17; Sallade and Braun (1982). Wagstaff (1976) and Wagstaff and Augustson (1982) report farmers on Melos will travel up to five hours to tend their most distant fields.

71 Osborne (1987a), 138.

72 For the Southern Argolid, see van Andel *et al.* (1986), 117; van Andel and Runnels (1987), 107–12, 117; for Southern Euboea, Keller (1985), 218–21; for Berbati, Wells *et al.* (1990), 237; for Melos, Wagstaff and Gamble (1982), 101; for Messenia, van Wersch (1972), 180–2; for Lakonia, Cartledge and Spawforth (1989), 170; for Methana, Mee *et al.* (1991), 228. For a modern

comparison from Keos: Whitelaw (1991). See Alcock (1989b), 25–6.

73 Off-site survey: Dunnell and Dancey (1983); Foley (1981); Thomas (1975). In the Mediterranean: Barker (1991), 5–6; Bintliff and Snodgrass (1988c); Cherry (1983b); Gallant (1986); Wright *et al.* (1990), 604–6.

74 For the evidence from Keos, Cherry *et al.* (1991), 37–54; from Nemea, Wright *et al.* (1990), 617; from Berbati, Wells *et al.* (1990), 232. On manuring: Bintliff and Snodgrass (1988c), 508. A wider variety of factors involved in the genesis of off-site scatters has been suggested by Wells *et al.* (1990), 237–8. For an exhaustive discussion of these problems, see Alcock *et al.* (in press).

75 Foxhall (1990).

76 On the law of "minimum effort": Chisholm (1962); Hall (1966). In a Mediterranean context: Sallade and Braun (1982). Tax-dodging: Corbier (1991), 227–8. For *latifundia*: Pliny, *HN* 18.35; White (1967), 73.

77 On profits to be made in years of food shortage: Garnsey (1988), 76–8; Grigg (1970), 115. Urban properties: Garnsey (1976). For conspicuous consumption in the Greco-Roman world, e.g. Finley (1985a), 144–5; cf. Clark and Haswell (1970), 135. This is not always the case; anthropologists elsewhere note a high correlation between social rank and a willingness to invest and experiment in order to maximize agricultural returns: Barlett (1980), 556; Cancian (1972), 135–59; Netting (1974), 41.

78 *Horses*: in Lakonia, Thessaly, Aetolia, *CIL* 6.33937; Larsen (1938), 485; in Thessaly, Aetolia, Akarnania, Arcadia, Argolid, Strabo 8.8.1; in Thessaly, Philostratus, *VS* 615; in Thessaly and Thrace, Virgil, *Georgics* 1.59, 2.90; in Arcadia, Arrian, *Anabasis* 2.16.5–6; Varro, *Rust.* 2.8.3; in Elis, Pausanias 6.24.2. *Cattle, sheep and goat*: in Epirus, Aelian, *De natura animalum* 3.34, 12.11; Varro, *Rust.* 2.1.1–2, 2.2.1; in Arcadia, Pliny, *HN* 25.94, 28.125; Strabo 8.8.1; Philostratus, *Vita Apollonii* (hereafter *VA*) 8.7.12; in Attica, Varro, *Rust.* 2.218. As for epigraphic data, boundary disputes involving grazing rights are known from the Late Hellenistic Argolid: Hodkinson (1988), 58; Jameson (forthcoming, b). Also, in Late Roman census records from Mytilene, a total of 70 percent of holdings listed grazing land: *IG* xii 2 76, 77, 78, 79, 80; Jones (1953); Mee *et al.* (1991), 230.

79 The ecological degradation in the Southern Argolid in Late Hellenistic times has also been attributed in part to increased pastoral activity: van Andel *et al.* (1986), 120; van Andel and Runnels (1987), 110. Payne (1985) details the currently limited data for the zooarchaeological study of animal husbandry in Greece. On the archaeology of pastoralism, Chang and Koster (1986). For an ethnoarchaeological perspective, Murray and Chang (1981). For the evidence from Methana, Mee *et al.* (1991), 228–30; from Arcadia, Lloyd (1991a), 191. *Mandrakia* (sheep pens) have been discovered for Late Roman (fourth–seventh centuries AD) Attica: Lohmann (1983), 114; (1985).

80 For inter-*poleis* tensions, see Osborne (1987a), 50–2. Grants of *epinomia* (pasturing rights) are known from earlier periods, but the formation of supralocal élite ties at this time would have eased potential conflicts. The best historical and epigraphic review of pastoralism for the Classical and Hellenistic

periods is provided by Hodkinson (1988) and the other papers in Whittaker (1988). On tax dodging: Dyson-Hudson and Dyson-Hudson (1980), 36–7; Mee *et al.* (1991), 230.

81 Aristotle, *Politics* 1321a.11; Grigg (1970), 160; Hodkinson and Hodkinson (1981), 279. Provision of water too would pose problems for many would-be specialized pastoralists: Semple (1932), 317–24; Wells (1970).

82 Chang and Koster (1986), 110.

83 For the need of small farmers for uncultivated land, see Burford-Cooper (1977/8), 173; Day (1942), 231–2; Garnsey (1988), 46, 53. The Keian *voli* system: Bennet and Voutsaki (1991), 377; Cherry *et al.* (1991), 468–9.

84 Finlay (1857), 59–64; Salmon (1974), 117. On the Late Roman decline: Boak (1955); Finley (1977b), 152. Sallares' arguments for a Malthusian crisis in the fourth century, leading inevitably to a massive decline in Hellenistic and Early Roman population levels, are not accepted here, since I prefer to regard population change as a more flexible and dependent variable in human social practice. In addition, a more critical attitude to the period's literary sources and the survey evidence is needed than Sallares allows: (1991), esp. 60–5, 100–7; cf. Bintliff (1985), 210–15. This more cautious interpretation of the Achaian depopulation is also adopted by Cartledge and Spawforth for Lakonia: (1989), 141–2.

85 See, for Methana, Mee *et al.* (1991), 223; for Boeotia, Sallares (1991), 469; cf. Fossey (1979). Hellenistic out-migration: Griffith (1935); McKechnie (1989); Rostovtzeff (1941), 1054–7; in-migration: Cohen (1983); Davies (1984), 265–8; Tarn and Griffith (1952), 103.

86 Finley (1985b), 81. Reassessment of the effects of the Hannibalic wars, once considered the "agent of universal destruction," is an interesting parallel to this argument; Frederiksen (1970/1), 339, 356. For an excellent assessment of the impact of warfare in the agricultural sphere, see Hanson (1983).

87 Will (1975), 515.

88 Obviously, these arguments go back to the work of Chayanov (1923). For anthropological studies: Barlett (1980), 557–8; Cowgill (1975a), 505–55; (1975b); Grigg (1976); White (1973); Wolf (1966). In a Greek context: Wood (1988), 55–6. On Greco-Roman family sizes and means of family limitation, see Eyben (1980–1).

89 For this argument in other social contexts: Brown and Podolefsky (1976), 229; Green (1980a); (1980b); Kirch (1980), 127–9.

90 On the concept of *agri deserti*, see Whittaker (1976); Shaw (1983), 149. Emphyteutic legislation: in Delphi, early second century AD, Jannoray (1944/5), 76–7; Garnsey and Saller (1987), 347, n. 52; in Thisbe, early third century AD, *IG* VIII 2226–7; *SIG*³ 884; Larsen (1938), 477; Abbott and Johnson (1926), 453–6; in Boeotia (undated), Jannoray (1944/5), 76 n. 2. Domitian's confiscation of the land of Hipparchus has been suggested as an attempt to help dispossessed small farmers: Geagan (1979), 385; Pleket (1961). Proselytizing for such emphyteutic schemes has been tentatively identified in Dio Chrysostom's *Euboean Discourse*: Jones (1978a), 60 and n. 21.

### 3 THE CIVIC LANDSCAPE

1 Jackson (1984), 18 and Shear (1981), 361. On the architectural framework of Roman Athens, see Boatwright (1983); Hoff (1989b); Thompson (1987); Willers (1990); Zanker (1988), 261–3; see also pp. 192–6. For Argos, see for example: Aupert (1987); Ginouvès (1972); for Corinth, Williams (1989).

2 Keos: Cherry *et al.* (1991), 337; Whitelaw and Davis (1991), 279–80. I must thank the directors of the Boeotia Survey for this information about their work at Hyettos. On the distribution of population in Boeotia, see Bintliff (n.d.).

3 For Haliartos, see Bintliff and Snodgrass (1988a), 176–8; (1988b), 61–5; for Askra, Bintliff and Snodgrass (1988b), 60–3; Snodgrass (1985). Thespiai's decline is especially interesting in view of the city's not inconsiderable history of sanctuary activity under the early empire, Alcock (in press, b); Bintliff and Snodgrass (1988a), 176–8; (1988b), 65–8; Bintliff (1991b).

4 For Phlius: Pausanias 2.12.3–15.2; Alcock (1991b), 460–2; Biers (1971); (1973); (1975); Wright *et al.* (1990), 617. For Methana, see Foxhall (1990), 108; *AR* (1984/95), 22. Strabo (8.6.15) uses the past tense when referring to this city, only one example of his unreliable testimony for many regions of Greece, Baladié (1980), 314.

5 For what it is worth, Strabo 8.6.12 also reports Hermione as *ouk asemos* (not unimportant); Pausanias 2.34.11–35.11; Philadelpheus (1909); Jameson (1953); (1959). For Karystos, Day (1951), 229–31 challenges the issue of the value of *Oration* 7 for Greek economic history in the Roman period. Evidence for the city's apparent expansion (public additions to the east, necropolis to south, domestic "suburb" to west) is reported in Keller (1985), 215, 222, 227, fig. 62. Ancient Melos: Sparkes and Cherry (1982). On Melian *negotiatores*: Sparkes (1982a), 51; *IG* XII 3 1078–9, 1234; *CIL* III 14203(10). Tanagra: Pausanias 9.22.2; Roller (1985); (1987); (1989). For Messenia and Phokis, see Wagstaff (1982), 118 and Fossey (1986), 99. John Patterson (1991), 163 has argued that the urban center of Balboura in Lycia, following a developmental sequence not unlike that traced here, expanded at this time.

6 On difficulties in judging a city's overall health and prosperity, see Hopkins (1978b), 70–1; (1980), 103 n. 8; Patterson (1987), 143–4; cf. Ward-Perkins (1984).

7 On settlement relocation in the Southern Argolid, Runnels and van Andel (1987), 318; on Melos, Wagstaff and Cherry (1982a), 170; on Keos, Cherry *et al.* (1991), 341–4 and figs. 17.10 and 17.11; table 17.5; in Lakonia, Cavanagh and Crouwel (1988), 81; Cartledge and Spawforth (1989), 170.

8 Even substantial settlements may have been abandoned in order to concentrate resources and functions within a single center; this has been suggested, for example, from the extensive survey of Opountian Lokris, see Fossey (1990), 134. Special-purpose sites: for Melos, see Cherry (1982); for the Southern Argolid, van Andel (1987), 309. Cf. Hodder and Orton (1976), 63, 85–6.

9 Cartledge and Spawforth (1989), 142; Foxhall (1990), 108; Lloyd (1991b).

10 Ecological, technological, economic, religious and socio-cultural factors all become involved. On the complexities of locational decision-making: cf. Blouet

(1972); Blok (1969); Demangeon (1927); (1962); Smith (1976a); (1976b); Toyne (1974); Trigger (1974); Wagstaff (1982).

11 Blouet (1971) and Whitehouse (1985) discuss cases where known hostilities left no trace in the landscape. On defense as only a partial explanatory force for settlement relocation: Rowlands (1972); Wagstaff (1969), 315; Wagstaff and Cherry (1982a), 145. On brigandage in Boeotia: Etienne and Knoepfler (1976), 244–5. I must thank Anthony Snodgrass for this observation about Boeotian settlement.

12 For the movement of slaves: Osborne (1991a), 244–6. Evidence from Italy, Hopkins (1978a); (1978b), 60; MacMullen (1974), 85; Patterson (1987), 142–4; (1991), 155–7.

13 Jameson (1977/8), 129.

14 On the dangers of specialization: cf. Garnsey (1988), 56; Netting (1974), 41. The increasing proximity of rural sites to urban centers in some regions could suggest their special use for cash cropping or market gardens; areas closer to the urban center tend to be dedicated to such purposes, as von Thünen's analysis suggests: Smith (1976a), 7; Hall (1966).

15 Millar (1981b), 72. For the Euboean rustics: Dio Chrysostom, *Oration* 7.15–18. Evidence for peasant mobility admittedly appears chiefly in Late Roman and Asian contexts: Libanius, *Oration* 47.17; Garnsey (1988), 62; Patlagean (1977), 179–81. Ancient examples of urban hiring markets: Finley (1985a), 223–4 and n. 28; MacMullen (1959), 213. Modern analogies: Netting (1974), 40; Barlett (1980), 557.

16 Tenancy is an elusive category for the Greek and Roman periods alike: Finley (1976), 104; Wood (1988), 181. On the flexibility allowed the small farmer by leasing land: Osborne (1988). For the political and social context of tenancy: Foxhall (1990).

17 Foxhall (1990), 109–11.

18 Finley (1976), 113; de Neeve (1984), 31–62.

19 Osborne (1988), 323. See also Finley (1976), 106; Standing (1981); Wood (1988), 183. On sharecropping: Cato 136–7; Pliny, *Epistulae* (hereafter *Ep.*) 9.37.3; Byres (1983), 12–15; de Ste. Croix (1981), 216–17, 256.

20 On the marble trade generally, see Dodge (1988); (1990); Baladié (1980), 197–210. Attic sources: Strabo 9.1.23; Walker (1985), 20–7; (1987), 68; Day (1942), 204–7; Langdon (1988). Lakonian sources: Strabo 8.5.7; Cartledge and Spawforth (1989), 169; Lambraki (1980), 32 n. 7. Karystian marbles: Hankey (1965); Lambraki (1980).

21 For the silver mines at Laurion, see Strabo 9.1.23; Davies (1935), 251; Healy (1978), 56, 62; Larsen (1938), 462, 486–7. Iron: for Boeotia, see Pliny, *HN* 36.128; Bakhuizen (1976), 52–6; (1979); Davies (1935), 245–6; for Gyaros, see Pliny, *HN* 8.222 quoting Theophrastus. On mining in Greece generally, see Davies (1935), 239–63.

22 For Patrai, see Pausanias 7.21.14; for Aulis, 9.19.8; for Chaironeia, 9.41.7; for Tithorea, 10.32.19. Pittinger (1975) and Sparkes (1982b) discuss the Melian mineral export, though this appears to be primarily a Late Roman phenomenon. Purple: in Bulis, Pausanias 10.37.3; in Lakonia, 3.21.6; in

Euboea, Dio Chrysostom, *Oration* 7.2; in Hermione, Plutarch, *Alexander* 36; Jameson (1969), 324 n. 31; Rudolph (1974), 108; also, in Thessaly, Philostratus, *Heroicus* 744. On purple generally, see Reinhold (1970); Charlesworth (1926), 125. Evidence for Spartan building activity: Cartledge and Spawforth (1989), 171.

23 Imperial confiscations: Larsen (1938), 463–4; Lambraki (1980); Baladié (1980), 209–10; Dodge (1988), 68–72. Tiberius is believed to have taken over many quarries in AD 17. On the economic isolation of quarries, see Fant (1989). One pre-Roman parallel for a local economic stimulus would be the development of the agricultural potential of the Laurion area to feed the servile mining communities, Osborne (1985b), 29–36; (1991a), 248–9; Lohmann (1985).

24 A modern case study from Bangladesh illustrates this possibility: Bhaduri *et al.* (1986). It is assumed that peasant households thus rely rather heavily upon agricultural income, but one external to their own independently owned farms.

25 Garnsey (1980), 38; Hodkinson and Hodkinson (1981), 284–6; Jameson (1977/8), 124; Wood (1988), 62.

26 Foxhall (1990), 111–13; Garnsey (1988), 58–63; Osborne (1987a), 59; Wallace-Hadrill (1990). For a discussion of rural patronage, see Garnsey and Woolf (1990). Libanius, *Oration* 47.17 illustrates the magnetic quality of the urban élite; for a modern Mediterranean example, Davis (1969), 181–3.

27 Hellenistic *sitoneia* schemes: Garnsey (1988), 79–82; for Thespiai, see Roesch (1965), 220–4; Migeotte (1985c), 314–16; for Thouria, see *IG* v 1 1379; Roebuck (1945), 153. For the provisions of Athens under the empire, see Dio Cassius 69.16.2; Philostratus, *VS* 526; Miller (1972a); (1972b); Spawforth and Walker (1985), 90; of Corinth: Wiseman (1979), 499, 505; cf. *IG* iv 795.

28 Cartledge and Spawforth (1989), 142, 156. For general analyses of euergetism and the social power of banqueting, see Gauthier (1985); Robert (1935), 444; Schmitt-Pantel (1981); (1985); Veyne (1976). Food distributions could accompany agonistic celebrations: Spawforth (1989), 197.

29 Elite control of access to resources: Blanton (1976), 257; Paynter (1982), 34–40; Smith (1975); (1976b); Standing (1981), 177. In pre-revolutionary Greece: Whitelaw (1991), 452–3.

30 On the Late Roman period: Garnsey (1980), 39; (1988), 18; Gregory (1984), 271; Jones (1953). Spatial analyses of feudalism: Dodgshon (1987), 192; Sack (1980), 182–5; Standing (1981), 174. Finley (1976), 116–17 does emphasize, however, the possibility of indebtment, and potential immobility, in the early imperial period as well.

31 Osborne (1987a), 134–5; Pečirka (1973), 118–19.

32 Finley (1985a), 135–8; (1977a).

33 Frederiksen (1975), 168; Hopkins (1978b); (1980); Millar (1981b), 72–3; Osborne (1991b). See also Engels (1990), esp. 121–30, though his assumption that ancient peasants had "approximately twice the surplus available to them" than has generally been thought rests on calculations of ancient agricultural productivity which are dubious in the extreme.

34 Osborne (1987a), 26.

35 Finley (1977a), 307; Hopkins (1978b), 73–4; Humphreys (1978).

36 Antioch in the fourth century had 150,000–300,000 inhabitants; its territory was at least 300 times the size of the city area: Finley (1977a), 326; Jones (1940), 259–60; Osborne (1987a), 193–4.

37 Sartre (1979), esp. 217; Rocchi (1988). Examples include quarrels between the Boeotian town of Koroneia and its neighbors: *IG* VII 2870; Fossey (1981); the Phokian communities of Amphissa, Delphi and Antikyrrha: Millar (1977), 436; and cities in the Southern Argolid: *IG* IV I² 76–7; *IG* IV 752, 791; Jameson (1953), 160–1; (forthcoming, b).

38 On the sanctuary of Artemis Limnatis, see Pausanias 4.4.2–3; Sartre (1979), 222; Alcock (1991a), 455; Cartledge and Spawforth (1989), 90, 95, 138–9, 187; *Ergon* (1988), 44–6. The presence of rural sanctuaries in border contexts has been noted in other Roman provinces, see Blagg (1986), 21; for Britain, see Hingley (1985); for Gaul, Drinkwater (1983). Other border markers mentioned in Pausanias 2.38.7; 3.3.1; 7.27.1; 8.34.6 (Hermes); 1.44.10; 2.35.2; 7.17.5; 8.11.1; 8.12.9; 8.25.1; 8.25.2 (other). On border deities and rituals in pre-Roman times: Kahn (1979); Sartre (1979), 216–23; Vernant (1983a); Vidal-Naquet (1986).

39 Elsner (forthcoming).

40 On roads in the province, see Axioti (1980); Baladié (1980), 265–77; Chevallier (1989), 140, 200; Purcell (1990), 12–14. For the Parthian campaign: Baladié (1980), 273–7; Robert (1963), 315. Skironian road: Wiseman (1978), 17.

41 Jackson (1984), 22–3.

42 On the *cursus publicus*: Baladié (1980), 333. Under Hadrian, the cities were relieved of their obligations to supply the costs of personnel and material for the postal system. Cf. Mitchell (1976).

43 Coulton (1987), 73.

44 Plutarch mentions tampering with aqueducts as one method of élite rivalry, *De fraterno amore* 487F–488A. On the Corinth aqueduct, see Pausanias 2.3.5; 8.22.3; Biers (1978); Engels (1990), 76–8; Puillon Boblaye (1836), 148; Tölle-Kastenbein (1990), 68. The section of this aqueduct shown in figure 41 may post-date the original Hadrianic construction, but it nonetheless probably formed part of the same overall system. The city of Argos could have tapped into this water source, but it may well have been served by a separate aqueduct system.

45 Corbier (1991), 222. For Athens, see *CIL* 3 549; Ziller (1877), 120–2; Kienast (1987), 167; Travlos (1971), 242–3; Kokkou (1970), 169–71. For Nikopolis, see Stillwell (1976), 626. For Epidauros, Pausanias 2.27.6; Habicht (1985), 10 and n. 53. Elaborate hydraulic systems are also known for private houses as well: for Patrai, see *AD* 32 (1977) B1: 80–2; 33 (1978) B1: 31; for the villa of Herodes Atticus in Thyreatis, Faklaris (1990), 98, pl. 32e.

46 Coulton (1987), 81. The famous example of Peirene fountain at Corinth is now believed to have been renovated by an unknown donor, not the otherwise ubiquitous Herodes Atticus. Walker (1987) discusses nymphaea in Corinth, Olympia, Athens, Argos.

4    THE PROVINCIAL LANDSCAPE

1 Evidence from other empires for *compulsory urbanism and foundations*: in the New World, see Morris (1972); de Montmollin (1987); Keatinge and Conrad (1983); Morris and Thompson (1970); for *population displacement*: in the New World, see Adams (1979a), 64; Kelly (1965); in the Old World, see Charanis (1960/1); Brinkman (1979); for *streamlining*: in the New World, see Redmond (1983), 121; Blanton *et al.* (1981), 18–20; cf. Flannery (1972); for a *"hands-off policy"*: Eisenstadt (1979); in the New World, see Menzel (1959); Hodge (1984). On city distributions in early modern Europe: de Vries (1984).

2 Aelius Aristides, *Roman Oration* ¶61; see Corbier (1991), 211; cf. Rostovtzeff (1957), 593 n. 4. On Roman urbanism in the west: Bekker-Nielsen (1989); Burnham and Johnson (1979).

3 Garnsey and Saller (1987), 32. It is true, however, that colonies were founded and cities encouraged in those areas which were still tribally organized and under-urbanized, see Bowersock (1965a), 62–72; Jones (1963), 3; Jones, A. (1971); Levick (1967).

4 On the interaction of centers and peripheries in other settings, see Adams (1979a), 62–7; Brumfiel (1983); Dyson (1985); Lattimore (1962); Trinkaus (1984), 46. On the importance of taxation systems, compare, for example, Hopkins (1980) and Murra (1980). On these points generally, see Alcock (1989a), 92–4; Schreiber (1987).

5 Finley (1973), 10.

6 Polybius 30.20.1–7; Strabo 9.2.30 (Haliartos). About Antony and Athens: see n. 30 below; for Sulla and Thebes: Plutarch, *Sulla* 19.6. For Dyme, see Purcell (1987), 75 n. 14; cf. Strabo 14.3.3.

7 *Buthrotum*, Strabo 7.7.5; Cicero, *Att.* 16.16a. *Dyme*, Strabo 8.7.5, 14.3.3. *Corinth*, Strabo 8.6.23. Hill (1946), 38 argues that the Corinthian territory was leased, not given, to Sikyon; cf. Strabo 8.6.23; Cicero, *De lege agraria* 1.5, 2.51. On the interregnum: Wiseman (1978), 15 n. 25; (1979), 491–6. The evidence for Corinth as provincial capital: Acts of the Apostles 18.12–17; Aelius Aristides, *Oration* 46. 27; cf. Engels (1990), 19 and 199 n. 41; Wiseman (1979), 501–2. Under Vespasian the city became *Colonia Laus Flavia Augusta Corinthiensis*, but the original title was restored under Domitian; Suetonius, *Vespasian* 17. The city received tax immunity from Hadrian; *IG* IV 1600. On Corinth's urban topography: Engels (1990); Wiseman (1978); (1979). The site has been excavated since the nineteenth century by the American School of Classical Studies.

8 Pausanias 7.18.6–7; 7.22.1, 6; 10.38.9; Purcell (1987), 78–82; Rizakis (1988); (1989). Archaeological investigation of the city has only recently begun in earnest; most of the work undertaken (up to 80 separate rescue excavations in a single year) is in the nature of rescue operations; cf. *AR* (1985/6), 31; (1987/8), 28.

9 Strabo 7.7.6, 10.2.2; Pausanias 5.23.3; cf. Chrysos (1987); Edmonson (1969); Jones (1987); Murray and Petsas (1989). On the city's institutional status: Bowersock (1965a), 94; Purcell (1987); Sarikakis (1970); cf. Mitchell (1979).

Amphiktyonic representation: Pausanias 10.8.3–5. Festivals: Suetonius, *Augustus* 18.2; Gagé (1936); Rieks (1970); Sarikakis (1965).

10 On the Nikopolitan synoecism: Strabo 7.7.5–6; 10.2.2–3; Pausanias 5.23.3; 7.18.8; 8.24.11; 10.38.4; Hoepfner (1987), 131–2; Kirsten (1987); Murray and Petsas (1989), 5 n. 25; Murray (1982), 356–64. Kassope and Ambrakia: Doukellis (1990a), 404 and nn. 28–9; *Ergon* (1977), 70–7.

11 Pausanias 10.38.9; Baladié (1980), 220; Rizakis (1989); (1990). Cf. Kahrstedt (1950) for problems of chronology. On a Macedonian synoecism to support a new city: *IGBulg* IV 2263; Garnsey and Saller (1987), 29–30.

12 Bommeljé and Doorn (1987). See *AR* (1986/7), 22 for fieldwork by the Patras Ephorate in Western Achaea.

13 Evidence for centuriation at Nikopolis and Ambrakia, Doukellis (1988b); (1990b); at Patrai, Rizakis (1985); at Corinth, Walbank (1986); cf. Chevallier (1958). From Macedon, possible cases of centuriation include those at the colonies of Dion and Pella, as well as Thessalonike; a definite pattern is argued for the Caesarian colony of Kassandreia in the Chalkidike by Doukellis (1988a). On the ideological force of "parceling up the world," see Purcell (1990), 20.

14 For the relationship of Augustus and Artemis: *CIL* 3 499, 510; Rizakis (1989), 184.

15 On east–west connections: Rougé (1966), 85; Slane (1986); Wright (1980). On the canal and the intentions of Caligula, Nero and Herodes Atticus: Suetonius, *Divus Julius* 44.3; *Caligula* 21; Pliny, *HN* 4.4.10; Engels (1990), 59–60; Wiseman (1978), 48–50. The *diolkos*, an overland causeway across the Isthmus, was also utilized during this period, for example by Octavian in 30 BC.

16 For the destructions in Epirus, see Ziolkowski (1986). On the situation in the region of Patrai: Pausanias 7.17.5–6; 7.18.6; Polybius 38.16.4–5; Rizakis (1989), 180. Administrative abuses: Cicero, *In Pisonem* 96.

17 Bowersock (1965a), 68; Purcell (1987), 72–5, 80–1, 89–90; Salmon (1969), 135. Landowners in western Achaia: Rizakis (1987/8); (1988). Augustan propaganda: Doukellis (1990a), 402–3.

18 On the "hellenization" of Corinth and Patrai: Bowersock (1965a), 69; Williams (1987); Wiseman (1979), 507–8.

19 Epirus: Bowersock (1965b), 288; Larsen (1938), 439–40 and n. 7; Keil (1936), 566. A new city, Hadrianopolis, created perhaps from a synoecism of an Epirote tribe, probably lay within this new province; Hierocles 651.8; Jones (1940), 65–6. Cf. Millar (1987), xiii; Mitchell (1987), 24.

20 Bowersock (1965a), 91. Less poetically, Larsen noted: "A more detailed survey will show that the number of flourishing cities in Greece was smaller under the Empire than it had previously been. Some cities had sunk into insignificance, others had disappeared entirely or been transformed into subject communities under the control of larger cities" (Larsen [1938], 467); cf. Picard (1989), 179.

21 Robert notes that other ancient authors shared this attitude; for example when Pliny reports that Larissa is gone, he means the loss of the independent *polis*, Robert (1951), 46 and n. 3; cf. Baladié (1980), 312–20. Examples of chronological vagueness would include Pausanias' mention of Arene, 5.6.2.

On the Boeotian cities, see Strabo, 9.2.25; Fossey (1988); Wallace (1972); (1979). For general discussion of the disappearance or movement of cities, see Demand (1990); Osborne (1987a), 55–6; (1991a), 247.

22 The text of Hierocles is dated to the early years of Justinian, but is probably based on information drawn from the first half of the fifth century AD; Gregory (1979), 273–7; Jones (1964), 716–17; Jones, A. (1971), 514–21, esp. 517.

23 On the transition to the Greek city of the Byzantine era, see Gregory (1982); (1984).

24 Kahrstedt (1954); cf. Jones (1956). Late Roman villas: in Halieis, Boyd and Rudolph (1978), 334; Rudolph (1979), 304–5; in Medeon, Fossey (1986), 26–9; in Epidauros Limera, Gregory (1984), 272.

25 On the Boeotian destructions: in Haliartos and Koroneia, Livy 42.63.3–12, 43.4.11; Fossey (1979), 562–71; in Thebes, Pausanias 7.15.9–10; in Lebadeia and Anthedon, Plutarch, *Sulla* 16, 26; Appian, *Mithridateios* 51; in Chorsiai, Fossey and Morin (1989), 166–79.

26 Papazoglou (1988) discusses the course of urbanism in the somewhat more militarily exposed province of Macedon.

27 Oliver (1953), 953–8; (1954).

28 On increasing financial pressures: Jones (1940); Migeotte (1984); (1985a); Millar (1983). Cities known to be in trouble: for Aigina, see *IG* IV 4; for Lykosoura, *SIG*³ 800; Rostovtzeff (1957), 254; for Sikyon, Griffin (1982), 90. Cities injured through warfare: for Gytheion, see *SIG*³ 748; for Tenos, *IG* XII 5 860; for Krannon, Migeotte (1984), 361; Austin (1981), 179–80. For Akraiphia, see Oliver (1971); Fossey (1979), 554–60.

29 Pre-conquest displacement of towns or people: for Pleuron, see Strabo 10.2.4; for Orneai, Pausanias 2.25.6; for Styra, Strabo 10.1.6; for Phokian cities, Pausanias 10.3.1–3, 10.33.8–9; for Tiryns, Strabo 8.6.11, Pausanias 2.25.8; for Thebes, Pausanias 9.23.5. Strabo (9.5.4) comments on a "fact which is common to, and true of, all countries, that whole regions and their several parts undergo changes in proportion to the power of those who hold sway."

30 For the Athenian evidence: Appian, *Bella Civilia* 5.7; Dio Cassius 69.16.2; Baladié (1980), 215–16; Larsen (1938), 467. Some ten years before (in 31 BC) Augustus had given Athens territory: Dio Cassius 38.39.2; Bowersock (1964); Hoff (1989a), 4; Kroll (1972). There is some confusion about the precise composition of these grants, see Day (1942), 134–6. For Sparta, see Cartledge and Spawforth (1989), 108–11.

31 On boundary competition: Hyginus 114, 12L; Brunt (1981), 165–6; Corbier (1991), 222; Sartre (1979), 213–18. Cf. Earle (1976) for a New World comparison.

32 On civic rivalry in Asia Minor, see Jones (1940), 249 and n. 73; Reynolds 1982; in Africa, Garnsey (1978), 245–6. See also Robert (1977); Syme (1981).

33 Megalopolis and Argos: Pausanias 8.27.1–2, 9.14.4; 2.25.6–8; cf. Moggi (1976). Medeon and Stiris: *SIG*³ 647; Austin (1981), no. 134; Fossey (1986), 99; Walbank (1981), 151–2. Aegean islands: Austin (1981), nos. 128, 133. Keos: Strabo 10.5.6; Cherry *et al.* (1991); Cherry and Davis (1991).

34 For Lykosoura, see Larsen (1938), 473. Other examples include villages to

Demetrias in Thessaly: Strabo 9.5.12; 9.5.15; Methydrion to Megalopolis: Pausanias 8.12.2; cities to Sparta: Pausanias 3.21.7; ?Chorsiai and Thisbe: Pliny, *HN* 4.3.8; Platon and Feyel (1938), 161 n. 1. Another potential case has been tentatively suggested by the investigators of the Methana survey project, on the basis of the landed interests of the Corinthian notable, L. Licinius Anteros, in Methana: Mee *et al.* (1991), 227. On dependent communities in other provinces: for Celaenae-Apamea, see Dio Chrysostom, *Oration* 35.14–15; for Nîmes, see Strabo 4.1.12; Pliny, *HN* 3.37.

35 Doyle (1986), 123–38, 198–231; Eisenstadt (1963), 175–83; Morris (1984). The development of a supralocal élite has been exceptionally well documented in the Aztec empire: Adams (1979a), 70; Hodge (1984); Smith (1986); for a Mayan comparison, Molloy and Rathje (1974).

36 For the evidence of Apuleius and Plutarch, see Millar (1981b), esp. 69 and Jones (1971b), ch. 5, "Plutarch's society: *domi nobiles,*" esp. 39–40; (1972). Historical and prosopographical examples of these alliances: Larsen (1953); Mitchell (1974); Oliver (1971); Spawforth (1974); (1978); (1980); (1984); (1985); (1986); Spawforth and Walker (1986); political allegiances over the imperial succession: Bowersock (1984), 178.

37 Patterson (1991), 152–6.

38 Cartledge and Spawforth (1989), 104.

39 Corinth: Spawforth and Walker (1985), 84, 86; Engels (1990), 69. Cornelius Pulcher was supposedly responsible for having Corinth declared free from taxation. On the Euryclids: Bowersock (1961); Biers (1985); Engels (1990), 70. Dedications from other non-Corinthian members of the Achaian élite, most notably Herodes Atticus, are also known in the capital. For the Athenian evidence: Spawforth and Walker (1985), 90–1; Jones (1978b). Other examples: Jones (1971b), 43 and n. 21. On élite traveling: Garnsey and Saller (1987), 99–100; Jones (1971b), 42 and nn. 16–17.

40 On Plutarch's background, Jones (1971b), 5–10. On the evidence from Argos, see Spawforth and Walker (1986), 101–2. Dio Chrysostom praised his town of Prusa, saying that despite frequent invitations from the chief cities of Greece, he never contemplated living elsewhere (*Oration* 44.6).

41 Rostovtzeff (1957), 254; cf. Juvenal: *Satires* 3.62. Italian urbanism: Garnsey (1983); Hopkins (1978a), 54–74; (1978b); W. Jongman, pers. comm. On the demographic effects of such a supercenter, compare Tenochtitlán in the New World, see Adams (1979a), 62.

42 Plutarch, *De vitando aere alieno* 831A; Rougé (1966), 88–9, 132–4; Gregory (1984), 271. Other cities too are described in positive terms by Strabo: Hermione, 8.6.12; Aigion, 8.7.5; Tegea, 8.8.2; Tanagra and Thespiai, 9.2.5, 9.2.25; Elateia, 9.3.2; Chalkis, 10.1.8, 11; Zakynthos, 10.2.18 and by Pausanias: Troizen, 2.30.10; Hermione, 2.34.11; Sparta, 3.11.2; Tanagra, 9.22.1–2; Lebadeia, 9.39.2; Elateia, 10.34.1; Amphissa, 10.38.4. The precise demographic or economic significance of such statements remains impossible to determine.

43 Patrai: Baladié (1980), 325; Papapostolou (1971); Rizakis (1989), 181. Athens: Shear (1981); Spawforth and Walker (1985); though Adams (1989),

11–12 rightly points out the archaeological evidence for "New Athens" remains undesirably sketchy.

44 See Engels (1990), 43–65 and Wiseman (1979) for a detailed description of the various attractions Corinth could boast.

45 Engels (1990), 84. These parameters are reached by using two different density figures: 100 people/hectare and 160 people/hectare; cf. 79–84. Water supply: Pausanias 2.3.5; Engels (1990), 76–8, 179–81; Robinson (1965), 29. For caveats on inferring population numbers from evidence such as this, see Fletcher (1981); Shaw (1980), 39.

46 Extensive surveys in the Corinthia, Engels (1990), 24; Wiseman (1978). Engels (1990), 27–33, 58 argues for the likelihood of imports; cf. Strabo 8.6.23. On the ceramic evidence, Slane (1986), 317.

47 Finley (1977a), 325.

48 Inland zones: Larsen (1938), 472–4, though see, for Arcadia, Lloyd (1991a), 190–1; for Phokis, Fossey (1986), 98–102. Examples of apparent coastal prosperity: Naupaktos: *AD* 26 (1975) B2: 315–19; Gytheion: *AD* 29 (1979) B2: 292–4. On the *cursus publicus*: pp. 121–2.

49 Bowersock (1965a), 5–13; (1969), 43–50; Crawford (1978); Jones (1978a), 116; Millar (1977), 494–5; cf. Plutarch, *Praecepta gerendae reipublicae* (hereafter *Praecepta*) 814C–D.

50 Elateia: Pausanias 10.34.2. For Athens, Cicero (*Pro Flacco* 26.62–3) asserted "the now shattered and weakened name of Greece is supported by the reputation of this city." On the Panhellenion: Spawforth and Walker (1985); Willers (1989). Hadrian as "savior and founder": Larsen (1938), 482–3 and n. 13. Sparta: Cartledge and Spawforth (1989), 190–211, esp. 210.

51 Pausanias 9.7.6; Plutarch, *Praecepta* 811B–C; Garnsey and Saller (1987), 30; Symeonoglou (1985), 148–55.

52 Other cases of *syngeneia*: Spawforth and Walker (1986), esp. 104. On similar processes elsewhere, see Garnsey (1978), 246 (Africa); Rogers (1991) (Asia).

53 For élite pedigrees, see Cartledge and Spawforth (1989), 162–5; Day (1942), 237–9; Herman (1987), 164; Jones (1971b), 40–2. On previous uses of the past: Alcock (1991a); Habicht (1961); Hedrick (1988).

54 For Hellenistic responses, see Davies (1984), 291; Gauthier (1972); Préaux (1978), 452–60; Tarn and Griffith (1952), 82–91; Walbank (1981), 141–58. Pausanias 7.16.9 reports the dissolution of leagues after the Achaean War.

55 On imperial encouragement of leagues, for Augustus, see Bowersock (1965a), 91; for Hadrian, Larsen (1938), 452; for Antoninus Pius, Oliver (1978), 190. For general discussion of leagues: Deininger (1965); Larsen (1955); (1968); Oliver (1978). League duties: Brunt (1961); Larsen (1955), 112–13, 123–4; Millar (1966), 389–90. Thessaly: *IG* ix 2 261; Larsen (1938), 442; Levick (1985), 62–3. Phokis: *IG* ix 1 61; Larsen (1938), 442.

56 Spawforth and Walker (1985), 81.

57 On the concept of "bridgehead" or "gateway" communities, see Galtung (1971); Burghardt (1971); Hirth (1978a).

58 For the behavior of provincial governors, see Burton (1975). Reports of embassies to Rome: Millar (1977), 394; Souris (1984). On Corinth and the

leagues: Oliver (1978), 191. It is worth mentioning, however, that numerous inscriptions dealing with the affairs of the province and with honors to provincial administrators have been discovered in Corinth: Wiseman (1979), 501–2 and n. 245.

59 On the origin of colonists: Engels (1990), 69–70. Italian influences in the colony: Engels (1990), 44, 62, 69. Numismatic evidence: Amandry (1988), 101.

60 Slane (1986), 317–18; also (1980). Until the mid-second century AD, western imports outnumbered those from the east, Slane (1989).

61 Williams (1989), 157. Walbank (1989), 394, for one, identified the Capitolium with Temple E in Corinth: "The recognition of the form and identity of the temple and its precinct highlights an aspect of Early Roman Corinth that is often overlooked, namely, that in layout, organization and religious practice, Corinth was a Roman colony and not simply a restoration of a Greek city."

62 Robinson (1974), esp. 484.

63 Engels (1990), 72, 101–2, 106.

64 The Isthmian Games "were wont to draw crowds of people": Strabo 8.6.20; on the games generally: Amandry (1988), 10–13, 101; Biers and Geagan (1970); Engels (1990), 52, 96–7, 212 n. 44; Geagan (1968); (1989). On the Roman arch: Gregory and Mills (1984).

65 On this distinction in other empires, see Brumfiel (forthcoming); Schreiber (1987), 266; Smith and Berdan (1992).

## 5   THE SACRED LANDSCAPE

1 For a range of archaeological studies of the sacred or ceremonial landscape, see Bradley (1984); (1990); Farrington (1992); Hall (1976); Kuper (1972); Kus (1989); Marcus (1973); Wheatley (1971).

2 Sourvinou-Inwood (1988); (1990); Jameson (1980); (1988).

3 Berve and Gruben (1963); Farnell (1896–1909); Ferguson (1989); Tomlinson (1976); though see Schachter (1967). The classic, if erratic, study of the positioning of sanctuaries is Scully (1979).

4 On the likelihood of religious development through time: Geertz 1966; Sourvinou-Inwood (1990), 300–1; Vernant (1983b). On the significance of sanctuary placement: de Polignac (1984), 41–92; Snodgrass (1986), 262–3. For recent research in this area, see Cole (forthcoming); Edlund (1987); Morgan (1990); Osborne (1987a), 165–92; (1985), 154–72.

5 Eisenstadt (1979); cf. Conrad and Demarest (1984).

6 Elsner (forthcoming); also Habicht (1985), esp. 20–1 and 165–75. For other recent work on Pausanias, see Hunt (1984), 391–401; Snodgrass (1987), 75–89; Veyne (1988), 3. For an excellent illustrated commentary, Papachatzis (1974–81).

7 Jost (1985), 549.

8 Tegea had benefited from an Archaic synoecism which resulted in the concentration of population and resources in the city; Strabo 8.8.2; Baladié (1980), 331–4. On Tegea's importance in the communication network of the

Peloponnese, see Sanders and Whitbread (1990).

9 Strabo 8.3.13; Baladié (1980), 335.

10 On Sulla's depredations, see Pausanias 9.33.6; 10.21.6. Caligula in turn had ordered the Zeus from Olympia be brought to Rome, Josephus, *Antiquitates Judaicae* 19.1.1; Suetonius, *Caligula* 22, 58.

11 The monuments on the Athenian acropolis are, of course, the best-known, if not the longest-lived, examples of ruins as "Mahnmale": see Schneider and Höcker (1990), 113–20. Among other unrepaired temples Pausanias mentions are those at Haliartos, known to have been destroyed by the Romans, but he seems somewhat confused about the destruction of this city, attributing it to the Persians, 9.32.4; 10.35.2; Habicht (1985), 99.

12 Roman looting: Larsen (1938), 313–25; Pollitt (1986), 153–6, 159–62. For the behavior of generals: on Mummius, Velleius Paterculus 1.13.4; Pollitt (1986), 158; on Marcellus, Plutarch, *Marcellus* 21.

13 Gordon (1979), 11 and n. 26.

14 See the discussion on pp. 140–1; Pollitt (1983), 66–74. Other examples include the depredations of Xerxes, who removed the Tyrannicides from Athens and an Apollo from Miletus; Alexander and Seleucus later returned these: Pausanias 1.8.5; 1.16.3. For the Pergamene reward: Pausanias 7.16.8.

15 Dio Chrysostom, on the other hand, counseled tolerance of the Roman deeds: "nor would the persons be any the worse off because, instead of being set up as offerings at Megara or Epidauros or in the market-place of Andros or Mykonos, [the statues] were set up in the sacred places of the Romans" (*Oration* 31.151).

16 Pollitt (1986), 160.

17 See Jost (1985), 542–4. All ancient references are to Pausanias. *Isis*: at Athens, see Walker (1979); at Megara, 1.41.3; at Phlius, 2.13.7; at Troizen, 2.32.6; at Methana, 2.34.1; at Bura, 7.25.9. *Serapis and Isis*: at Corinth, 2.4.6, see also Smith (1977); at Hermione, 2.34.10; at Boiai, 3.22.13; at Thouria, 4.32.6; at Aigeira, 7.26.7. *Serapis*: at Oitylos, 3.25.10; at Kopai, 9.24.1–2; at Patrai, 7.21.13. *Ammon*: at Gytheion, 3.21.8; at Thebes, 8.16.1. *Didymenian Mother and Attis*: at Patrai, 7.20.3; at Dyme, 7.17.8. Apart from Tithorea, another non-urban example is the cult of Isis and Serapis dedicated by L. Vibullius Spanios and his wife (second century AD) in Hylai, a *kome* of Thespiai: Schachter (1981), 201. Cf. Solmsen (1979).

18 A similar proliferation occurred in Asia Minor, though the present study does not collect the evidence for Achaia as fully as Price (1984), esp. 78–100, maps II–V, has done for that province. In any case, no Achaian *kome* is known to have possessed the necessary size and autonomy either to wish, or to be able, to conduct imperial cult, Price (1984), 78–86, 136–46. Pausanias provides several examples of cult in smaller Achaian cities: in Megara, 1.40.2; in Sikyon, 2.8.1; in Asopos, 3.22.9; in Kynaitha, 8.19.1–2. On Arcadia: Jost (1985), 541. For the behavior of free cities, see Benjamin and Raubitschek (1959), 73.

19 In the traditional civic cults of the Classical epoch, the entire urban framework was utilized, since cities for the most part lacked a centralized and unified cult center: Martin (1974), 253. Pausanias (9.22.2) approved Tanagra's urban layout, with spatially distinct zones for residence and sanctuaries.

20 Olympieion: Pausanias 1.18.6–7; Abramson (1974); Vermeule (1977), 85; Wycherley (1964). For the Roman acropolis: Schneider and Höcker (1990), 222–34. Oddly enough, Pausanias does not mention the Roma and Augustus temple: Binder (1969); Kawerau (1888); Mellor (1975), 101–5; Travlos (1971), 494. For the Roman Parthenon: Pausanias 1.24.7; Caroll (1982); Oliver (1983), 102; Smith (1896), 339; *AR* (1984/5), 6. For Julia Domna: Oliver (1965), 179. *Arae Augusti* in Athens: Benjamin and Raubitschek (1959), 84–5. On altars to Augustus and to Hadrian: Benjamin (1963); Price (1984), 69. Roman agora: Benjamin and Raubitschek (1959), 85; Camp (1986), 184.
21 Cartledge and Spawforth (1989), 108, 127–8.
22 Messene: Habicht (1985), 42–6, 58; on the possible re-identification of the precinct: *AR* (1987/8), 20. Orchomenos: Alcock (1991a), 462–3. Gytheion: *SEG* IX 923; Price (1984), 109 and nn. 58, 111. Images of Hadrian and his family in the Theater of Dionysos at Athens (blocking the view) are also worth mentioning, Vermeule (1968), 19–20. This list makes no pretense at comprehensiveness; for a regional survey of imperial shrines in Achaia, see Trummer (1980); Vermeule (1968).
23 Murray and Petsas (1989), 86; see also Carter (1977); Doukellis (1990a), 405–6. For the setting of triumphal arches generally: Clavel-Lévêque and Lévêque (1982). Arch of Hadrian: *IG* II² 5185; Travlos (1971), 253–7; the new theory is that of Adams (1989). For the arch at Isthmia, see p. 169, fig. 58.
24 Jost (1985), 541–2; Spawforth (1978), 255–6.
25 For evidence on festival crowds, see Lucian, *Peregrinus* 1; Plutarch, *Quaestiones conviviales* 628A (Athens), 638B, 674F (Delphi), 723A (Corinth); Jones (1970); (1971b), 42. On the Boeotian festivals: Schachter (1981), 216–19; (1986), 147–53, 156–79. In general, Spawforth (1989).
26 On other "Olympia"s: Cartledge and Spawforth (1989), 187; Spawforth (1986), 327–31; (1989), 194. Metroon: Pausanias 5.20.9; Hitzl (1991); Price (1984), 160–1. Nymphaeum of Herodes Atticus: Bol (1984); Tomlinson (1976), 64; Vermeule (1977), 84; Walker (1987).
27 For Peregrinus it was "at the height of the festival, all but in the theatre, that he plans to roast himself," but the final event actually took place immediately afterwards and some way from the sanctuary, Lucian, *Peregrinus* 19–21, 35–6; Jones (1986), 117–32.
28 *Delphi*: one of the three Marmaria temples held statues of a "few Roman emperors," the other two were abandoned, Pausanias 10.8.6. Domitian undertook restorations here: *SIG*³ 821; Millar (1977), 450; Tomlinson (1976), 70. The Amphiktyonic League continued to play a part in provincial life, though it was now used and modified by imperial policy, for example in the prominent role given to Nikopolis by Augustus, cf. Larsen (1958). The prosperous condition of *Isthmia* has already been discussed (p. 169). *Nemea* was in a somewhat different state, for the games had been moved to Argos before 100 BC. Pausanias reported an abandoned temple and a missing cult image, which may well have been transferred to Argos: Pausanias 2.15.2, 2.24.2; Miller (1990), 20, 23–4, 57, 141–2, 193.
29 Strabo 8.8.2; Baladié (1980), 336 and n. 239.
30 Shear (1981), 365; Camp (1986), 184–7; Thompson and Wycherley (1972),

160–8; Thompson (1962). *Temple of Ares*: Dinsmoor (1940); McAllister (1959); Townsend (1955). *Zeus Agoraios*: Shear (1981), 365; Stillwell (1933), 140–8; Thompson (1952), 91–3. *Southwest and Southeast Temples*: Dinsmoor (1974); (1982); Thompson (1960), 339–43. Dinsmoor dates the Southeast Temple to the first half of the second century AD; the Southwest to the first half of the first century AD. For the Odeion of Agrippa, see Thompson (1950). It should be noted, however, that the Temple of Nemesis at Rhamnous (possibly part of the same fifth-century building program as the Acharnai and Sounion temples) was left in place and indeed repaired and rededicated to Livia in AD 45/6; Broneer (1932); Miles (1989). Eliakis (1980) attributes temple repairs there to the reign of Julian.

31 Oliver (1972) dates the decree *IG* II² 1035 to 27/26 BC; Culley (1975); (1977) dates it to between 10/9 and 3/2 BC. Shear (1981), 366–7 opts for a Claudian date. Salamis may be especially prominent in this program owing to its recent restoration to Athens by Julius Nikanor, the "New Homer and New Themistocles," Jones (1978b), 222–8. The hoplite general, king archon and other important officials were given responsibility for implementing this legislation.

32 Shear (1981), 362.

33 Shear (1981), 362–3; cf. Camp (1986), 187. For an echo of the *De finibus* (hereafter *Fin.*), one can turn to Byron's "Childe Harold's Pilgrimage" (II.88), "Where'er we tread 'tis haunted, holy ground . . ."

34 Bowersock (1984), esp. 174.

35 Shear (1981), 360. Zeus Eleutherios: Thompson (1966); Thompson and Wycherley (1972), 102–3. Claudius: *IG* II–III² 3274. Livia as Artemis Boulaia: Oliver (1965); Thompson and Wycherley (1972), 166.

36 On the reuse of Athenian monuments: on the acropolis, Dinsmoor (1920); in the agora, Vanderpool (1959). For the Aemilius Paullus monument, see Pollitt (1986), 156–8. On reuse or sharing of temples: Pausanias 1.40.2; Price (1984), 146–62. Hadrian as eponymous hero: Pausanias 1.5.5; Graindor (1934), 83–4; Oliver (1983), 103–4. Hellenistic rulers previously had been granted that status.

37 Price (1984), 119. On Lucius' appeal: Millar (1981b), 66; Price (1984), 119, 192–3. Manumissions also occurred at the shrines to Egyptian deities and at the panhellenic center of Delphi: Hopkins (1978a), 133–71; Schachter (1981), 200–5.

38 Obvious examples include Messene, where a member of the prominent Saethida family was high priest, and his son was made a Roman senator by Hadrian: Habicht (1985), 58 and n. 80. In Sparta, Eurycles was the founder and almost certainly the first high priest of the city's imperial cult, which was subsequently held "by inheritance": Cartledge and Spawforth (1989), 99. On the festival of the Megala Ptoia and Kaisareia: Schachter (1981), 209.

39 Price (1984), 100, also 126–32; cf. Zanker (1988), 302–6.

40 All the following references are to Pausanias. Extra- or peri-urban sanctuaries: 2.12.2 (Hera); 2.36.2 (Apollo); 2.36.8 (Athena Saitis); 3.22.10 (Athena); 7.22.11 (Triclaria); 8.41.10 (Aphrodite); 8.53.11 (Artemis); 8.54.5 (Apollo);

10.38.8 (Poseidon); 8.35.5 (Artemis Sciatis). Urban sanctuaries: 2.7.6 (Artemis); 2.9.7 (Apollo Lykeios); 2.11.2 (various); 2.24.3 (Larisean Zeus); 2.34.10 (Athena); 8.14.4 (Athena); 8.24.6 (Aphrodite); 8.30.4 (The Mother); 8.31.9 (Athena, Hera); 9.33.3 (anonymous); 10.38.13 (Asklepios).

41 Frazer (1898), xiv.

42 At least one of the examples cited in the *De defectu oraculorum*, the Ptoion sanctuary, is known to have survived long after Plutarch pronounced it dead. A late first-century date is suggested for Plutarch's composition, but epigraphic evidence shows that the Ptoia were still celebrated into the third century AD. The sanctuary did, however, have periodic breakdowns in its celebration owing to economic difficulties; in at least two episodes, wealthy local men had to come to the sanctuary's rescue. See *IG* VII 2712; *SEG* XV 330; Fossey (1979), 589; Ogilvie (1967); Schachter (1981), 72. *Warfare*: in Haliartos, Pausanias 9.33.3; in Alalkomenai, 9.33.5–6. *Economic distress*: Jost (1985), 550–1. What must be avoided above all is the attribution of defunct sanctuaries to a growing disillusionment with traditional pagan cults. Christianizing attitudes about the debasement of religious life during this period tend to color such arguments, and suggestions that paganism continued only "fitfully" under the Principate have now largely been dismissed. Compare Festugière (1972) and Tomlinson (1976), 23–4 with Lane Fox (1986) and MacMullen (1981).

43 On these issues, see Elsner (forthcoming); Cartledge and Spawforth (1989), 190–211. "Tour guides": Hunt (1984), 397–9. It remains an intriguing point that to Pausanias an empty temple appears to form as significant a landmark as any functioning sanctuary.

44 Skinner (1964), 38. For related studies in other contexts, see Farrington (1992); Geertz (1977); Kertzer (1988), 22–3; Tuan (1977), 161–78; Turner (1974), 193–6.

45 Callaghan (1978); Hood and Smyth (1981), 20–3; Shaw (1986), 222–35; cf. Harrison (1991); Sanders (1982), 36–40. I must thank Peter J. Callaghan for his thoughts on this subject.

46 Imperial gifts included a gold crown and purple robe from Nero, and a golden peacock from Hadrian. Of a statue of Orestes before the entrance: "they say . . . that it represents the Emperor Augustus" (Pausanias 2.17.3). Hadrian's image was put up within the temple, possibly in recognition of his financial support for public works; poorly preserved inscriptions commemorate his donations: Strabo 8.6.10; Pausanias 2.17.1–6; Caskey and Amandry (1952), 219–21 and n. 32; Waldstein (1905) I, 134–6. For Hadrianic interest in another rural cult, the sanctuary of Horse Poseidon at Mantineia, see Pausanias 8.10.2.

47 On Phigaleia: Jost (1985) 88, 96, 546. Whether or not the Helos region was still an official part of Spartan territory at this time is unclear, but the land was still closely linked with the city, see Cartledge and Spawforth (1989), 137–8. For the region, see Wagstaff (1982).

48 Bintliff and Snodgrass (1985), 158–60, table 7; Habicht (1985), 35–6.

49 To some extent, the effect of the Megalopolitan synoecism of the fourth century BC upon the Arcadian religious landscape can be seen as a forerunner to this development in imperial times. At the time of that synoecism, while some

sanctuaries were allowed to disappear, others were maintained in the former cities, symbolizing the new center's control over the most sacred places in the territory, and thus the territory itself; Jost (1985), 548–50. Argive territorial expansion followed a similar tactic, cf. Pausanias 2.25.6.

50 NVAP sites: Wright *et al.* (1990), 610–12. I thank the project directors for these observations. A similar drop in rural sanctuary numbers is apparent in the Southern Argolid, given the decline of "special-purpose" sites; Runnels and van Andel (1987), 309. On the island of Keos, the shrine at Ayia Irini was in use until the third century BC: Caskey (1981), 127. On the Attic sites, Fowden (1988), 56–7, where he assumes "most of their visitors were simple local people"; cf. Langdon (1976).

51 Crawford (1981), 160; Blagg (1985); Frederiksen (1976), 353–4.

52 On élite benefactions in various cities: Graindor (1930); Jost (1985), 126–7, 551; Migeotte (1985b); Oliver (1971); Spawforth (1989), 196–7. Apart from individual benefactors, groups of citizens could still contribute through collective donations (*epidoseis*): Migeotte (1985c), 316; cf. (1984) for earlier Hellenistic parallels. Other signs of élite pre-eminence: Pausanias 9.3.6–8, 10.32.15; Small (1987).

53 For the Lykosoura dedications, see Spawforth (1978), 253; (1985), 222–4; Cartledge and Spawforth (1989), 103. Priesthoods too, especially hereditary priesthoods, served similar purposes, being restricted to a small cadre of prominent families. While hereditary priesthoods were not an imperial development (as the priestly aristocracies in Classical Sparta and Athens demonstrate), there nonetheless existed a close connection between the heroic pedigrees cultivated by wealthy families, and civic priesthoods: Cartledge and Spawforth (1989), 194–5.

54 Cartledge and Spawforth (1989), 170; Spawforth (1989), 196. Apart from Sparta, other profitable festival locations would be Argos, Corinth, Athens, Epidauros and Thespiai (although this last shows no sign of benefiting from the demands of the Erotideia or Mouseia crowds). On the profitability of landownership around Epidauros, and the presence of the family of the Statilii: Spawforth (1985), 248–58. Lykosoura too was believed to attract revenues from visitors: Jones (1940), 140. On the financial impact of a major Italian sanctuary: Blagg (1985), 46.

55 Cartledge and Spawforth (1989), 137–8, 194; on the family of Brasidas: Spawforth (1985), 224–44.

56 As in the ancient tradition of sacrificing to the children of Glauke at Corinth: "after Corinth was laid waste by the Romans and the old Corinthians were wiped out, the new settlers broke the custom" (Pausanias 2.3.7); Williams (1987). Agonistic festivals: Spawforth (1989). Interesting studies of individual cults: Kabirion, Schachter (1986), 66–110, esp. 104–6; Eleusinian Demeter, Walker (1989); and of individual cities, Rogers (1991).

57 On cultic landscapes in other Roman provinces: Blagg (1986); Hingley (1985); King (1990); Picard (1983); Wilson (1973). Cf. Henig and King (1986).

58 Attitudes to religious resistance, see Garnsey (1978), 253 *contra* Benabou (1976); cf. Curchin (1991), 180–90. Suppression of the Druids: Clavel-

Lévêque (1985); King (1990), 232–4. For religious tension in other empires: Appadurai and Breckenridge (1976); Carrasco (1961); Farriss (1984); Miller and Farriss (1979).

59 This incident with Athena occurred in 21 BC, see Bowersock (1964); Hoff (1989a), esp. 269; (1989b), 4. Other instances of possible symbolic ambivalence might include the occasional imperial temple reported as deserted by Pausanias, such as in Elis (6.24.10): "adjoining the market place is an old temple surrounded by pillars; the roof has fallen down, and I found no image in the temple. It is dedicated to the Roman emperors." One abandoned temple in Mantineia had been dedicated to Aphrodite as Ally, commemorating the Mantineian alliance with Octavian at Actium. Motivations for the cult apparently proved, as Jost put it, "too circumstantial": Pausanias 8.9.6; Jost (1985), 550. Cf. Deininger (1971).

## 6 GREECE WITHIN THE EMPIRE

1 I am obliged to Dr. Antony Spawforth for many ideas about the potential effects of Late Roman taxation which he will develop in detail elsewhere. On coastal sites: Melos, where these harbors appear to be linked to the export of raw minerals (p. 111), see Wagstaff and Cherry (1982a), 145–6; for Methana, see Mee *et al.* (1991), 227; for the Southern Argolid, where local manufactures of amphorae have also been noted, see Runnels and van Andel (1987), 319, 326. For some background on trends in Late Roman taxation, see Jones (1964); MacMullen (1976); Whittaker (1980).

2 For the behavior of *decuriones*: Bowersock (1965a), 148–9; Jones (1963), 8; Millar (1983). Discussions of the Late Antique city in the Greek east include Ellis (1988); Foss (1977); Gregory (1982); (1984); Kennedy (1985).

3 Some scholars have considered the possible *loss* of external supplies (for example to feed Constantinople) to explain Late Roman agricultural intensification, e.g. van Andel and Runnels (1987), 116–17; for a proposed cultic response, Langdon (1976), 7–8, 73–6, 94–5. For some problems in understanding Late Roman commerce, Wickham (1988). One comparison of Late Roman trajectories in the eastern and western empires may be found in Bintliff and Snodgrass (1988a).

4 Adams (1979a), 69; see also Dyson (1985), 5.

5 Advocates of developmental studies: Deman (1975); Michel (1975); cf. Leveau (1978), but they are strongly criticized by Thompson (1982). On the underdeveloped Roman economy: Garnsey and Saller (1987), 43.

6 Hopkins (1980), 101; Garnsey and Saller (1987), 95–7. Achaia is not specifically mentioned in either of these discussions.

7 On the Guadalquivir Valley: Ponsich (1974); (1979); Curchin (1991), 126–8. On the Libyan evidence, Barker and Jones (1985); Buck and Mattingly (1985); Mattingly (1988); for other references, see Mattingly (1989), 275 n. 3. For diversity within these provinces, see Dyson (1991), 28 and Mattingly (1989).

8 Lower Moesia: Garnsey and Saller (1987), 90–1; Poulter (1979). For the

Neothermal Dalmatia Project, see Chapman and Shiel (1991), esp. 72; Chapman *et al.* (1987). For a recent synthesis of British data, see Millett (1990), esp. 201–5.

9 Two recent useful collections of data are Barker and Lloyd (1991) and Greene (1986).

10 Such a response is clear in a variety of other imperial settings; for example in New World contexts: Blanton *et al.* (1981), 26–7; Earle *et al.* (1987); Redmond (1983), 176.

11 Patterson (1991), esp. 164–5; (1987). One difference between the two areas is that Lycia was under compulsion to pay tax, "exacerbating the general tendencies paralleled by the situation in Samnium, where tax-collection was not a significant factor."

12 Lloyd (1991a) extends Patterson's model to the Greek upland region of Arcadia.

13 Nicolet (1988), 206.

14 Aidepsos: Plutarch, *De fraterno amore* 487F; Gregory (1979). It was while Sulla was at Aidepsos that he was presented with a gift of fish by men of Halai (one of his victims during the Mithridatic wars) earning the retort "What, is any man of Halai still alive?" (Plutarch, *Sulla* 26.3–4). Pausanias also mentions hot baths some 30 stades from the town of Ancient Methana; "it wells up hot and exceedingly salt" (2.34.1).

15 On the pleasures of Asia, see Bowersock (1965a), 75. A Greek education became the fashion of the sons of wealthy Romans; see, for example, Bowersock (1965a), 75–80; Camp (1989). On Sparta: *Daily Telegraph* 17–12–91, p. 12; Cartledge and Spawforth (1989), 207–11. Spencer (1954), 48–54 discusses the "sentiment of place" felt by Roman tourists in Greece.

16 Eisner (1991), 30 and *passim*.

17 Jones (1978a), 50–3, 56–64 on some of the literary influences perceptible in these orations.

18 Snell (1953), 282; Williams (1970), 65–70, esp. 67 on *Eclogue* 1; Jenkyns (1989), esp. 39. For references to Arcadia in the *Eclogues*: 4.58; 7.4–5; 10.26–7, 32–3. Other discussions of Virgil's Arcadia: Alpers (1979); Leach (1974); Segal (1981), 285–8; van Sickle (1967). For later interpretations of the concept, see Crook (1989); Panofsky (1955). Crook (1989), 52 quotes Burne-Jones on the "Arcadian vision": "a beautiful romantic dream of something that never was, never will be – in a light better than any light that ever shone – in a land no one can define or remember, only desire."

19 Angelomatis-Tsougarakis (1990), 13 and 25. See also Constantine (1984); (1989), 9–12; Hibbert (1987), 219–29; Spencer (1954), 54–85. The accounts of the early modern travelers cover a broad spectrum of responses to Greece; to be fair, more sympathetic and detailed accounts (such as those of Colonel W. M. Leake) do exist, but they are exceptional. The nature of the exact expectations laid upon Greece changed through time; "Hellenism" was hardly a static concept, and varied from one European country to another; cf. Turner (1981).

20 Tsigakou (1981), 30. On misapprehensions about the appearance of the Greek countryside: Jenkyns (1980), 171; Rackham (1983), 345–6; Snodgrass (1987),

69–71. See Tsigakou (1981), 9–78 for a detailed discussion of the artistic "rediscovery" of Greece. Eighteenth- and nineteenth-century representations of the newly explored South Pacific (considered an "Arcadian" setting by some) provides a parallel case: "the artist had rarely been more than an illustrator of the convictions of the group to which he belonged, or which employed him" (Smith [1950], esp. 100).

21 McNeal (1991), esp. 50; Schneider and Höcker (1990). On the "modern" presentation of the Parthenon marbles in the British Museum, see Osborne (1987b).

22 Eco (1986), 39.

23 The quotation is taken from a proclamation by Alexandros Ypsilantis in 1821, quoted in Tsigakou (1981), 48. For Herzfeld's ideas, (1982), 3–23, esp. 23. Competing constructions of Greek identity (the "Hellenist" thesis *vs.* the more introspective and self-critical "Romeic") emerged within the new nation, although in the early years the former was easily dominant, responding as it did to "the European image of Classical Greece" (p. 20).

24 John Galt, *Letters from the Levant* (1813), quoted in Angelomatis-Tsougarakis (1990), 92. McNeal (1991), 50–1, 61–3 discusses the Greek rejection of certain periods of their past. For some background on European influences upon the fledgling nation, see Clogg (1979), 43–104.

25 Finlay (1857), xix.

# Bibliography

Abbott, F. F. and Johnson, A. C. (1926) *Municipal Administration in the Roman Empire*, Princeton.

Abrams, P. (1978) "Towns and economic growth: some theories and problems," in Abrams, P. and Wrigley, E. A., eds., *Towns in Societies: Essays in Economic History and Historical Sociology*, 9–33. Cambridge.

Abramson, H. (1974) "The Olympieion in Athens and its connections with Rome," *California Studies in Classical Antiquity* 7: 1–25.

Accame, S. (1946) *Il dominio romano in Grecia dalla Guerra Acaica ad Augusto*, Rome.

Adams, A. (1989) "The arch of Hadrian at Athens," in Walker and Cameron, eds., 10–16.

Adams, R. McC. (1979a) "Late Hispanic empires of the New World," in Larsen, ed., 59–73.

(1979b) "Common concerns but different viewpoints: a commentary," in Larsen, ed., 393–404.

Åkerström-Hougen, G. (1974) *The Calendar and Hunting Mosaics of the Villa of the Falconer in Argos*, Stockholm.

Alcock, S. E. (1989a) "Archaeology and imperialism: Roman expansion and the Greek city," *JMA* 2: 87–135.

(1989b) "Roman imperialism in the Greek landscape," *JRA* 2: 5–34.

(1991a) "Tomb cult and the post-classical polis," *AJA* 95: 447–67.

(1991b) "Urban survey and the polis of Phlius," *Hesperia* 60: 421–63.

(in press, a) "Breaking up the Hellenistic world: survey and society," in Morris, I., ed., *Classical Greece: Ancient Histories and Modern Archaeologies*, Cambridge.

(in press, b) "Changes on the ground in early imperial Boeotia," in Bintliff, J., ed., *Proceedings of the 6th International Congress on Boiotian Antiquities*, Liverpool.

(forthcoming) "Nero at play? The emperor's Grecian odyssey," in Elsner, J. and Masters, J., eds., *Culture and Society in the Age of Nero*, London.

Alcock, S. E., Cherry, J. F. and Davis, J. L. (in press) "Intensive survey, agricultural practice and the Classical landscape of Greece," in Morris, I., ed., *Classical Greece: Ancient Histories and Modern Archaeologies*, Cambridge.

Alpers, P. (1979) *The Singer of the Eclogues: A Study of Virgilian Pastoral*, Berkeley.

Amandry, M. (1988) *Le Monnayage des duovirs corinthiens* (*BCH* Supplement 15), Paris.

Ameling, W. (1983) *Herodes Atticus II: Inschriftenkatalog*, Hildesheim.

# Bibliography

Ammerman, A. J. and Feldman, M. W. (1978) "Replicated collection of site surfaces," *AAnt* 43: 734–40.

Anderson-Stojanovic, V. R. (1987) "The chronology and function of ceramic unguentaria," *AJA* 91: 105–22.

Angelomatis-Tsougarakis, H. (1990) *The Eve of the Greek Revival: British Travellers' Perceptions of Early Nineteenth-Century Greece*, London.

Appadurai, A. and Breckenridge, C. A. (1976) "The South Indian temple: authority, honor and redistribution," *Contributions to Indian Sociology* 10: 187–211.

Argoud, G. (1987) "Eau et agriculture en Grèce," in Louis, P., Métral, F. and Métral, J., eds., *L'Homme et l'eau en Méditerranée et au Proche-Orient IV: L'eau dans l'agriculture*, Lyons.

Asheri, D. (1966) *Distribuzioni di terre nell'antica Grecia* (Memoria dell'accademia delle scienze di Torino, Series 4, no. 10), Turin.

Athanasiadis, N. (1975) "Zur postglazialen Vegetationsentwicklung von Litochoro Katerinis und Pertouli Trikalon (Griechenland)," *Flora* 164: 99–132.

Athanassakis, A. N. (1983) "A new frontier for the archaeology of Epirus: a preliminary survey of Ano Radovyzia," *The Ancient World* 8: 47–66.

Aupert, P. (1987) "Pausanias et l'Asclépieion d'Argos," *BCH* 111: 511–17.

Austin, M. M. (1981) *The Hellenistic World from Alexander to the Roman Conquest*, Cambridge.

Axioti, K. (1980) "Romaikoi dromoi tes Aitoloakarnanias," *AD* 35 A: 186–205.

Badian, E. (1972) *Publicans and Sinners*, Oxford.

Bakhuizen, S. C. (1976) *Chalcis-in-Euboea: Iron and Chalcidians Abroad* (Chalcidian Studies III), Leiden.

(1979) "On Boeotian iron," *Teiresias* Supplement 2 (Proceedings of the Second International Conference on Boeotian Antiquities), 19–21. Montreal.

(1985) *Studies in the Topography of Chalcis on Euboea*, Leiden.

Baladié, R. (1980) *Le Péloponnèse de Strabon*, Paris.

Barker, G. (1991) "Approaches to archaeological survey," in Barker and Lloyd, eds., 1–9.

Barker, G. and Hodges, R. (1981) "Archaeology in Italy, 1980: new directions and misdirections," in Barker and Hodges, eds., 1–16.

Barker, G. and Hodges R., eds. (1981) *Archaeology and Italian Society: Prehistoric, Roman and Medieval Studies* (BAR International Series 102), Oxford.

Barker, G. and Jones, B. (1985) "Investigating ancient agriculture on the Saharan fringe: the UNESCO Libyan Valleys Survey," in Macready, S. and Thompson, F. H., eds., *Archaeological Field Survey in Britain and Abroad* (Society of Antiquaries Occasional Paper 6), 225–41. London.

Barker, G. and Lloyd J., eds. (1991) *Roman Landscapes: Archaeological Survey in the Mediterranean Region* (Archaeological Monographs of the British School at Rome 2), London.

Barker, G., Lloyd, J. and Webley, D. (1978) "A classical landscape in Molise," *PBSR* 33: 35–51.

Barlett, P. F. (1980) "Adaptive strategies in peasant agricultural production," *AnnRevAnth* 9: 545–73.

Barrett, J., Bradley, R. and Green, M. (1991) *Landscape, Monuments and Society: The*

*Prehistory of Cranborne Chase*, Cambridge.

Behr, C. A. (1981) *P. Aelius Aristides, The Complete Works. Volume 2: Orations XVII– LIII*, Leiden.

Bekker-Nielsen, T. (1989) *The Geography of Power: Studies in the Urbanization of Roman North-West Europe* (BAR International Series 477), Oxford.

Beloch, K. J. (1927) *Griechische Geschichte* (Volume 4), Berlin.

Benabou, M. (1976) *La Résistance africaine à la romanisation*, Paris.

Benjamin, A. S. (1963) "The altars of Hadrian in Athens and Hadrian's panhellenic program," *Hesperia* 32: 57–86.

Benjamin, A. S. and Raubitschek, A. E. (1959) "Arae Augusti," *Hesperia* 28: 65–85.

Bennet, D. J. L. (1986) Aspects of the administrative organization of LMII–IIIB Crete: a study based on archaeological and textual data. Unpublished Ph.D. dissertation, University of Cambridge.

Bennet, J. and Voutsaki, S. (1991) "A synopsis and analysis of travelers' accounts of Keos (to 1821)," in Cherry *et al.*, 365–82.

Bentley, J. W. (1987) "Economic and ecological approaches to land fragmentation: in defense of a much-maligned phenomenon," *AnnRevAnth* 16: 31–67.

Bernhardt, R. (1971) *Imperium und Eleutheria: die römische Politik gegenüber den freien Städten des griechischen Ostens*, Hamburg.

(1977) "Der Status des 146 v.Chr. unterworfenen Teils Griechenlands bis zur Einrichtung der Provinz Achaia," *Historia* 26: 62–73.

(1980) "Die Immunitas der Freistädte," *Historia* 29: 190–207.

(1985) *Polis und römische Herrschaft in der späten Republik, 149–31 v.Chr.*, Berlin.

Berve, H. and Gruben, G. (1963) *Greek Temples, Theatres and Shrines*, London.

Bhaduri, A., Rahman, H. Z. and Arn, A.-L. (1986) "Persistence and polarisation: a study in the dynamics of agrarian contradiction," *Journal of Peasant Studies* 13: 82–9.

Biers, J. C. (1985) *The Great Bath of the Lechaion Road* (Corinth Volume XVIII), Princeton.

Biers, W. R. (1971) "Excavations at Phlius, 1970," *Hesperia* 40: 242–7.

(1973) "Excavations at Phlius, 1972," *Hesperia* 42: 102–20.

(1975) "The theater at Phlius: excavations 1973," *Hesperia* 44: 51–68.

(1978) "Water from Stymphalos?" *Hesperia* 47: 171–84.

Biers, W. R. and Geagan, D. J. (1970) "A new list of victors in the Caesarea at Isthmia," *Hesperia* 39: 79–93.

Binder, W. (1969) *Der Roma-Augustus Monopteros auf der Akropolis in Athen und sein typologischer Ort*, Stuttgart.

Bintliff, J. L. (1985) "Greece: The Boeotia Survey," in Macready, S. and Thompson, F. H., eds., *Archaeological Field Survey in Britain and Abroad* (Society of Antiquaries Occasional Paper 6), 196–216. London.

(1991a) "The contribution of an *Annaliste*/structural history approach to archaeology," in Bintliff, J. L., ed., *The Annales School and Archaeology*, 1–33. Leicester.

(1991b) "The Roman countryside in Central Greece: observations and theories from the Boeotia survey (1978–1987)," in Barker and Lloyd, eds., 122–32.

(n.d.) "Further considerations on the population of ancient Boeotia." Unpublished paper.

Bintliff, J. L. and Snodgrass, A. M. (1985) "The Cambridge/Bradford Boeotian Expedition: the first four years," *JFA* 12: 123–61.

(1988a) "The end of the Roman countryside: a view from the east," in Jones, R., Bloemers, H., Dyson, S. and Biddle, M., eds., *First Millennium Papers: Western Europe in the First Millennium AD* (BAR International Series 401), 175–217. Oxford.

(1988b) "Mediterranean survey and the city," *Antiquity* 62: 57–71.

(1988c) "Off-site pottery distributions: a regional and interregional perspective," *Current Anthropology* 29: 506–13.

(1989) "From *polis* to *chorion* in south-west Boeotia," in Beister, H. and Buckler, J., eds., *Boiotika (Vorträge vom 5.Internationalen Böotien-Kolloquium zu Ehren von Professor Dr. Siegfried Lauffer)*, 285–99. Munich.

Blagg, T. F. C. (1985) "Cult practice and its social context in the religious sanctuaries of Latium and Southern Etruria: the sanctuary of Diana at Nemi," in Malone, C. and Stoddart, S., eds., *Papers in Italian Archaeology IV. Part iv: Classical and Medieval Archaeology* (BAR International Series 246), 33–50. Oxford.

(1986) "Roman religious sites in the British landscape," *Landscape History* 8: 15–25.

Blanton, R. E. (1976) "Anthropological studies of cities," *AnnRevAnth* 5: 249–64.

Blanton, R. E., Kowalewski, S. A., Feinman, G. and Appel, J. (1981) *Ancient Mesoamerica: A Comparison of Change in Three Regions*, Cambridge.

Blok, A. (1969) "South Italian agro-towns," *CSSH* 11: 121–35.

Blouet, B. W. (1971) "Rural settlement in Malta," *Geography* 56: 112–18.

(1972) "Factors influencing the evolution of settlement patterns," in Ucko, P. J., Tringham, R. and Dimbleby, G. W., eds., *Man, Settlement and Urbanism*, 3–15. London.

Boak, A. E. R. (1955) *Manpower Shortage and the Fall of the Roman Empire in the West*, Ann Arbor.

Boatwright, M. T. (1983) "Further thoughts on Hadrianic Athens," *Hesperia* 52: 173–6.

Bol, R. (1984) *Das Statuenprogramm des Herodes-Atticus-Nymphäums*, Berlin.

Bommeljé, S. and Doorn, P. K. (1984) *Strouza Region Project (1981–83): An Historic-Topographic Fieldwork. 1983: Second Interim Report*, Utrecht.

(1985) *Strouza Region Project (1981–4): An Historic-Topographic Fieldwork. 1984: Third Interim Report*, Utrecht.

(1987) *Aetolia and the Aetolians* (Studia Aetolica 1), Utrecht.

Bottema, S. (1982) "Palynological investigations in Greece with special reference to pollen as an indicator of human activity," *Paleohistoria* 24: 257–89.

Bowersock, G. W. (1961) "Eurycles of Sparta," *JRS* 51: 112–18.

(1964) "Augustus on Aegina," *CQ* 14: 120–1.

(1965a) *Augustus and the Greek World*, Oxford.

(1965b) "Zur Geschichte des römischen Thessaliens," *Rheinisches Museum* 108: 277–89.

(1969) *Greek Sophists in the Roman Empire*, Oxford.

ed. (1974) *Approaches to the Second Sophistic*, University Park, PA.

(1984) "Augustus and the East: the problem of the succession," in Millar, F. and Segal, E., eds., *Caesar Augustus: Seven Aspects*, 169–88. Oxford.

Bowie, E. L. (1974) "Greeks and their past in the Second Sophistic," in Finley, M. I.,

# Bibliography

ed., *Studies in Ancient Society*, 166–209. London.

Boyd, T. D. and Rudolph, W. W. (1978) "Excavations at Porto Cheli and vicinity, preliminary report IV: the lower town of Halieis, 1970–77," *Hesperia* 47: 333–55.

Bradley, R. (1984) *The Social Foundations of Prehistoric Britain: Themes and Variations in the Archaeology of Power*, London.

Bradley, R., ed. (1990) *Monuments and the Monumental* (= *WA* 22.2), London.

Braudel, F. (1973) *The Mediterranean and the Mediterranean World in the Age of Philip II* (Volumes 1 and 2, 2nd edn), London.

Brinkman, J. A. (1979) "Babylonia under the Assyrian empire, 745–627 BC," in Larsen, ed., 223–50.

Briscoe, J. (1974) "Rome and the class struggle in the Greek states: 200–146 BC," in Finley, M.I., ed., *Studies in Ancient Society*, 53–73 (= *Past and Present* 36 (1967): 3–20). London.

Broneer, O. (1932) "Some Greek inscriptions of Roman date from Attica," *AJA* 36: 397–400.

Broughton, T. R. S. (1934) "Roman landholding in Asia Minor," *Transactions of the American Philological Association* 65: 207–39.

Brown, P. and Podolefsky, A. (1976) "Population density, agricultural intensity, land tenure and group size in the New Guinea highlands," *Ethnology* 15: 211–38.

Brumfiel, E. (1983) "Aztec state making: ecology, structure and the origin of the state," *American Anthropologist* 85: 261–84.

(forthcoming) "The effects of expansion and contraction on subordinate communities: Aztec expansion in the Valley of Mexico," in Small, D., ed., *The Archaeology of Imperial Control*, Cambridge.

Bruneau, P. (1985) "Tendances de la mosaïque en Grèce à l'époque impériale," *ANRW* II.12.2: 320–46.

Brunt, P. A. (1961) "Charges of provincial maladministration under the early Principate," *Historia* 10: 189–227.

(1971) *Italian Manpower 225 BC–AD 14*, Oxford.

(1976) "The Romanization of the local ruling classes in the Roman Empire," in Pippidi, D.M., ed., *Assimilation et résistance à la culture gréco-romaine dans le monde ancien*, 161–73. Paris.

(1981) "The revenues of Rome": review of Neesen (1980), *JRS* 71: 161–72.

Buck, D. J. and Mattingly, D. J., eds. (1985) *Town and Country in Roman Tripolitania* (BAR International Series 274), Oxford.

Burford-Cooper, A. (1977/8) "The family farm in Greece," *CJ* 73: 162–75.

Burghardt, A. F. (1971) "A hypothesis about gateway cities," *Annals of the Association of American Geographers* 61: 269–85.

Burnham, B. C. and Johnson, H. B., eds. (1979) *Invasion and Response: The Case of Roman Britain* (BAR British Series 73), Oxford.

Burton, G. P. (1975) "Proconsuls, assizes, and the administration of justice under the empire," *JRS* 65: 92–106.

(1979) "The *curator rei publicae*: towards a reappraisal," *Chiron* 9: 465–88.

Bury, J. B. and Meiggs, R. (1975) *A History of Greece to the Death of Alexander the Great* (4th edn), London.

Busing, H. and Busing-Kolbe, A. (1972) "Chorsiai. Eine Boiotische Festung," *AA* 87: 74–87.

Byres, T. J. (1983) "Historical perspectives on sharecropping," *The Journal of Peasant Studies* 10: 7–40.

Callaghan, P. J. (1978) "KRS 1976: excavations at a shrine of Glaukos, Knossos," *BSA* 73: 1–30.

Camp, J. M. (1986) *The Athenian Agora: Excavations in the Heart of Classical Athens*, London.
  (1989) "The philosophical schools of Roman Athens," in Walker and Cameron, eds., 50–5.

Cancian, F. (1972) *Change and Uncertainty in a Peasant Economy*, Stanford.

Caroll, K. K. (1982) *The Parthenon Inscription*, Durham.

Carrasco, P. (1961) "The civil-religious hierarchy in Mesoamerican communities: pre-Spanish background and colonial development," *American Anthropologist* 63: 483–97.

Carter, J. M. (1977) "A new fragment of Octavian's inscription at Nicopolis," *ZPE* 24: 227–32.

Cartledge, P. and Spawforth, A. (1989) *Hellenistic and Roman Sparta: A Tale of Two Cities*, London.

Cary, M. (1951) *A History of the Greek World from 323 to 146 BC* (2nd edn), London.

Caskey, J. L. and Amandry, P. (1952) "Investigations at the Heraion of Argos, 1949," *Hesperia* 21: 165–221.

Caskey, M. E. (1981) "Ayia Irini, Kea: the terracotta statues and the cult in the temple," in Hägg, R. and Marinatos, N., eds., *Sanctuaries and Cults in the Aegean Bronze Age: Proceedings of the First International Symposium at the Swedish Institute in Athens, 12–13 May, 1980*, 127–35. Stockholm.

Castrén, P. (1989) "The post-Herulian revival of Athens," in Walker and Cameron, eds., 45–9.

Cavanagh, W. G. (1991) "Surveys, cities and synoecism," in Rich, J. and Wallace-Hadrill, A., eds., *City and Country in the Ancient World*, 97–118. London.

Cavanagh, W. G. and Crouwel, J. (1988) "Laconia Survey 1983–86," *Lakonikai Spoudai*, 77–88.

Champion, T. C., ed. (1989) *Centre and Periphery: Comparative Studies*, London.

Chang, C. and Koster, H. A. (1986) "Beyond bones: towards an archaeology of pastoralism," in Schiffer, M. B., ed., *Advances in Archaeological Method and Theory* (Volume 9), 97–148. New York.

Chapman, J. and Shiel, R. S. (1991) "Settlement, soils and societies in Dalmatia," in Barker and Lloyd, eds., 62–75.

Chapman, J., Shiel, R. S. and Batovic, S. (1987) "Settlement patterns and land use in Neothermal Dalmatia, Yugoslavia: 1983–1984 seasons," *JFA* 14: 123–46.

Charanis, P. (1960/1) "The transfer of population as a policy in the Byzantine Empire," *CSSH* 3: 140–54.

Charlesworth, M. P. (1926) *Trade-routes and Commerce of the Roman Empire*, Cambridge.

Chayanov, A. (1923) *The Theory of the Peasant Economy* (Reprinted 1986), Wisconsin.

Cherf, W. J. (1987) "The Roman borders between Achaia and Macedonia," *Chiron* 17: 135–42.

Cherry, J. F. (1982) "Appendix A: register of archaeological sites on Melos," in Renfrew and Wagstaff, eds., 291–309.
  (1983a) "Evolution, revolution, and the origins of complex society in Minoan

Crete," in Krzyszkowska, O. and Nixon, L., eds., *Minoan Society*, 33–45. Bristol.

(1983b) "Frogs round the pond: perspectives on current archaeological survey projects in the Mediterranean region," in Keller, D. R. and Rupp, D. W., eds., *Archaeological Survey in the Mediterranean Area* (BAR International Series 155), 375–416. Oxford.

(1984) "Common sense in Mediterranean survey?" *JFA* 11: 117–20.

(1988) "Pastoralism and the role of animals in the pre- and proto-historic economies of the Aegean," in Whittaker, ed., 6–34.

Cherry, J. F., ed. (1992) *Archaeology of Empires* (= *WA* 23.3), London.

Cherry, J. F. and Davis, J. L. (1991) "The Ptolemaic base at Koressos on Keos," *BSA* 86: 9–28.

Cherry, J. F., Davis, J. L., Demitrack, A., Mantzourani, E., Strasser, T. and Talalay, L. (1988) "Archaeological survey in an artifact-rich landscape: a Middle Neolithic example from Nemea, Greece," *AJA* 92: 159–76.

Cherry, J. F., Davis, J. L. and Mantzourani, E. (1991) *Landscape Archaeology as Long-Term History: Northern Keos in the Cycladic Islands* (Monumenta Archaeologica 16), Los Angeles.

Chevallier, R. (1958) "Pour une interprétation archéologique de la couverture aérienne grecque: note sur les centuriations romaines de Grèce," *BCH* 82: 635–6.

(1989) *Roman Roads* (Revised edn), London.

Chisholm, M. (1962) *Rural Settlement and Land Use*, London.

Chrysos, E., ed. (1987) *Nicopolis I* (Proceedings of the First International Symposium on Nicopolis, 23–29 September 1984), Preveza.

Chysostomou, P. (1982) "To nymphaio ton Rizon Prevezes," *AAA* 15: 10–21.

Clark, C. and Haswell, M. (1970) *The Economics of Subsistence Agriculture* (4th edn), London.

Clavel-Lévêque, M. (1985) "Mais ou sont les druides d'antan . . . ? Tradition religieuse et identité culturelle en Gaule," *Dialogues d'histoire anciennes* 11: 557–604.

Clavel-Lévêque, M. and Lévêque, P. (1982) "Impérialisme et sémiologie: l'espace urbain à Glanum," *Mélanges d'archéologie et d'histoire de l'Ecole Française de Rome* 94: 675–98.

Clogg, R. (1979) *A Short History of Modern Greece*, Cambridge.

Cohen, G. M. (1983) "Colonization and population transfer in the Hellenistic world," in van 't Dack, E., van Dessel, P. and van Gucht, W., eds., *Egypt and the Hellenistic World*, 63–74. Leuven.

Cohen, R. (1981) "Evolutionary epistemology and human values," *Current Anthropology* 22: 201–18.

Cole, S. G. (forthcoming) *Bodies of Water and Fields of Grain: Ritual Constructions of the Female in the Ancient Greek City*.

Conrad, G. W. and Demarest, A. A. (1984) *Religion and Empire: The Dynamics of Aztec and Inca Expansionism*, Cambridge.

Constantine, D. (1984) *Early Greek Travellers and the Hellenic Ideal*, Cambridge.

(1989) "The question of authenticity in some early accounts of Greece," in Clarke, G. W., ed., *Rediscovering Hellenism: The Hellenic Inheritance and the English Imagination*, 1–22. Cambridge.

# Bibliography

Corbier, M. (1991) "City, territory and taxation," in Rich, J. and Wallace-Hadrill, A., eds., *City and Country in the Ancient World*, 211–39. London.

Cornell, T. and Matthews, J. (1982) *Atlas of the Roman World*, Oxford.

Cosgrove, D. E. (1984) *Social Formation and Symbolic Landscape*, London.

Cosgrove, D. E. and Daniels, S., eds. (1988) *The Iconography of Landscape: Essays on the Symbolic Representation, Design and Use of Past Environments*, Cambridge.

Coulton, J. J. (1987) "Roman aqueducts in Asia Minor," in Macready and Thompson, eds., 72–84.

Cowgill, G. L. (1975a) "On the causes and consequences of ancient and modern population changes," *American Anthropologist* 77: 505–55.

(1975b) "Population pressure as a non-explanation," *AAnt* 40: 127–31.

Crawford, D. J. (1976) "Imperial estates," in Finley, M. I., ed., *Studies in Roman Property*, 35–70. Cambridge.

Crawford, M. H. (1975) "Finance, coinage and money from the Severans to Constantine," *ANRW* II.2: 560–93.

(1977) "Rome and the Greek world," *Economic History Review* 30: 42–52.

(1978) "Greek intellectuals and the Roman aristocracy in the first century BC," in Garnsey, P. and Whittaker, C. R., eds., *Imperialism in the Ancient World*, 193–207. Cambridge.

(1981) "Italy and Rome," *JRS* 71: 153–60.

(1986) "Introduction," in Crawford, M. H., ed., *L'impero romano e le strutture economiche e sociali delle province* (Biblioteca di Athenaeum 4), 9–12. Como.

Crook, J. M. (1989) "The Arcadian vision: neoclassicism and the picturesque," in Clarke, G. W., ed., *Rediscovering Hellenism: The Hellenic Inheritance and the English Imagination*, 43–59. Cambridge.

Culley, G. R. (1975) "The restoration of sanctuaries in Attica: *IG*, II², 1035," *Hesperia* 44: 207–23.

(1977) "The restoration of sanctuaries in Attica, II. The structure of *IG*, II², 1035 and the topography of Salamis," *Hesperia* 46: 282–98.

Curchin, L. A. (1991) *Roman Spain: Conquest and Assimilation*, London.

Davidson, D. and Tasker, C. (1982) "Geomorphological evolution during the late Holocene," in Renfrew and Wagstaff, eds., 82–94.

Davidson, G. R. (1952) *The Minor Objects* (Corinth Volume XVII), Princeton.

Davies, J. K. (1984) "Cultural, social, and economic features of the Hellenistic world," in Walbank, F. W., Astin, A. E., Frederiksen, M. W. and Ogilvie, R. M., *CAH² 7.1, The Hellenistic World*, 257–320. Cambridge.

Davies, O. (1935) *Roman Mines in Europe* (Reprinted 1979), New York.

Davis, J. (1969) "Town and country," *Anthropological Quarterly* 42: 171–85.

(1977) *People of the Mediterranean: An Essay in Comparative Social Anthropology*, London.

Davis, J. L. (1991) "Contributions to a Mediterranean rural archaeology: historical case studies from the Ottoman Cyclades," *JMA* 4: 131–216.

Day, J. (1942) *An Economic History of Athens under Roman Domination*, New York.

(1951) "The value of Dio Chrysostom's *Euboean Discourse* for the economic historian," in Coleman-Norton, P., ed., *Studies in Roman Economic and Social History in Honor of A. C. Johnson*, 209–35. Princeton.

Deininger, J. (1965) *Die Provinziallandtage der Römischen Kaiserzeit von Augustus bis zum Ende dritte Jahrhunderts n. Chr.*, Munich.

(1971) *Der politische Widerstand gegen Rom in Griechenland, 217–86 BC*, Berlin.

Deman, A. (1975) "Matériaux et réflexions pour servir à une étude du développement et du sous-développement dans les provinces de l'empire romain," *ANRW* II.3: 3–97.

Demand, N. (1990) *Urban Relocation in Archaic and Classical Greece: Flight and Consolidation*, Bristol.

Demangeon, A. (1927) "La géographie de l'habitat rural," *Annales de géographie* 36: 1–24, 97–115.

(1962) "The origins and causes of settlement types," in Wagner, P. L. and Mikesell, M. W., eds., *Readings in Cultural Geography*, 506–16. Chicago.

Deniaux, E. (1987) "Atticus et l'Epire," in Cabanes, P., ed., *L'Illyrie méridionale et l'Epire dans l'antiquité*, 245–54. Clermont-Ferrand.

Dickson, D. B. (1989) "Out of Utopia: Runnels and van Andel's non-equilibrium growth model of the origins of agriculture," *JMA* 2: 297–302.

Dinsmoor, W. B. (1920) "The monument of Agrippa at Athens" (abstract), *AJA* 24: 83.

(1940) "The temple of Ares at Athens," *Hesperia* 9: 1–52.

Dinsmoor, W. B., Jr. (1974) "The temple of Poseidon: a missing sima and other matters," *AJA* 78: 211–38.

(1982) "Anchoring two floating temples," *Hesperia* 51: 410–52.

Dodge, H. (1988) "Decorative stone for architecture in the Roman Empire," *OJA* 7: 65–80.

(1990) "The architectural impact of Rome in the East," in Henig, M., ed., *Architecture and Architectural Sculpture in the Roman Empire* (Oxford University Committee for Archaeology Monograph No. 29), 108–20. Oxford.

Dodgshon, R. A. (1987) *The European Past: Social Evolution and Spatial Order*, London.

Doukellis, P. N. (1988a) "Biens fonciers et territoire en Chalcidique," *Dialogues d'histoire anciennes* 14: 155–8.

(1988b) "Cadastres romains en Grèce: traces d'un réseau rural à Actia Nicopolis," *Dialogues d'histoire anciennes* 14: 159–66.

(1990a) "Actia Nicopolis: idéologie impériale, structures urbaines et développement régional," *JRA* 3: 399–406.

(1990b) "Ena diktuo agrotikon orion sten pediada tes Artas," *Meletemata* 10: 269–83.

Doyle, M. W. (1986) *Empires*, Ithaca.

Drinkwater, J. F. (1983) *Roman Gaul: The Three Provinces, 58 BC–AD 260*, London.

Dunant, C. and Thomopoulos, J. (1954) "Inscriptions de Céos," *BCH* 78: 316–48.

Duncan-Jones, R. P. (1976) "Some configurations of landholding in the Roman empire," in Finley, M. I., ed., *Studies in Roman Property*, 7–33. Cambridge.

Dunnell, R. C. (1980) "Evolutionary theory and archaeology," in Schiffer, M. B., ed., *Advances in Archaeological Method and Theory* (Volume 3), 35–99. New York.

Dunnell, R. C. and Dancey, W. S. (1983) "The siteless survey: a regional scale data collection strategy," in Schiffer, M. B., ed., *Advances in Archaeological Method and Theory* (Volume 6), 267–87. New York.

# Bibliography

Dyson, S. L. (1978) "Settlement patterns in the Ager Cosanus. The Wesleyan University Survey, 1974–6," *JFA* 5: 251–68.

(1981a) "A classical archaeologist's response to the 'new archaeology,'" *Bulletin of the American Schools of Oriental Research* 242: 7–13.

(1981b) "Settlement reconstruction in the Ager Cosanus and the Albegna Valley: Wesleyan University Research, 1974–79," in Barker, G. and Hodges, R., eds., *Archaeology and Italian Society: Prehistoric, Roman and Medieval Studies* (BAR International Series 102), 269–74. Oxford.

(1982) "Archaeological survey in the Mediterranean Basin: a review of recent research," *AAnt* 47: 87–98.

(1985) "Introduction," in Dyson, S. L., ed., *Comparative Studies in the Archaeology of Colonialism* (BAR International Series 233), 1–7. Oxford.

(1991) "The romanization of the countryside," in Barker and Lloyd, eds., 27–8.

Dyson-Hudson, R. and Dyson-Hudson, N. (1980) "Nomadic pastoralism," *AnnRevAnth* 9: 15–61.

Earle, T. (1976) "A nearest-neighbor analysis of two Formative settlement systems," in Flannery, ed., 196–223.

Earle, T. K., D'Altroy, T. N., LeBlanc, C. J., Hastorf, C. A. and Levine, T. Y. (1987) *Archaeological Field Research in the Upper Mantaro, Peru 1982–83: Investigations of Inka Expansion and Exchange*, Los Angeles.

Eco, U. (1986) *Travels in Hyperreality*, London.

Edlund, I. E. M. (1987) *The Gods and the Place. Location and Function of Sanctuaries in the Countryside of Etruria and Magna Graecia (700–400 BC)* (Skrifter utgivna av Svenska institutet i Rom. 4), Stockholm.

Edmonson, C. N. (1969) "Augustus, Actium and Nikopolis" (abstract), *AJA* 73: 235.

Edwards, G. R. (1975) *Corinthian Hellenistic Pottery* (Corinth Volume VII.2). Princeton.

Eisenstadt, S. N. (1963) *The Political Systems of Empires*, New York.

(1979) "Observations and queries about sociological aspects of imperialism in the ancient world," in Larsen, ed., 21–33.

Eisner, R. (1991) *Travelers to an Antique Land: The History and Literature of Travel to Greece*, Ann Arbor.

Ekholm, K. and Friedman, J. (1979) "'Capital' imperialism and exploitation in ancient world systems," in Larsen, ed., 41–58.

Eliakis, K. (1980) "E anakataskeve tes anatolikes opses tou naou tes Nemeses sto Ramnounta – mia episkeve sta chronia tou aftokratora Ioulianou?" *AD* 35 A: 206–23.

Ellis, S. (1988) "The end of the Roman house," *AJA* 92: 565–76.

Elsner, J. (forthcoming) *Art and the Roman Viewer*, Cambridge.

Empéreur, J.-Y. and Garlan, Y. (1986) *Recherches sur les amphores grecques* (*BCH* Supplément 13), Paris.

Empéreur, J.-Y. and Picon, M. (1986) "Des ateliers d'amphores à Paros et à Naxos," *BCH* 110: 495–511.

(1989) "Les régions de production d'amphores impériales en Méditerranée orientale," in *Amphores romaines et historie économique. Dix ans de recherche. Actes du Colloque de Sienne* ( = *Collection de l'Ecole Française à Rome* 114), 223–48. Rome.

# Bibliography

Engels, D. (1990) *Roman Corinth: An Alternative Model for the Classical City*, Chicago.

Etienne, R. and Knoepfler, D. (1976) *Hyettos de Béotie et la chronologie des archontes fédéraux entre 250 et 171 av. J.-C.* (*BCH* Supplément 3), Paris.

Eyben, E. (1980/1) "Family planning in Graeco-Roman antiquity," *Ancient Society* 11/12: 5–81.

Faklaris, P. (1990) *Archaia Kunouria*, Athens.

Fant, J. C., ed. (1988) *Ancient Marble Quarrying and Trade* (BAR International Series 453), Oxford.

(1989) "*Poikiloi lithoi*: the anomalous economics of the Roman imperial marble quarry at Teos," in Walker and Cameron, eds., 206–18.

Faraklas, N. (1972) *Troizinia, Kalaureia, Methana* (Ancient Greek Cities 10), Athens.

Farnell, L. R. (1896–1909) *The Cults of the Greek States* (5 volumes), Oxford.

Farrington, I. S. (1992) "Ritual geography, settlement patterns and the characterization of the provinces of the Inka heartland," *WA* 23: 368–85.

Farriss, N. M. (1984) *Maya Society under Colonial Rule: The Collective Enterprise of Survival*, Princeton.

Ferguson, J. (1989) *Among the Gods: An Archaeological Exploration of Ancient Greek Religion*, London.

Ferguson, W. S. (1911) *Hellenistic Athens*, London.

Festugière, A. J. (1972) *Etudes de religion grecque et hellénistique*, Paris.

Feyel, M. (1942) *Polybe et l'histoire de Béotie au III^e siècle avant notre ère*, Paris.

Finlay, G. (1857) *Greece Under the Romans* (2nd edn), Edinburgh.

Finley, M. I. (1973) "Introduction," in Finley, M. I. ed., *Problèmes de la terre en Grèce ancienne*, 9–12. Paris.

(1976) "Private farm tenancy in Italy before Diocletian," in Finley, M. I., ed., *Studies in Roman Property*, 103–21. Cambridge.

(1977a) "The ancient city: from Fustel de Coulanges to Max Weber and beyond," *CSSH* 19: 305–27.

(1977b) *Aspects of Antiquity* (2nd edn), Harmondsworth.

(1978) "Empire in the Greco-Roman world," *Greece and Rome* 25: 1–15.

(1983) *Politics in the Ancient World*, Cambridge.

(1985a) *The Ancient Economy* (2nd edn), London.

(1985b) *Ancient History: Evidence and Models*, London.

(1986) "Archaeology and history," in *The Use and Abuse of History* (2nd edn), 87–101. London.

Flannery, K. V. (1972) "The cultural evolution of civilizations," *Annual Review of Ecology and Systematics* 3: 399–426.

ed. (1976) *The Early Mesoamerican Village*, New York.

Fletcher, R. (1981) "People and space: a case study in material behaviour," in Hodder, I., Isaac, G. and Hammond, N. eds., *Pattern of the Past: Studies in Honour of David Clarke*, 97–128. Cambridge.

Foley, R. (1981) "Off-site archaeology: an alternative approach for the short-sited," in Hodder, I., Isaac, G. and Hammond, N., eds., *Pattern of the Past: Studies in Honour of David Clarke*, 157–83. Cambridge.

Follet, S. (1976) *Athènes au II^e et au III^e siècle*, Paris.

Forbes, H. A. (1976) " 'We have a little bit of everything': the ecological basis of some

# Bibliography

agricultural practices in Methana, Trizinia," in Dimen, M. and Friedl, E., eds., *Regional Variation in Modern Greece and Cyprus: Toward a Perspective on the Ethnography of Greece* (Annals of the New York Academy of Sciences 268), 236–50. New York.

Forte, B. (1972) *Rome and the Romans as the Greeks Saw Them* (Papers and Monographs of the American Academy of Rome 24), Rome.

Foss, C. (1977) "Archaeology and the '20 cities' of Byzantine Asia," *AJA* 81: 469–86.

Fossey, J. M. (1979) "The cities of the Kopais in the Roman period," *ANRW* II.7.1: 548–91.

   (1981) "The city archive at Koroneia, Boeotia," *Euphrosyne* 11: 46–60 .

   (1986) *The Ancient Topography of Eastern Phokis*, Amsterdam.

   (1988) *Topography and Population of Ancient Boiotia* (Volume I), Chicago.

   ed. (1989) *Boeotia Antiqua I. Papers on Recent Work in Boiotian Archaeology and History*, Amsterdam.

   (1990) *The Ancient Topography of Opountian Lokris*, Amsterdam.

Fossey, J. M. and Morin, J. (1989) "The Khostia project: excavation and survey," in Fossey, ed., 165–74.

Fowden, G. (1988) "City and mountain in Late Roman Attica," *JHS* 108: 48–59.

Fowler, H. N. and Stillwell, R. (1932) *Introduction: Topography, Architecture* (Corinth Volume I.I). Cambridge, MA.

Foxhall, L. (1990) "The dependent tenant: landleasing and labor in Italy and Greece," *JRS* 80: 97–114.

Foxhall, L., Mee, C., Forbes, H., and Gill, D. W. J. (1989) "The Ptolemaic base of Methana" (abstract), *AJA* 93: 247–8.

Frantz, A. (1988) *Late Antiquity: AD 267–700* (The Athenian Agora Volume XXIV), Princeton.

Frazer, J. G. (1898) *Pausanias' Description of Greece* (Volume I), London.

Frederiksen, M. W. (1970/1) "The contribution of archaeology to the agrarian problem in the Gracchan period," *Dialoghi di Archeologia* 4/5: 330–67.

   (1975) "Theory, evidence and the ancient economy," *JRS* 65: 164–71.

   (1976) "Changes in the patterns of settlement," in Zanker, P., ed., *Hellenismus in Mittelitalien*, 34–55. Göttingen.

Friedl, E. (1962) *Vasilika: A Village in Modern Greece*, New York.

Frost, F. J. (1977) "Phourkari. A villa complex in the Argolis, Greece," *International Journal of Nautical Archaeology and Underwater Exploration* 6: 233–8.

Fuks, A. (1984) *Social Conflict in Ancient Greece*, Jerusalem.

Fulford, M. (1986) "Pottery and precious metals in the Roman world," in Vickers, M., ed., *Pots and Pans: A Colloquium on Precious Metals and Ceramics*, 153–60. Oxford.

   (1989) "To east and west: the Mediterranean trade of Cyrenaica and Tripolitania in antiquity," *Libyan Studies* 20: 169–91.

Gaffney, C. F. and Gaffney, V. L. (1986) "From Boeotia to Berkshire: an integrated approach to geophysics and rural field survey," *Prospezione Archeologiche* 10: 65–71.

Gagé, J. (1936) "Actiaca," *Mélanges d'archéologie et d'histoire de l'Ecole Française de Rome* 53: 37–100.

# Bibliography

Gall, P. L. and Saxe, A. A. (1977) "The ecological evolution of culture: the state as predator in succession theory," in Earle, T. K. and Ericson, J. E., eds., *Exchange Systems in Prehistory*, 255–68. New York.

Gallant, T. W. (1982) An examination of two island polities in antiquity: the Lefkas-Pronnoi survey. Unpublished Ph.D. thesis, University of Cambridge.

(1986) "Background noise and site definition: a contribution to survey methodology," *JFA* 13: 403–18.

(1991) Review of van Andel and Runnels (1987), *CJ* 86: 184–6.

Gallo, L. (1979) "Recenti studi di demografia greca (1971–8)," *Annali della Scuola Normale Superiore di Pisa* S. III, 9: 1571–1646.

(1980) "Popolosità è scarsità: contributo allo studio di un topos," *Annali della Scuola Normale Superiore di Pisa* S. III, 10: 1233–70.

(1984) *Alimentazione e demografia della grecia antica*, Salerno.

Galtung, J. (1971) "A structural theory of imperialism," *Journal of Peace Research* 8: 81–117.

Garnsey, P. (1976) "Urban property investment," in Finley, M. I., ed., *Studies in Roman Property*, 123–36. Cambridge.

(1978) "Rome's African empire under the principate," in Garnsey, P. and Whittaker, C. R., eds., *Imperialism in the Ancient World*, 223–54. Cambridge.

(1979) "Where did Italian peasants live?" *Proceedings of the Cambridge Philological Society* 25: 1–25.

(1980) "Non-slave labour in the Roman world," in Garnsey, P., ed., *Non-slave Labour in the Greco-Roman World*. (Cambridge Philological Society, Supplementary Volume 6), 34–47. Cambridge.

(1983) "Grain for Rome," in Garnsey, P., Hopkins, K. and Whittaker, C. R., eds., *Trade in the Ancient Economy*, 118–30. London.

(1988) *Famine and Food Supply in the Graeco-Roman World*, Cambridge.

Garnsey, P., Gallant, T. and Rathbone, D. (1984) "Thessaly and the grain supply of Rome during the second century BC," *JRS* 74: 30–44.

Garnsey, P. and Saller, R. (1987) *The Roman Empire: Economy, Society, and Culture*, London.

Garnsey, P. and Woolf, G. (1990) "Patronage of the rural poor in the Roman world," in Wallace-Hadrill, ed., 153–70.

Gauthier, P. (1972) Review of Vatin (1970), *Revue des études grecques* 85: 208–13.

(1985) *Les Cités grecques et leurs bienfaiteurs* (*BCH* Supplément 12). Paris.

Geagan, D. J. (1968) "Notes on the agonistic institutions of Roman Corinth," *GRBS* 9: 69–80.

(1979) "Roman Athens: some aspects of life and culture I. 86 BC–AD 267," *ANRW* II.7.1: 371–437.

(1989) "The Isthmian dossier of P. Licinius Priscus Juventianus," *Hesperia* 58: 349–60.

Geertz, C. (1966) "Religion as a cultural system," in Banton, M., ed., *Anthropological Approaches to the Study of Religion*, 1–46. London.

(1977) "Center, kings and charisma: reflections on the symbolics of power," in Ben-David, J. and Clark, T. N., eds., *Culture and its Creators*, 140–71. Chicago.

Georgiou, H. and Faraklas, N. (1985) "Ancient habitation patterns of Keos:

locations and nature of sites on the northwest part of the island," *Ariadne* 3: 207–66.

Gill, D. W. J. (1986) "Classical Greek fictile imitations of precious metal vases," in Vickers, M., ed., *Pots and Pans: A Colloquium on Precious Metals and Ceramics*, 9–30. Oxford.

Gilliam, J. F. (1965) "Romanization of the Greek East: the role of the army," *Bulletin of the American Society of Papyrologists* 2: 65–73.

Ginouvès, R. (1972) *Le Théâtron à gradins droits et l'Odéion d'Argos*, Paris.

Giovannini, A. (1978) *Rome et la circulation monétaire en Grèce au II<sup>e</sup> siècle avant Jésus-Christ*, Basel.

Glotz, G. (1936) *Histoire grecque* (Volume 3), Paris.

Gordon, R. L. (1979) "The real and the imaginary: production and religion in the Graeco-Roman world," *Art History* 2: 5–34.

Gossage, A. J. (1954) "The date of *IG* v² 516 (*SIG*³ 800)," *BSA* 49: 51–6.

Graindor, P. (1927) *Athènes sous Auguste*, Cairo.

(1930) *Un milliardaire antique: Hérode Atticus et sa famille*, Cairo.

(1931) *Athènes sous Tibère à Trajan*, Cairo.

(1934) *Athènes sous Hadrien* (Reprinted 1973, New York), Cairo.

Green, S. W. (1980a) "Broadening least-cost models for expanding agricultural systems," in Earle, T. K. and Christenson, A. L., eds., *Modelling Change in Prehistoric Subsistence Economies*, 209–41. New York.

(1980b) "Toward a general model of agricultural systems," in Schiffer, M. B., ed., *Advances in Archaeological Method and Theory* (Volume 3), 311–55. New York.

Greene, K. (1986) *The Archaeology of the Roman Economy*, London.

Gregory, T. (1979) "Roman inscriptions from Aidepsos," *GRBS* 20: 255–77.

(1982) "The fortified cities of Byzantine Greece," *Archaeology* 35: 14–21.

(1984) "Cities and social evolution in Roman and Byzantine south-east Europe," in Bintliff, J. L., ed., *European Social Evolution: Archaeological Perspectives*, 267–76. Bradford.

Gregory, T. E. and Mills, H. (1984) "The Roman arch at Isthmia," *Hesperia* 53: 407–45.

Greig, J. R. A. and Turner, J. (1974) "Some pollen diagrams from Greece and their archaeological significance," *Journal of Archaeological Science* 1: 177–94.

Griffin, A. (1982) *Sikyon*, Oxford.

Griffith, G. T. (1935) *Mercenaries of the Hellenistic World*, Cambridge.

Grigg, D. (1970) *The Harsh Lands: A Study in Agricultural Development*, London.

(1976) "Population pressure and agricultural change," in Board, C., Chorley, R. J., Haggett, P., and Stoddart, D. R., eds., *Progress in Geography: International Reviews of Current Research Volume 8*, 133–76. London.

Grote, G. (1862) *A History of Greece* (Volume 8), London.

Gruen, E. S. (1984a) *The Hellenistic World and the Coming of Rome*, Berkeley.

(1984b) "Material rewards and the drive for empire," in Harris, W. V., ed., *The Imperialism of Mid-Republican Rome* (Papers and Monographs of the American Academy in Rome 29), 59–88. Rome.

Guiraud, P. (1893) *La Propriété foncière en Grèce jusqu'à la conquête romaine*, Paris.

Gunneweg, J. (1987) "Roman pottery trade in the eastern Mediterranean," *Acta Rei*

*Cretariae Romanae Fautorum* 25/6: 119–29.

Habicht, C. (1961) "Falsche Urkunden zur Geschichte Athens im Zeitalter der Perserkriege," *Hermes* 89: 1–35.

(1985) *Pausanias' Guide to Ancient Greece*, Berkeley.

Halfmann, H. (1986) *Itinera Principum: Geschichte und Typologie der Kaiserreisen im Römischen Reich*, Stuttgart.

Hall, P., ed. (1966) *Von Thünen's Isolated State*, Oxford.

Hall, R. L. (1976) "Ghosts, water barriers, corn and sacred enclosures in the eastern woodlands," *AAnt* 41: 360–4.

Halstead, P. J. L. (1987) "Traditional and ancient rural economy in Mediterranean Europe: plus ça change?" *JHS* 107: 77–87.

Hammond, N. G. L. (1967) *Epirus*, Oxford.

(1986) *A History of Greece to 322 BC* (3rd edn), Oxford.

Hankey, V. (1965) "A marble quarry at Karystos," *Bulletin du Musée de Beyrouth* 18: 53–9.

Hanson, V. D. (1983) *Warfare and Agriculture in Classical Greece* (Bibliotheca di Studi Antichi 40), Pisa.

Harden, D. B. (1987) *Glass of the Caesars*, Milan.

Harrison, G. (1991) "Changing patterns in land tenure and land use in Roman Crete," in Barker and Lloyd, eds., 115–21.

Haselgrove, C. (1987) "Culture process on the periphery: Belgic Gaul and Rome during the late Republic and early Empire," in Rowlands *et al.*, eds., 104–24.

Hatzfeld, J. (1919) *Les Trafiquants italiens dans l'orient hellénique* (Reprinted 1975), New York.

Hayes, J. W. (1972) *Late Roman Pottery*, London.

(1973) "Roman pottery from the South Stoa at Corinth," *Hesperia* 42: 416–70.

(1980) *A Supplement to Late Roman Pottery*, London.

(1983) "The Villa Dionysos excavations, Knossos," *BSA* 78: 97–169.

Healy, J. F. (1978) *Mining and Metallurgy in the Greek and Roman World*, London.

Hedeager, L. (1987) "Empire, frontier and the barbarian hinterland: Roman and northern Europe from AD 1–400," in Rowlands *et al.*, eds., 125–40.

Hedrick, C. W., Jr. (1988) "The temple and cult of Apollo Patroos in Athens," *AJA* 92: 185–210.

Helly, B. (1973) *Gonnoi I. La Cité et son histoire II: Les Inscriptions*, Amsterdam.

Henig, M. and King, A., eds. (1986) *Pagan Gods and Shrines of the Roman Empire* (Oxford University Committee for Archaeology Monograph No. 8), Oxford.

Hennig, D. (1977) "Der Bericht des Polybios über Böotien und die Lage von Orchomenos in der 2. Hälfte des 3. Jhds. v. Chr.," *Chiron* 7: 119–48.

Herman, G. (1987) *Ritualised Friendship and the Greek City*, Cambridge.

Hertzberg, G. F. (1866–75) *Die Geschichte Griechenlands unter der Herrschaft der Römer* (3 volumes), Halle.

Herzfeld, M. (1982) *Ours Once More: Folklore, Ideology and the Making of Modern Greece*, Austin.

(1987) *Anthropology Through the Looking-Glass: Critical Ethnography in the Margins of Europe*, Cambridge.

Hibbert, C. (1987) *The Grand Tour*, London.

Hill, H. (1946) "Roman revenues from Greece after 146 BC," *CPhil* 41: 35–42.

Hingley, R. (1985) "Location, function and status: a Romano-British 'religious complex' at the Noah's Ark Inn, Frilford (Oxfordshire)," *OJA* 4: 201–14.

(1989) *Rural Settlement in Roman Britain*, London.

Hirth, K. G. (1978a) "Inter-regional trade and the formation of prehistoric gateway communities," *AAnt* 43: 25–45.

(1978b) "Problems in data recovery and measurement in settlement archaeology," *JFA* 5: 125–31.

Hitzl, K. (1991) *Die Kaiserzeitliche Statuenausstattung des Metroon*, Berlin.

Hodder, I. and Orton, C. (1976) *Spatial Analysis in Archaeology*, Cambridge.

Hodge, M. G. (1984) *Aztec City States* (Memoirs of the Museum of Anthropology, University of Michigan 18), Ann Arbor.

Hodkinson, S. (1988) "Animal husbandry in the Greek polis," in Whittaker, ed., 35–74.

Hodkinson, S. and Hodkinson, H. (1981) "Mantineia and the Mantinike: settlement and society in a Greek polis," *BSA* 76: 239–96.

Hoepfner, W. (1987) "Nikopolis – Zur Stadtgründung des Augustus," in Chrysos, ed., 129–33.

Hoff, M. C. (1989a) "Civil disobedience and unrest in Augustan Athens," *Hesperia* 59: 267–76.

(1989b) "The early history of the Roman agora at Athens," in Walker and Cameron, eds., 1–8.

Holleaux, M. (1938) "Discours prononcé par Néron à Corinthe en rendant aux Grecs la liberté," *Etudes d'épigraphie et d'histoire grecques I*: 165–85.

Hood, S. and Smyth, D. (1981) *Archaeological Survey of the Knossos Area* (*BSA* Supplement 14), London.

Hope Simpson, R. (1984) "The analysis of data from surface surveys," *JFA* 11: 115–17.

Hopkins, K. (1978a) *Conquerors and Slaves*, Cambridge.

(1978b) "Economic growth and towns in classical antiquity," in Abrams, P. and Wrigley, E. A., eds., *Towns in Societies: Essays in Economic History and Historical Sociology*, 35–77. Cambridge.

(1980) "Taxes and trade in the Roman empire (200 BC–AD 400)," *JRS* 70: 101–25.

(1988) "Graveyards for historians," in Hinard, F., ed., *Le Mort, les morts et l'au-delà dans le monde romain (Actes du Colloque de Caen, 20–22 novembre 1985)*, 113–26. Caen.

Horsfall, N. (1989) "Atticus brings home the bacon," *Liverpool Classical Monthly* 14: 60–2.

Hoskins, W. G. (1955) *The Making of the English Landscape*, London.

Howell, R. (1970) "A survey of eastern Arcadia in prehistory," *BSA* 65: 79–127.

Humphreys, S. C. (1978) "Town and country in ancient Greece," in Humphreys, S. C., *Anthropology and the Greeks*, 130–5. London.

Hunt, E. D. (1984) "Travel, tourism and piety in the Roman empire: a context for the beginnings of Christian pilgrimage," *EMC/CV* 28, n.s. 3: 391–417.

Inden, R. (1986) "Orientalist constructions of India," *Modern Asian Studies* 20: 401–46.

Isaac, B. (1988) Review of Parker (1986), *JRS* 78: 240–1.

# Bibliography

Jackson, J. B. (1984) *Discovering the Vernacular Landscape*, New Haven.

(1986) "The vernacular landscape," in Penning-Rowsell, E. C. and Lowenthal, D., eds., *Landscape Meanings and Values*, 65–81. London.

Jameson, M. H. (1953) "Inscriptions from the Peloponnese," *Hesperia* 22: 148–71.

(1959) "Inscriptions of Hermione, Hydra, and Kasos," *Hesperia* 28: 109–20.

(1969) "Excavations at Porto Cheli and vicinity, preliminary report, 1: Halieis 1962–8," *Hesperia* 38: 311–42.

(1977/8) "Agriculture and slavery in Classical Athens," *CJ* 73: 122–45.

(1980) "Apollo Lykeios in Athens," *Archaiognosia* 1: 213–35.

(1988) "Sacrifice and animal husbandry in Classical Greece," in Whittaker, ed., 87–119.

(forthcoming, a) "Agricultural labor in Classical Greece," in Wells, B., ed., *Agriculture in Classical Greece*, Stockholm.

(forthcoming, b) "Supplementary note on the border dispute between Hermion and Epidauros," in Jameson *et al.*, eds.

Jameson, M., Runnels, C. and van Andel, T., eds. (forthcoming) *A Greek Countryside: The Southern Argolid from Prehistory to the Present Day*, Stanford.

Jannoray, J. (1944/5) "Thrigkoi epi stelais: à propos d'une série de blocs de corniche inscrits, à Delphes," *BCH* 68/9: 75–93.

Jenkyns, R. (1980) *The Victorians and Ancient Greece*, Oxford.

(1989) "Virgil and Arcadia," *JRS* 79: 26–39.

Jones, A. H. M. (1940) *The Greek City*, Oxford.

(1953) "Census records of the later Roman empire," *JRS* 43: 49–64.

(1956) Review of Kahrstedt (1954), *CR* 6: 53–4.

(1963) "The Greeks under the Roman empire," *Dumbarton Oaks Papers* 17: 3–19.

(1964) *The Later Roman Empire: 284–602 AD* (2 volumes), Oxford.

(1971) *The Cities of the Eastern Roman Provinces* (2nd edn), Oxford.

(1974) "Taxation in antiquity," in Jones, A. H. M. and Brunt, P. A., eds., *The Roman Economy: Studies in Ancient Economic and Administrative History*, 151–86. Oxford.

Jones, C. P. (1970) "A leading family from Roman Thespiae," *HSCP* 74: 223–55.

(1971a) "The levy at Thespiae under Marcus Aurelius," *GRBS* 12: 45–8.

(1971b) *Plutarch and Rome*, Oxford.

(1972) "Two friends of Plutarch," *BCH* 96: 263–7.

(1978a) *The Roman World of Dio Chrysostom*, Cambridge, MA.

(1978b) "Three foreigners in Attica," *Phoenix* 32: 222–34.

(1986) *Culture and Society in Lucian*, Cambridge.

Jones, J. E. (1987) "Cities of victory – patterns and parallels," in Chrysos, ed., 99–108.

Jones, J. E., Graham, A. J. and Sackett, L. H. (1973) *An Attic Country House Below the Cave of Pan at Vari*, London.

Jost, M. (1985) *Sanctuaires et cultes d'Arcadie* (Ecole Française d'Athènes, Etudes Péloponnésiennes 9), Paris.

Kabbani, R. (1986) *Europe's Myths of Orient*, London.

Kahn, L. (1979) "Hermès, la frontière et l'identité ambiguë," *Ktema* 4: 201–11.

Kahrstedt, U. (1950) "Die Territorien von Patrai und Nikopolis in der Kaiserzeit,"

*Historia* 1: 549–61.

(1954) *Das wirtschaftliche Gesicht Griechenlands in der Kaiserzeit*, Bern.

Kapetanopoulos, E. (1965) "The evidence of Athens," *Bulletin of the American Society of Papyrologists* 2: 47–55.

Kase, E. W. and Wilkie, N. C. (1977) "The Phokis-Doris expedition," *AD* 32 B1: 110–13.

Katzoff, R. (1986) "Where did the Greeks of the Roman period practice wrestling?" *AJA* 90: 437–40.

Kawerau, G. (1888) *Der Tempel der Roma und des Augustus auf der Akropolis von Athen*, Berlin.

Keatinge, R. W. and Conrad, G. W. (1983) "Imperialist expansion in Peruvian prehistory: Chimu administration of a conquered territory," *JFA* 10: 255–83.

Keil, J. (1936) "The Greek provinces," in Cook, S. A., Adcock, F. E. and Charlesworth, M. P., eds., *CAH XI, The Imperial Peace, AD 70–192*, 555–605. Cambridge.

Keller, D. R. (1985) Archaeological survey in Southern Euboea, Greece: a reconstruction of human activity from Neolithic times through the Byzantine period. Unpublished Ph.D. thesis, Indiana University.

Keller, D. R. and Wallace, M. (1986) "The Canadian Karystia Project," *EMC/CV* 30, n.s. 5: 155–9.

(1987) "The Canadian-Karystia Project, 1986," *EMC/CV* 31, n.s. 6: 225–7.

Kelly, K. (1965) "Land-use regions in the central and northern portions of the Inca empire," *AAAG* 55: 327–39.

Kennedy, H. (1985) "From polis to madina: urban change in late antique and early Islamic Syria," *Past and Present* 106: 3–27.

Kertzer, D. I. (1988) *Ritual, Politics and Power*, New Haven.

Kienast, H. (1987) "Athen," in *Die Wasserversorgung Antiker Städte*, 167–71. Mainz.

King, A. (1990) "The emergence of Romano-Celtic religion," in Blagg, T. F. C. and Millett, M., eds., *The Early Roman Empire in the West*, 220–41. Oxford.

Kirch, P. V. (1980) "The archaeological study of adaptation: theoretical and methodological issues," in Schiffer, M. B., ed., *Advances in Archaeological Method and Theory* (Volume 3), 101–56. New York.

Kirsten, E. (1987) "The origins of the first inhabitants of Nikopolis," in Chrysos, ed., 91–8.

Kleiner, D. E. E. (1983) *The Monument of Philopappos in Athens*, Rome.

Knapp, A. B., ed. (1992) *Archaeology, Annales, and Ethnohistory*, Cambridge.

Knauss, J., Heinrich, B. and Kalcyk, H. (1984) *Die Wasserbauten der Minyer in der Kopais: Die älteste Flussregulierung Europas*, Munich.

Kohl, P. (1987a) "The ancient economy, transferable technologies and the Bronze Age world-system: a view from the northeastern frontier of the Ancient Near East," in Rowlands *et al.*, eds., 13–24.

(1987b) "The use and abuse of world systems theory: the case of the pristine west Asian state," in Schiffer, M. B., ed., *Advances in Archaeological Method and Theory* (Volume 11), 1–35. New York.

Kokkou, A. (1970) "Hadrianeia erga eis tas Athenas," *AD* 25 A: 150–73.

Kosso, C. (n.d.) Public policy and agricultural practice: an archaeological and textual study of Late Roman Greece. Unpublished Ph.D. thesis, University of Illinois.

Kroll, J. H. (1972) "Two hoards of Athenian bronze coins," *AD* 27 A: 86–120.

Kuper, H. (1972) "The language of sites in the politics of space," *American Anthropologist* 74: 411–25.

Kus, S. (1989) "Sensuous human activity and the state: towards an archaeology of bread and circuses," in Miller *et al.*, eds., 140–54.

Laet, S. J. de (1949) *Portorium. Etude sur l'organisation douanière chez les Romains, surtout à l'époque du Haut-Empire*, Bruges.

Lambraki, A. (1980) "Le cipolin de la Karystie: contribution à l'étude des marbres de la Grèce exploités aux époques romaines et paléochrétiennes," *RA* 1: 31–62.

Lane Fox, R. (1986) *Pagans and Christians*, Harmondsworth.

Langdon, M. K. (1976) *A Sanctuary of Zeus on Mount Hymettos* (*Hesperia* Supplement 16), Princeton.

(1988) "Hymettiana II. An ancient quarry on Mount Hymettos," *AJA* 92: 75–83.

Larsen, J. A. O. (1935) "Was Greece free between 196–146 BC?" *CPhil* 30: 193–214.

(1938) "Roman Greece," in Frank, T., ed., *An Economic Survey of Ancient Rome IV*, 259–498. Baltimore.

(1953) "A Thessalian family under the Principate," *CPhil* 48: 86–95.

(1955) *Representative Government in Greek and Roman History*, Berkeley.

(1958) "The policy of Augustus in Greece," *Acta Classica* 1: 123–30.

(1968) *Greek Federal States*, Oxford.

Larsen, M. T., ed. (1979) *Power and Propaganda: A Symposium on Ancient Empires*, Copenhagen.

Lattimore, O. (1962) "The frontier in history," in Lattimore, O., *Studies in Frontier History: Collected Papers 1928–1958*, 469–91. London.

Laumonier, A. (1977) *La Céramique hellénistique à relief I. Ateliers "ioniens"* (Délos Fascicule 31), Paris.

Lazenby, J. F. and Hope Simpson, R. (1972) "Greco-Roman times: literary tradition and topographical commentary," in McDonald and Rapp, eds., 81–99.

Leach, E. (1974) *Vergil's Eclogues: Landscapes of Experience*, Ithaca.

Leveau, Ph. (1978) "La situation coloniale de l'Afrique romaine," *Annales (E.S.C.)* 33: 89–92.

Lévêque, P. and Morel, J. P., eds. (1980) *Céramiques hellénistiques et romaines*, Paris.

(1987) *Céramiques hellénistiques et romaines II*, Paris.

Levick, B. (1967) *Roman Colonies in Southern Asia Minor*, Oxford.

(1985) *The Government of the Roman Empire: A Sourcebook*, London.

(forthcoming) "Greece," in *CAH²* XI, *The Imperial Peace, AD 70–192*, Cambridge.

Lloyd, J. A. (1991a) "Farming the highlands: Samnium and Arcadia in the Hellenistic and Early Roman imperial periods," in Barker and Lloyd, eds., 180–93.

(1991b) "Forms of rural settlement in the Early Roman empire," in Barker and Lloyd, eds., 233–40.

Lloyd, J. A. and Barker, G. (1981) "Rural settlement in Roman Molise: problems of archaeological survey," in Barker, G. and Hodges, R., eds., *Archaeology and Italian Society* (BAR International Series 102), 375–416. Oxford.

Lohmann, H. (1983) "Atene, eine attische Landgemeinde klassischer Zeit," *Hellenika Jahrbuch*, 98–117.

(1985) "Landleben im klassischen Attika," *Ruhr-Universität Bochum Jahrbuch*, 71–96.

Lukermann, F. E. and Moody, J. (1978) "Nichoria and vicinity: settlements and circulation," in Rapp, G. Jr. and Aschenbrenner, S. E., eds., *Excavations at Nichoria in South-west Greece. Volume I: Site, Environs, and Techniques*, 78–112. Minneapolis.

McAllister, M. H. (1959) "The Temple of Ares at Athens: a review of the evidence," *Hesperia* 28: 1–64.

McDonald, W. A. (1984) "The Minnesota Messenia survey: a look back," in *Studies Presented to Sterling Dow on his Eightieth Birthday*, 185–91. Durham, NC.

McDonald, W. A. and Hope Simpson, R. (1972) "Archaeological exploration," in McDonald and Rapp, eds., 117–47.

McDonald, W. A. and Rapp, G. R., Jr., eds. (1972) *The Minnesota Messenia Expedition: Reconstructing a Bronze Age Regional Environment*, Minneapolis.

McKechnie, P. (1989) *Outsiders in the Greek Cities in the Fourth Century BC*, London.

MacMullen, R. (1959) "Roman imperial building in the provinces," *HSCP* 64: 207–35.

(1974) *Roman Social Relations 50 BC–AD 284*, New Haven.

(1976) *Roman Government's Response to Crisis, AD 235–337*, New Haven.

(1981) *Paganism in the Roman Empire*, New Haven.

McNeal, R. A. (1991) "Archaeology and the destruction of the later Athenian acropolis," *Antiquity* 65: 49–63.

MacNeice, L. (1966) *Collected Poems*, London.

Macready, S. and Thompson, F. H., eds. (1987) *Roman Architecture in the Greek World* (The Society of Antiquaries Occasional Papers 10), London.

Mahaffy, J. P. (1890) *The Greek World under Roman Sway: From Polybius to Plutarch*, London.

(1892) *Problems in Greek History*, London.

Marcus, J. (1973) "Territorial organisation of the lowland Classic Maya," *Science* 180: 911–16.

Martin, R. (1974) *L'Urbanisme dans la Grèce antique* (2nd edn), Paris.

Mattingly, D. J. (1988) "Oil for export? A comparison of Libyan, Spanish and Tunisian olive oil production in the Roman empire," *JRA* 1: 33–56.

(1989) "Field survey in the Libyan valleys," *JRA* 2: 275–80.

Mee, C., Gill, D., Forbes, H. and Foxhall, L. (1991) "Rural settlement change in the Methana peninsula, Greece," in Barker and Lloyd, eds., 223–32.

Mellor, R. (1975) *ΘEA PΩMH: The Worship of the Goddess Roma in the Greek World* (*Hypomnemata* 42), Göttingen.

Mendoni, L. (1985/90) "Symbole sten topographia tes notioanatolikes Keas," *Epeteris Etaireias Kykladikon Meleton* 13: 311–28.

Mendoni, L. G. and Mourtzas, N. D. (1990) "An archaeological approach to coastal sites: the example of the ancient harbor of Karthaia," in *Praktika Triemerou Aigaiou: 21–23 Dekembriou 1989*, 387–403. Athens.

Mendoni, L. and Papageorgiadou, H. (1989) "A surface survey of Roman Kea," in

Walker and Cameron, eds., 169–73.

Menzel, D. (1959) "The Inca occupation of the south coast of Peru," *Southwestern Journal of Anthropology* 15: 125–42.

Michel, J.-H. (1975) "L'insuffisance des investissements: signe ou cause de sous-développement dans deux provinces romaines (l'Espagne et l'Afrique du Nord)," *ANRW* 11.3: 84–7.

Migeotte, L. (1984) *L'Emprunt public dans les cités grecques*, Paris.

(1985a) "Endettement des cités béotiennes autour des années 200 avant J.-C.," *Teiresias* Supplement 3 (Proceedings of the Third International Conference on Boeotian Antiquities 1979), 103–7. Montreal.

(1985b) "Réparation de monuments publics à Messène au temps d'Auguste," *BCH* 109: 597–607.

(1985c) "Souscriptions publiques en Béotie," in Roesch, P. and Argoud, G., eds., *La Béotie antique* (Colloques Internationaux du Centre National de la Recherche Scientifique), 311–16. Paris.

Miles, M. M. (1989) "A reconstruction of the temple of Nemesis at Rhamnous," *Hesperia* 58: 137–249.

Millar, F. (1966) Review of Deininger (1965), *CR* 16: 388–90.

(1969) "P. Herennius Dexippus: the Greek World and the third century invasions," *JRS* 59: 12–29.

(1977) *The Emperor in the Roman World*, London.

(1981a) *The Roman Empire and its Neighbours* (2nd edn), London.

(1981b) "The world of the Golden Ass," *JRS* 71: 63–75.

(1983) "Empire and city, Augustus to Julian: obligations, excuses, and status," *JRS* 73: 76–96.

(1984) "The Mediterranean and the Roman revolution: politics, war and the economy," *Past and Present* 102: 3–24.

(1987) "Introduction," in Macready and Thompson, eds., ix–xv.

Miller, A. G. and Farriss, N. M. (1979) "Religious syncretism in Colonial Yucatan: the archaeological and ethnohistorical evidence from Tancah, Quintana Roo," in Hammond, N. and Willey, G. R., eds., *Maya Archaeology and Ethnohistory*, 223–40. Austin.

Miller, D. (1989) "The limits of dominance," in Miller *et al.*, eds., 63–79.

Miller, D., Rowlands, M. and Tilley, C., eds. (1989) *Domination and Resistance*, London.

Miller, S. G. (1972a) "A Roman monument in the Athenian agora," *Hesperia* 41: 50–95.

(1972b) "Addendum to a Roman monument in the Athenian agora," *Hesperia* 41: 475–6.

(1990) *Nemea: A Guide to the Site and Museum*, Berkeley.

Miller, S. Grobel (1972) "A mosaic floor from a Roman villa at Anaploga," *AJA* 41: 332–54.

Millett, M. (1990) *The Romanization of Britain: An Essay in Archaeological Interpretation*, Cambridge.

(1991a) "Pottery: population or supply patterns? The *Ager Tarraconensis* approach," in Barker and Lloyd, eds., 18–26.

(1991b) "Roman towns and their territories: an archaeological perspective," in Rich, J. and Wallace-Hadrill, A., eds., *City and Country in the Ancient World*, 169–89. London.

Mitchell, S. (1974) "The Plancii in Asia Minor," *JRS* 64: 27–39.

(1976) "Requisitioned transport in the Roman empire: a new inscription from Pisidia," *JRS* 66: 106–31.

(1979) "Iconium and Ninica: two double communities in Roman Asia Minor," *Historia* 30: 409–38.

(1987) "Imperial building in the eastern Roman provinces," in Macready and Thompson, eds., 18–25.

Mitford, W. (1820) *The History of Greece* (Volume 10), London.

Moggi, M. (1976) *I sinecismi interstatali Greci*, Pisa.

Molloy, J. P. and Rathje, W. J. (1974) "Sexploitation among the Late Classic Maya," in Hammond, N., ed., *Mesoamerican Archaeology: New Approaches*, 431–43. London.

Montmollin, O. de (1987) "Forced settlement and political centralization in a Classic Maya polity," *Journal of Anthropological Archaeology* 6: 220–62.

Moretti, L. (1981) "Iscrizioni di Tespie della prima età imperiale," *Athenaeum* 69: 71–7.

Morgan, C. (1990) *Athletes and Oracles: The Transformation of Olympia and Delphi in the 8th Century BC*, Cambridge.

Morris, C. (1972) "State settlements in Tawantinsuyu: a strategy of compulsory urbanism," in Leone, M. P., ed., *Contemporary Archaeology*, 393–401. Carbondale.

Morris, C. and Thompson, D. E. (1970) "Huanuco Viejo: an Inca administrative center," *AAnt* 35: 344–62.

Morris, P. (1984) "Introduction," in Morris, P., ed., *Africa, America and Central Asia: Formal and Informal Empire in the 19th Century* (Exeter Studies in History No. 9), 1–9. Exeter.

Munn, M. (1985) "A late Classical rural settlement phenomenon in the Southern Argolid, Greece" (abstract), *AJA* 89: 343.

(1988) "En methoriois tes Attikes kai tes Boiotias," *Epeteris tes Etaireias Boiotikon Meleton, Tomos A', Teuchos a'*, 363–71. Athens.

(1989) "New light on Panakton and the Attic–Boiotian frontier," in Beister, H. and Buckler, J., eds., *Boiotika (Vorträge vom 5.Internationalen Böotien-Kolloquium zu Ehren von Professor Dr. Siegfried Lauffer)*, 231–44. Munich.

Munn, M. H. and Munn, M. L. Z. (1989a) "The Stanford Skourta Plain Project: the 1987 and 1988 seasons of survey on the Attic–Boiotian frontier" (abstract), *AJA* 93: 274–5.

(1989b) "Studies on the Attic–Boiotian Frontier: the Stanford Skourta Project, 1985," in Fossey, ed., 73–127.

(1990) "On the frontiers of Attica and Boiotia: the results of the Stanford Skourta Plain Project," in Schachter, A., ed., *Essays in the Topography, History and Culture of Boiotia*, 33–40. Montreal.

Murra, J. V. (1980) *The Economic Organization of the Inka State*, Greenwich, CT.

Murray, P. and Chang, C. (1981) "An ethnoarchaeological study of a contemporary herder's site," *JFA* 8: 372–81.

Murray, W. M. (1982) The coastal sites of Western Akarnania: a topographical-historical survey. Unpublished dissertation, University of Pennsylvania.

Murray, W. M. and Petsas, P. M. (1989) *Octavian's Campsite Memorial for the Actian War* (Transactions of the American Philosophical Society 79.4), Philadelphia.

Neesen, L. (1980) *Untersuchungen zu den direkten Staatsabgaben der römischen Kaiserzeit*, Bonn.

Neeve, P. W. de (1984) *Colonus: Private Farm Tenancy in Roman Italy during the Republic and the Early Principate*, Amsterdam.

Netting, R. McC. (1974) "Agrarian ecology," *AnnRevAnth* 3: 21–57.

Nicolet, C. (1988) *L'Inventaire du monde*, Paris.

Nisbet, R. G. M., ed. (1961) *Cicero's* In L. Calpurnium Pisonem, Oxford.

Nutton, V. (1978) "The beneficial ideology," in Garnsey, P. and Whittaker, C. R., eds., *Imperialism in the Ancient World*, 209–22. Cambridge.

Ogilvie, R. M. (1967) "The date of the *De defectu oraculorum*," *Phoenix* 21: 108–19.

Oliver, J. H. (1951) "New evidence on the Attic Panhellenion," *Hesperia* 20: 31–3.

(1953) *The Ruling Power* (Transactions of the American Philosophical Society 43.4), Philadelphia.

(1954) "The Roman Governor's permission for a decree of the polis," *Hesperia* 23: 163–7.

(1965) "Livia as Artemis Boulaia at Athens," *CPhil* 60: 179.

(1968) *The Civilizing Power* (Transactions of the American Philosophical Society 58), Philadelphia.

(1970) *Marcus Aurelius: Aspects of Civic and Cultural Policy in the East* (*Hesperia* Supplement 13), Princeton.

(1971) "Epaminondas of Acraephia," *GRBS* 12: 221–37.

(1972) "On the Hellenic policy of Augustus and Agrippa in 27 BC," *AJP* 92: 190–7.

(1973) "Imperial commissioners in Achaia," *GRBS* 14: 389–405.

(1978) "Panachaeans and Panhellenes," *Hesperia* 47: 185–91.

(1983) *The Civic Tradition and Roman Athens*, Baltimore.

Orlandos, A. K. (1915) "Peri ton anastelotikon ergasion en Orchomeno tes Boiotias," *AD* 1 B: 51–3.

Osborne, R. (1985a) "Building and residence on the land in Classical and Hellenistic Greece: the contribution of epigraphy," *BSA* 80: 119–28.

(1985b) *Demos: The Discovery of Classical Attika*, Cambridge.

(1985c) "The land-leases from Hellenistic Thespiai: a re-examination," in Roesch, P. and Argoud, G., eds., *La Béotie antique* (Colloques Internationaux du Centre National de la Recherche Scientifique), 317–23. Paris.

(1987a) *Classical Landscape with Figures: The Ancient Greek City and its Countryside*, London.

(1987b) "The viewing and obscuring of the Parthenon frieze," *JHS* 107: 98–105.

(1988) "Social and economic implications of the leasing of land and property in Classical and Hellenistic Greece," *Chiron* 18: 279–323.

(1991a) "The potential mobility of human populations," *OJA* 10: 231–52.

(1991b) "Pride and prejudice, sense and subsistence: exchange and society in the Greek city," in Rich, J. and Wallace-Hadrill, A., eds., *City and Country in the*

*Ancient World*, 119–45. London.

Owens, E. J. (1976) "Increasing Roman domination of Greece in the years 48–27 BC," *Latomus* 35: 719–29.

Pailes, R. A. and Whitecotton, J. W. (1979) "The greater Southwest and the Mesoamerican 'world' system: an exploratory model of frontier relationships," in Savage, W. W. and Thompson, S., eds., *The Frontier: Comparative Studies* (Volume 2), 105–21. Norman, Oklahoma.

Panofsky, E. (1955) "*Et in Arcadia ego*: Poussin and the elegiac tradition," in Panofsky, E., *Meaning in the Visual Arts*, 295–326. Garden City, NY.

Papachatzis, N. D. (1974–81) *Pausaniou Ellados Periegesis* (5 volumes), Athens.

Papapostolou, J. A. (1971) "Topographika ton Patron," *AAA* 4: 305–19.

Papazoglou, F. (1988) *Les Villes de Macédoine à l'époque romaine* (*BCH* Supplément 16), Paris.

Parker, S. T. (1986) *Romans and Saracens: A History of the Arabian Frontier*, Winona Lake, IN.

Patlagean, E. (1977) *Pauvreté économique et pauvreté sociale à Byzance 4ᵉ–7ᵉ siècles* (Ecole des Hautes Etudes en Sciences Sociales, Civilisations et Sociétés 48), Paris.

Patterson, J. R. (1987) "Crisis: what crisis? Rural change and urban development in imperial Apennine Italy," *PBSR* 55: 115–46.

  (1991) "Settlement, city and elite in Samnium and Lycia," in Rich, J. and Wallace-Hadrill, A., eds., *City and Country in the Ancient World*, 149–68. London.

Payne, S. (1985) "Zoo-archaeology in Greece: a reader's guide," in Wilkie, N. C. and Coulson, W. D. E., eds., *Contributions to Aegean Archaeology: Studies in Honor of W. A. McDonald*, 211–44. Minneapolis.

Paynter, R. (1981) "Social complexity in peripheries: problems and models," in van der Leeuw, S. E., ed., *Archaeological Approaches to the Study of Complexity*, 117–34. Amsterdam.

  (1982) *Models of Spatial Inequality: Settlement Patterns in Historical Archaeology*, New York.

Pečirka, J. (1973) "Homestead farms in Classical and Hellenistic Hellas," in Finley, M. I., ed., *Problèmes de la terre en Grèce ancienne*, 113–47. Paris.

Pédech, P. (1971) "La géographie urbaine chez Strabon," *Ancient Society* 2: 234–53.

Percival, J. (1976) *The Roman Villa*, London.

Perlzweig, J. (1961) *Lamps of the Roman Period* (The Athenian Agora Volume VII), Princeton.

Petrochilos, N. K. (1974) *Roman Attitudes to the Greeks*, Athens.

Philadelpheus, A. (1909) "Ai en Ermionidi anaskaphai," *Praktika tes en Athenais Archaiologikes Etaireias*, 172–84.

Picard, G. C. (1983) "Les centres civiques ruraux dans l'Italie et la Gaule romaine," in *Architecture et société: de l'archaïsme grec à la fin de la république romaine (Actes du colloque international organisé par le CNRS et l'Ecole française de Rome, 2–4 décembre 1980, Rome)*, 415–23. Paris.

Picard, O. (1989) "Thasos dans le monde romain," in Walker and Cameron, eds., 174–9.

Pittinger, J. (1975) "The mineral products of Melos in antiquity and their identification," *BSA* 70: 191–7.

Platon, N. and Feyel, M. (1938) "Inventaire sacré de Thespies," *BCH* 62: 149–66.

Pleket, H. W. (1961) "Domitian, the Senate and the provinces," *Mnemosyne* 14: 296–315.

(1976) Review of Helly (1973), *Mnemosyne* 29: 325–8.

Plog, S., Plog, F. and Wait, W. (1978) "Decision making in modern surveys," in Schiffer, M. B., ed., *Advances in Archaeological Method and Theory* (Volume 1), 383–421. New York.

Polignac, F. de (1984) *La Naissance de la cité grecque*, Paris.

Pollitt, J. J. (1983) *The Art of Rome: Sources and Documents*, Cambridge.

(1986) *Art in the Hellenistic Age*, Cambridge.

Pomeroy, S. (1983) "Infanticide in Hellenistic Greece," in Cameron, A. and Kuhrt, A., eds., *Images of Women in Antiquity*, 207–22. London.

Ponsich, M. (1974) *Implantation rurale antique sur le Bas-Guadalquivir I*, Madrid.

(1979) *Implantation rurale antique sur le Bas-Guadalquivir II*, Paris.

Potter, T. W. (1978) "Population hiatus and continuity: the case of the South Etruria survey," in Blake, H., Potter, T. W. and Whitehouse, D. B., eds., *Papers in Italian Archaeology I: The Lancaster Seminar, Part I* (BAR Supplementary Series 41.1), 99–116. Oxford.

(1979) *The Changing Landscape of Southern Etruria*, London.

Poulter, A. G. (1979) "Rural communities (*vici* and *komai*) and their role in the organization of the limes of Moesia Inferior," in Hanson, W. S. and Keppie, L. J. F., eds., *Roman Frontier Studies, Part III* (BAR International Series 71), 729–44. Oxford.

Pounds, N. J. G. (1973) *An Historical Geography of Europe, 450 BC–AD 1330*, Cambridge.

Prakash, G. (1990) "Writing post-Orientalist histories of the Third World: perspectives from Indian historiography," *CSSH* 32: 383–408.

Préaux, C. (1978) *Le Monde hellénistique*, Paris.

Price, B. J. (1980) "The Truth is not in accounts but in account books: on the epistemological status of history," in Ross, E. B., ed., *Beyond the Myths of Culture: Essays in Cultural Materialism*, 155–80. New York.

Price, S. R. F. (1984) *Rituals and Power: The Roman Imperial Cult in Asia Minor*, Cambridge.

Puillon Boblaye, M. E. (1836) *Expédition scientifique de Morée. Recherches géographiques sur les ruines de la Morée*, Paris.

Purcell, N. (1987) "The Nicopolitan synoecism and Roman urban policy," in Chrysos, ed., 71–90.

(1990) "The creation of provincial landscape: the Roman impact," in Blagg, T. and Millett, M., eds., *The Early Roman Empire in the West*, 7–29. Oxford.

Quass, F. (1982) "Zur politischen Tätigkeit der munizipalen Aristokratie des griechischen Ostens in der Kaiserzeit," *Historia* 31: 188–213.

Rackham, O. (1983) "Observations on the historical ecology of Boeotia," *BSA* 78: 291–351.

Ramsden, S. E. (1972) Roman mosaics in Greece: the mainland and the Ionian islands. Unpublished Ph.D. thesis, University of London.

Redmond, E. M. (1983) *A Fuego y Sangre: Early Zapotec Imperialism in the Cuicatlan*

*Canada, Oaxaca* (Studies in Latin American Ethnohistory and Archaeology 1), Ann Arbor.

Reed, M., ed. (1984) *Discovering Past Landscapes*, London.

Reid, J. S. (1913) *The Municipalities of the Roman Empire*, Cambridge.

Reinhold, M. (1970) *History of Purple as a Status Symbol in Antiquity* (Collection Latomus 116), Brussels.

Renfrew, C. and Wagstaff, M., eds. (1982) *An Island Polity: The Archaeology of Exploitation in Melos*, Cambridge.

Reynolds, J. (1982) *Aphrodisias and Rome* (Journal of Roman Studies Monograph No. 1), London.

Rhomaios, K. A. (1930) "To Eroon tes Alyzias," *Archaiologike Ephemeris* 1930: 141–59.

Rieks, R. (1970) "Sebasta und Aktia," *Hermes* 98: 96–116.

Riley, J. A. (1979) "The coarse pottery from Benghazi," in Lloyd, J. A., ed., *Excavations at Sidi Khrebish Benghazi (Berenice) II*, 91–497. Tripoli.

(1981) "Italy and the Eastern Mediterranean in the Hellenistic and Early Roman periods: the evidence of the coarse pottery," in Barker, G. and Hodges, R., eds., *Archaeology and Italian Society: Prehistoric, Roman and Medieval Studies* (BAR International Series 102), 69–78. Oxford.

Rizakis, A. (1984) "Munera Gladiatoria à Patras," *BCH* 108: 533–42.

(1985) "Cadastres romains en Grèce," *Dialogues d'histoire ancienne* 11: 761–2.

(1987/8) "E Romaike Politike sten Peloponneso kai e Achaike Sympoliteia," *Praktika tou tritou Diethnous Synedriou Peloponnesiakon Spoudon*, 2–36.

(1988) "Le port de Patras et les communications avec l'Italie sous la République," *Cahiers d'histoire* 33: 453–72.

(1989) "La colonie romaine de Patras en Achaie: le témoignage épigraphique," in Walker and Cameron, eds., 180–6.

(1990) "A contribution to the history of Roman colonization in the N.W. Peloponnese" (abstract), *Meletemata* 10.

Robert, L. (1935) "Etudes sur les inscriptions et la topographie de la Grèce centrale," *BCH* 59: 438–52.

(1951) *Etudes de numismatique grecque*, Paris.

(1963) "Nouvelles inscriptions d'Iasos," *Revue des études anciennes* 65: 298–329.

(1977) "La titulature de Nicée et de Nicomédie: la gloire et la haine," *HSCP* 81: 1–39.

Robinson, H. S. (1959) *Pottery of the Roman Period* (The Athenian Agora Volume v), Princeton.

(1965) *The Urban Development of Ancient Corinth*, Athens.

(1974) "A monument of Roma at Corinth," *Hesperia* 43: 470–84.

Rocchi, G. D. (1988) *Frontiera e confini nella Grecia antica*, Rome.

Roebuck, C. A. (1941) *A History of Messenia from 369 to 146 BC*, Chicago.

(1945) "A note on Messenian economy and population," *CPhil* 40: 149–65.

Roesch, P. (1965) *Thespies et la confédération béotienne*, Paris.

Rogers, G. M. (1991) *The Sacred Identity of Ephesos: Foundation Myths of a Roman City*, London.

Roller, D. W. (1985) "Tanagra during the Roman period," in Argoud, G. and

Roesch, P., eds., *La Béotie antique* (Colloques Internationaux du Centre National de la Recherche Scientifique), 277–81. Paris.

(1987) "Tanagra Survey Project 1985. The site of Grimadha," *BSA* 82: 213–32.

(1989) "Recent investigations at Grimadha (Tanagra)," in Fossey, ed., 129–63.

Rossiter, J. J. (1989) "Roman villas of the Greek east and the villa in Gregory of Nyssa *Ep.* 20," *JRA* 2: 101–10.

Rostovtzeff, M. I. (1941) *The Social and Economic History of the Hellenistic World* (3 volumes), Oxford.

(1957) *The Social and Economic History of the Roman Empire* (2 volumes, 2nd edn; revised by P. M. Fraser), Oxford.

Rotroff, S. I. (1982) *Hellenistic Pottery: Athenian and Imported Moldmade Bowls* (The Athenian Agora Volume XXII), Princeton, NJ.

Rougé, J. (1966) *Recherches sur l'organisation du commerce maritime en Méditerranée sous l'empire romain*, Paris.

Rowlands, M. J. (1972) "Defence: a factor in the organization of settlements," in Ucko, P. J., Tringham, R. and Dimbleby, G. W., eds., *Man, Settlement, and Urbanism*, 447–62. London.

Rowlands, M. J., Larsen, M. and Kristiansen, K., eds. (1987) *Centre and Periphery in the Ancient World*, Cambridge.

Roy, J., Lloyd, J. A. and Owens, E. J. (1988) "Tribe and polis in the chora at Megalopolis: changes in settlement pattern in relation to synoecism," *Praktika tes en Athenais Archaiologikes Etaireias* 1988, 179–82.

(1989) "Megalopolis under the Roman empire," in Walker and Cameron, eds., 146–50.

Rudolph, W. W. (1974) "Excavations at Porto Cheli and vicinity, preliminary report, III: excavations at Metochi 1970," *Hesperia* 43: 105–31.

(1979) "Excavations at Porto Cheli and vicinity, preliminary report, V: the early Byzantine remains," *Hesperia* 48: 294–320.

Runnels, C. N. and van Andel, T. H. (1987) "The evolution of settlement in the Southern Argolid, Greece: an economic explanation," *Hesperia* 56: 303–34.

Ruschenbusch, E. (1985) "Die Zahl der griechischen Staaten und Arealgrösse und Bürgerzahl der 'Normalpolis,'" *ZPE* 59: 253–63.

Rutter, J. B. (1983) "Some thoughts on the analysis of ceramic data generated by site surveys," in Keller, D. R. and Rupp, D. W., eds., *Archaeological Survey in the Mediterranean Area* (BAR International Series 155), 137–42. Oxford.

Sack, R. D. (1980) *Conceptions of Space in Social Thought: A Geographic Perspective*, London.

Sackett, L. H., Hankey, V., Howell, R. J., Jacobsen, T. W. and Popham, M. R. (1966) "Prehistoric Euboea: contributions towards a survey," *BSA* 61: 33–112.

Said, E. (1978) *Orientalism*, New York.

Ste. Croix, G. E. M. de (1981) *The Class Struggle in the Ancient Greek World*, London.

Sallade, J. K. and Braun, D. P. (1982) "Spatial organization of peasant agricultural subsistence territories: distance factors and crop location," in Tooker, E. and Sturtevant, W. C., eds., *Ethnography by Archaeologists*, 19–41. Washington, DC.

Sallares, J. R. (1991) *The Ecology of the Ancient Greek World*, London.

Salmon, E. T. (1969) *Roman Colonization under the Republic*, London.

Salmon, P. (1974) *Population et dépopulation dans l'Empire romain* (Collection Latomus 137), Brussels.

Sanders, G. D. R. and Whitbread, I. K. (1990) "Central places and major roads in the Peloponnese," *BSA* 85: 333–61.

Sanders, I. (1982) *Roman Crete*, Warminster.

Sarikakis, T. (1965) "Aktia ta en Nikopolei," *Archaiologike Ephemeris* 1965, 145–62.

(1970) "Nicopolis d'Epire: était-elle une colonie ou une ville grecque?" *Balkan Studies* 11: 91–6.

Sartre, M. (1979) "Aspects économiques et aspects religieux de la frontière dans les cités grecques," *Ktema* 4: 213–24.

Schachter, A. (1967) "A Boiotian cult-type," *BICS* 14: 1–16.

(1981) *Cults of Boiotia I. Acheloos to Hera* (*BICS* Supplement 38.1), London.

(1986) *Cults of Boiotia II. Herakles to Poseidon* (*BICS* Supplement 38.2), London.

Schmitt-Pantel, P. (1981) "Le festin dans la fête de la cité grecque hellénistique," in *La Fête, pratique et discours* (Centre de Recherches D'Histoire Ancienne 42), 85–95. Paris.

(1985) "Banquet et cité grecque: quelques questions suscitées par les recherches récentes," *Mélanges d'archéologie et d'histoire de l'Ecole Française de Rome* 97: 135–58.

Schneider, J. (1977) "Was there a pre-capitalist world-system?" *Peasant Studies* 6: 20–9.

Schneider, L. and Höcker, C. (1990) *Die Akropolis von Athen. Antikes Heiligtum und modernes Reiseziel*, Cologne.

Schreiber, K. (1987) "Conquest and consolidation: a comparison of the Wari and Inka occupations of a Highland Peruvian valley," *AAnt* 52: 266–84.

Scully, V. (1979) *The Earth, the Temple and the Gods* (Revised edn), New Haven.

Segal, C. (1981) *Poetry and Myth in Ancient Pastoral: Essays on Theocritus and Virgil*, Princeton.

Semple, E. (1932) *The Geography of the Mediterranean Region: Its Relation to Ancient History*, London.

Shaw, B. D. (1980) "Archaeology and knowledge: the history of the African provinces of the Roman empire," *Florilegium* 2: 28–60.

(1982/3) " 'Eaters of flesh, drinkers of milk': the ancient Mediterranean ideology of the pastoral nomad," *Ancient Society* 13/14: 5–31.

(1983) "Soldiers and society: the army in Numidia," *Opus* 2: 133–57.

Shaw, J. W. (1986) "Excavations at Kommos (Crete) during 1984–1985," *Hesperia* 55: 219–69.

Shear, T. L. (1930) *The Roman Villa* (Corinth Volume v), Cambridge, MA.

Shear, T. L., Jr. (1981) "Athens: from city-state to provincial town," *Hesperia* 50: 356–77.

Sheehan, M. C. and Whitehead, D. R. (1981) "The late-postglacial vegetation history of the Argolid peninsula, Greece," *National Geographic Society Research Reports* 13: 693–708.

Sherk, R. K. (1957) "Roman imperial troops in Macedonia and Achaea," *AJP* 78: 52–62.

Shipley, G. (1987) *A History of Samos, 800–188 BC*, Oxford.

Skinner, G. W. (1964) "Marketing and social structure in rural China: Part 1,"

*Journal of Asian Studies* 24: 3–43.

Slane, K. W. (1986) "Two deposits from the Early Roman Cellar Building, Corinth," *Hesperia* 55: 271–318.

(1987) "Roman pottery from east of the theater: quantifying the assemblages," *AJA* 91: 483–5.

(1989) "Corinthian ceramic imports: the changing pattern of provincial trade in the first and second centuries AD," in Walker and Cameron, eds., 219–25.

Small, D. (1987) "Social correlations to the Greek cavea in the Roman period," in Macready and Thompson, eds., 85–93.

Small, D. ed. (forthcoming) *The Archaeology of Imperial Control*, Cambridge.

Smith, B. (1950) "European vision and the South Pacific," *Journal of the Warburg and Courtauld Institutes* 13: 65–100.

Smith, C. (1896) "Archaeology in Greece, 1895–96," *JHS* 16: 335–56.

Smith, C. A. (1975) "Examining stratification systems through peasant marketing arrangements: an application of some models from economic geography," *Man* 10: 95–122.

(1976a) "Analyzing regional social systems," in Smith, C. A., ed., *Regional Analysis, Volume II: Social Systems*, 3–20. New York.

(1976b) "Exchange systems and the spatial distribution of elites: the organization of stratification in agrarian societies," in Smith, C. A., ed., *Regional Analysis, Volume II: Social Systems*, 309–74. New York.

Smith, D. E. (1977) "The Egyptian cults of Corinth," *Harvard Theological Review* 70: 201–31.

Smith, D. M. (1990) "Introduction: the sharing and dividing of geographical space," in Chisholm, M. and Smith, D. M., eds., *Shared Space: Divided Space. Essays on Conflict and Territorial Organization*, 1–21. London.

Smith, M. E. (1986) "The role of social stratification in the Aztec empire: a view from the provinces," *American Anthropologist* 88: 70–91.

Smith, M. E. and Berdan, F. (1992) "Archaeology and the Aztec empire," *WA* 23: 353–67.

Snell, B. (1953) "Arcadia: the discovery of a spiritual landscape," in Snell, B., *The Discovery of the Mind: The Greek Origins of European Thought* (Translated by T. G. Rosenmeyer), 281–309. Oxford.

Snodgrass, A. M. (1980) *Archaic Greece: The Age of Experiment*, London.

(1982) "La prospection archéologique en Grèce et dans le monde Méditerranéen," *Annales (E.S.C.)* 37: 800–13.

(1985) "The site of Askra," in Argoud, G. and Roesch, P., eds., *La Béotie antique* (Colloques Internationaux du Centre National de la Recherche Scientifique), 87–95. Paris.

(1986) Review of de Polignac (1984), *CR* 36: 261–5.

(1987) *An Archaeology of Greece: The Present State and Future Scope of a Discipline*, Berkeley.

(1990) "Survey archaeology and the rural landscape of the Greek city," in Murray, O. and Price, S., eds., *The Greek City: From Homer to Alexander*, 113–36. Oxford.

Solmsen, F. (1979) *Isis among the Greeks and Romans*, Cambridge, MA.

Souris, G. (1984) Studies in provincial diplomacy under the Principate. Unpublished Ph.D. thesis, University of Cambridge.

Sourvinou-Inwood, C. (1988) "Further aspects of polis religion," *Annali, Istituto Orientale di Napoli: Archeologia e storia antica* 10: 259–74.

(1990) "What is polis religion?" in Murray, O. and Price, S., eds., *The Greek City from Homer to Alexander*, 295–322. Oxford.

Sparkes, B. A. (1982a) "Classical and Roman Melos," in Renfrew and Wagstaff, eds., 45–52.

(1982b) "Production and exchange in the Classical and Roman periods," in Renfrew and Wagstaff, eds., 228–35.

Sparkes, B. A. and Cherry, J. F. (1982) "A note on the topography of the ancient settlement at Melos," in Renfrew and Wagstaff, eds., 53–7.

Spawforth, A. J. S. (1974) "The Appaleni of Corinth," *GRBS* 15: 295–303.

(1978) "Balbilla, the Euryclids, and memorials for a Greek magnate," *BSA* 73: 249–60.

(1980) "Sparta and the family of Herodes Atticus: a reconsideration of the evidence," *BSA* 75: 203–20.

(1984) "Notes on the third century AD in Spartan epigraphy," *BSA* 79: 263–88.

(1985) "Families at Roman Sparta and Epidaurus: some prosopographical notes," *BSA* 80: 191–258.

(1986) "A Severan statue group and an Olympic festival at Sparta," *BSA* 81: 313–32.

(1989) "Agonistic festivals in Roman Greece," in Walker and Cameron, eds., 193–7.

Spawforth, A. J. S. and Walker, S. (1985) "The world of the Panhellenion: i. Athens and Eleusis," *JRS* 75: 78–104.

(1986) "The world of the Panhellenion: ii. Three Dorian cities," *JRS* 76: 88–105.

Spencer, T. (1954) *Fair Greece, Sad Relic: Literary Philhellenism from Shakespeare to Byron*, Bath.

Spurr, M. S. (1986) *Arable Cultivation in Roman Italy*, c. 200 BC–c. AD 100, London.

Standing, G. (1981) "Migration and modes of exploitation: social origins of immobility and mobility," *Journal of Peasant Studies* 8: 173–211.

Stillwell, R. (1933) "Architectural studies," *Hesperia* 2: 112–48.

ed. (1976) *The Princeton Encyclopaedia of Classical Sites*, Princeton.

Stobart, J. C. (1911) *The Glory that was Greece*, London.

Sutton, R. F., Jr. (1991) "Ceramic evidence for settlement and land use in the Geometric to Hellenistic period," in Cherry *et al.*, 245–63.

Sutton, R. F., Jr., Cherry, J. F., Davis, J. L. and Mantzourani, E. (1991). "Gazetteer of archaeological sites," in Cherry *et al.*, 69–156.

Sutton, S. B. (1988) "What is a 'village' in a nation of migrants?" *Journal of Modern Greek Studies* 6: 187–215.

Syme, R. (1979a) "The Greeks under Roman rule," in Syme, R., *Roman Papers II*, 566–81. Oxford.

(1979b) "Problems about Janus," *AJP* 100: 188–212.

(1981) "Rival cities, notably *Tarraco* and *Barcino*," *Ktema* 6: 271–85.

(1988) "Greeks invading the Roman Government," in Syme, R., *Roman Papers IV*,

1–20. Oxford.

Symeonoglou, S. (1985) *The Topography of Thebes*, Princeton.

Tarn W. W. (1925) "The social question in the third century," in Bury, J. B. *et al.*, *The Hellenistic Age: Aspects of Hellenistic Civilization*, 108–40. Cambridge.

Tarn, W. W. and Griffith, G. T. (1952) *Hellenistic Civilisation* (3rd edn), London.

Thirlwall, C. (1844) *A History of Greece* (Volume 8), London.

Thomas, D. H. (1975) "Non-site sampling in archaeology: up the creek without a site?" in Mueller, J. W., ed., *Sampling in Archaeology*, 61–81. Tucson.

Thompson, H. A. (1950) "The Odeion in the Athenian Agora," *Hesperia* 19: 31–141.

(1952) "Excavations in the Athenian Agora: 1951," *Hesperia* 21: 83–113.

(1959) "Athenian twilight: AD 267–600," *JRS* 49: 61–72.

(1960) "Activities in the Athenian Agora: 1959," *Hesperia* 29: 327–68.

(1962) "Itinerant temples of Attica" (abstract), *AJA* 66: 200.

(1966) "The Annex to the Stoa of Zeus in the Athenian Agora," *Hesperia* 35: 171–87.

(1981) "Athens faces adversity," *Hesperia* 50: 343–55.

(1987) "The impact of Roman architects and architecture on Athens: 170 BC–AD 170," in Macready and Thompson, eds., 1–17.

Thompson, H. A., Thompson, D. B. and Rotroff, S. I. (1987) *Hellenistic Pottery and Terracottas*, Princeton.

Thompson, H. A. and Wycherley, R. E. (1972) *The Agora of Athens: The History, Shape and Uses of an Ancient City Center* (The Athenian Agora Volume XIV), Princeton.

Thompson, L. A. (1982) "On 'development' and 'underdevelopment' in the Early Roman empire," *Klio* 64: 383–401.

Tölle-Kastenbein, R. (1990) *Antike Wasserkultur*, Munich.

Tolstoy, P. and Fish, S. K. (1975) "Surface and subsurface evidence for community size at Coapexco, Mexico," *JFA* 2: 97–104.

Tomlinson, R. A. (1972) *Argos and the Argolid*, London.

(1976) *Greek Sanctuaries*, London.

Touloumakos, I. (1967) *Der Einfluss Roms auf die Staatsform der griechischen Stadtstaaten des Festlandes und der Inseln im ersten und zweiten Jhdt. v. Chr.*, Göttingen.

Townsend, E. (1955) "A Mycenaean chamber tomb under the Temple of Ares," *Hesperia* 24: 187–219.

Toyne, P. (1974) *Organisation, Location and Behaviour: Decision Making in Economic Geography*, London.

Travlos, J. (1971) *Pictorial Dictionary of Ancient Athens*, London.

Trigger, B. G. (1974) "The archaeology of government," *WA* 6: 95–106.

Trinkaus, K. M. (1984) "Boundary maintenance strategies and archaeological indicators," in DeAtley, S. P. and Findlow, F. J., eds., *Exploring the Limits: Frontiers and Boundaries in Prehistory* (BAR International Series 223), 35–49. Oxford.

Trummer, R. (1980) Die Denkmäler des Kaiserkults in der römischen Provinz Achaia. Dissertationen der Universität Graz 52, Graz.

Tsigakou, F.-M. (1981) *The Rediscovery of Greece: Travellers and Painters of the Romantic Era*, London.

Tuan, Y.-F. (1971) "Geography, phenomenology and the study of human nature,"

*Canadian Geographer* 15: 181–92.

(1974) *Topophilia: A Study of Environmental Perception, Attitudes and Fears*, Englewood Cliffs, NJ.

(1977) *Space and Place: The Perspective of Experience*, London.

Turner, F.M. (1981) *The Greek Heritage in Victorian Britain*, New Haven.

Turner, V. (1974) *Dramas, Fields and Metaphors*, Ithaca.

Upham, S. (1982) *Polities and Power*, New York.

Valmin, M. N. (1938) *The Swedish Messenia Expedition*, Lund.

van Andel, T. H. and Runnels, C. N. (1987) *Beyond the Acropolis: A Rural Greek Past*, Stanford.

van Andel, T. H., Runnels, C. N. and Pope, K. O. (1986) "Five thousand years of land use and abuse in the Southern Argolid, Greece," *Hesperia* 55: 103–28.

van Sickle, J. B. (1967) "The unity of the *Eclogues*: Arcadian forest, Theocritean trees," *Transactions and Proceedings of the American Philological Association* 98: 491–508.

van Wersch, H. J. (1972) "The agricultural economy," in McDonald and Rapp, eds., 177–87.

Vanderpool, E. (1959) "Athens honors the emperor Tiberius," *Hesperia* 28: 86–90.

(1970) "Some Attic inscriptions," *Hesperia* 39: 40–6.

Vatin, C. (1970) *Recherches sur le mariage et la condition de la femme mariée à l'époque hellénistique* (Bibliothèque des Ecoles Françaises d'Athènes et de Rome, Fasc. 216), Paris.

Vermeule, C. C. (1968) *Roman Imperial Art in Greece and Asia Minor*, Cambridge, MA.

(1977) *Greek Sculpture and Roman Taste*, Ann Arbor.

Vernant, J.-P. (1983a) "Hestia-Hermes: the religious expression of space and movement in ancient Greece," in Vernant, J.-P., *Myth and Thought among the Greeks*, 127–75. London.

(1983b) "Space and political organization in ancient Greece," in Vernant, J.-P., *Myth and Thought among the Greeks*, 212–34. London.

Veyne, P. (1976) *Le Pain et le cirque*, Paris.

(1988) *Did the Greeks Believe Their Myths?* (Translated by Paula Wissing), Chicago.

Vickers, M. (1985) "Artful crafts: the influence of metalwork on Athenian painted pottery," *JHS* 105: 108–28.

(1986) "Silver, copper and ceramics in ancient Athens," in Vickers, M., ed., *Pots and Pans: A Colloquium on Precious Metals and Ceramics*, 137–51. Oxford.

Vidal-Naquet, P. (1986) "The Black Hunter and the origin of the Athenian *ephebeia*," in Vidal-Naquet, P., *The Black Hunter: Forms of Thought and Forms of Society in the Greek World* (Translated by A. Szegedy-Maszak), 106–28. Baltimore.

Vries, J. de (1984) *European Urbanization, 1500–1800*, London.

Vroom, J. (1987) "Fact and fiction in Aetolian ceramic research," in Bommeljé and Doorn, eds., 27–31.

Wagstaff, J. M. (1969) "The study of Greek rural settlement: a review of the literature," *Erdkunde* 23: 306–17.

(1976) *Aspects of Land Use in Melos*, Southampton.

(1982) *The Development of Rural Settlement: A Study of the Helos Plain in Southern Greece*, Trowbridge.

ed. (1987) *Landscape and Culture: Geographical and Archaeological Perspectives*, Oxford.

Wagstaff, J. M. and Augustson, S. (1982) "Traditional land use," in Renfrew and Wagstaff, eds., 106–33.

Wagstaff, J. M. and Cherry, J. F. (1982a) "Settlement and population change," in Renfrew and Wagstaff, eds., 136–55.

(1982b) "Settlement and resources," in Renfrew and Wagstaff, eds., 246–63.

Wagstaff, J. M. and Gamble, C. (1982) "Island resources and their limitations," in Renfrew and Wagstaff, eds., 95–105.

Walbank, F. W. (1979) *A Historical Commentary on Polybius* (Volume 3), Oxford.

(1981) *The Hellenistic World*, Glasgow.

Walbank, M. E. H. (1986) "The nature of Early Roman Corinth" (abstract), *AJA* 90: 220–1.

(1989) "Pausanias, Octavia and Temple E at Corinth," *BSA* 84: 361–94.

Waldstein, C. (1905) *The Argive Heraeum*, Boston.

Walker, S. (1979) "A sanctuary of Isis on the south slope of the Athenian acropolis," *BSA* 74: 243–57.

(1985) *Memorials to the Roman Dead*, London.

(1987) "Roman nymphaea in the Greek world," in Macready and Thompson, eds., 60–71.

(1989) "Two Spartan women and the Eleusinion," in Walker and Cameron, eds., 130–41.

Walker, S. and Cameron, A., eds. (1989) *The Greek Renaissance in the Roman Empire* (*BICS* Supplement 55), London.

Wallace, P. W. (1972) "Boiotia in the time of Strabo," *Teiresias* Supplement 1 (Acts of the First International Conference on Boiotian Antiquities), 71–7.

(1979) *Strabo's Description of Boeotia: A Commentary*, Heidelberg.

Wallace-Hadrill, A., ed. (1990) *Patronage in Ancient Society*, London.

Wallerstein, I. (1974) *The Modern World-System*, New York.

(1980) *The Modern World-System II*, New York.

Walton, C. S. (1929) "Oriental senators in the service of Rome," *JRS* 19: 38–63.

Wardman, A. (1976) *Rome's Debt to Greece*, London.

Ward-Perkins, B. (1984) *From Classical Antiquity to the Middle Ages: Urban Public Building in Northern and Central Italy, AD 300–850*, Oxford.

Ward-Perkins, B., Mills, N., Gadd, D. and Delano Smith, C. (1986) "Luni and the Ager Lunensis: the rise and fall of a Roman town and its territory," *PBSR* 54: 81–146.

Waywell, S. E. (1979) "Roman mosaics in Greece," *AJA* 83: 293–321.

Weiss, H. (1977) "Periodization, population, and early state formation in Khuzistan," in Levine, L. D. and Young, T. C., Jr., eds., *Mountains and Lowlands: Essays in the Archaeology of Greater Mesopotamia* (Bibliotheca Mesopotamica 7), 347–69. Malibu.

Weller, C. H. (1906) "The extent of Strabo's travel in Greece," *CPhil* 1: 339–56.

Wells, B., Runnels, C. and Zangger, E. (1990) "The Berbati-Limnes archaeological survey, the 1988 season," *Opuscula Atheniensia* 18: 207–38.

Wells, D. (1970) "The water requirements of particular stock producing systems," in Taylor, J. A., ed., *The Role of Water in Agriculture*, 121–32. Oxford.

Welter, G. (1941) *Troizinia und Kalaureia*, Berlin.

Wenke, R. J. (1987) "Western Iran in the Partho-Sasanian period: the imperial transformation," in Hole, F., ed., *The Archaeology of Western Iran*, 251–81. Washington DC.

Whallon, R. (1979) *An Archaeological Survey of the Keban Reservoir Area of East-Central Turkey* (Memoirs of the Museum of Anthropology, University of Michigan 11), Ann Arbor.

Wheatley, P. (1971) *The Pivot of the Four Quarters*, Edinburgh.

White, B. (1973) "Demand for labor and population growth in colonial Java," *Human Ecology* 1: 217–36.

White, K. D. (1967) "Latifundia," *BICS* 14: 62–79.

Whitehouse, D. (1985) "Raiders and invaders: the Roman campagna in the first millennium AD," in Malone, C. and Stoddart, S., eds., *Papers in Italian Archaeology IV. Part iv: Classical and Medieval Archaeology* (BAR International Series 246), 207–13. Oxford.

Whitelaw, T. W. (1991) "The ethnoarchaeology of recent rural settlement and land use in Northwest Keos," in Cherry *et al.*, 403–54.

Whitelaw, T. W. and Davis, J. L. (1991) "The *polis* center of Koressos," in Cherry *et al.*, 265–81.

Whittaker, C. R. (1976) "Agri deserti," in Finley, M. I., ed., *Studies in Roman Property*, 137–65. Cambridge.

  (1980) "Inflation and the economy in the fourth century AD," in King, C. E., ed., *Imperial Revenue, Expenditure and Monetary Policy in the Fourth Century AD* (BAR International Series 76), 1–22. Oxford.

  ed. (1988) *Pastoral Economies in Classical Antiquity* (Cambridge Philological Society Supplementary Volume 14), Cambridge.

Wickham, C. (1988) "Marx, Sherlock Holmes and Late Roman commerce," *JRS* 78: 183–93.

Wilkes, J. J. (1989) "Civil defence in third-century Achaia," in Walker and Cameron, eds., 187–92.

Will, E. (1975) "Le monde hellénistique," in Will, E., Mossé, C. and Goukowsky, P., eds., *Le Monde grec et l'orient*, 337–645. Paris.

  (1982) *Histoire politique du monde hellénistique ( 323–30 av. J.-C.)* (Volume 2, 2nd edn), Nancy.

Willers, D. (1989) "The redesigning of Athens under Hadrian," in Walker and Cameron, eds., 9.

  (1990) *Hadrians panhellenisches Programm: Archäologische Beiträge zur Neugestaltung Athens durch Hadrian*, Basel.

Williams, C. K. II. (1987) "The refounding of Corinth: some Roman religious attitudes," in Macready and Thompson, eds., 26–37.

  (1989) "A re-evaluation of Temple E and the west end of the Forum of Corinth," in Walker and Cameron, eds., 156–62.

Williams, C. K. II and Zervos, O. H. (1983) "Corinth, 1982: east of the theater," *Hesperia* 52: 1–47.

Williams, G. (1970) *The Nature of Roman Poetry*, London.

Williamson, T. and Bellamy, L. (1987) *Property and Landscape: A Social History of Land*

*Ownership and the English Countryside*, London.

Wilson, A. J. N. (1966) *Emigration from Italy in the Republican Age of Rome*, Manchester.

Wilson, D. R. (1973) "Temples in Britain: a topographical survey," *Caesarodunum* 8: 24–44.

Wilson, R. J. A. (1990) *Sicily under the Roman Empire: The Archaeology of a Roman Province, 36 BC–AD 535*, Warminster.

Winter, J. E. and Winter, F. E. (1990) "Some disputed sites and itineraries of Pausanias in the northeast Peloponnesos," *EMC/CV* n.s. 9: 221–61.

Wiseman, J. (1978) *The Land of the Ancient Corinthians* (Studies in Mediterranean Archaeology 50), Gothenburg.

(1979) "Corinth and Rome, I," *ANRW* 7.1: 438–548.

Wolf, E. R. (1966) *Peasants*, Englewood Cliffs, NJ.

(1982) *Europe and the People without a History*, Berkeley.

Wood, E. M. (1988) *Peasant-Citizen and Slave: The Foundations of Athenian Democracy*, London.

Woodell, S. R. J., ed. (1985) *The English Landscape: Past, Present and Future* (Wolfson College Lectures 1983), Oxford.

Woodhouse, W. J. (1897) *Aetolia. Its Geography, Topography and Antiquities* (Reprinted 1973), New York.

Woodward, A. M. (1925/6) "Excavations at Sparta, 1926. The inscriptions," *BSA* 27: 210–54.

Woolf, G. (1990) "World-systems analysis and the Roman empire," *JRA* 3: 44–58.

Wright, J., Cherry, J. F., Davis, J. L. and Mantzourani, E. (1985) "To ereunitiko archaiologiko programma sten koilada tes Nemeas kata ta ete 1984–85," *AAA* 18: 86–104.

Wright, J., Cherry, J. F., Davis, J. L., Mantzourani, E., Sutton, S. B. and Sutton, R. F., Jr. (1990) "The Nemea Valley Archaeological Project: a preliminary report," *Hesperia* 59: 579–659.

Wright, K. S. (1980) "A Tiberian pottery deposit from Corinth," *Hesperia* 49: 135–77.

Wycherley, R. E. (1964) "The Olympieion at Athens," *GRBS* 5: 161–79.

Zanker, P. (1988) *The Power of Images in the Age of Augustus* (Translated by Alan Shapiro), Ann Arbor.

Ziller, E. (1877) "Untersuchungen über die antiken Wasserleitungen Athens," *Mitteilungen des deutschen archäologischen Institutes in Athen* 2: 107–31.

Ziolkowski, A. (1986) "The plundering of Epirus in 167 BC: economic considerations," *PBSR* 54: 69–80.

# Index

# Index

Attica: landed properties in, 78; landless population in, 106; marble quarries of, 110; restoration of sanctuaries in, 194; rural sanctuaries in, 209; survey in, 35, 39–40
Atticus, 13, 65
Attis, 180
Augustus [Octavian], 13, 78, 111, 133, 136, 140, 143, 152, 163, 176–7, 181–2, 184, 186, 190, 193, 214
Aulis (**26**), 111, 154

Baetica, 222–3
Baladié, R., 177
Bassae (**104**): Temple of Apollo at, 204, 206
baths, Roman: generally, 125; at Athens, 125, 127; at Berbati, 43; at Halieis, 68; on Melos, 101; in Messenia, 68; at villa sites, 64, 67–8
battle: of Actium, 14, 90, 133, 149, 184, 186, 217; of Chaironeia, 3
Berbati (**110**), 43, 65; Berbati-Limnes survey project, 43, 68, 83–4
Bernhardt, R., 22
Bithynia, 186
Blagg, T. F. C., 210
Boeotia, 9, 13, 35, 50, 73, 149, 151, 154, 199–200, 208, 219; Boeotian League, 153; *civitates liberae*, 147; depopulation, 89, 97, 99; iron-working, 110; land leasing, 82; *negotiatores*, 75; *publicani*, 20; roads, 121; settlements, 54, 63; survey in, 37–9, 53, 57–9, 96–9; warfare in, 89, 106
Boiai (**88**), 205
Bolina, 136
booty, 13, 63, 89
boundaries, 118–28, 152–3, 202–10
Bowersock, G. W., 2, 195
Brasidas, 212
Braudel, F., 9
Brauron, 176
Britain, 213, 220, 222
building materials, 111
Bulis (**44**), 111
Bura (**69**), 10
burial monuments, 67, 70
Buthrotum (**128**), 133, 143
Byllis, 134, 143
Byron, Lord (George Gordon), 1, 31, 215
*byssos* (flax), 80, 111

cadastral organization, 137, 139–40
Caesar, C. Julius, 13, 133, 163, 182
Caligula, 178–9
Callaghan, P. J., 202
Caracalla, 8–9, 18
Carrara, 110
Carthage, 133
Cassas, L. F., 228
center–periphery models, 5, 131–2
Chaironeia (**58**), 3, 111, 123, 149, 154, 157, 217
Chalkis (**24**), 76, 110, 123, 167
Chemtou, 110
Chios, 110
Chorsiai (**43**), 39, 149
chronology: problems of, 49–51, 105, 217–20; standard for Greece, 35
Cicero, 13, 25, 226; *Ad Familiares*, 31; attacks on L. Calpurnius Piso, 20; remarks about Achaia, 26
cities: benefactions to, 163–4; distribution within Roman empire, 130; economic vitality, 101–2, 152–64; excavations at, in Roman Greece, 93, 96; expansion, 152–3; "extinct," 145–7; favorable positions, 162; financial pressure on, 151; foundation of, 132–45; free, 22–3, 181, 223; government, 150; and imperial cult, 181–99; number in Achaia, 130–1; and their past, 163–4, 171; population, 116, 158–60, 171; relationships between, 164; relationship to countryside, 93–4; rivalry between, 152–3, 164, 172, 199, 208; sanctuaries and territorial definition, 202–10; sizes, 157–62, 171; as sources of alternative employment for farmers, 107; status of, 94, 153, 171; successful, 157–64; survival of, 152–64; and water supply, 125–6
Claudius, 16, 178, 190, 195
Cleopatra, 197
*coloni*, 114, 220
colonies, 77, 134, 143
Constantinople, 220
Corinth (**79**), 23, 31, 50, 52, 93, 156, 167, 200, 213, 219; Aphrodite Hoplismeni, 168; aqueducts, 124–5, 160; as bridgehead community, 116–19; cadastral organization, 137; canal across the isthmus, 141–2, Capitolium,

# Index

euergetism, 77–8, 113–14, 126, 154, 156, 210

Eurycles, C. Iulius, 78, 182

Eurycles Herculanus L. Vibullius Pius, C. Iulius, 187

Euryclids, 156, 210–11

Eurynome, 206

Evander, 164

*evocatio*, 179

Fabius Maximus, 179

farmsteads, 54, 59–60, 96; agro-pastoral symbiosis, 87–8; along communication routes, 102; leasing arrangements, 109; status of owners, 61–2, 108–9

Finlay, G., 229

Finley, M. I., 132, 160

Flamininus, T. Quinctius, 9, 16, 169

Flavia Domitilla (Maior), 190; (Minor), 190

Foxhall, L., 108

Fowden, G., 209

Frazer, J. G., 200

Frederiksen, M., 210

Freeman, E., 215, 229

Gaius Caesar, 195

Gallo, L., 27

Galtung, J., 19

Garnsey, P., 221–2

Gaudos, 152

Gaul, 221

Gebel Dokhan, 110

Gebel Fatireh, 110

geomorphology, 80–1

Geronthrai, 20

Gonnoi (**131**), 10

Gordon, R., 179

Gortys, 167, 203

"Graeculi," 28, 157, 168

Grote, G., 3

Guadalquivir Valley, 222

Gyaros (**4**), 110–11

Gytheion (**94**), 76, 162, 182–3, 205

Hadrian, 17, 80, 93, 156, 160, 164, 166, 169; and Antinoos, 186–7; aqueduct construction, 124–5, 160, 228; Arch in Athens, 184, 187; bath construction, 127; corn dole at Athens, 113; development of Athens, 93, 158, 163;

as an eponymous hero in Athens, 197; and Olympieion in Athens, 181; and Panhellenion, 17, 156, 163; priest of, 156; road construction, 121; territorial gifts of, 152

Halai (**56**), 149

Haliartos (**40**), 38, 90, 97, 132, 149, 200

Halieis (**85**), 40, 59, 68

Halstead, P. J. L., 61, 95

Harma (**27**), 154

Helos (**91**), 203–5, 212; sanctuary of Demeter and Kore, 212

Hera: at Argos, 202–3

Heracles, 119

Heraia (**115**), 120

Hermes, 119

Hermione (**84**), 101–2, 111, 120–1, 125, 162, 180, 206, 212; sanctuary of Demeter Chthonia, 206

herms, 119

Herod the Great, 190

Herodes Atticus, 2, 74, 125, 210; estates of, 66–7, 78; nymphaeum at Olympia, 190–2

Herzfeld, M., 1, 31–2, 229

Hesiod, 97

Hierapytna, 167

Hierocles, 145, 147–8

Hipparchos, grandfather of Herodes Atticus, 74

historical sources on Achaia: negative tone of, 25–6; range of, 24–5; reliability of, 30; source criticism of, 25–32; *topoi* in, 30; written by the "winners," 24

history of Greece: in the early imperial Roman period, 8–24; European construction of, 3–5

Hoff, M., 214

Homer, 147, 208, 227

*honestiores*, 220

Hopkins, K., 21, 221

Horace, 1–2, 25–6

*humiliores*, 220

Hyettos (**52**), 96–7, 106

Hymettos, Mount, 110; sanctuary of Zeus, 209

Hypata (**65**), 157, 167

Hysiai, 154

Iasos, 110

Ikos, 182